BUTTERWORTHS COMPANY LAW GUIDE

General Editor

MICHAEL RENSHALL OBE, MA, FCA

Consultant Editor

KEITH WALMSLEY LLB, FCIS, *Solicitor*

LONDON
BUTTERWORTHS
1985

United Kingdom	Butterworth & Co (Publishers) Ltd, 88 Kingsway, London WC2B 6AB and 61A North Castle Street, Edinburgh EH2 3LJ
Australia	Butterworths Pty Ltd, Sydney, Melbourne, Brisbane, Adelaide, Perth, Canberra and Hobart
Canada	Butterworth & Co (Canada) Ltd, Toronto and Vancouver
New Zealand	Butterworths of New Zealand Ltd, Wellington and Auckland
Singapore	Butterworth & Co (Asia) Pte Ltd, Singapore
South Africa	Butterworth Publishers (Pty) Ltd, Durban and Pretoria
USA	Butterworth Legal Publishers, St Paul, Minnesota, Seattle, Washington, Boston Massachusetts, Austin, Texas and D & S Publishers, Clearwater, Florida

© Butterworth & Co (Publishers) Ltd 1985

ISBN 0 406 19700 8

Set by Colset Pte Ltd, Singapore
and Printed by Billing & Sons Ltd.,
Worcester

Preface

This work is intended as a companion volume to *Butterworth's Company Law Handbook*.

The general aims are:

- to give a broad general guide to and commentary on the Act for practitioners and others concerned with company law and administration — accountants, solicitors, company secretaries and directors

- to provide a primary source of reference to the provisions of the statute and leading authorities

- to set the Act in the context of common practice and explain its application to practical problems

The Companies Act 1985 is the thirteenth British Companies Act this century and the fourth consolidation measure (previous consolidations were in 1908, 1929 and 1948).

It is a measure of the increasing complexity of business legislation that the 462 sections and 18 schedules of the 1948 Act have swollen in the present Act to 747 sections and 25 schedules. This is after transfer from the old companies legislation into new statutes of the provisions relating to business names (now set out in the Business Names Act 1985) and the insider dealing provisions (now transferred to the Company Securities (Insider Dealing) Act 1985).

Unusually for consolidation measures the Department of Trade and Industry sought external views in preparing the Consolidation Bill. There were three separate rounds of consultation, the first seeking views on the general approach, the others inviting comments on details of texts. The first point for consultation concerned the question whether the new legislation should take the form of one principal Act or a number of smaller Acts dealing with separate subjects. On that occasion responses were evenly divided between these options. However following a later round of consultation the view clearly emerged that the measures should be amalgamated into one statute except for those provisions governing insider dealings, business names and the consequential provisions and this is the shape the legislation has finally taken.

The 1985 Act is illustrative of the adage 'Everything is different, nothing is changed', for in essence the law is as before, though opportunity has been taken to clarify meaning or correct anomalies in a number of instances. A full list of such changes will be found in the Companies Acts (Pre-Consolidation Amendments) Orders, 1984 SIs Nos 134 and 1169.

Generally, those familiar with the previous legislation will find the structure of the new Act more logical and accessible, though it may take a little while for the new section numbers to become familiar.

The editors are grateful to all the contributors for their efforts in producing their material on time and the staff at Butterworths who first conceived the idea of the work, and without whose help support and labours the work would still be struggling to be born.

Michael Renshall
General Editor
July 1985

Notes on contributors

Michael Renshall OBE MA FCA is a Partner in Peat Marwick Mitchell, London. He was Technical Director of the Institute of Chartered Accountants in England and Wales from 1969–1977. Amongst his publications are *Added Value Statements* (1978), *The Companies Act Handbook 1981* and *Purchase of Own Shares* (1983).

Keith Walmsley LLB FRICS, a Solicitor, is Manager, Legal Services, The Stock Exchange. A member of the Council of the Institute of Chartered Secretaries and Administrators, he is Editor of the Institute of Chartered Secretaries and Administrators Official Manual *Company Secretarial Practice* and of *Butterworth's Company Law Handbook*.

Professor L H Leigh BA LLB PhD is Professor of Criminal Law in the University of London (London School of Economics and Political Science). His publications include *Introduction to Company Law* (Third Edition), *Economic Crime in Europe* (1980) and *Control of Commercial Fraud* (1982).

W Ratford FCA is a partner in Peat Marwick Mitchell, London. An insolvency specialist, he is a member of the Council of the Insolvency Practitioners' Association and its President for 1985–86.

E R Hardy Ivamy is professor of law at the University of London. A leading authority on insurance and shipping law, his major books include *General Principles of Insurance Law*, *Fire and Motor Insurance*, *Marine Insurance* and *Personal Accident, Life and Other Insurances*. He is the editor of volume 25 (Insurance) and volume 43 (Shipping and Navigation) of Halsbury's Laws of England and of *Chalmers' Marine Insurance Act 1906*. He is the author of *Payne and Ivamy's Carriage of Goods by Sea* and the *Encyclopedia of Shipping Law Sources (UK)*.

Sally A Jones, a law lecturer at Nottingham University, is the joint author with D Bellringer of *Share Capital*.

Peter Castle, a barrister, is a member of the Middle Temple and Lincoln's Inn. He is a former lecturer in law at Surrey University and now practices at the Chancery Bar.

Derek Foster CA is a partner in Arthur Young and the firm's national Director of Accounting. He is Chairman of the Auditing Practices

Committee of the Consultative Committee of Accontancy Bodies, and a former member of the Company Law Committee and Ethics Committee of the Institute of Chartered Accountants of Scotland. He is author of *Guide to the requirements of the Companies Act 1981* and its accompanying booklet *Model reports and accounts* published by the Institute of Chartered Accountants of Scotland. He was greatly assisted in the preparation of his material on company accounts in the present work by Alwine Jones MA ACA, a member of the Arthur Young National Technical Department.

Contents

Table of abbreviations

ACT	Advance Corporation Tax
ASC	Accounting Standards Committee
BA 1914	Bankruptcy Act 1914
CA 1948	Companies Act 1948
CA 1976	Companies Act 1976
CA 1981	Companies Act 1981
CA 1985	Companies Act 1985
CCAB	Consultative Committee of Accountancy Bodies
CC(CP)A 1985	Companies Consolidation (Consequential Provisions) Act 1985
DTI	Department of Trade and Industry
ED	Exposure Draft
FA 1973	Finance Act 1973
FIFO	First in, first out
ICAEW	Institute of Chartered Accountants in England and Wales
LIFO	Last in, first out
LPA 1925	Law of Property Act 1925
NIC	National Insurance Contributions
PAYE	Pay As You Earn Tax
PF(I)A	Prevention of Fraud (Investments) Act 1958
RDG	Regional Development Grant
SSAP's	Statements of Standard Accounting Practice (CCAB)
Table A, 1985 Regs	Companies (Tables A—F) Regulations, SI 1985 No 805 (as amended by SI 1985 No 1052)
TR	Technical Release (CCAB)
VAT	Value Added Tax

Table of statutes

References in **bold** type indicate where the section of the Act is set out in part or in full.
References in *italic* type are to pages of the Appendices, Tables and Examples.

Table of cases

1 The creation of the company

Professor E R Hardy Ivamy

Introduction

1.01 A person wishing to form a company must first consider the type of company most suitable for his purpose.[1] There are certain formalities required.[2] The memorandum[3] and articles of association[4] are the two chief documents which need to be drafted. The name [5] and the objects[6] of the company must be set out in the memorandum. The memorandum and other documents must be sent to the Registrar of Companies for registration.[7] A company which has been registered may be re-registered as a different type of company.[8] There are various ways in which a person may become a member.[9] A company can usually commence business as soon as it has been registered, but this is not always so.[10] There are certain rules about the company's capacity to enter into contracts, and the form which they must take.[11]

[1] See paras 1.02–1.15, below.
[2] See para 1.16, below.
[3] See paras 1.17–1.18, below.
[4] See paras 1.19–1.23, below.
[5] See paras 1.24–1.34, below.
[6] See paras 1.35–1.39, below.
[7] See paras 1.40–1.52, below.
[8] See paras 1.53–1.66, below.
[9] See paras 1.67–1.71, below.
[10] See para 1.72, below.
[11] See paras 1.73–1.77, below.

TYPES OF COMPANY

Introduction

1.02 The main types of company recognised by the Act are:—(1) registered; (2) oversea; (3) public; (4) private; (5) unregistered; (6) limited by shares; (7) limited by guarantee; (8) unlimited; (9) small; (10) medium; (11) dormant; (12) investment; and (13) special category. These are described briefly below.

Registered company

1.03 A registered company is a company registered in any part of the United Kingdom under the Joint Stock Companies Acts or under the legislation (past or present) relating to companies in Great Britain.[1]

[1] CA 1985, s 735.

Oversea company

1.04 An oversea company is

(a) a company incorporated elsewhere than in Great Britain which after 1 July 1985, establishes a place of business in Great Britain; and
(b) a company so incorporated which has, before that date, established a place of business and continues to have a place of business in Great Britain at that date.[1]

---

[1] CA 1985, s 744. As to oversea companies generally see para 9.28, below.

Public company

1.05 A public company is a company limited by shares[1] or limited by guarantee[2] and having a share capital, being a company

(a) the memorandum[3] of which states that it is to be a public company, and
(b) in relation to which the provisions of the Companies Act 1985 as to the registration[4] or re-registration[5] of a company as a public company have been complied with on or after 22 December 1980.[6]

---

[1] See para 1.08, below.
[2] See para 1.09, below.
[3] See para 1.17, below.
[4] See para 1.40, below.
[5] See para 1.53, below.
[6] CA 1985, s 1(3).

Private company

1.06 A private company is a company that is not a public company.[1]

---

[1] CA 1985, s 1(3).

Unregistered company

1.07 An unregistered company includes any trustee savings bank certified under the enactments relating to such banks and any partnership (whether limited or not) and any association and any company with the following exceptions:

(a) a railway company incorporated by Act of Parliament;
(b) a company registered in any part of the United Kingdom under the Joint Stock Companies Acts or under the legislation (past or present) relating to companies in Great Britain;
(c) a partnership, association or company which consists of less than eight members and is not a foreign partnership, association or company;
(d) a limited partnership registered in England, and Wales or Northern Ireland.[1]

[1] CA 1985, s 665. A partnership consisting of less than 8 members can only be wound up under the Partnership Act 1890. If it has 8 or more members it may be wound up under that Act, but also as an unregistered company under CA 1985.

Company limited by shares

1.08 A company limited by shares is a company having the liability of its members limited by the memorandum to the amount, if any, unpaid on the shares respectively held by them.[1]

[1] CA 1985, s 1(2)(a).

Company limited by guarantee

1.09 A company limited by guarantee is a company having the liability of its members limited by memorandum[1] to such amount as the members may respectively thereby undertake to contribute to the assets of the company in the event of its being wound up.[2]

[1] As to the memorandum, see para 1.17, post.
[2] CA 1985, s 1(2)(b).

Unlimited company

1.10 An unlimited company is a company not having any limit on the liability of its members.[1]

[1] CA 1985, s 1(2)(c).

Small company

1.11 A small company is a company which in a financial year satisfies two or more of the following conditions:

    (a) the amount of its turnover for the year is not more than £1.4 million;
    (b) its balance sheet total[1] is not more than £700,000;
    (c) the average number of persons employed by the company[2] in the year (determined on a weekly basis) does not exceed 50.[3]

[1] 'Balance sheet total' means in relation to a company's financial year
  (a) where in the company's accounts Format 1 of the balance sheet formats set out in Pt I of Sch 4 is adopted, the aggregate of the amounts shown in the balance sheet under the headings corresponding to items A to D in that Format, and
  (b) where Format 2 is adopted, the aggregate of the amount shown under the general heading 'Assets': CA 1985, s 248(3).
[2] The average number of persons employed is determined by applying the method of calculation prescribed by para 56(2) and (3) of Sch 4 for determining the number required by sub-para 1(a) of that paragraph to be stated in a note to the company's accounts: ibid, s 248(4).
[3] CA 1985, s 248(1). In applying this sub-section to a period which is a company's financial

year but not in fact a year, the maximum figures for turnover in para (a) of the subsection are to be proportionately adjusted: ibid, s 248(5).

Medium-sized company

1.12   A medium-sized company is a company which in a financial year satisfies two or more of the following conditions:

(a)   the amount of its turnover for the year is not more than £5.75 million;

(b)   the balance sheet total[1] is not more than £2.8 million;

(c)   the average number of persons[2] employed by the company in the year (determined on a weekly basis) does not exceed 250.[3]

[1] For the meaning of balance sheet total, see para 1.11, note 1, above.

[2] For the method of determining the average number of persons employed, see para 1.11, note 2, above.

[3] CA 1985, s 248(2). In applying this sub-section to a period which is a company's financial year but not in fact a year, the maximum figures for turnover in para (a) of that subsection are to be proportionately adjusted: ibid, s 248(5).

Dormant company

1.13   A dormant company is one which is dormant during any period in which no transaction occurs that is for the company a significant accounting transaction.[1]

Further, to qualify as a dormant company the company must be one which is not a special category company,[2] is not obliged to file group accounts,[3] and which would qualify to file modified accounts as for a small company.[4]

[1] CA 1985, s 252(5). A 'significant accounting transaction' is one which is required by s 221 to be entered in the company's accounting records (disregarding any which arises from the taking of shares in a company by a subscriber to the memorandum in pursuance of an undertaking of his in the memorandum): ibid, s 252(5). See also paras 9.229–9.233, below.

[2] For a 'special category company', see para 2.14, below.

[3] As to group accounts, see paras 9.156 et seq, below.

[4] For a 'small company', see para 1.11, above.

Investment company

1.14   An investment company is a public company which has given notice in the prescribed form (which has not been revoked) to the Registrar of Companies of its intention to carry on business as an investment company, and has since the date of that notice complied with the following requirements:

(a)   that the business of the company consists of investing its funds mainly in securities, with the aim of spreading investment risk and giving members of the company the benefits of the results of the management of its funds;

(b)   that none of the company's holdings in companies (other than those which are for the time being in investment companies) represents more than 15 per cent by value of the investing company's investments;

(c) that distribution of the company's capital profits is prohibited by its memorandum or articles of association; and

(d) that the company has not retained, otherwise than in compliance with Part VIII[1] of the Companies Act 1985, in respect of any accounting reference period[2] more than fifteen per cent of the income it derives from securities.[3]

[1] Which relates to 'Distribution of Profits and Assets'. See paras 4.71–4.76, below.
[2] As to 'accounting reference period', see para 9.20, below.
[3] CA 1985, s 266.

Special category company

1.15 This is a company which is a banking company, a shipping company or an insurance company.[1]

A 'banking company' means a company which is a recognised bank for the purposes of the Banking Act 1979 or is a licensed institution within that Act.[2]

A 'shipping company' means a company which, or a subsidiary of which, owns ships or includes among its activities the management or operation of ships and which satisfies the Secretary of State that it ought in the national interest to be treated under Part VII[3] of CA 1985 as a shipping company.[4]

An 'insurance company' means an insurance company to which Part II of the Insurance Companies Act 1982 applies.[5]

A special category company is entitled to certain privileges under CA 1985, mainly relating to the form and content of accounts.[6]

[1] CA 1985, s 257(1).
[2] Ibid.
[3] Which concerns 'Accounts and Audit.' See Chapters 9 and 10, below.
[4] CA 1985, s 257(1).
[5] Ibid.
[6] See paras 9.10–9.14, below.

FORMATION OF COMPANY

Mode of formation

1.16 Any two or more persons associated for a lawful purpose[1] may, by subscribing their names to a memorandum of association[2] and otherwise complying with the requirements of CA 1985 in respect of registration,[3] form an incorporated company, with or without limited liability.[4]

[1] The Registrar of Companies must not register an unlawful association: *R v Registrar of Companies, ex Bowen* [1914] 3 KB 1161. A company formed for the purpose of dealing in lottery bonds is illegal: *Re International Securities Corpn Ltd* (1908) 99 LT 581.
[2] See para 1.17, below.
[3] See para 1.40, below.
[4] CA 1985, s 1(1).

THE MEMORANDUM OF ASSOCIATION

Requirements of the memorandum

1.17   The memorandum of every company must state:[1]

(a)   the name of the company;[2]
(b)   whether the registered office of the company is to be situated in England and Wales,[3] or in Scotland; and
(c)   the objects of the company.[4]

The memorandum of a company limited by shares or by guarantee must also state that the liability of its members is limited.[5]

The memorandum of a company limited by guarantee must also state that each member undertakes to contribute to the assets of the company if it should be wound up while he is a member or within one year after he ceases to be a member

(i)   for payment
    (a)   of the debts and liabilities of the company contracted before he ceases to be a member; and
    (b)   of the costs, charges and expenses of winding up; and
(ii)   for adjustment of the rights of the contributories among themselves,

such amount as may be required not exceeding a specified amount.[6]

In the case of a company having a share capital

(a)   the memorandum must also (unless it is an unlimited company) state the amount of the share capital with which the company proposes to be registered and the division of the share capital into shares of a fixed amount;
(b)   no subscriber of the memorandum may take less than one share; and
(c)   there must be shown in the memorandum against the name of each subscriber the number of shares he takes.[7]

The memorandum must be signed by each subscriber in the presence of at least one witness.[8]

A company cannot alter the conditions contained in its memorandum except in the cases, in the mode and to the extent for which express provision is made by the Companies Act 1985.[9]

---

[1] CA 1985, s 2(1).

[2] For the name of the company, see paras 1.24–1.34, below.

[3] Alternatively, the memorandum must contain a statement that the company's registered office is to be situated in Wales: CA 1985, s 2(2). A company whose registered office is situated in Wales may by special resolution alter its memorandum so as to provide that the registered office is to be so situated: ibid, s 2(2). For the registered office, see para 7.08, below. For special resolutions, see paras 8.122–8.125, below.

[4] For the objects of the company, see paras 1.35–1.39, below.

[5] CA 1985, s 2(3).

[6] Ibid, s 2(4).

[7] Ibid, s 2(5).

[8] Ibid, s 2(6).

[9] Ibid, s 2(7). As to the alteration of the name of the company, see para 1.27, below. As to the alteration of the objects of the company, see para 1.36, below.

Forms of memorandum

1.18   The form of a memorandum of

(i)   a public company, being a company limited by shares;

(ii)   a public company being a company limited by guarantee and having a share capital;[1]

(iii)   a private company limited by shares;

(iv)   a private company limited by guarantee and not having a share capital;

(v)   a private company limited by guarantee and having a share capital;[2] and

(vi)   an unlimited company having a share capital

must be as specified for such companies by regulations made by the Secretary of State, or as near to that form as circumstances admit.[3]

Regulations must be made by statutory instrument subject to annulment in pursuance of a resolution by either House of Parliament.[4]

---

[1] As from 22 December 1980 a company cannot be formed as, or become, a company limited by guarantee with a share capital: CA 1985, s 1(4).

[2] Ibid, s 1(4).

[3] Ibid, s 3(1). The regulations at present in force are the Companies (Tables A–F) Regulations 1985 (SI 1985/805) as amended by SI 1985/1052.

[4] CA 1985, s 3(2).

THE ARTICLES OF ASSOCIATION

Function of articles

1.19   The articles are the rules for the internal management of the company. They are concerned with such matters as e g (i) share capital and variation of rights;[1] (ii) liens on shares;[2] (iii) calls on shares;[3] (iv) forfeiture of shares;[4] (v) alteration of capital;[5] (vi) general meetings;[6] (vii) notice of general meetings;[7] (viii) proceedings at general meetings;[8] (ix) votes of members;[9] (x) the remuneration and powers of directors;[10] (xi) borrowing powers of the company;[11] (xii) the managing director;[12] (xiii) the secretary;[13] (xiv) the seal;[14] (xv) dividends;[15] (xvi) accounts;[16] (xvii) capitalisation of profits;[17] and (xviii) audit.[18]

---

[1] See para 3.26, below.

[2] See para 8.36, below.

[3] See para 3.18, below.

[4] See paras 8.33–8.35, below.

[5] See para 3.26, below.

[6] See paras 8.94 et seq, below.

[7] See para 8.101, below.

[8] See paras 8.94 et seq, below.

[9] See paras 8.118–8.120, below.

[10] See paras 6.07, 6.12 and 6.17, below.

[11] See para 4.78, below.

[12] See paras 6.12–6.13, below.

[13] See para 6.39, below.

14 See para 7.05, below.
15 See para 4.68, below.
16 See paras 9.33–9.38, below.
17 See para 4.71, below.
18 See Chapter 10, below.

Need for articles

1.20 There may in the case of a company limited by shares, and there must in the case of a company limited by guarantee or of an unlimited company, be registered with the memorandum articles of association signed by the subscribers to the memorandum and prescribing regulations for the company.[1]

In the case of an unlimited company having a share capital,[2] the articles must state the amount of share capital with which the company proposes to be registered.[3]

Articles must

(a) be printed;
(b) be divided into paragraphs numbered consecutively; and
(c) be signed by each subscriber to the memorandum in the presence of at least one witness who must attest the signature.[4]

1 CA 1985, s 7(1).
2 As to share capital, see paras 3.18 et seq, below.
3 CA 1985, s 7(2).
4 Ibid, s 7(3).

Tables A, C, D and E

1.21 Table A is as prescribed by regulations made by the Secretary of State.[1] A company may for its articles adopt the whole or any part of that Table.[2]

In the case of a company limited by shares, if articles are not registered, or, if articles are registered, in so far as they do not exclude or modify Table A, that Table[3] constitutes the company's articles, in the same manner and to the extent as if articles in the form of that Table had been duly registered.[4]

If in consequence of regulations made by the Secretary of State Table A is altered, the alteration does not affect a company registered before the alteration takes effect, or repeal as respects that company any portion of the Table.[5]

The form of the articles of association of

(i) a company limited by guarantee and not having a share capital;
(ii) a company limited by guarantee and having a share capital
(iii) unlimited company having a share capital

must be respectively in accordance with Table C, D or E prescribed by regulations made by the Secretary of State, or as near to that form as circumstances admit.[6]

Regulations must be made by statutory instrument subject to annulment in pursuance of a resolution of either House of Parliament.[7]

1 CA 1985, s 8(1). The regulations at present in force are the Companies (Tables A to F) Regulations 1985 (SI 1985/805) as amended by SI 1985/1052.

2 CA 1985, s 8(1).

3 So far as applicable, and as in force at the date of the company's registration. Nothing in the Companies Act 1985 affects the application of Table A in the Companies Act 1948 (or the predecessors of that Act) to any company existing immediately before 1 July 1985: Companies Consolidation (Consequential Provisions) Act 1985, s 31(8)(b).

4 CA 1985, s 8(2).

5 Ibid, s 8(3).

6 Ibid, s 8(4). For the forms see the Companies (Alteration of Tables A to F, etc.) Regulations 1985 (SI 1985/805).

7 CA1985, s 8(5).

Alteration of articles by special resolution

1.22 Subject to the provisions of the Companies Act 1985 and to the conditions contained in the memorandum, a company may by special resolution alter its articles.[1]

Alterations so made in the articles are (subject to the Act) as valid as if originally contained in them, and are subject in like manner to alteration by special resolution.[2]

1 CA 1985, s 9(1). As to special resolutions, see paras 8.122–8.125, below.

2 CA 1985, s 9(2).

Validity of alteration

1.23 An alteration is valid only where it is made in good faith for the benefit of the 'company as a whole'.[1] This term means the members as a general body.[2]

An alteration which is to benefit the company as a whole is valid even though it seriously affects the position of individual shareholders.[3]

The majority of the members may even alter the articles to take power to exclude the majority where this is done bona fide for the benefit of the company.[4]

Further, an alteration may be held to be valid even where it alters the whole structure of the company.[5]

Any alteration of the articles which purports to compel a member to subscribe for more shares than he has at the date of the alteration, or in any way to increase his liability, will not be binding on him unless he agrees in writing, either before or after the alteration to be bound by it.[6]

Where the articles provide that the consent of a class of shareholders is needed before their rights can be altered, any alteration without such consent will not be binding on them.[7]

A company may alter its articles in breach of a contract not to do so made between the company and a third party, but may render itself liable in damages to him for so doing.[8]

1 *Greenhalgh v Arderne Cinemas Ltd* [1951] Ch 286, CA.

2 Ibid at 1126 (per Sir Raymond Evershed MR).

3 *Allen v Gold Reefs of West Africa Ltd* [1900] 1 Ch 656.

4 *Sidebottom v Kershaw, Leese & Co* [1920] 1 Ch 154. For the rights of a minority, see chap 8.

5 *Andrews v Gas Meter Co* [1897] Ch 361.

6 CA 1985, s 16(1).

7 As to the variation of class rights, see paras 8.11 et seq, below.

8 *Punt v Symons & Co Ltd* [1903] 2 Ch 506; *Southern Foundries (1926) Ltd v Shirlaw* [1940] 2 All ER 445.

NAME

(1) Provisions of the Companies Act 1985

Name as stated in memorandum

1.24   The name of a public company must end with the words 'public limited company'.[1]

In the case of a company limited by shares or by guarantee (not being a public company) the name must have 'limited' as its last word[2] except where it is exempted under s 30[3] from this requirement.[4]

1 CA 1985, s 25(1). If the memorandum states that the company's registered office is to be situated in Wales, the words 'cwmni cyfyngedig cyhoeddus' may be used instead of 'public limited company': ibid, s 25(1).

2 Ibid, s 25(2).

3 See para 1.29, below.

4 CA 1985, s 25(2). As to the last word of the company's name where the memorandum states that its registered office is to be situated in Wales, see ibid, s 25(2).

Prohibition on registration with certain names

1.25   A company must not be registered by a name

(a) which includes, otherwise than at the end of the name, any of the words or expressions 'limited', 'unlimited' or 'public limited company';[1]

(b) which includes, otherwise than at the end of the name, an abbreviation of any of those words or expressions;

(c) which is the same as a name appearing in the Registrar of Companies' index of company names;

(d) the use of which by the company would in the opinion of the Secretary of State constitute a criminal offence; or

(e) which in the opinion of the Secretary of State is offensive.[2]

Except with the approval of the Secretary of State a company must not be registered by a nàme which

(a) in the opinion of the Secretary of State would be likely to give the impression that the company is connected in any way with Her Majesty's Government or with any local authority;[3] or

(b) includes any word or expression for the time being specified in regulations made under s 29[4] by the Secretary of State.[5]

In determining whether one name is the same as another, there are to be disregarded

(a) the definite article, where it is the first word of the name;
(b) the following words and expressions[6] where they appear at the end of the name
    'company',
    'and company',
    'company limited',
    'and company limited',
    'limited',
    'unlimited', and
    'public limited company';
(c) abbreviations of any of those words and expressions where they appear at the end of the name.
(d) type and case of letters, accents, spaces between letters and punctuation marks;

and 'and' and '&' are to be taken as the same.[7]

---

[1] Or their Welsh equivalents: 'cwmni cyfyngedig cyhoeddus'.

[2] CA 1985, s 26(1).

[3] 'Local authority' means any local authority within the meaning of the Local Government Act 1972, the Common Council of the City of London or the Council of the Isles of Scilly: ibid, s 26(2).

[4] See para 1.28, below.

[5] CA 1985, s 26(2).

[6] Or their Welsh equivalents.

[7] CA 1985, s 26(3).

Alternatives of statutory designations

1.26 A company which is either required or entitled to include in its name, as its last part the words 'limited' or 'public limited company'[1] may instead of those words include as the last part of the name the alternative of 'Ltd' or 'plc' respectively.[2]

---

[1] Or their Welsh equivalents.

[2] CA 1985, s 27(1), (3). A reference in the Act to the name of a company or to the inclusion of any of those words in a company's name includes a reference to the name [including (in place of any of the words so specified) the appropriate alternative] or to the inclusion of the appropriate alternative, as the case may be: ibid, s 27(2).

Change of name

1.27 A company may by special resolution[1] change its name.[2]

Where a company has been registered by a name which

(a) is the same as or, in the opinion of the Secretary of State, too like a name appearing at the time of registration in the Registrar's index of company names, or
(b) is the same as, or in the opinion of the Secretary of State, too like a name which should have appeared in that index at that time,

the Secretary of State may within twelve months of that time, direct the company to change its name within such period as he may specify.[3]

If it appears to the Secretary of State that misleading information has been given for the purpose of a company's registration with a particular name,[4] he may within five years of the date of its registration with that name in writing direct the company to change its name within such period as he may specify.[5]

Where a direction to change the name has been given the Secretary of State may, by a further direction in writing, extend the period within which the company is to change its name at any time before the end of that period.[6]

A company which fails to comply with a direction, and any officer of it who is in default, is liable to a fine and, for continued contravention, to a daily default fine.[7]

Where a company changes its name the Registrar of Companies must[8] enter the new name of the company on the register in place of the former name.[9] He must issue a certificate of incorporation[10] altered to meet the circumstances of the case.[11] The change of name has effect from the date on which the altered certificate is issued.[12]

A change of name does not affect any rights or obligations of the company or render defective any legal proceedings by or against it.[13] Any legal proceedings which might have been continued or commenced against it by its former name may be continued or commenced against it by its new name.[14]

---

[1] As to special resolution, see paras 8.122–8.125, below.

[2] CA 1985, s 28(1). But if it appears to the Secretary of State that a company, which is exempt under s 30 from the requirement to use the word 'limited' as part of its name (see para   , below, (a) has carried on any business other than the promotion of any of the objects mentioned in s 30(3) or (b) has applied any of its profits or other income otherwise than in promoting such objects or (c) has paid a dividend to any of its members, the Secretary of State may direct the company to change its name by resolution of the directors: ibid, s 28(1).

[3] CA 1985, s 28(2). S 26(3) applies in determining whether a name is the same as or too like another: ibid, s 28(2).

[4] Or undertakings or assurances have been given for that purpose and have not been fulfilled.

[5] CA 1985, s 28(3).

[6] Ibid, s 28(4).

[7] Ibid, s 28(5). The fine is one-fifth of the statutory maximum: ibid, s 730 and Sch 24. The default fine is one-fiftieth of the statutory maximum: ibid. The 'statutory maximum' means the prescribed sum under the Magistrates' Courts Act 1980, s 32.

[8] Subject to CA 1985, s 26. See para 1.25, above.

[9] CA 1985, s 28(6).

[10] As to the certificate of incorporation, see para 1.44, below.

[11] CA 1985, s 28(6).

[12] Ibid, s 28(6).

[13] Ibid, s 28(7).

[14] Ibid, s 28(7).

Regulations about names

1.28   The Secretary of State may by regulations

(i)   specify words or expressions for the registration of which as, or as part of, a company's name approval is required;[1] and

(ii)   in relation to any such word or expression, specify the Government department or other body to whom a request must be made to indicate whether and if so why it has any objections to the company's proposal to have it as, or as part of, its corporate name.[2]

The person to make the request is generally the person who made the statutory declaration[3] in connection with the registration of the company.[4]

The person who has made the request must submit to the Registrar of Companies a statement that it has been made and a copy of any response received from that body together with

(i) the requisite statutory declaration, or

(ii) a copy of the special resolution changing the company's name,

as the case may be.[5]

---

[1] Under CA 1985, s 26(2)(b). See para 6.2, above.

[2] CA 1985, s 29(1). The regulations at present in force are the Company and Business Names Regulations 1981 (SI 1981/1685), as amended by SI 1982/1653. In Column 1 of the Schedule of the regulations the words and expressions for the registration of which as, or as part of, a company's name the approval of the Secretary of State is required are set out. In Column 2 each Government department or other body to whom a request must be made to indicate whether and if so why it has any objections to the company's proposal to have it or as part of its corporate name are set out opposite the word or expression concerned.

Columns 1 and 2 of the Schedule are set out in the table appearing below:

Column (1)	Column (2)
Word or expression	Relevant body
Abortion	Department of Health and Social Security
Apothecary	Worshipful Society of Apothecaries of London or Pharmaceutical Society of Great Britain
Association	
Assurance	
Assurer	
Authority	
Benevolent	
Board	
Breed	
Breeder	Ministry of Agriculture, Fisheries and Food
Breeding	
British	
Building Society	
Chamber of Commerce	
Chamber of Industry	
Chamber of Trade	
Charitable	Charity Commission or Scottish Home and Health Department
Charity	
Charter	
Chartered	
Chemist	
Chemistry	
Contact Lens	General Optical Council
Co-operative	
Council	
Dental	General Dental Council
Dentistry	
District Nurse	Panel of Assessors in District Nurse Training

Column (1)	Column (2)
Word or expression	Relevant body
Duke	Home Office or Scottish Home and Health Department
England	
English	
European	
Federation	
Foundation	
Friendly Society	
Fund	
Giro	
Great Britain	
Group	
Health Centre	} Department of Health and Social
Health Service	} Security
Health Visitor	Council for the Education and Training of Health Visitors
Her Majesty	} Home Office or Scottish Home and
His Majesty	} Health Department
Holding	
Industrial and Provident Society	
Institute	
Institution	
Insurance	
Insurer	
International	
Ireland	
Irish	
King	Home Office or Scottish Home and Health Department
Midwife	} Central Midwives Board or Central
Midwifery	} Midwives Board for Scotland
National	
Nurse	General Nursing Council for England } and Wales or General Nursing Council
Nursing	} for Scotland
Nursing Home	Department of Health and Social Security
Patent	
Patentee	
Police	Home Office or Scottish Home and Health Department
Polytechnic	Department of Education and Science
Post Office	
Pregnancy Termination	Department of Health and Social Security
Prince	} Home Office or Scottish Home and
Princess	} Health Department
Queen	
Reassurance	
Reassurer	

Column (1)	Column (2)
Word or expression	Relevant body
Register Registered Reinsurance Reinsurer Royal Royale Royalty Scotland Scottish Sheffield Society	} Home Office or Scottish Home and Health Department
Special School	Department of Education and Science
Stock Exchange Trade Union Trust United Kingdom	
University	Department of Education and Science
Wales Welsh	
Windsor	Home Office or Scottish Home and Health Department

3 Under CA 1985, s 12(3). See para 8.4, below.

4 CA 1985, s 12(2).

5 Ibid, s 29(3). Ss 709 and 710 (public rights of inspection of documents kept by the Registrar of Companies) do not apply to documents kept under this subsection: ibid, s 29(4). The regulations must be made by statutory instrument, to be laid before Parliament after it is made: CA 1985, s 29(6). They cease to have effect at the end of 28 days beginning with the day on which they were made (but without prejudice to anything previously done by virtue of them or to the making of new regulations) unless during that period they are approved by resolution of each House: ibid, s 29(6). In reckoning that period no account is to be taken of any time during which Parliament is dissolved or prorogued or during which both Houses are adjourned for more than 4 days: ibid, s 29(6).

Exemption from requirement of 'limited'

1.29 A private company limited by guarantee is exempt from the need[1] to use 'limited' as part of its name if it complies with the following requirements:

   (i) the objects of the company are (or, in the case of a company about to be registered, are to be) the promotion of commerce, art, science, education, religion, charity or any profession, and anything incidental or conducive to any of those objects; and

   (ii) the company's memorandum or articles

      (a) require its profits (if any) or other income to be applied in promoting its objects,

      (b) prohibit the payment of dividends to its members, and

      (c) require all the assets which would otherwise be available to its members generally to be transferred on its winding up either to another body with objects similar to its own or to another body the objects of which are the promotion of charity and anything incidental or conducive thereto (whether or not the body is a member of the company).[2]

A statutory declaration that a company complies with the above requirements may be delivered to the Registrar of Companies, who may accept the declaration as sufficient evidence of the matters stated in it.[3] He may refuse to register a company by a name which does not include the word 'limited' unless such a declaration has been delivered to him.[4]

The statutory declaration must be in the prescribed form and be made

(i)   in the case of a company to be formed, by a solicitor engaged in its formation or by a person named[5] as director or secretary; and

(ii) in the case of a company proposing to change its name so that it ceases to have the word 'limited' as part of its name, by a director or secretary of the company.[6]

A company which is exempt from the need to use the word 'limited' and whose name does not include 'limited' must not alter its memorandum or articles of association so that it ceases to comply with the requirements mentioned above as to the objects of the company and the provisions which have to be stated in the memorandum or articles of association.[7]

A company which alters its memorandum or articles of association in contravention of these provisions, and any officer who is in default, is liable to a fine, and for continued contravention, to a daily default fine.[8]

If it appears to the Secretary of State that such a company

(a)   has carried on any business other than the promotion of the objects mentioned above, or

(b)   has applied any of its profits or other income otherwise than in promoting such objects, or

(c)   has paid a dividend to any of its members,

he may, in writing, direct the company to change its name by resolution of the directors within such period as may be specified in the direction, so that its name ends with 'limited'.[9]

A company which fails to comply with a direction by the Secretary of State and any officer of the company who is in default, is liable to a fine and, for continued contravention, to a daily default fine.[10]

A copy of a resolution passed by the directors of a company in compliance with a direction by the Secretary of State must, within fifteen days after it has been passed, be forwarded to the Registrar of Companies and recorded by him.[11] It must be either a printed copy or else a copy in some other form approved by him.[12]

A company which has received a direction must not thereafter be registered by a name which does not include 'limited' without the approval of the Secretary of State.[13]

---

[1] Under CA 1985, s 25. See para 1.24, above.

[2] CA 1985, s 30(2), (3).

[3] Ibid, s 30(4).

[4] Ibid, s 30(4).

[5] In the statement delivered under CA 1985, s 10(2). See para 8.1, below.

6 CA 1985, s 30(5).

7 Ibid, s 31(1).

8 Ibid, s 31(5). The fine is the statutory maximum and the daily default fine is one-tenth of the statutory maximum: ibid, s 730 and Sch 24. The 'statutory maximum' means the prescribed sum under the Magistrates' Courts Act 1980, s 32: ibid, Sch 24.

9 CA 1985, s 31(2).

10 Ibid, s 31(6). The fine is one-fifth of the statutory maximum, and the daily default fine is one-fiftieth of the statutory maximum: ibid, s 730 and Sch 24. The 'statutory maximum' means the prescribed sum under the Magistrates' Courts Act 1980, s 32: ibid, Sch 24.

11 CA 1985, ss 31(2), 380(1)(4)(e). If a company fails to forward a copy of the resolution to the Registrar of Companies within 15 days, the company and every officer of it who is in default is liable to a fine and, for continued contravention, to a daily default fine: ibid, s 380(5). The fine is one-fifth of the statutory maximum, and the daily default fine is one-fiftieth of the statutory maximum: ibid, s 730 and Sch 24. For the 'statutory maximum', see n 8, above.

12 CA 1985, ss 31(2), 380(1)(4)(e).

13 Ibid, s 31(3).

Power to require company to abandon misleading name

1.30　If in the Secretary of State's opinion the name by which a company is registered gives so misleading an indication of the nature of its activities as to be likely to cause harm to the public, he may direct it to change its name.[1]

The direction must, if not duly made the subject of an application to the court, be complied with within a period of six weeks from the date of the direction or such longer period as the Secretary of State may think fit to allow.[2]

The company may, within a period of three weeks from the date of the direction, apply to the court to set it aside.[3] The court may set the direction aside or confirm it.[4] If the court confirms the direction, it must specify a period within which it must be complied with.[5]

If a company makes default in complying with a direction, it is liable to a fine and, for continued contravention, to a daily default fine.[6]

Where a company changes its name under the above provisions, the Registrar of Companies must enter the new name in the register in place of the former name.[7] He must issue a certificate of incorporation[8] to meet the circumstances of the case.[9] The change of name has effect from the date on which the altered certificate is issued.[10]

A change of name under the above provisions does not affect any of the rights or obligations of the company, or render defective any legal proceedings by or against it.[11] Any legal proceedings which might have been continued or commenced against it by its former name may be continued or commenced against it by its new name.[12]

---

1 CA 1985, s 32(1).

2 Ibid, s 32(2).

3 Ibid, s 32(3).

4 Ibid, s 32(3).

5 Ibid, s 32(3).

6 Ibid, s 32(4). The fine is one-fifth of the statutory maximum, and the daily default fine is one-fiftieth of the statutory maximum: ibid, s 730 and Sch 24. For the 'statutory maximum', see para 1.29 n 8, supra.

7 CA 1985, s 32(5).

8 As to the certificate of incorporation, see para 1.44, below.

9 CA 1985, s 32(5).

10 Ibid, s 32(5).

11 Ibid, s 32(5).
12 Ibid, s 32(5).

Prohibition on trading under misleading name

1.31   A person who is not a public company is guilty of an offence if he carries on any trade, profession or business under a name which includes, as its last part, the words 'public limited company'.[1] A person guilty of such an offence, and if that person is a company, any officer of the company who is in default is liable to a fine and, for continued contravention, to a daily default fine.[2]

A public company is guilty of an offence if, in circumstances in which the fact that it is a public company is likely to be material to any person, it uses a name which may reasonably be expected to give the impression that it is a private company.[3] If a public company does so, the company and any officer who is in default is liable to a fine and, for continued contravention, to a daily default fine.[4]

---

[1] CA 1985, s 33(1). The position is the same where the Welsh equivalent of the words 'public limited company' is used: ibid, s 33(1).
[2] Ibid, s 33(3). The fine is one-fifth of the statutory maximum and the daily default fine is one-fiftieth of the statutory maximum: ibid, s 730 and Sch 24. The 'statutory maximum' means the prescribed sum under the Magistrates' Courts Act 1980, s 32: ibid, Sch 24.
[3] Ibid, s 33(2).
[4] Ibid, s 33(3). The fine is one-fifth of the statutory maximum and the daily default fine is one-fiftieth of the statutory maximum: ibid, s 730 and Sch 24. For the meaning of the 'statutory maximum', see n 2, above.

Penalty for improper use of 'limited'

1.32   If any person trades or carries on business under a name or title of which 'limited'[1] or any contraction or imitation of those words, is the last word, that person, unless duly incorporated with limited liability, is liable to a fine and, for continued contravention, to a daily default fine.[2]

---

[1] Or the Welsh equivalent: cyfyngedig.
[2] CA 1985, s 34. The fine is one-fiftieth of the statutory maximum, and the daily default fine is one-fiftieth of the statutory maximum: ibid, s 730 and Sch 24. The 'statutory maximum' means the prescribed sum under the Magistrates' Courts Act 1980, s 32: ibid, Sch 24.

---

(2) Provisions of other Acts

1.33   It is unlawful for any person, without the authority of the Defence Council to use for any purpose whatsoever the designation 'Red Cross', 'Geneva Cross', 'Red Crescent' or 'Red Lion and Sun'.[1]

The words 'common good' must not, without the consent of the Charity Commissioners, be used in the name of any institution other than a body corporate established by Royal Charter.[2]

Where the use by an association of any name has been protected by an Order in Council,[3] a person must not without the authority of the association, use the name the use of which is so protected or any name so closely resembling the name the use of which is so protected as to lead to the belief that it is that name.[4]

It is unlawful to use in connection with any trade, business, calling or profession the word 'Anzac' or any word closely resembling that word without the authority of the Secretary of State, given on the request of the Government of the Commonwealth of Australia or of the Dominion of New Zealand.[5]

[1] Geneva Conventions Act 1957, s 6(1). For the penalty, see ibid, s 7(3).

[2] Charities Act 1960, s 31(2). For the penalty see ibid, s 31(3).

[3] See e g Chartered Associations (British Legion) Protection Order 1927 (SR & O 1931, No 929); Chartered Associations (Scout Association) Protection Order 1967 (SI 1967/1673); Chartered Associations (Girl Guides Association) Protection Order 1970 (SI 1970/1944).

[4] Chartered Associations (Protection of Names and Uniforms) Act 1926, s 1(3). For the penalty, see ibid, s 1(4).

[5] 'Anzac' (Restriction on Trade Use of Word) Act 1916, s 1(1). For the penalty, see ibid, s 1(2).

(3) Provisions of the common law

Passing off action

1.34 A company should not select a name so like that of an existing company or firm as to lead to confusion in the minds of the public, for if it does so, the other party is entitled to bring an action for 'passing off'.[1]

The other party may claim damages and/or an injunction to restrain the company from continuing the use of the name concerned.[2]

[1] *Ewing v Buttercup Margarine Co Ltd* [1917] 2 Ch 1, CA.

[2] Ibid.

OBJECTS

Purpose of objects clause

1.35 The purpose of the objects clause is to enable the members and the creditors of the company to ascertain the scope of the transactions into which the company may enter.[1]

[1] *Cotman v Brougham* [1918] AC 514, HL.

Alteration of objects

1.36 A company may by special resolution[1] alter its memorandum with respect to the objects of the company, so far as may be required to enable it

(i) to carry on its business more economically or more efficiently; or

    (ii)   to attain its main purpose by new or improved means; or

    (iii) to enlarge or change the local area of its operations; or

    (iv) to carry on some business which under existing circumstances may conveniently or advantageously be combined with the business of the company; or

    (v)   to restrict or abandon any of the objects specified in the memorandum;[2] or

    (vi) to sell or dispose of the whole or any part of the undertaking of the company; or

    (vii) to amalgamate with any other company or body of persons.[3]

If an application is made under the following provisions, the alteration does not have effect except in so far as it is confirmed by the court.[4]

---

[1] As to special resolutions, see paras 8.122–8.125, below.

[2] See *Re Hampstead Garden Suburb Trust Ltd* [1962] Ch 806.

[3] CA 1985, s 4.

[4] Ibid, s 4.

Objection to alteration

1.37 Where a company's memorandum has been altered by special resolution, an application may be made to the court for the alteration to be cancelled.[1]

Such an application may be made

    (a) by the holders of not less in the aggregate than 15 per cent in nominal value of the company's issued share capital[2] or any class of it, or, if the company is not limited by shares, not less than fifteen per cent of the company's members; or

    (b) by the holders of not less than fifteen per cent of the company's debentures[3] entitling the holders to object to an alteration of the objects.[4]

But an application cannot be made by any person who has consented to or voted in favour of the alteration.[5]

The application must be made within 21 days after the date on which the resolution altering the company's objects was passed. It may be made on behalf of the persons entitled to make it by such one or more of their number as they may appoint in writing for the purpose.[6]

The court may on such an application make an order confirming the alteration either wholly or in part and on such terms and conditions as it thinks fit.[7]

If it thinks fit, the court may adjourn the proceedings in order that an arrangement may be made to its satisfaction for the purchase of the interests of dissentient members.[8] It may give such directions and make such orders as it thinks expedient for facilitating or carrying into effect any such arrangement.[9]

The court's order may, if the court thinks fit, provide for the purchase by the company of any of the shares of the company, and for the reduction accordingly of its capital, and may make such alterations in the company's memorandum and articles as may be required in consequence of that alteration.[10]

If the court's order requires the company not to make any, or any specified, alteration in its memorandum or articles, the company does not then have power without the leave of the court to make any such alteration in breach of that requirement.[11]

An alteration in the memorandum or articles of a company made by virtue of an order, other than one made by resolution of the company, is of the same effect as if duly made by resolution.[12]

[1] CA 1985, s 5(1).

[2] As to issued share capital, see para 3.18, below.

[3] The debentures entitling the holders to object to an alteration of a company's objects are any debentures secured by a floating charge which were issued or first issued before 1 December 1947 or form part of the same series as any debentures so issued: CA 1985, s 5(8). A special resolution altering a company's objects requires the same notice to the holders of any such debentures as to members of the company: ibid, s 5(8). For debentures, see para 4.78, below, and for a floating charge, see para 4.79, below.

[4] CA 1985, s 5(2).

[5] Ibid, s 5(2).

[6] Ibid, s 5(3).

[7] Ibid, s 5(4).

[8] Ibid, s 5(4).

[9] Ibid, s 5(4).

[10] Ibid, s 5(5).

[11] Ibid, s 5(6).

[12] Ibid, s 5(7). The Act applies accordingly to the memorandum or articles as so altered: ibid, s 5(7).

Notices to registrar

1.38 If a company passes a resolution altering its objects then, if no application[1] objecting to the alteration is made, the company must within fifteen days of the end of the period for making such an application deliver to the Registrar of Companies a printed copy of its memorandum as so altered.[2]

If an application objecting to the alteration is made the company must give notice in the prescribed form (form 6) of that fact to the Registrar.[3] Further, within fifteen days from the date of any order cancelling or confirming the alteration, deliver to the Registrar an office copy of the order, and, in the case of an order confirming the alteration, a printed copy of the memorandum as altered.[4]

If a company makes default in notice or delivering the document to the Registrar the company and every officer of it who is in default is liable to a fine and for continued contravention, to a daily default fine.[5]

[1] Under CA 1985, s 5.

[2] CA 1985, s 6(1)(a).

[3] Ibid, s 6(1)(b)(i).

[4] Ibid, s 6(1)(b)(ii). The court may by order at any time extend the time for the delivery of the documents to the Registrar for such period as it may think proper: ibid, s 6(2).

[5] Ibid, s 6(3). The fine is one-fifth of the statutory maximum, and the daily default fine is one-fiftieth of the statutory maximum: ibid, s 730 and Sch 24. The 'statutory maximum' means the prescribed sum under the Magistrates' Courts Act 1980, s 32: ibid, Sch 24

Validity of alteration

1.39 The validity of an alteration of a company's memorandum with respect to the objects of the company cannot be questioned on the ground that it was not authorised[1] except in proceedings taken for the purpose[2] before the expiration of 21 days after the date of the resolution concerned.[3]

[1] Under s 4.
[2] Whether under s 5 or otherwise.
[3] CA 1985, s 6(4). Where such proceedings are taken otherwise than under s 5, sub-ss (1) to (3) of s 6 apply in relation to the proceedings as if they had been taken under that section, and as if an order declaring the alteration invalid were an order cancelling it, and as if an order dismissing the proceedings were an order confirming the alteration: ibid, s 6(5).

REGISTRATION

Documents to be sent to Registrar of Companies

1.40 The company's memorandum and articles (if any) must be delivered to the Registrar of Companies.[1] Articles must be registered by a company limited by guarantee or unlimited.[2] If a company limited by shares does not register articles, Table A (in the form extant at the time of registration) will constitute the company's articles.[3]

With the memorandum there must be delivered a statement in the prescribed form (form 10) containing the names and requisite particulars[4] of

(i) the person who is, or the persons who are to be the first director or directors of the company; and
(ii) the person who is, or the persons who are to be the first secretary or joint secretaries of the company.[5]

The statement must be signed by or on behalf of the subscribers of the memorandum.[6] It must contain a consent signed by each of the persons named, in it as a director, as secretary or as one of joint secretaries to act in the relevant capacity.[7]

Where a memorandum is delivered by a person as agent for the subscribers, the statement must specify that fact and the person's name and address.[8]

An appointment by any articles delivered with the memorandum of a person as director or secretary of the company is void unless he is named as a director or secretary in the statement.[9]

In the statement there must be specified the situation of the company's registered office[10] on incorporation.[11]

[1] CA 185, s 10(1).
[2] Ibid, s 7(1).
[3] Ibid, s 8(2).
[4] The requisite particulars in each case are those set out in ibid, Sch 1.
[5] CA 1985, s 10(2).
[6] Ibid, s 10(3).
[7] Ibid, s 10(3).
[8] Ibid, s 10(4).
[9] Ibid, s 10(5).
[10] For the registered office, see para 7.08, below.
[11] CA s 10(6).

Capital duty

1.41 Where a company is to be incorporated with limited liability and is to have a share capital a statement in the prescribed form (form PUC 1) and containing the prescribed particulars must be delivered to the Registrar of Companies in addition to the memorandum and articles.[1]

The statement is registered by the Registrar upon payment of the appropriate stamp duty.[2] Unless the statement is registered, he must not register the memorandum and articles.[3]

---

[1] FA 1973, s 47(3). The form and particulars are those prescribed by the Commissioners of Inland Revenue; ibid, s 47(1).
[2] Ibid, s 47(3). The rate is set out in ibid, s 47(5) and Sch 19, Part II.
[3] Ibid, s 47(3).

Minimum authorised capital

1.42 When a memorandum delivered to the Registrar of Companies states that the association to be registered is a public company, the amount of the share capital[1] stated in the memorandum to be that with which the company proposed to be registered must not be less than the 'authorised minimum'.[2]

The 'authorised minimum' means £50,000 or such other sum as the Secretary of State may by order made by statutory instrument specify instead.[3]

---

[1] As to share capital, see para 3.18, below.
[2] CA 1985, s 11.
[3] Ibid, s 118.

Duty of Registrar of Companies

1.43 The Registrar of Companies must not register a company's memorandum which has been delivered to him[1] unless he is satisfied that all the requirements of the Act in respect of registration and of matters precedent and incidental to it have been complied with.[2]

The Registrar must retain and register the memorandum and articles (if any) delivered to him.[3]

A statutory declaration in the prescribed form (form 12) by

(a) a solicitor engaged in the formation of a company; or
(b) a person named as a director or secretary of the company in the statement delivered under s 10(2)[4]

that those requirements have been complied with must be delivered to the Registrar.[5] The Registrar may accept such a declaration as sufficient evidence of compliance.[6]

---

[1] Under s 10. See para 1.40, above.
[2] CA 1985, s 12(1).
[3] Ibid, s 12(2).
[4] See para 1.40, above.
[5] CA 1985, s 12(3).
[6] Ibid, s 12(3).

Effect of registration

1.44   On the registration of a company's memorandum the Registrar of Companies must give a certificate that the company is incorporated and, in the case of a limited company, that it is limited.[1]

The certificate may be signed by the Registrar, or authenticated by his official seal.[2]

From the date of incorporation mentioned in the certificate the subscribers[3] of the memorandum, together with such other persons as may from time to time become members[4] of the company, are a body corporate by the name contained in the memorandum.[5]

The body corporate is then capable of exercising all the functions of an incorporated company, but with such liability on the part of its members to contribute to its assets in the event of its being wound up[6] as is provided by the Act.[7] But in the case of a public company an additional certificate as to the amount of its allotted share capital[8] is necessary before it can commence business.[9]

The persons named in the statement under s 10[10] as directors, secretary or joint secretaries are, on the company's incorporation, deemed to have been respectively appointed as its first directors, secretary or joint secretaries.[11]

Where the Registrar registers an association's memorandum which states that the association is to be a public company, the certificate of incorporation must contain a statement that the company is a public company.[12]

A certificate of incorporation given in respect of an association is conclusive evidence

(a) that the requirements of the Act in respect of registration and of matters precedent and incidental to it have been duly complied with, and that the association is a company authorised to be registered, and is duly registered, under the Act; and

(b) if the certificate contains a statement that the company is a public company, that the company is such a company.[13]

---

[1] CA 1985, s 13(1).
[2] Ibid, s 13(2).
[3] As to subscribers of the memorandum, see para 1.17, above.
[4] As to members of the company, see para 1.67, below.
[5] CA 1985, s 13(3).
[6] As to winding up, see chapter 11, below.
[7] CA, s 13(4).
[8] Under s 117.
[9] CA 1985, s 13(4). As to the commencement of business, see para 1.72, below.
[10] See para 1.40, above.
[11] CA 1985, s 13(5).
[12] Ibid, s 13(6).
[13] Ibid, s 13(7).

Effect of memorandum and articles

1.45   The memorandum and articles, when registered, bind the company and its members to the same extent as if they respectively had been signed and sealed by each member, and contained covenants on the part of each member to observe all the provisions of the memorandum and of the articles.[1]

The articles are a binding contract between the company and a member only in his capacity of a member.[2] Thus, where a person is appointed by the articles as a solicitor and he subsequently becomes a member, he cannot claim against the company under the articles if it fails to appoint him.[3]

One member is not entitled to enforce the articles against another member, and can do so only through getting the company to bring the action to do so.[4]

No contract between the company and a third party is constituted by the articles,[5] so, where they provide that a person is to be employed as the company's solicitor and he is not appointed, he cannot sue under the articles.[6]

---

[1] CA 1985, s 14(1).

[2] *Bisgood v Henderson's Transvaal Estates Ltd* [1908] 1 Ch 743.

[3] *Eley v Positive Government Security Life Assurance Co* (1876) 1 Ex D 88, CA.

[4] *Welton v Saffery* [1897] AC 299, HL.

[5] *Hickman v Kent or Romney Marsh Sheep Breeders' Association* [1915] 1 Ch 881; *Beattie v E and F Beattie Ltd* [1938] 3 All ER 214.

[6] *Re Rhodesian Properties Ltd* (1901) 45 Sol Jo 580.

Memorandum and articles of company limited by guarantee

1.46 In the case of a company limited by guarantee and not having a share capital, every provision in the memorandum or articles, or in any resolution of the company purporting to give any person a right to participate in the divisible profits of the company otherwise than as a member, is void.[1]

Every provision in the memorandum or articles, or in any resolution, of a company so limited purporting to divide the company's undertaking into shares or interests is to be treated as a provision for a share capital, notwithstanding that the nominal amount or number of the shares or interests is not specified by the provision.[2]

---

[1] CA 1985, s 15(1).

[2] Ibid, s 15(2).

Effect of alteration on company's members

1.47 A member[1] of a company is not bound by an alteration in the memorandum or articles after the date on which he became a member, if and so far as the alteration

(a) requires him to take or subscribe for more shares than the number held by him at the date on which the alteration is made; or

(b) in any way increases his liability as at that date to contribute to the company's share capital or otherwise to pay money to the company.[2]

---

[1] As to the membership of a company, see paras 1.67–1.71, below.

[2] CA 1985, s 16(1). This sub-s operates notwithstanding anything in the memorandum or articles: ibid, s 16(2). But it does not apply in a case where the member agrees in writing, either before or after the alteration is made, to be bound by the alteration: ibid, s 16(2).

Conditions in memorandum which could have been in articles

1.48 In general, a condition in a company's memorandum which could lawfully have been contained in articles of association instead of in the memorandum may be altered by the company by special resolution.[1] But if an application[2] is made to the court for the alteration to be cancelled, the alteration does not have effect except in so far as it is confirmed by the court.[3]

But this provision is subject to s 16[4] and to Part XVII of the Act.[5]

Further, the provision does not apply where the memorandum itself provides for or prohibits the alteration of all or any of the conditions above referred to, and does not authorise any variation or abrogation of the special rights of any class of members.[6]

---

[1] CA 1985, s 17(1). As to special resolution, see paras 8.122–8.125, below.

[2] As regards the application, s 5 (except sub-ss 2(b) and 8 and 6(1) to (3) apply in relation to any alteration and to any application under s 17 as they apply in relation to alterations and applications under ss 4 to 6: ibid, s 17(3). As to ss 5 and 6, see paras 1.37–1.38, above.

[3] CA 1985, s 17(1).

[4] See para 1.47, above.

[5] CA 1985, s 17(2)(a).

[6] CA 1985, s 17(2)(b).

Registration of amendments of memorandum or articles

1.49 Where an alteration is made in a company's memorandum or articles by any statutory provision, whether contained in an Act or in an instrument made under an Act, a printed copy of the Act or instrument, must, not less than fifteen days after that provision comes into force, be forwarded to the Registrar of Companies and recorded by him.[1]

Where a company is required[2] to send to the Registrar any document making or evidencing an alteration in the company's memorandum or articles,[3] the company must send with it a printed copy of the memorandum or articles as altered.[4]

If a company fails to comply with the above provisions, the company and any officer of it who is in default is liable to a fine and, for continued contravention, to a daily default fine.[5]

---

[1] CA 1985, s 18(1).

[2] By s 18 or otherwise.

[3] Other than a special resolution under s 4 to alter the objects of the company. See para 1.36, above.

[4] CA 1985, s 18(2).

[5] Ibid, s 18(3). The fine is one-fifth of the statutory maximum: ibid, s 730 and Sch 24. The daily default fine is one-fiftieth of the statutory maximum: ibid, s 730 and Sch 24. The 'statutory maximum' means the prescribed sum under the Magistrates' Courts Act 1980, s 32: ibid, Sch 24.

Copies of memorandum and articles to be given to members

1.50 A company must, on being so required by any member, send to him a copy of the memorandum and of the articles (if any), and a copy of any Act which alters the memorandum, subject to payment

(i) in the case of a copy of the memorandum and of the articles, of 5p or such less sum as the company may prescribe, and

(ii) in the case of a copy of an Act, of such sum not exceeding its published price as the company may require.[1]

If a company makes default in complying with this provision, the company and every officer of it who is in default, is liable for each offence to a fine.[2]

---

[1] CA 1985, s 19(1).

[2] Ibid, s 19(2). The fine is one-fifth of the statutory maximum: ibid, s 730 and Sch 24. The 'statutory maximum' means the prescribed sum under the Magistrates' Courts Act 1980, s 32: ibid, Sch 24.

Issued copy of memorandum to embody alterations

1.51 Where an alteration is made in a company's memorandum, every copy of the memorandum issued after the date of the alteration must be in accordance with the alteration.[1]

If, where any such alteration has been made, the company at any time after the date of the alteration issues any copies of the memorandum which are not in accordance with the alteration, it is liable to a fine, and so too is every officer of the company who is in default.[2]

---

[1] CA 1985, s 20(1).

[2] Ibid, s 20(2). The fine is one-fifth of the statutory maximum for each occasion on which copies are so issued after the date of the alteration: ibid, s 730 and Sch 24. The 'statutory maximum', is the prescribed sum under the Magistrates' Courts Act 1980, s 32: ibid, Sch 24.

Registered documentation of Welsh companies

1.52 Where a company is to be registered with a memorandum stating that its registered office[1] is to be situated in Wales, the memorandum and articles to be delivered may be in Welsh.[2] But, if they are, they must be accompanied by a certified translation into English.[3]

Where a company whose registered office is situated in Wales has altered its memorandum as allowed by s 2(2),[4] it may deliver to the Registrar of Companies for registration a certified translation into Welsh of its memorandum and articles.[5]

A company whose memorandum states that its registered office is to be situated in Wales may comply with any provision of the Companies Act 1985 requiring it to deliver any document to the Registrar of Companies by delivering to him that document in Welsh (or, if it consists of a prescribed form, completed in Welsh), together with a certified translation into English.[6]

---

[1] As to the registered office, see para 7.08, below.

[2] CA 1985, s 21(1).

[3] Ibid s 21(1).

[4] For the provisions of s 2(2), see para 1.17, above.

[5] CA 1985, s 21(2).

[6] Ibid, s 21(3).

RE-REGISTRATION

1.53
Part II of the Act contains provisions by which a company may alter its status (e g from private to public) by re-registration. The changes in status provided are: (1) private company to public company; (2) limited company to unlimited; (3) unlimited company to limited; and (4) public company to private company. These are discussed below.

(1) Private company becoming public

Mode of re-registration

1.54   A private company (other than a company not having a share capital)[1] may be re-registered as a public company if:

- (i)   a special resolution[2] that it should be so re-registered is passed; and
- (ii)   an application for re-registration is delivered to the Registrar of Companies, together with the necessary documents.[3]

The special resolution must

- (a)   alter the company's memorandum[4] so that it states that the company is to be a public company; and
- (b)   make such other alterations in the memorandum as are necessary to bring it (in substance and in form) into conformity with the requirements of the Act with respect to the memorandum of a public company;[5] and
- (c)   make such alterations in the company's articles[6] as are requisite in the circumstances.[7]

The application must be in the prescribed form (form 43(3)) and be signed by a director or secretary of the company.[8]
The documents to be delivered with it are

- (i)   a printed copy of the memorandum and articles as altered in pursuance of the resolution;
- (ii)   a copy of a written statement by the company's auditors that in their opinion the relevant balance sheet[9] shows that at the balance sheet date the amount of the company's net assets[10] was not less than the aggregate of its called-up share capital[11] and undistributable reserves;
- (iii)   a copy of the relevant balance sheet together with an unqualified report[12] by the company's auditors in relation to that balance sheet;
- (iv)   if s 44 of the Act applies,[13] a copy of the valuation report; and
- (v)   a statutory declaration in the prescribed form (form 43(3)(e)) by a director or secretary of the company
    - (a)   that the special resolution has been passed and that the conditions of ss 44[14] and 45[15] (so far as applicable) have been satisfied; and
    - (b)   that between the balance sheet date and the application for re-registration, there has been no change in the company's financial situation that has resulted in the amount of its net assets

becoming less than the aggregate of its called-up share capital and undistributable reserves.[16]

A resolution that a company be re-registered as a public company may change the company name by deleting the word 'company' or the words 'and company' including any abbreviation of them.[17]

---

[1] But a private company cannot be re-registered if it has previously been re-registered as unlimited: CA 1985, s 43(1).

[2] As to special resolutions, see paras 8.122–8.125, below.

[3] CA 1985, s 43(1). As to the documents required, see infra.

[4] See para 1.17, above.

[5] The alterations must also comply with s 25(1) as regards the company's name: CA 1985, s 43(2)(b). For the provisions of s 25(1) see para 1.24, above.

[6] See paras 1.22–1.23, above.

[7] CA 1985, s 43(2).

[8] Ibid, s 43(3).

[9] I e a balance sheet prepared at a date not more than 7 months before the company's application: ibid, s 43(4).

[10] Within the meaning of s 264(2): ibid, s 43(4). As to the company's net assets, see para   , below.

[11] As to called-up share capital, see para 3.18, below.

[12] As defined in s 46. See para 1.57, below.

[13] See para 1.55, below.

[14] See para 1.55, below.

[15] See para 1.56, below.

[16] CA 1985, s 43(3).

[17] Ibid, s 43(5).

Valuation of consideration for shares recently allotted

1.55 If shares have been allotted[1] by the company between the date as at which the relevant balance sheet[2] was prepared and the passing of the resolution, and those shares were allotted as fully or partly paid up as to their nominal value or any premium on them otherwise than in cash,[3] the Registrar of Companies must not entertain an application by the company for re-registration unless further requirements are satisfied.[4]

These requirements are that

(i)   the consideration for the allotment has been independently valued;[5] and

(ii) a report with respect to the value of the consideration has been made[6] by an independent person qualified to be appointed as the company's auditor during the six months immediately preceding the allotment of the shares.[7]

---

[1] As to allotment, see para 3.18, below.

[2] For the meaning of 'relevant balance sheet', see para 1.54, above.

[3] See para 4.03, below.

[4] CA 1985, s 44(1).

[5] In accordance with s 108.

[6] In accordance with s 108.

[7] CA 1985, s 44(2). For exceptions to the operation of this subsection, see ibid, s 44(3)(4)(5)(6).

Additional requirements relating to share capital

1.56 For a private company to be re-registered as a public company, the following conditions with respect to its share capital must be satisfied at the time the special resolution is passed:

(a) the nominal value of the company's allotted[1] shares must be not less than the authorised minimum;[2] and

(b) each of the company's allotted shares must be paid up at least as to one-quarter of the nominal value of that share and the whole of any premium[3] on it.[4]

If any shares in the company or any premium on them have been fully or partly paid up by an undertaking given by any person that he or another should do work or perform services (whether for the company or any other person), the undertaking must have been performed or otherwise discharged.[5]

If shares have been allotted as fully or partly paid up as to their nominal value or any premium otherwise than in cash and the consideration for the allotment consists of or includes an undertaking to the company,[6] then either:

(a) the undertaking must have been performed or otherwise discharged; or

(b) there must be a contract between the company and some person pursuant to which the undertaking is to be performed within five years from the time the special resolution is passed.[7]

For determining whether these requirements have been met certain shares in the company may be disregarded. They are (a) any shares allotted before 22 June 1982 and (b) shares allotted in connection with an employees share scheme.[8]

---

[1] As to allotment, see para 3.18, below.
[2] I e £50,000 or such other sum as the Secretary of State may by order made by statutory instrument specify instead: CA 1985, s 118(1).
[3] As to a premium, see para 4.02, below.
[4] CA 1985, s 45(1)(2).
[5] Ibid, s 45(3).
[6] Other than one to which s 45(3) applies.
[7] CA 1985 s 45(4).
[8] See ibid s 45(5)(6)(7).

Meaning of 'unqualified report'

1.57 If the balance sheet was prepared in respect of an accounting reference period of the company, the reference in s 43(3)(c)[1] to an 'unqualified report' of the auditors means a report stating without material qualification[2] that in their opinion the balance sheet:

(i) has been properly prepared in accordance with the Act, and

(ii) gives a true and fair view of the state of the company's affairs as at the balance sheet date.[3]

If the balance sheet was not prepared in respect of an accounting reference period the reference in s 43(3)(c) is to a report stating without material qualification that in the auditors' opinion the balance sheet relating to the form and content of company accounts

(a) complies with the applicable accounting provisions,[4] and
(b) gives a true and fair view of the state of the company's affairs as at the balance sheet date.[5]

Provided that certain requirements are fulfilled, the auditors' report in the case of 'special category companies'[6] does not have to state that the balance sheet gives a true and fair view of the company's state of affairs as at the balance sheet date.[7]

---

[1] See para 1.54, above.

[2] A qualification is not material if, but only if, the auditors in their report state that the thing giving rise to the qualification is not material for the purpose of determining (by reference to the balance sheet) whether at the balance sheet date the amount of the company's net assets was not less than the aggregate of its called-up share capital and undistributable reserves: CA 1985, s 46(5).

[3] Ibid, s 46(2).

[4] The accounting provisions concerned are ss 228 and 238(1) in Chapter I of Part VII and (where applicable) s 258 in Chapter II of that Part: ibid, s 46(3).

[5] CA 1985, s 46(3).

[6] I e banking companies, shipping companies and insurance companies, as defined by ibid, s 257(1), see para 1.15, above.

[7] CA 1985, s 46(4).

Certificate of re-registration

1.58 If the Registrar of Companies is satisfied that a company may be re-registered as a public company, he must

(a) retain the application and other documents delivered to him; and
(b) issue the company with a certificate of incorporation stating that the company is a public company.[1]

The Registrar may accept a declaration under s 43(3)(e)[2] as sufficient evidence that the special resolution has been passed and the other conditions of re-registration have been satisfied.[3]

He must not issue the certificate if it appears to him that the court has made an order confirming a reduction of the company's capital,[4] which has the effect of bringing the nominal value of the company's allotted share capital below the authorised minimum.[5]

On the issue to the company of a certificate of incorporation

(a) the company becomes a public company; and
(b) any alterations in the memorandum and articles set out in the resolution take effect accordingly.[6]

The certificate is conclusive evidence

(a) that the requirements of the Act in respect of re-registration and of matters precedent and incidental to it have been complied with; and
(b) that the company is a public company.[7]

¹ CA 1985, s 47(1).
² See para 1.54, above.
³ CA 1985, s 47(2).
⁴ As to the reduction of capital, see para 4.43, below.
⁵ CA 1985, s 47(3). As to the 'authorised minimum', see para 1.42, below.
⁶ CA 1985, s 47(4).
⁷ Ibid, s 47(5).

Modification for unlimited company re-registering

1.59   Where an unlimited company applies for re-registration, the special resolution must in addition to the matters mentioned above:

(a) state that the liability of the members is to be limited by shares, and what the company's share capital is to be; and

(b) make such alterations in the company's memorandum as are necessary to bring it in substance and in form into conformity with the requirements of the Act with respect to the memorandum of a company limited by shares.[1]

Further, the certificate of incorporation, in addition to stating that the company is a public company, must also state that the company has been incorporated as a company limited by shares.[2]

The company by virtue of the issue of the certificate becomes a public company so limited.[3] The certificate is conclusive evidence of the fact that it is such a company.[4]

¹ CA 1985, s 48(2). As to the requirements of the Act with respect to the memorandum of a company limited by shares, see para 1.17, above.
² CA 1985, s 48(3).
³ Ibid, s 48(3).
⁴ Ibid, s 48(3).

(2) Limited company becoming unlimited

1.60   A limited company may apply to be re-registered as an unlimited company, but is not entitled to do so if:

(i)   it is limited by virtue of re-registration under s 51;[1] or

(ii) it is a public company;[2] or

(iii) it is a company which has previously been re-registered as unlimited.[3]

The application must be in the prescribed form (form 49(1)) and be signed by a director or secretary of the company. It must be lodged with the Registrar of Companies together with the documents specified below.[4]

The application must set out such alterations in the company's memorandum as:

(a) if it is to have a share capital, are requisite to bring it (in substance and in form) into conformity with the requirements of the Act with respect to the memorandum of a company to be formed as an unlimited company having a share capital;[5] or

(b) if it is not to have a share capital, are requisite in the circumstances.[6]

If articles have been registered, the application must set out such alterations in them as

(a) if the company is to have a share capital, are requisite to bring the articles (in substance and in form) into conformity with the requirements of the Act with respect to the articles of a company to be formed as an unlimited company having a share capital;[7] or

(b) if the company is not to have a share capital, are requisite in the circumstances.[8]

If articles have not been registered, the application must have annexed to it, and request the registration of, printed articles.[9]

These articles must comply with the requirements of the Act with respect to the articles of a company to be formed as an unlimited company having a share capital, and if the company is not to have a share capital they must be articles appropriate to the circumstances.[10]

The documents to be lodged with the Registrar are:

(i) the prescribed form of assent (form 49(8)(a)) to the company's being registered as unlimited, subscribed by or on behalf of all the members of the company;

(ii) a statutory declaration (form 49(8)(b)) made by the directors of the company
   (a) that the persons by whom or on whose behalf the form of assent is subscribed constitute the whole membership of the company, and
   (b) if any of the members have not subscribed the form themselves, the directors have taken all reasonable steps to satisfy themselves that each person who subscribed it on behalf of a member was lawfully empowered to do so;

(iii) a printed copy of the memorandum incorporating the alterations in it set out in the memorandum; and

(iv) if articles have been registered, a printed copy of them incorporating the alterations set out in the application.[11]

---

[1] CA 1985, s 49(2). As to s 51, see para 1.62, below.
[2] CA 1985, s 49(3).
[3] Ibid, s 49(3).
[4] Ibid, s 49(4).
[5] As to these requirements, see para 1.17, above.
[6] CA 1985, s 49(5).
[7] As to these requirements, see para 1.21, above.
[8] CA 1985, s 49(6).
[9] Ibid, s 49(7).
[10] Ibid, s 49(7).
[11] Ibid, s 49(8). Subscription to a form of assent by the legal personal representative of a deceased member of a company is deemed to be subscription by him: ibid, s 49(9). A trustee in bankruptcy of a member of a company is, to the exclusion of the latter, deemed a member of the company: ibid, s 49(9).

Certificate of re-registration

1.61   The Registrar of Companies must retain the application and other documents lodged with him, and must:

(a) if articles are annexed to the application, register them; and

(b) issue to the company a certificate of incorporation appropriate to the status to be assumed by it.[1]

On the issue of the certificate

(i) the status of the company is changed from limited to unlimited; and
(ii) the alterations in the memorandum set out in the application and (if articles have been previously registered) any alterations to the articles so set out take effect as if duly made by resolution of the company; and
(iii) the provisions of the Act apply accordingly to the memorandum and articles as altered.[2]

The certificate is conclusive evidence that the requirements in respect of re-registration and of matters precedent and incidental to it have been complied with, and that the company was authorised to be re-registered and was duly so re-registered.[3]

---

[1] CA 1985, s 50(1).
[2] Ibid, s 50(2).
[3] Ibid, s 50(3).

---

(3) Unlimited company becoming limited

1.62 A company which is registered as unlimited may be re-registered as limited if a special resolution[1] that it should be so re-registered is passed, and the requirements mentioned below are complied with in respect of the resolution and otherwise.[2]

But an unlimited company cannot be re-registered as a public company.[3] Further, an unlimited company cannot be re-registered as a limited company if it is unlimited by virtue of re-registration under s 49.[4]

The special resolution must state whether the company is to be limited by shares or by guarantee and:

(a) *if it is to be limited by shares*, must state what the share capital is to be and provide for the making of such alterations in the memorandum as are necessary to bring it (in substance and in form) into conformity with the requirements of the Act with respect to the memorandum of a company so limited,[5] and such alterations in the articles as are requisite in the circumstances;

(b) *if it is to be limited by guarantee*, must provide for the making of such alterations in its memorandum and articles as are necessary to bring them (in substance and in form) into conformity with the requirements of the Act with respect to the memorandum and articles of a company so limited.[6]

A copy of the special resolution must be forwarded to the Registrar of Companies within fifteen days after it is passed and must be recorded by him.[7] It must be either a printed copy or else a copy in some other form approved by him.[8] If a company fails to comply with this provision, the company and every officer who is in default, is liable to a fine, and, for continued contravention, to a daily default fine.[9]

The application for the company to be re-registered as limited, framed in the prescribed form (form 51) and signed by a director or by the secretary of the company, must be lodged with the Registrar of Companies, together with the necessary documents, not earlier than the day on which the copy of the special resolution which has been forwarded to him, has been received by him.[10]

The documents to be lodged with the Registrar of Companies are:

(i) a printed copy of the memorandum as altered in pursuance of the special resolution; and

(ii) a printed copy of the articles as so altered.[11]

---

[1] As to a special resolution, see below.

[2] CA 1985, s 51(1).

[3] Ibid, s 51(2).

[4] Ibid, s 51(2).

[5] For these requirements, see para 1.17, above.

[6] CA 1985, s 51(3).

[7] Ibid, ss 51(3), 380.

[8] Ibid, ss 51(3), 380.

[9] The fine is one-fifth of the statutory maximum: ibid, s 730 and Sch 24. The daily default fine is one-fiftieth of the statutory maximum: ibid, s 730 and Sch 24. The 'statutory maximum' means the prescribed sum under the Magistrates' Courts Act 1980, s 32: ibid, Sch 24.

[10] CA 1985, s 51(4).

[11] Ibid, s 51(5).

Certificate of re-registration

1.63 The Registrar of Companies must retain the application and other documents lodged with him.[1] He must issue to the company a certificate of incorporation appropriate to the status to be assumed by the company.[2]

On the issue of the certificate:

(a) the status of the company is changed from unlimited to limited; and

(b) the alterations in the memorandum specified in the special resolution and the alterations in, and additions to, the articles so specified take effect.[3]

The certificate is conclusive evidence that the requirements in respect of re-registration and of matters precedent and incidental to it and have been complied with and that the company was authorised to be re-registered and was duly so re-registered.[4]

---

[1] CA 1985, s 52(1).

[2] Ibid, s 52(1).

[3] Ibid, s 52(2).

[4] Ibid, s 52(3).

---

(4) Public company becoming private

Mode of re-registration

1.64 A public company may be re-registered as a private company if:

(i) a special resolution[1] that it should be so re-registered is passed and has not been cancelled by the court;[2]

(ii) an application in the prescribed form (form 53) and signed by a director or the secretary of the company is delivered to the Registrar of Companies, together with a printed copy of the memorandum and articles as altered by the resolution; and

(iii) the period during which an application for the cancellation of the resolution may be made has expired without any such application having been made; or

(iv) where such an application has been made, the application has been withdrawn or an order confirming the resolution has been made by the court,[3] and a copy of the order has been delivered to the Registrar of Companies.[4]

The special resolution must alter the company's memorandum so that it no longer states that the company is to be a public company, and must make such other alterations in the company's memorandum and articles as are requisite in the circumstances.[5]

A public company cannot be re-registered otherwise than as a private company limited by shares or by guarantee.[6]

---

[1] As to a special resolution, see paras 8.122–8.125, below.
[2] Under s 54. See para 1.65, below.
[3] Under s 54(5). See para 1.65, below.
[4] CA 1985, s 53(1).
[5] Ibid, s 53(2).
[6] Ibid, s 53(3).

Application to cancel resolution

1.65   Where a special resolution by a public company to be re-registered as a private company has been passed, an application may be made to the court for the cancellation of the resolution.[1]

The application may be made:

(a) by the holders of not less in the aggregate than five per cent in nominal value of the company's issued share capital[2] or any class[3] of it;

(b) if the company is not limited by shares, by not less than five per cent of its members; or

(c) by not less than 50 of the company's members.[4]

But an application cannot be made by a person who has consented to or voted in favour of the resolution.[5]

The application must be made within 28 days of the passing of the resolution, and may be made on behalf of the persons entitled to make the application by such one or more of their number as they may in writing appoint for the purpose.[6]

If such an application is made, the company must forthwith give notice in the prescribed form (form 54) of that fact to the Registrar of Companies.[7] A company which fails to do so, and any officer of it who is in default, is liable to a fine and, for continued contravention, to a daily default fine.[8]

On the hearing of the application, the court must make an order either cancelling or confirming the resolution, and:

(a) may make that order on such terms and conditions as it thinks fit, and may, if it thinks fit, adjourn the proceedings in order that an arrangement may be made to the satisfaction of the court for the purchase of the interests of dissentient members; and

(b) may give such directions and make such orders as it thinks expedient for facilitating or carrying into effect any such arrangement.[9]

The court's order may, if the court thinks fit, provide for the purchase by the company of the shares of any of its members, and for the reduction accordingly of the company's capital,[10] and may make such alterations in the company's memorandum and articles as may be required in consequence of that provision.[11]

The company must, within fifteen days from the making of the court's order, or within such longer period as the court may at any time by order direct, deliver to the Registrar of Companies an office copy of the order.[12] A company which fails to do so, and any officer of it who is in default, is liable to a fine and, for continued contravention, to a daily default fine.[13]

If the court's order requires the company not to make any, or any specified, alteration in its memorandum or articles, the company has not then power without the leave of the court to make any such alteration in breach of the requirement.[14]

An alteration in the memorandum or articles made by an order of the court under the above provisions, if not made by resolution of the company, is of the same effect as if duly made by resolution.[15] The Act applies accordingly to the memorandum and articles so altered.[16]

---

[1] CA 1985, s 54(1).

[2] As to issued share capital, see para 3.18, below.

[3] As to classes of shares, see para 8.05, below.

[4] CA 1985, s 54(2).

[5] Ibid, s 54(2).

[6] Ibid, s 54(3).

[7] Ibid, s 54(4).

[8] Ibid, s 54(10). The fine is one-fifth of the statutory maximum: ibid, s 730 and Sch 24. The daily default fine is one-fiftieth of the statutory maximum; ibid, s 730 and Sch 24. The 'statutory maximum' means the prescribed sum under the Magistrates' Courts Act 1980, s 32: ibid, Sch 24.

[9] CA 1985, s 54(5).

[10] As to reduction of capital, see para 4.42, below.

[11] CA 1985, s 54(6).

[12] Ibid, s 54(7).

[13] Ibid, s 54(10). The fine is one-fifth of the statutory maximum: ibid, s 730 and Sch 24. The daily default fine is one-fiftieth of the statutory maximum: ibid, s 730 and Sch 24. The 'statutory maximum' means the prescribed sum under the Magistrates' Courts Act 1980, s 32: ibid, Sch 24.

[14] CA 1985, s 54(8).

[15] Ibid, s 54(9).

[16] Ibid, s 54(9).

Certificate of re-registration

1.66   If the Registrar of Companies is satisfied that a company may be re-registered as a private company, he must:

(a) retain the application and other documents delivered to him; and
(b) issue the company with a certificate of incorporation appropriate to a private company.[1]

On the issue of the certificate:

(i) the company becomes a private company; and
(ii) the alterations in the memorandum and articles set out in the resolution take effect accordingly.[2]

The certificate is conclusive evidence

(a) that the requirements in respect of re-registration and of matters precedent and incidental to it have been complied with; and
(b) that the company is a private company.[3]

---

[1] CA 1985, s 55(1).
[2] Ibid, s 55(2).
[3] Ibid, s 55(3).

A COMPANY'S MEMBERSHIP

Definition of 'member'

1.67   The subscribers of a company's memorandum are deemed to have agreed to become members of the company and on its registration must be entered as such in its register of members.[1]

Every other person who agrees to become a member of a company and whose name is entered on its register of members, is a member of the company.[2]

---

[1] CA 1985, s 22(1).
[2] CA 1985, s 22(2).

Membership of holding company

1.68   In general, a body corporate cannot be a member of a company which is its holding company; and any allotment or transfer of shares[1] in a company to its subsidiary[2] is void.[3]

But this does not prevent a subsidiary which was, on 1 July 1948, a member of its holding company, from continuing to be a member.[4]

Further, the above provision does not apply where the subsidiary is concerned as personal representative, or where it is concerned as a trustee, unless the holding company or subsidiary of it is beneficially interested[5] under the trust and is not so interested only by way of security for the purposes of a transaction entered into by it in the ordinary course of a business which includes the lending of money.[6]

---

[1] As to the allotment or transfer of shares, see paras 3.18 and 5.01, respectively. In relation to a company limited by guarantee or unlimited which is a holding company, the reference to shares

(whether or not the company has a share capital) includes the interest of its members as such, whatever the form of that interest: CA 1985, s 23(5).

2 For the meaning of 'subsidiary', see below.

3 CA 1985, s 23(1). This sub-s applies in relation to a nominee for a body corporate which is a subsidiary, as if references to such a body corporate included a nominee for it: ibid, s 23(3).

4 Ibid, s 23(2). But subject to s 23(4), the subsidiary has no right to vote at meetings of the holding company or any class of its members: ibid, s 23(2).

5 For the meaning of 'beneficially interested', see ibid, Sch 2.

6 Ibid, s 23(4).

Agreement to become member

1.69 The agreement to become a member may be an express one e g where a person proposes to take shares and there are an acceptance of the proposal by the company and a communication of the acceptance to him by allotment to him.[1]

An agreement to become a member may also be implied from a person's conduct.[2]

1 As to the allotment of shares, see para 3.18, below.

2 See e g *Re Bank of Hindustan, China and Japan, Campbell's Case, Hippisley's Case* (1873) 9 Ch App 1; *New Brunswick and Canada Rly and Land Co Ltd v Boore* (1858) 3 H & N 249.

Minor

1.70 A contract by a minor to take shares is voidable, and he is entitled to repudiate his membership during his minority or on attaining the age of 18.[1]

1 *Newry and Enniskillen Rly Co v Coombe* (1849) 3 Exch 565.

Minimum membership for carrying on business

1.71 If a company carries on business without having at least two members and does so for more than six months, a person who, for the whole or any part of the period that it so carries on business after those six months:

(a) is a member of the company; and
(b) knows that it is carrying on business with only one member,

is liable (jointly and severally with the company) for the payment of the company's debts contracted during the period or, as the case may be, that part of it.[1]

1 CA 1985, s 24.

COMMENCEMENT OF BUSINESS

1.72 A private company is entitled to commence business from the date of incorporation mentioned in the certificate of incorporation issued by the Registrar of Companies.[1]

But a company registered as a public company on its original incorporation must not do business or exercise any borrowing powers unless the Registrar of Companies has issued an additional certificate as to the amount of the allotted share capital[2] or the company is re-registered[3] as a private company.[4]

The Registrar must issue a company with such a certificate if, on an application made to him by the company in the prescribed form (form 117), he is satisfied that the nominal value of the company's allotted share capital is not less than the authorised minimum,[5] and there is delivered to him a statutory declaration complying with the following requirements.[6]

The statutory declaration must be in the prescribed form (included in form 117) and must be signed by a director or secretary of the company.[7] It must:

(i) state that the nominal value of the company's allotted share capital is not less than the authorised minimum;

(ii) specify the amount paid up, at the time of the application, on the allotted share capital of the company;

(iii) specify the amount, or estimated amount of the company's preliminary expenses and the persons by whom those expenses have been paid or are payable; and

(iv) specify the amount or benefit paid or given, or intended to be paid or given, to any promoter[8] of the company, and the consideration for the payment or benefit.[9]

The Registrar may accept a statutory declaration, which is delivered to him under the above provisions, as sufficient evidence of the matters stated in it.[10]

A certificate in respect of a company is conclusive evidence that the company is entitled to do business and exercise any borrowing powers.[11]

If a company does business or exercises borrowing powers in contravention of the above provisions, the company and any officer of it who is in default is liable to a fine.[12]

If the above provisions are contravened, any transaction entered into by the company is still valid.[13]

But if a company enters into a transaction in contravention of the provisions and fails to comply with its obligations within 21 days from being called upon to do so, the directors are jointly and severally liable to indemnify the other party to the transaction in respect of any loss or damage suffered by him by reason of the company's failure to comply with those obligations.[14]

---

[1] CA 1985, s 13(4). As to the certificate of incorporation, see para 1.44, above.

[2] As to the allotted share capital, see para 3.18, below.

[3] As to re-registration as a private company, see para 1.64, above.

[4] CA 1985, s 117(1).

[5] I e £50,000 or such other sum as the Secretary of State may by order made by statutory instrument specify instead: ibid, s 118(1).

[6] CA 1985, s 117(2). For the purposes of this sub-section a share allotted in respect of an employees' share scheme must not be taken into account in determining the nominal value of the company's allotted share capital unless it is paid up at least as to one-quarter of the nominal value of the share and the whole of any premium on the share: ibid, s 117(4).

[7] Ibid, s 117(3).

[8] As to promoters, see paras 2.01 et seq, below.

[9] CA 1985, s 117(3).

[10] Ibid, s 117(5).

[11] Ibid, s 117(6).

[12] Ibid, s 117(7). On conviction on indictment the fine is one of an unlimited amount, and on summary conviction the fine is the statutory maximum: ibid, s 730 and Sch 24. The 'statutory maximum' is the prescribed sum under the Magistrates' Courts Act 1980, s 32: ibid, Sch 24.

[13] CA 1985, s 117(8).
[14] Ibid, s 117(8).

CONTRACTS

Company's capacity

1.73   Where a company makes a contract which is outside the powers given to it by the memorandum, the contract is void and cannot be enforced by the company even though all the shareholders purport to ratify it.[1]

But in favour of a person dealing with a company in good faith, any transaction decided on by the directors is deemed to be one which it is within the capacity of the company to enter into, and the power of the directors to bind the company is deemed to be free of any limitation under the memorandum or articles.[2]

A party to a transaction so decided on is not bound to enquire as to the capacity of the company to enter into it or as to any such limitation on the powers of the directors, and is presumed to have acted in good faith unless the contrary is proved.[3]

[1] *Ashbury Rly Carriage and Iron Co v Riche* (1875) LR 7 HL 653.
[2] CA 1985, s 35(1).
[3] Ibid, s 35(2).

Form of company's contracts

1.74   A contract which if made between private persons would be by law required to be in writing and, if made according to the law of England to be under seal, may be made on behalf of the company in writing under the company's common seal.[1]

A contract which if made between private persons would be by law required to be in writing, signed by the parties to be charged therewith, may be made on behalf of the company in writing signed by any person acting under its authority, express or implied.[2]

A contract which if made between private persons would by law be valid although made by parol only, and not reduced into writing, may be made by parol on behalf of the company by any person acting under its authority, express or implied.[3]

A contract made in accordance with the above provisions:

(i)   is effectual in law, and binds the company and its successors and all other parties to it;

(ii)   may be varied or discharged in the same manner.[4]

[1] CA 1985, s 36(1)(a). As to the company's common seal, see para 7.05, below.
[2] CA 1985, s 36(1)(b).
[3] Ibid, s 36(1)(c).
[4] Ibid, s 36(2).

Pre-incorporation contracts

1.75   Where a contract purports to be made by a company, or by a person as agent for a company, at a time when the company has not been formed, then, subject to any agreement to the contrary, the contract has effect as one entered into by the person purporting to act for the company or as agent for it, and he is personally liable on the contract accordingly.[1]

[1] CA 1985, s 36(4).

Bills of exchange and promissory notes

1.76   A bill of exchange or promissory note is deemed to have been made, accepted or endorsed on behalf of a company if made, accepted or endorsed, in the name of, or by or on behalf of or on account of, the company by a person acting under its authority.[1]

[1] CA 1985, s 37.

Execution of deeds abroad

1.77   A company may, by writing under its common seal,[1] empower any person, either generally or in respect of any specified matters, as its attorney, to execute deeds on its behalf in any place elsewhere than in the United Kingdom.[2]

A deed signed by such an attorney on behalf of the company and under his seal binds the company and has the same effect as if it were under the company's common seal.[3]

[1] As to the company's common seal, see para 7.05, below.
[2] CA 1985, s 38(1).
[3] Ibid, s 38(2).

2   Promoters and Prospectuses

Sally A Jones

PROMOTERS

2.01   Neither the Companies Act 1985[1] nor the common law provides a general definition of promoter, but it would appear that it has a wide meaning and that any person 'who undertakes to form a company with reference to a given project and to set it going and who takes the necessary steps to accomplish that purpose'[2] is a promoter. It is clear therefore that a promoter may be promoting a private or public company though it is more usual to use the term promoter in relation to public companies. In practice two distinct types of promoter are discernible, the professional promoter whose job it is to form the company for someone else's benefit and once formed ceases to have anything to do with it, and the manager/promoter who wishes to incorporate a business with which he is associated and will continue to be associated with after incorporation. No distinction is made between these types of promoters at law but two particular considerations should be borne in mind:

(a)   there may be a greater temptation for the professional promoter to abuse his position and relationship with the company than the manager/promoter who is likely to be a shareholder, director or creditor of the newly formed company;

(b)   as a general principle promoters, like all fiduciaries, are not entitled to remuneration as of right. There must be a valid contract;[3] however where the promoter is a professional it would be easier to imply that he is entitled to payment than in the case of the manager/promoter, who might be rewarded indirectly by his participation in the new company. Whether a person is a promoter or not is a question of fact based on what he actually did.[4]

Although the word promoter appears to cover a wide range of people, professional advisers to promoters are not usually within this range. So, for example, a solicitor or accountant providing a promoter with the usual professional services will not be a promoter for the purposes of company law.[5] Of course if a professional person provides more than the usual services of a person in that profession he may be held to be a promoter.[6] Merely signing the memorandum of association as a subscriber was not thought to be sufficient to make a person a promoter, but the Second EEC Directive on Company Law[7] assumes that any subscriber is a promoter. There is now a statutory duty imposed on a public company to obtain an independent expert's valuation on non-cash assets which are to be used to purchase shares by a subscriber to the memorandum.[8] Although a professional person may not be a promoter he does not necessarily escape liability completely but could be liable for negligent misstatement under *Hedley Byrne v Heller*.[9]

Failure to define the word promoter not only leads to questions as to who is a promoter and for how long he is a promoter but as the duties are imposed on promoters, who must carry out those duties?

---

[1] But see CA 1985, s 67(3), n 5 below.

[2] Per Cockburn CJ in *Twycross v Grant* (1877) 2 CPD 469 at 541.

[3] Note that an agreement between the promoter and the non-existent company for remuneration will be ineffective.

[4] *Lydney and Wigpool Iron Ore Co v Bird* (1886) 33 Ch D 85 at 93, CA.

[5] *Re Great Wheal Polgooth Co* (1883) 53 LJ Ch 42 and CA 1985, s 67 specifically excludes any person by reason of his acting in a professional capacity for persons engaged in the formation of the company: CA 1985, s 67(3).

[6] *Bagnall v Carlton* (1877) 6 Ch D 371, CA.

[7] And now see CA 1985, s 104.

[8] CA 1985, s 104, see para 4.12.

[9] [1964] AC 465.

PROMOTER'S REMUNERATION

2.02   The promoter can neither be the agent nor a trustee of a non-existent company,[1] in fact the promoter cannot make any contract with the company which has not yet come into existence. In this respect the promoter risks getting no payment for his work. Payment for promoters, like promoters themselves, takes a variety of forms. A fairly common arrangement is for the promoter to agree with the directors of the company that they will provide for payment in the articles of association. This has two major drawbacks, firstly if the company is never formed there will be no provision for payment and secondly, even if the company is formed with appropriate articles, a promoter is an outsider as far as enforcement of the articles is concerned and cannot sue under CA 1985, s 14 for breach of the contract in the articles.[2] The promoter may persuade the directors to make themselves personally liable for the promoter's remuneration. The promoter's position is made more difficult by the fact that he is not even able to claim reimbursement of costs incurred on behalf of the company in connection with the formation, e g registration fees, unless he has a valid contract providing for such.[3]

Other methods of paying a promoter are:

(a) by shares or an option to take up shares[4] at a preferential price or by the issue for cash of a special class of shares with valuable rights, e g voting or preferential dividend entitlement;

(b) by the promoter selling his business to the new company and keeping the profit on the sale;[5]

(c) by commission, e g an issuing house may be employed to float a public company and payment for this will be a commission on the shares. CA 1985, s 97 provides for the sale of shares to underwriters with a commission of up to ten per cent of the nominal value which can be taken as a discount on the price of the shares;[6]

(d) by profit on the resale of shares, e g a common method of floating a company is for an issuing house to agree to subscribe for the whole issue and then receive payment for its work in the form of a profit on the resale of those shares.

However payment is made, the promoter as a fiduciary[7] must disclose any payment to the company. The 'company' for these purposes would appear to be either an entirely independent board of directors or the existing or potential members as a whole. Disclosure of payment could be made in the prospectus, articles or other document. In the case of a public issue of shares requiring a prospectus, disclosure of the details of payment to any promoter given within the two preceding years or intended to be given *must* be included in the prospectus.[8]

---

[1] *Lagunas Nitrate Co v Lagunas Syndicate* [1899] 2 Ch 392 at 426, CA.

[2] See para 1.45.

[3] *Melhado v Porto Alegre Rly Co* (1874) LR 9 CP 503.

[4] However, note that CA 1985, s 99(2) provides that a *public* company may not issue shares for an undertaking 'to do work or perform services for a company', moreover there may be problems in such an issue on the basis that a promoter's services may be regarded as past consideration: *Re Eddystone Marine Ins* [1893] 3 Ch 9, CA.

[5] If the company is a public company such a sale in exchange for shares would require an independent expert's valuation of the consideration in accordance with CA 1985, s 103 and see paras 4.08–4.13 and 10.46–10.50, above.

[6] See para 4.14, below.

[7] See para 2.03, below.

[8] CA 1985, s 56 and Sch 3, Part I, para 10.

PROMOTER'S DUTIES

2.03 Promoters are not trustees nor are they agents of the non-existent company. However, they are in a position of trust and thus the usual fiduciary duties are imposed on them.[1] There are generally three main fiduciary duties:

(1) a duty not to put oneself in a position of conflict of interest and duty;
(2) a duty not to make any secret profit;
(3) a duty to act bona fide for the benefit of the company.

The duties are technically to the company itself and thus the company is the only person entitled to the remedy for breach, but because it is not yet in existence the duties are said to be owed to the potential shareholders.

The duties are fiduciary, i e derived from equitable principles, and the remedy available is an equitable one. The promoter in breach will not merely be liable for damages for the loss suffered by the company as a result of his breach but the promoter will be *liable to account* for the profit made by him, which may be greater than the company's loss.

The typical breach of promoter's duty involves all three of the fiduciary duties, e g a promoter sells his own property to the company he is promoting and fails to make appropriate disclosure of the facts (see para 2.04, below).

(1) This is a breach of the duty not to place oneself in a position of conflict of interest and duty. The promoter's personal interest is to get the best possible price for his property, his duty to the company is to obtain the property at the most competitive price. It would appear to make no

difference to the question of whether or not there is a breach that the promoter sold the property at the prevailing market price.[2]

(2) This situation, whether or not the price was reasonable, would be a breach of the second duty, not to make a secret profit. The essence of this duty is that the profit is made secretly, thus no breach is committed if the promoter discloses the terms of the transaction to those entitled, generally the shareholders.[3]

(3) The given example might also be a breach of the duty to act bona fide for the benefit of the company. In relation to the commission of this breach the amount received by the promoter from the company for the property may go to the issue of good faith.

---

[1] *Erlanger v New Sombrero Phosphate Co* (1878) 3 App Cas 1218.

[2] *Aberdeen Rly v Blaikie Bros* (1854) 2 Eq Rep 1281, HL.

[3] See para 2.04, below.

DISCLOSURE AND REMEDIES

2.04 The fiduciary duties mentioned above are similar to those imposed on directors.[1] The usual basis for the imposition of these duties is that the person concerned is entrusted with looking after another's property and there is considerable temptation for abuse. But whereas directors have control of the company's own property, the promoter has no control over the company's property as the company is not yet in a position to own its own property, thus it is easier for a promoter to escape liability by disclosure than for a director.

The key to avoiding liability for breach of these duties is disclosure. Remuneration of a promoter is a particular example of a breach of fiduciary duty. This is acceptable as long as the promoter discloses to an independent board[2] or the existing or potential members as a whole. This applies in relation to other breaches. It has been said that the promoter must ensure that 'the real truth is disclosed to those who are induced by the promoters to join the company'.[3] In *Salomon v Salomon & Co*,[4] for example, the court held that Salomon was not liable as a promoter for breach of his fiduciary duty because all the shareholders knew of the transaction between the promoter and the company. Of course a promoter cannot avoid liability by making disclosure to directors or shareholders under his control. The promoter may make disclosure in a number of ways, either in the company's memorandum or articles or by communicating with the shareholders or within the prospectus. A promoter is bound to give details of any payments to him in the prospectus.[5]

If the promoter does not disclose or does not make adequate disclosure of his secret profit then the company's major remedy is to make him liable to account for the profit.

As an alternative to making a promoter liable to account for any secret profit it seems that the company may sue for damages for breach of fiduciary duty.[6] This would be particularly useful where the promoter has not made any secret profit for himself but where the company has suffered a loss.

In addition to the promoter's liability to account for any secret profit and any action for damages the company is able to have the transaction entered in breach of duty set aside.[7] The company would cease to be bound by the contract and the agreement would be treated as having ended. This right to rescind may be lost in certain circumstances, in particular rescission is based on restoring the parties to their pre-contractual position. If this is no longer possible then neither is rescission. A company does not have to rescind the contract in order to make the promoter liable, the two remedies are quite distinct.[8] The company may wish to adopt the transaction and can do so without prejudice to the promoter's liability to account or pay damages.

Other remedies by the company may also be available, e g (1) tort of deceit on proof of fraud, (2) negligence, under *Hedley Bryne v Heller*,[9] (3) a promoter may also be liable under CA 1985, s 631[10] (damages against deliquent directors section) and if the promoter is a subscriber to the memorandum he may be liable under CA 1985, s 104.[11]

---

[1] See para (*Director's Duties*).

[2] *Erlanger v New Sombrero Phosphate Co*, supra.

[3] *Lagunas Nitrate Co v Lagunas Syndicate* [1899] 2 Ch 392 at 422, CA.

[4] [1897] AC 22.

[5] CA 1985, Sch 3, Pt I, para 10, see Appendix A.

[6] *Re Leeds & Hanley Theatres of Varieties Ltd* [1902] 2 Ch 809, CA.

[7] *Erlanger*, above.

[8] *Gluckstein v Barnes* [1900] AC 240.

[9] [1964] AC 465. Note that an action for non-fraudulent misrepresentation will probably not lie in this case because only parties to the contract may take advantage of the Misrepresentation Act 1967, s 2(1) and a promoter is not usually a party to the contract.

[10] This section also applies to breaches committed by directors, see paras 6.23-6.24.

[11] I e prohibition on sale of goods by subscriber to the memorandum of a public company without an expert's report of value of goods.

LIABILITY OF PROMOTERS

2.05 So far only the promoter's relationship with the company he is promoting has been considered. Important problems occur in connection with the promoter's relationship with third parties. The usual problem is that a promoter purports to enter into contracts on behalf of the company when the company has not yet been formed. Before the company is formed it has no capacity and thus cannot enter into legally binding agreements. There are two major questions, is a promoter liable on the contract and what remedies does the third party have?

PRE-INCORPORATION CONTRACTS

Common law

2.06 A promoter is not technically an agent of a company until it is formed, thus he can never create a contract between the unformed company and a third party, but he may be personally liable if he contracts as principal or acts on behalf of an undisclosed principal in the same way as an agent may be liable. When a promoter is acting on behalf of an unformed company it is assumed that he intends the contract to be binding and as he is the only person with capacity, the contract is binding on him personally.[1] The promoter can rebut this presumption by expressly contracting as the company.[2] In such a case there is no contract at all, the company has no capacity and the contract cannot be binding on the promoter. *Kelner v Baxter*[3] is an unfortunate exception[4] to the general agency principle that an agent is not usually liable on a contract made on behalf of another and certainly there is no assumption in all cases that where the principal is non-existent, the agent is personally liable. The question to be asked to determine the promoter's liability on such a contract is 'what is the real intent as revealed in the contract, and did the agent intend to become a party to the contract?'[5] An alternative basis for imposing liability on the agent would be the tortious[6] action of breach of implied warranty of authority.[7] This action has been used where a principal ceased to have capacity but the agent continued to act.

Where a promoter purports to contract on behalf of the unformed company and the company on formation ratifies that action, this will be ineffective. Ratification operates restrospectively to validate the transaction at the time the agent entered into it, but in relation to the pre-incorporation contract the company had no capacity at the time the promoter entered into the contract and it cannot by ratification extend its capacity to a period before its incorporation.[8]

---

[1] *Kelner v Baxter* (1866) LR 2 CP 174.

[2] *Leopold Newborne v Sensolid Ltd* [1954] 1 QB 45.

[3] See above.

[4] Probably because on the particular facts of the case, the goods had been supplied by the third party and consumed by the company, thus restitution was impossible.

[5] *Phonogram Ltd v Lane* [1982] QB 938.

[6] Or quasi-contractual action, see Fridman, *The Law of Agency*.

[7] *Collen v Wright* (1857) 8 E & B 647.

[8] Compare this with ratification of director's excesses of authority by shareholders in general meeting, para . . .

PRE-INCORPORATION CONTRACTS

CA 1985, s 36(4)[1]

2.07 Many of the problems referred to above in relation to pre-incorporation contracts have been overcome by CA 1985, s 36(4) which provides that:

> 'Where a contract purports to be made by a company, or by a person as agent for a company, at a time when the company has not been formed, then subject to any agreement to the contrary the contract has effect as one entered into by the person purporting to act for the company or as agent for it, and he is personally liable on the contract accordingly.'

It clearly imposes personal liability on the contract on the promoter in whatever capacity he acts. However, it is still open to the promoter to expressly exclude his personal liability under s 36(4) as it is said to be 'subject to any agreement to the contrary'. Though in *Phonogram Ltd v Lane*[2] the Court of Appeal considered signing as an agent or as the principal (as in

Newborne's case[3]) insufficient, only an *express* exclusion of liability would be regarded as adequate.[4]

The section may be too harsh on promoters for there is no provision for liability to be transferred to the company once formed. The promoter would appear to remain personally liable on the contract irrespective of the existence of the company.[5]

Novation, i e making a new contract and discharging the old one, and assignment, i e transferring the contract to the company, are other methods open to the promoter to enable him to transfer his liabilities to the company after formation. But such procedures need the approval of the third party and agreement by the company and of course if the company is never formed these procedures are not available. The promoter could make the continuance of the contract dependent on adoption by the company once the company is formed thus limiting his liability to the period beginning with the making of the contract and ending at the time of formation of the company. Often a draft contract between the company and the third party is drawn up for completion on formation of the company and a clause inserted in the articles or memorandum that a contract will be entered into. Novation need not be a formal procedure but can be inferred from the conduct of the parties after incorporation,[6] but not where the company's conduct is due to an erroneous belief that the contract was binding on it anyway.[7] Assignment would need to be a formal procedure. Mere ratification of the contract of the company as recommended by the Jenkin's Committee[8] to relieve the promoter of liability once the company is formed does not seem possible on the wording of CA 1985, s 36(4).

Pre-incorporation contracts should not be confused with provisional contracts. Under the old companies legislation a public company could not trade between its incorporation and the acquisition of a trading certificate,[9] and such contracts were not binding on the company if entered into during that period. CA 1948, s 109 was repealed by CA 1980 but a new public company cannot commence any business after incorporation until it has complied with certain requirements.[10] Consistent with the doctrine of protection of third parties any contract made between incorporation and the granting of a s 117 certificate is valid but the sanctions for breach of s 117 are criminal. Moreover, if any third party suffers as a result of the company and directors' breach, i e the company fails to carry out its obligations under the contract, the directors are jointly and severally liable to indemnify that person.[11] Provisional contracts are valid in all respects even though the s 117 certificate has not been, or never is granted because s 117(8) provides that nothing in this section 'affects the validity of any transaction entered into by a company . . .'

---

[1] Implementing the Second European Directive on Company Law.

[2] [1982] QB 938.

[3] *Leopold Newborne v Sensolid Ltd* [1954] 1 QB 45.

[4] Per Lord Denning at p 187.

[5] The Companies Bill 1973 would have dealt with these defects but was never implemented and the Companies Consolidation (Consequential Provisions) Act 1985 failed to remedy this defect.

[6] *Howard v Patent Ivory Manufacturing Co* (1888) 38 Ch D 156.

[7] *Re Northumberland Ave Hotel Co* (1886) 33 Ch D 16, CA.

[8] Cmnd 1749.

9 CA 1948, s 109.
10 CA 1985, s 117. See para 1.44.
11 CA 1985, s 117(8).

PUBLIC ISSUES OF SHARES

2.08   Most companies start life as private companies and convert to public companies if and when they need to do so. Despite the increase in formalities[1] and costs[2] required for conversion from a private to a public company, it is still uncommon for a public company to be formed initially. Only public companies may offer their shares to the public, indeed it is a criminal offence for a private company to do so.[3] Thus any private company wishing to offer its shares to the public must first re-register as a public company.[4]

Public companies wishing to offer their securities for sale to the public usually apply for a listing on The Stock Exchange,[5] though shares may also be publicly traded on the Unlisted Securities Market or over the counter.

The common methods of raising finance from the public are:

(1) direct method or prospectus issue, i e company issues prospectus inviting subscriptions;
(2) offers for sale, i e company sells new issue to issuing house which then offers the securities for sale;
(3) placings, i e issuing house agrees to find purchasers.

The rules relating to issue of shares and prospectuses apply equally to debentures, i e to all the company's securities, unless there is an indication to the contrary.

1 E g compliance with CA 1985, s 117.
2 E g costs of changing all company stationery to read plc instead of Ltd.
3 CA 1985, s 81.
4 See paras 1.53 et seq.
5 The U K gave effect to the 'Admission Directive', the Listing Particulars Directive and the Interim Reports Directive of the European Community by Stock Exchange (Listing) Regulations 1984 (SI 1984/716). This necessitated a new edition of The Yellow Book which came into operation 1 January 1985. The detailed provisions of the Admission Interim Reports and Listing Particulars Directives are outside the scope of this work.

OTHER METHODS OF RAISING CAPITAL

Rights issues

2.09   With minor exceptions, listed and USM companies are required and, unless they can avail themselves of the disapplication provisions, all other companies are obliged to offer any new shares first to their existing shareholders in proportion to their existing holding.[1] These pre-emption rights are designed to protect the value of the existing shareholder's holding. Such issues are important to the company as a source of capital and are administratively simpler than public issues as no prospectus is required.

Companies may also make a conversion issue, by offering debenture-holders shares as an alternative to redemption.

Bonus issues or capitalisation issues

These are also popular, but in fact do not increase the company's total assets. A bonus issue is an issue to existing shareholders of additional shares in proportion to their current holding. Such shares are issued out of balances on the company's profits or quasi-capital account.[2] Clearly a bonus issue will not be an offer of shares to the public requiring compliance with the prospectus rules.

---

[1] CA 1985, s 89. See para 3.06, below. S 95 disapplies pre-emption rights in certain circumstances; see s 308 below, Ed.

[2] See para 3.19, below.

COMPANIES LEGISLATION: PROSPECTUSES

2.10 The most important legislative provisions controlling a public issue of shares are those relating to prospectuses. All public companies offering their shares or debentures for sale to the public must publish a prospectus (but note there is an important exception for listed companies which provide listing particulars under The Stock Exchange Listing Regulations).[1] Such prospectuses must contain certain details proscribed by statute. Both the requirement of a prospectus and the contents of a prospectus are strict, reflecting the many public share scandals of the nineteenth century. It is not only the contents of the prospectus that are prescribed but it is a general principle that promoters give the overall picture and do not include information which could be misleading.

> 'Promoters are responsible for drafting the prospectus with strict and scrupulous accuracy and not only to abstain from stating as fact that which is not so, but to omit no one fact within their knowledge, the existence of which might in any degree affect the nature or extent or quality, of the privileges and advantages which the prospectus holds out as inducements to take shares.'[2]

A prospectus is 'any prospectus, notice, circular, advertisement, or other invitation, offering to the public for subscription or purchase any shares in or debentures of a company'.[3] The definition is not limited to offers made by the company itself but deems any document by which the offer for sale is made to be a prospectus for all purposes,[4] i e an offer for sale. Only such prospectuses are prospectuses for the purposes of the companies legislation. S 744 needs further comment.

(a) *'Any prospectus, notice, circular, advertisement, or other invitation, offering shares or debentures.'* It is an example of the strictness with which the prospectus rules are applied that the words used in s 744 of offer, invitation are not limited to their meaning in the context of the law of contract and questions of communication of offer etc are not relevant.

(b) . . . *'to the public'*. Public is not restricted to the public at large but includes any section of the public, e g the members or debenture-holders of a particular company or clients of an issuing house.[5] A rights issue for example in principle is a prospectus issue, so too placings. However, offers which are essentially the domestic concern of the company are excluded from the definition of 'the public'.[6] Offers are domestic if they are not calculated to result in the securities becoming available for purchase by persons other than those receiving the offer, or otherwise the company's domestic concern. Note that a restriction in a company's articles or in companies legislation on offering shares to the public will not prohibit a company offering its shares to its members, even though they are 'the public' for the purposes of CA 1985, s 60(2), otherwise private companies would be committing a criminal offence under CA 1985, s 81 whenever they were complying with their statutory duty to grant their shareholders pre-emption rights. Similarly offers of shares to employees under an existing employee share scheme will not be a public issue.[7] Offers of listed securities to professional dealers are not deemed offers to the public.[8]

If a company makes an offer to its existing members or debenture-holders whether or not it is a public issue within CA 1985, s 59 may depend on whether the company's letters of allotment are renounceable or non-renounceable. If non-renounceable only the shareholder addressed may accept the offer and thus s 59 is not relevant, where the allotment is renounceable it could be taken up by any person and would be an offer to the public.

(c) *'Subscription or purchase . . .'* S 744 applies to subscription or purchase. Subscription refers to a cash acquisition of unissued shares or debentures from the company, whereas purchase names the acquisition for cash of shares or debentures from another person to whom the company has previously allotted the shares, e g an issuing house.[9] A bonus issue does not involve a purchase or subscription element and is outside of s 59 and the prospectus requirements generally. Moreover, issues in return for assets, in particular shares in other companies do not involve purchase or subscription and thus do not require a prospectus.[10]

---

[1] The issue of application forms for the purchase of shares or debentures is unlawful unless accompanied by a prospectus complying with the statutory requirements: CA 1985, s 56(2). The exception for listed companies is provided in para 7(1)(a) of The Stock Exchange (Listing) Regulations 1984, SI 1984/716.
[2] *New Brunswick Co v Muggeridge* (1860) 1 Drew and Sm 363 at 383.
[3] CA 1985, s 744.
[4] Ibid, s 58.
[5] Ibid, s 59.
[6] Ibid, s 60.
[7] CA 1985, s 60(6).
[8] Ibid, s 60(8).
[9] *Government Stock and Other Securities Investment Co Ltd v Christopher* [1956] 1 All ER 490, following *Re V G M Holdings Ltd* [1942] Ch 235.
[10] CA 1985, s 103. Note that for listed companies making large acquisitions listing particulars may nevertheless be required: Listing Particulars Directive, Art 6, Ed.

Contents of a prospectus

2.11   CA 1985, s 56 requires all prospectuses[1] to contain those details specified in Part I of Sch 3 to the 1985 Act and to include reports outlined in Part II of Sch 3.[2] The aim of the details is to provide potential investors with sufficient information about the company to enable them to make a commercial decision regarding the investment. The overriding principle is that the prospectus must not contain untruths or half-truths which could mislead the investor.[3] Details of the directors and the promoter and any benefit they might obtain from the issue must be disclosed. The company must disclose its past financial record and give full details of the new issue, how much is needed, for what purpose it is to be used and so forth. Details of every material contract must be given, though the Act gives no guidance on what might be regarded as material. Whether a contract is material or not is a question of fact but the major consideration is whether mention of the contract would influence the investor in deciding whether or not to invest in the company.

Every contract is material 'the knowledge of which might have an effect upon a reasonable subscriber for shares in determining him to give or withhold faith in the promoter, director or trustee issuing the prospectus.'[4]

All purchases of property would appear to be material, so too all underwriting contracts. Copies of all relevant material contracts must be filed with the registrar of companies.[5]

---

[1] Subject to a few exceptions, see para 2.14, below.

[2] For listed companies the prospectus requirements are effectively superseded by the Listing Particulars in The Stock Exchange (Listing) Regulations: see Arts 1 and 4.1.

[3] See paras 2.17, et seq, below.

[4] *Gover's Case* (1875) 1 Ch D 182 at 200.

[5] CA 1985, s 65(2).

Minimum subscription

2.12 Prior to CA 1980[1] very little attempt had been made to prevent the formation of under-capitalised companies. S 47 of CA 1948 (now CA 1985, s 83) was the only real safeguard. This section provides that the first prospectus of a company issued in respect of shares of the company must state the minimum capital which in the opinion of the directors must be raised to meet the following costs:

(1) the purchase of property;
(2) preliminary expenses of formation;
(3) to repay loans; and
(4) working capital.

The statute does not suggest or lay down a minimum amount or percentage. The quantification of the necessary amount is within the directors' discretion though an unreasonable error constitutes a material misstatement which may have both civil and criminal consequences.[2]

If the minimum amount is not subscribed within forty days of the first issue of the prospectus, the issue is deemed to have failed and the offer automatically lapses and the company is required to return all monies received. If the money is not repaid within the following eight days, every director becomes personally liable to repay the sum involved plus interest unless he can show that the default in payment was not due to his negligence or misconduct.[3]

---

[1] Now see CA 1985, s 117.

[2] See paras 2.18–2.33, below.

[3] CA 1985, s 83.

Prospectus reports

2.13   The reports to be included in the prospectus are:

(1)   a report by the company's auditors dealing with the company's profit and losses for the preceding five years;

(2)   where the proceeds of the issue are to be used directly or indirectly to purchase a business or acquire a company, an independent accountant's report on the profits and losses of that business or company for the preceding five financial years.[1]

Where the prospectus includes an expert's report, it must also contain a statement that the expert has consented to its inclusion and has not withdrawn his consent to the prospectus.[2] The expert's consent must be registered, along with the report, with the registrar of companies.[3]

[1] CA 1985, Sch 3, Part II.
[2] CA 1985, s 61.
[3] CA 1985, s 64(1)(b).

Exceptions

2.14   The prospectus provisions of s 56 do not apply where the issue is to existing members or debenture holders, whether or not the applicant has the right to renounce the offer, i e generally a rights issue. Nor do they apply where the prospectus relates to shares or debentures which are in all respects uniform with shares or debentures already issued and listed on The Stock Exchange.[1]

It is unlawful to issue any form of application for shares unless the form is accompanied by a prospectus,[2] but this sub-section does not apply to an issue of shares or debentures where the form of application is issued in connection with a bona fide invitation to a person to agree to underwrite the securities or where the offer is not a public one.[3]

[1] CA 1985, s 56(5).
[2] Ibid, s 56(2).
[3] Ibid, s 56(3).

Failure to comply with prospectus requirements

2.15   No sanction either criminal or civil is imposed in respect of a breach of s 56(1), but breaches of s 56(2), i e prohibition on issue of application forms not complying with s 56(1) makes the person in breach liable to a fine. It might therefore be thought that no penalty would lie for contravention of s 56(1). However, s 66 states that in the event of non-compliance or contravention of *any* of the requirements of s 56, a director or other person, e g the promoter, responsible for the prospectus will not be liable if he proves that:

(a)   as regards matters not disclosed, he was not cognisant thereof;

(b)   he proves that the breach arose from an honest mistake of fact on his part; or

(c) the court is satisfied that the breach was immaterial or having regard to all the circumstances, reasonably to be excused, thus implying that some remedy lies for breach of s 56(1). In *Re South of England Natural Gas Co Ltd*,[1] where certain information had not been disclosed in the prospectus, the allottee was unable to rescind the contract for the purchase of shares against the company but he was able to sue for damages those responsible for the unsatisfactory prospectus.

S 56(1) appears to be limited to those prospectuses issued by or on behalf of a company, or by or on behalf of a promoter of it, ignoring the wider definition of prospectus used elsewhere in the Act.[2] It is suggested that the wider definition was intended but this is not consistent with the wording of s 56.[3]

---

[1] [1911] 1 Ch 573.
[2] I e by virtue of CA 1985, s 58.
[3] For fuller discussion see *Gower*, pp 390–391.

Formalities

2.16 A prospectus must be signed by all those people mentioned in it as directors and the prospectus must be dated.[1] The date is taken as the date of publication of the prospectus unless the contrary is proved.[2]

The prospectus must state that a copy of it has been delivered to the registrar and two copies must have been filed with the registrar before publication,[3] along with copies of the reports to be annexed to the prospectus and any other documents required to be annexed. Date of publication of the prospectus may be important in determining liability under CA 1985, ss 56 and 64 though it would appear that no liability would be incurred merely for omission of a detail required by s 56(1) to be included in the prospectus unless the prospectus is issued. Whether the date of publication is the issue date or the issue date is when there is a general distribution is not clear. In *Nash v Lynde*[4] the prospectus was not issued when a managing director sent the prospectus to another director who used it to induce another to become a director of the company, which occurred, and the new director also purchased some shares.

Where a general prospectus has been issued at least three working days must elapse before applications can become binding contracts. This gives potential investors time to study the prospectus and obtain professional advice on the proposed issue.[5] On the other hand revocation of application is not possible until after the expiration of three working days after issue of the prospectus,[6] this prevents those investors hoping for a quick profit on the shares from revoking their applications if the market looks less promising.

---

[1] CA 1985, s 63.
[2] Ibid, s 63.
[3] Ibid, s 64.
[4] [1929] AC 158, HL.
[5] CA 1985, s 82(1).
[6] Ibid, s 82(7).

LIABILITY IN RESPECT OF PROSPECTUSES

2.17   This area is complex and the various developments both at common law and in legislation have been reactions to particular abuses. The law has developed piecemeal and consequently there are many sources of liability for misstatements and omissions in prospectuses.

Liability in respect of prospectuses will be dealt with under the following headings:

(1) criminal liability;
(2) civil liability—common law;
(3) civil liability—non-companies legislation;
(4) civil liability—companies legislation.

Criminal liability

(a) Companies Act 1985, s 70

2.18   Prima facie an offence will be committed under s 70 if the prospectus contains an untrue statement and any person who authorised the issue of the prospectus is prima facie guilty of the offence. Commission of this offence is not limited to directors or officers of the company. An untrue statement not only covers statements positively false but those statements which although literally correct are misleading.[1] Statements in any report or other document annexed to the prospectus are deemed to be in the prospectus. The accused may prove that the statement, although untrue, was immaterial or that he had reasonable ground to believe and did believe that the statement was true to escape liability, but contrary to the usual principle the onus is on him to satisfy the conditions of the defence. No intent to defraud is required for commission of the offence, mere negligence is sufficient, subject to the defences. Punishment for contravention of s 70 is provided in the section itself, and on conviction a person is liable to a fine or up to two years imprisonment or both.[2]

There are a number of other criminal sanctions imposed for breach of specific prospectus rules, e g s 56(4), and there are sections imposing criminal liability generally for misstatements.

---

[1] CA 1985, s 71(a).
[2] Ibid, s 70.

(b) Prevention of Fraud (Investments) Act 1958 (as amended by the Banking Act 1979)

2.19   This act is designed to prohibit dealing in securities by unlicensed persons. No licence is required by members of any recognised stock exchange or recognised association of dealers in securities. Two sections of this Act need consideration in the context of public issues of securities: ss 13 and 14.

2.20   *(i) Prevention of Fraud (Investments) Act 1958, s 13.* A person is guilty of an offence under s 13(1) if he recklessly (dishonestly or otherwise) makes a statement which is misleading, false or deceptive, or dishonestly conceals material facts and induces or attempts to induce a person to make any form of investment, whether in securities or other property.

A statement is made recklessly if it is made 'heedless of whether the person making it has any real facts on which to base the statement or promise.'[1] This offence is punishable by up to seven years imprisonment.[2]

---

[1] *R v Grunwald* [1963] 1 QB 935 at 939, per Paull J.
[2] PF (I) A 1958, s 13(1).

2.21   *(ii) Prevention of Fraud (Investments) Act 1958, s 14.* S 14 imposes the most severe of the criminal sanctions in relation to prospectuses. It prohibits the distribution, or possession for the purposes of distribution, of any document offering to acquire or dispose of securities which is not a prospectus complying with the prospectus rules in Sch 3. S 13 requires the personal conditions of liability plus commission of the particular acts outlined, s 14 only requires commission of the specified acts. But a person commits no offence under s 14 if he does not know that the document is a circular or that it contains prohibited information or invitation.[1] Nor is any offence committed if the circulars are distributed in connection with a bona fide invitation to enter into an underwriting agreement or to the company's, or its subsidiary's, holders of securities, creditors or employees or to a person whose business involves the acquisition or disposal or the holding of securities.[2] The offence under s 14 is punishable by up to two years imprisonment or a fine or both.

---

[1] PF (I) A 1958, s 14(1).
[2] Ibid, s 14(2), (3) and (5).

(c) Theft Act 1968

2.22   Where an officer of a company publishes a written statement which to his knowledge is or may be misleading, false or deceptive in a material particular, with intent to deceive members or creditors of the company, he commits an offence punishable by up to seven years imprisonment.[1] The prosecution must show that there was an untrue statement and that the accused knew it to be untrue. In *R v Kylsant*[2] it was held that a statement is untrue if it conveys a misleading impression even though it is correct.

---

[1] Theft Act 1968, s 19.
[2] [1932] 1 KB 442, decided under the Larceny Act 1861, the fore-runner of s 19.

(d) Banking Act 1979

2.23   Subject to a few specific exceptions, no person may take a deposit in the course of carrying on a deposit-taking business unless it is a recognised bank or a licensed institution.[1] The Bank of England is made responsible for the recognition and licensing system and it has the power to revoke the recognition or licence.

---

[1] Banking Act 1979, s 1.

Civil liability

Misrepresentation

2.24   Where an investor has been induced to purchase securities on the basis of a misleading statement, he may wish either to make a claim against the company or against the person responsible for the misrepresentation for rescission or damages. The claim is brought by the person who has purchased the securities may be for fraudulent, negligent or innocent misrepresentation at common law or for non-fraudulent misrepresentation under the Misrepresentation Act 1967. These various actions will be considered in turn.

2.25   *Rights against the company.* Where an allottee has relied on a misstatement in a prospectus, as a general principle he has the right to rescind the contract of purchase against the company, and in some cases he will have the right to damages. Only the original allottee will have this right because he has purchased the securities directly from the company and only parties to a contract have the right to rescind. Neither a shareholder who has purchased shares on the market but on the basis of a prospectus issued by a company, nor the person in whose favour the shares are renounced has the right to rescind against the company.

In order to claim rescission the allottee must show:

(1)   that there was a misrepresentation and that it was a misrepresentation of fact;
(2)   that the misrepresentation was material; and
(3)   that he relied on the misrepresentation to enter into the contract.[1]

Rescission is available whether the misrepresentation is fraudulent, negligent or innocent.

The allottee may claim damages against the company where either he can show fraudulent misrepresentation, i e tort of deceit, or where damages can be awarded in lieu of rescission for non-fraudulent misrepresentation.[2] In order to prove fraudulent misrepresentation the allottee must show (1)–(3) above, and:

(4)   that the misrepresentation was fraudulent;
(5)   that those making the misrepresentation were authorised by the company; and
(6)   that he has suffered loss or damage as a result of the misrepresentation.[3]

In order to show non-fraudulent misrepresentation under s 2(1), a person must have entered into a contract after a misrepresentation had been made to him, which if it had been made fraudulently would render the person making it liable in damages, i e (1)–(6) above, but excluding (4). However, the person making the statement may escape liability if he can show that he had reasonable ground to believe and did believe that the facts represented were true. Although this section is intended to be analogous with CA 1985, s 67 it may in fact be more extensive. It would appear that the allottee may sue the company for damages under this section, a remedy which is not possible under s 67.[4]

The common law doctrine of misstatement has undergone considerable change since the seminal nineteenth century case on company prospectuses, *Derry v Peek*.[5]

In *Hedley Byrne v Heller*[6] liability for negligent misstatement was held to lie if there was a duty of care owed by the person making the statement to the person relying on it and that a duty of care of this type could exist in the absence of a contractual or other fiduciary relationship. While the range of circumstances in which a duty of care will arise is not entirely clear, even the most restrictive definition of duty of care would include those people responsible for publishing a prospectus.[7]

The allottee will usually find an easier route to a remedy via s 67 or s 2(1) of the Misrepresentation Act 1967. S 67 does not require the plaintiff to show that a duty of care existed, once the plaintiff has shown that he has suffered loss as a result of an untrue statement in a prospectus, the onus is on the defendant to show that he was not responsible for the statement.

Similarly, the plaintiff does not need to show a duty of care for s 2(1) though the misleading statement must be addressed to the plaintiff.[8]

If a person can show fraudulent misrepresentation, i e a false representation made knowingly, or without belief in its truth, or recklessly, without caring whether it be true or false or negligent misrepresentation, he is entitled to damages for the loss suffered, but where the action is for innocent misrepresentation, only rescission is available unless the plaintiff can rely on non-fraudulent misrepresentation within s 2(1) where damages are available in lieu of rescission.[9]

---

[1] See for example *Edgington v Fitzmaurice* (1885) 29 Ch D 459.
[2] Misrepresentation Act 1967, s 2(1).
[3] *Derry v Peek* (1889) 14 App Cas 337.
[4] See para 2.31, below.
[5] (1889) 14 App Cas 337.
[6] [1964] AC 465.
[7] See for example *Mutual Life and Citizens' Association Co Ltd v Evatt* [1971] AC 793.
[8] See para 2.29, below.
[9] Misrepresentation Act 1967, s 2(2).

2.26 *Rights against others.* The allottee may have remedies against the company by virtue of the contractual nexus between the parties, e g a remedy under the Misrepresentation Act 1967, s 2(1) will only be possible if the shares were purchased directly from the company. There is even some doubt as to whether a purchase as a result of an offer for sale would be direct enough to give the shareholder a remedy.[1] Moreover it was held in *Houldsworth v City of Glasgow Bank*[2] that damages against the company for fraudulent misrepresentation would only lie if the contract were also rescinded. If this is correct the action for damages would be of little use for if rescission is granted the purchase price would be returned to the allottee with interest and no damage would have been suffered. In the absence of a remedy against the company the shareholder may wish to pursue a remedy against others, e g the promoter or experts who made statements in the prospectus, the directors of the company or even the transferor of securities.

---

[1] Despite CA 1985.
[2] (1880) 5 App Cas 317.

2.27   *Damages*. An action for damages for the tort of deceit i e fraudulent misrepresentation will lie against any person who has made a false statement intending that it should be relied on. However, an action for non-fraudulent misrepresentation under the Misrepresentation Act 1967 will not lie except against the other party to the contract. It could be argued that where the shareholder purchases shares from someone other than the company and the company registers that person as a member, a contract then exists between the company and the member under CA 1985, s 14 and this contract could provide the necessary relationship for the Misrepresentation Act 1967 to apply. Where the claim is framed as a common law action under *Hedley Byrne v Heller*[1] any person who owes a duty of care to the shareholder may be liable in damages; this can extend to directors, experts, promoters and even to the issuing house or broker in the case of an offer for sale or placing.

[1] [1964] AC 465.

2.28   *Rescission*. Rescission against the other contracting party is the primary remedy for misrepresentation. Where the company is the other party, rescission is available as outlined earlier, but the shareholder may have purchased his securities from another person. The right to rescind for misrepresentation used to be lost if the contract was executed and a contract for the sale of shares is executed once the company registers the purchaser as a member. The Misrepresentation Act 1967 provides that the right to rescind the contract is available 'where a person has entered into a contract after a misrepresentation has been made to him, and the misrepresentation has become a term of the contract or the contract has been performed . . .' Thus it is no longer a bar to rescinding against the other party that the contract has been executed. However the purchaser must show that the vendor was in some way responsible for the misrepresentation and knew that the purchaser was entering into the contract in reliance on the misrepresentation which subsequently turned out to be untrue.

2.29   *Loss of right to rescind*. The remedy of rescission is based on restitution, i e restoring the parties to their pre-contractual position. Where the contract has been affirmed the innocent party will lose his right to rescind. Affirmation will usually be by the innocent party, with knowledge of the misrepresentation, electing to carry on with the contract, e g by accepting a dividend or voting at a general meeting. Affirmation may be a question of lapse of time, i e a failure to rescind within a reasonable time of the misrepresentation.[1] If the rescission would affect the rights of an innocent third party it will not be possible. For example, if the company goes into liquidation it is too late to rescind as the rights in liquidation will be fixed. However this might not be the case where the purchaser is claiming rescission against the vendor who is not the company.

[1] *Bwlch-y-Plwn Lead Mining Co v Baynes* (1867) LR 2 Exch 324.

2.30   *Breach of contract*. Clearly the major remedy for misstatement in prospectuses is rescission of the contract for the tort of misrepresentation. However, since s 1 of the Misrepresentation Act 1967 has put it beyond doubt, a remedy for breach of contract may also lie for misrepresentation where the misleading statement has become a term of the contract. The major advantage of an action in contract over an action in tort is the measure of damages.[1] As a general principle, in contract a person is entitled to his bargain profit or loss whereas in tort he is only to be restored to the pre-contractual position.

---

[1] Though doubt has been shed on whether there is any difference between damages in tort and damages in contract, e g *Ross v Caunters* [1980] Ch 297 and *Junior Books Ltd v Veitchi Co Ltd* [1983] 1 AC 520.

2.31 *CA 1985, s 67*. The plaintiff need only show that he has suffered loss as a result of an untrue statement in a prospectus to be able to claim damages[1] against the promoter, director or a person responsible for issuing the prospectus. The defendant can only escape liability by showing that he believed that the statement was true and had reasonable grounds for believing it was true. This section was intended to remove the need for any common law or other statutory remedies relating to misstatements in prospectuses. In some respects it is wider than the other possible remedies, but in other respects it is narrower.

---

[1] On the same basis as the tort of deceit.

2.32 *Wider*. The usual onus of proof is reversed, the plaintiff shows the circumstances of the breach and it is up to the defendant to show that he was not responsible. The remedy under Misrepresentation Act 1967, s 2 requires the untrue statement to be addressed to the plaintiff, and other actions require reliance on the statement or incorporation into the contract. S 67 on the other hand appears to give a remedy to any person who subscribes on the faith of the prospectus whether or not it was addressed to him. 'On the faith of' seems weaker than reliance.

2.33 *Narrower*. S 67 gives a remedy only to subscribers, i e allottees of the company not subsequent purchasers. The company is not liable under s 67, only directors, promoters and those responsible for issuing the prospectus. This may include an expert. However, an expert has additional defences under s 68(2). He can show that he withdrew his consent to the prospectus either:

(a) before the prospectus was registered; or
(b) on becoming aware of the untruth after the prospectus was registered but before any allotments were made, having given adequate (reasonable) public notice of his withdrawal and his reasons. The withdrawal of consent must be in writing.

PRIVATE ISSUE OF SHARES

2.34 A private issue is not limited to private companies. There are two categories of private issue of shares, those offered by public companies where the offer is of domestic concern only, e g to existing members or existing employees,[1] and those shares offered by private companies, all of which must be private offers because of the prohibition on offering their shares to the public.

None of the limitations discussed above[2] apply to private issues of shares and thus a public company making a non-public offer and a private company offering its shares privately can go straight to allotment. Before considering allotment of shares generally, consideration must be given to the form of application for shares. These are dealt with in the next chapter.

---

[1] CA 1985, s 60(4).
[2] See paras 2.8–2.33.

3 Issue of shares and share capital

Sally A Jones

ISSUE OF SHARES: GENERALLY

Application for shares

3.01 An application for shares does not need to be in any particular form. The investor is the person making an offer to purchase the shares and the company has the choice to accept or reject as it pleases. The investor may revoke his offer at any time up to acceptance by the company, except that if it is a prospectus issue this common law rule is reversed. The applicant may not revoke his application until three days have elapsed since the opening of the subscription lists.[1] Without this 'breathing space' the company will have no idea of the success of the issue, because the offers could be revoked.

An application can be conditional and if the company allots shares in ignorance of the condition, the allotment will be ineffective, i e the company purports to accept an offer which the applicant has not made.[2]

Although no particular form is required for the application it is common for companies to send out application forms in order to standardize procedure. No such form of application may be sent unless accompanied by a prospectus, or either the offer is a non-public one or the application is a bona fide invitation to an underwriter to underwrite the shares.[3]

---

[1] CA 1985, s 82(7).
[2] *Re Universal Banking Co, Rogers' Case & Harrison's Case* (1868) 3 Ch App 633.
[3] CA 1985, s 56(2).

Acceptance of application

3.02 Acceptance of the applicant's offer must be communicated to the applicant, allotment of the shares it not usually sufficient.[1] However as the parties can agree to any mode of acceptance they wish, the allotment could be expressly provided to be the acceptance.

The offer made by the applicant may only be accepted if it has not already been revoked or lapsed; an offer will lapse after the expiration of a reasonable time.[2] What is a reasonable time is a question of fact dependent on the particular circumstances of the case.

---

[1] *Re Richmond Hill Hotel Co Pellatt's Case* (1867) 2 Ch App 527.
[2] *Ramsgate Victoria Hotel v Montefiore* (1866) LR 1 Exch 109.

Restrictions on allotment of shares

3.03   The prospectus rules and other restrictions on issue mentioned so far relate to the negotiations leading up to issue and allotment. In addition to these restrictions, controls are imposed on companies at the time of issue and allotment. Three categories of restrictions are discernible, those applicable to all companies, those applicable to public companies generally and those applicable to public issues by public companies.

All companies

(1) Authority for issue

3.04   Firstly the company must have power to issue shares. A specific authority in the articles is not usually required, for it will be assumed that the directors can issue shares under their general management power.[1] Secondly, since 1980 the directors must be authorised by the articles or shareholders to make an issue.[2]

The power to issue shares exercised by directors sometimes led to abuse, in particular directors issuing shares to themselves or their supporters in order to perpetuate their control of the company.[3] S 80 returns control of issues of shares to the shareholders. Directors must now obtain authority to make an issue of shares in respect of an issue of relevant securities. Authority can be by ordinary resolution or provided for in the articles. The authority may be general or limited to a particular issue and may be conditional or unconditional. The authority must state the maximum amount of the relevant securities to be allotted and the date on which it expires, which in any case cannot be made more than five years from the date on which the authority was granted. Moreover, any authority, whether included in the articles or a resolution of the company, can be revoked or varied before the expiry date by an ordinary resolution of the general meeting at any time.[4]

Relevant securities are shares in the company other than those taken by subscribers to the memorandum or shares issued as part of an employee share scheme and any right to subscribe for or to convert any security into shares in the company other than shares so alloted.[5] This last requirement is designed to prevent directors avoiding the requirement of authority by issuing convertible debentures which carry no similar restriction, but which on conversion into shares could cause the type of problem the section is designed to prevent.

Consistent with the policy of protecting investors, any share issued in contravention of s 80 is valid[6] but any director who knowingly and wilfully contravenes the section is liable to a fine.[7]

---

[1] See, e g Table A, Art 70.
[2] CA 1985, s 80.
[3] E g *Clemens v Clemens Bros* [1976] 2 All ER 268.
[4] CA 1985, s 80(8).
[5] Ibid, s 80(2).
[6] Ibid, s 80(10).
[7] Ibid, s 80(9).

(2) Proper purposes doctrine[1]

3.05 Shares must be issued for a proper purpose and for the benefit of the company. In *Hogg v Cramphorn*[2] the court held that an issue of shares made for the purpose of defeating a take-over bid and not for the purpose of raising additional capital was an issue for a collateral purpose and therefore a breach of directors' duty.

It is not now correct to say that the only proper purpose for the issue of shares is raising capital, other purposes are acceptable as long as the primary purpose is the raising of capital.[3] Where an issue is made for the director's own interest and not in the best interest of the company or where the ulterior motive of the issue is to alter voting rights the issue is void[4] but it is not clear whether all issues for an improper purpose will render the issue void. In *Hogg v Cramphorn*[5], for example, the shares issued in breach were validated by a vote of the shareholders in general meeting independent of the votes attached to the shares issued in breach, whereas in *Clemens v Clemens Bros*[6] the resolutions proposing an issue of shares to the majority shareholder and the other directors were set aside, i e no shares had actually been issued.

---

[1] And see chap 6 (director's duties).
[2] [1967] Ch 254.
[3] *Howard Smith Ltd v Ampol Petroleum Ltd* [1974] AC 821.
[4] *Piercy v S Mills & Co Ltd* [1920] 1 Ch 77.
[5] Supra.
[6] [1976] 2 All ER 268.

---

(3) Pre-emption rights

3.06 The 1980 Act introduced pre-emption rights. These statutory pre-emption rights are now contained in CA 1985, s 89 and grant a right to every existing shareholder to have allotted to him a proportionate part of any new issue of shares. The main effect of the pre-emption rights is to prevent a dilution of a shareholder's shareholding by the issue of new shares.[1] Only certain shareholders are entitled to pre-emption rights and only certain shares are subject to pre-emption rights.

(a) Shares entitled to pre-emption rights. The shares entitled to pre-emption rights are described as relevant shares and relevant employee shares. All holders of these shares are entitled to be offered new shares in proportion to their existing shareholding. Relevant shares are all shares except:

(i) shares not participating in capital and dividend, e g preference shares participating in capital or dividend
(ii) shares held or to be held in employee share schemes,

Relevant employee shares are those shares which would be relevant shares except for the fact that they are held under an employee share scheme.

(b) Shares subject to pre-emption rights. The company must offer all new equity securities to those shareholders entitled to pre-emption rights as defined above. Equity securities are defined in CA 1985, s 94(2) as a relevant share or a right to subscribe for, or convert, any security into a relevant share. Any reference to the allotment of equity securities includes

references to the grant of a right to subscribe for, or to convert any securities, into relevant shares. It should be noted in particular that convertible debentures would fall into this definition, an anti-avoidance measure.

---

[1] As for, e g in *Clemens v Clemens Bros*, above.

Formalities of pre-emption issue

3.07   Shareholders must be given at least 21 days to accept a pre-emption offer.[1] During this time the offer cannot be withdrawn unless all shares have been accepted or refused.[2] The company may not go to allotment until this period has expired. The pre-emption offer must be made to shareholders on the same or more favourable terms than it was proposed to offer the shares to outsiders.[3]

Once the pre-emption offer has been made, the Act is silent on what is to happen to the shares if shareholders do not wish to take them up. The company's articles may provide what is to happen in this situation and in small companies it is usual to provide that the rejected shares should be offered to the accepting shareholders in proportion to their new holding and so on until all the shares are taken up. As the Act is silent in this respect it is assumed that there is no further restriction on offer and the shares can in the absence of an article to the contrary be offered to non-shareholders.

---

[1] CA 1985, s 90(6).

[2] Ibid, s 89.

[3] Ibid, s 89(1)(a).

Disapplication of pre-emption rights[1]

3.08   Pre-emption rights do not apply in the following circumstances:

(i)   where the offer of new equity securities is for non-cash consideration;

(ii)   where the equity securities would be held under an employees share scheme;

(iii)   where they are inconsistent with any other general statutory provision, i e the pre-emption rights are subject to any general prohibitions contained in other statutory provisions.

A company's articles may provide for pre-emption rights but the statutory pre-emption rights will still apply unless the articles provide for pre-emption rights in relation to particular classes of shares, i e unless the pre-emption rights in the company's articles are more favourable to the shareholders. Where reliance on the company's own pre-emption rights is made it may be that unless all the new shares are taken up in accordance with those rights, the remaining shares must be offered in proportion to the existing holdings of members, otherwise the pre-emption rights in the articles would be less favourable than those in the Act and this would be inconsistent with the spirit of the Act if not the precise wording.

Pre-emption rights can also be excluded in certain cases. Private companies may exclude them by provision in the memorandum or articles, and any provision of pre-emption in the memorandum or articles will exclude the statutory provisions in so far as they are inconsistent. Directors may be empowered to dispense with or modify the pre-emption rights. This applies to public and private companies where the directors have been authorised to make an issue of new relevant securities under CA 1985, s 80. Such power to dispense with or modify the pre-emption rights can only be exercised whilst the authority for issue under s 80 is current. If the directors have a general authority to issue shares the power to dispense with or modify the pre-emption rights can be given either in the articles or by a special resolution. Where the authority under s 80 is only for a particular issue, the power to dispense with or modify the pre-emption rights must be granted by a special resolution, recommended by the directors. In making the recommendation the directors must state their reasons for it, the amount to be paid to the company in respect of the particular shares and the directors' justification of that amount. This recommendation must accompany the notice of the meeting at which it is proposed to pass the requisite special resolution.

---

[1] CA 1985, s 95.

Sanctions

3.09 Failure to comply with the pre-emption rights is subject to civil and criminal sanctions. Any person who should have been offered shares but has not, has a claim for compensation against the company and every officer who knowingly authorised or permitted the breach. Compensation is for any loss, damages, costs or expenses incurred as a result of the failure to be offered the shares.[1] Finally any inclusion in the directors' statement, required before the power to dispense or modify the pre-emption rights can be exercised, which is misleading false or deceptive in a material particular, renders the person knowingly or recklessly authorising or permitting its inclusion, guilty of a criminal offence.[2]

---

[1] CA 1985, s 92.
[2] Ibid, s 95(6).

Other pre-emption rights[1]

3.10 In this discussion of pre-emption rights mention has only been made of the statutory rights, but there are two other sources of pre-emption: the company's own articles and The Stock Exchange rules. Pre-emption rights can be granted in two situations: on the issue of new shares or on the transfer of shares. The Companies Acts are only concerned with the protection of shareholders against pre-emption at the time of a new issue, but it is common for companies, particularly private companies, to include pre-emption rights on transfer in their articles. The common form of article requires any member selling his shares to offer them first to the existing shareholders, usually in proportion to their shareholding. Often a shareholder in a company incorporating such a clause in its articles, finds himself trapped into keeping the shares if the shareholders do not wish to buy them, especially if there is no alternative, i e the shareholder may become a locked-in minority, with little hope of selling his shares, and if he is a minority will have little hope of changing the position.[2] Such a provision ensures that membership of the company is kept to a small, known group and was a common restriction on transfer when this was a necessary part of the definition of a private company prior to 1980.

The Stock Exchange also imposes pre-emption rights and any company wishing to obtain or retain a listing is obliged to offer any new shares issued for cash to its existing equity holders first, and in the same proportion as their existing holding.[3]

[1] And see chap 8 (pre-emption rights).

[2] The clause contained in the articles could be altered in the usual way, i e special resolution of the members. The shareholder may also have a remedy under CA 1985 s 459 or be able to petition for a winding up on the 'just and equitable' ground: CA 1985, s 517(g). See further chap 8 (minority rights).

[3] The Stock Exchange Regulations for Admission of Securities to Listing require pre-emption rights in the Listing Agreement, para 13.

PUBLIC COMPANIES: GENERALLY

Minimum share capital[1]

3.11   Before a public company may commence business or exercise borrowing powers it must obtain a certificate of compliance with certain minimum share capital requirements.[2] If the company fails to do this it must re-register as a private company.

The minimum capital requirement is that the company must have allotted share capital of not less than £50,000.[3] The prohibition on commencing business or exercising borrowing powers does not apply to the issue of shares or at least not to the issue of shares to comply with this minimum requirement. Although this is a separate requirement from the minimum subscription on a prospectus issue, there is a link in that the newly formed public company must state that its minimum subscription is at least £50,000.[4]

In order for a public company to obtain its s 117 certificate it must also deliver to the registrar of companies a statutory declaration.[5] This must contain a statement that the nominal value of the company's allotted shares is not less than the statutory minimum and give details of the amount already paid up on the allotted shares. The declaration must also contain details regarding formation expenses and who has been paid or to whom these expenses are payable and finally details of any amount or benefit given or intended to be given to any promoter.[6]

[1] See para 1.72, above.

[2] CA 1985, s 117.

[3] Ibid, s 118, the authorised minimum of £50,000 may be altered by order of the Secretary of State.

[4] See para 3.14, below.

[5] CA 1985, s 117(2).

[6] Ibid, s 117(3).

Minimum paid-up for allotted shares

3.12 On every issue of shares by a public company, including the issue to comply with the minimum share capital requirements the company must obtain payment of at least one-quarter of the nominal amount of the share allotted and the whole of any premium.[1] Where payment on shares is indefinitely postponed in part or in full, creditors of the company may be misled into believing that the company has use of money which it has never received. The aim of this provision is to ensure that the company has the use of some of its share capital at the time of issue. The requirement applies every time a public company makes an issue and not just on formation of the company.

Shares allotted in contravention of the section are treated as if the requirement had been complied with and the shareholder is liable for that amount plus interest on it at the appropriate rate.[2] Moreover, any person who becomes the holder of shares allotted in breach is jointly and severally liable with that shareholder to pay that amount unless he is a bona fide purchaser or derived his title from a person who was not liable for the contravention, i e a person who became a holder after the contravention.[3]

Employee shares subject to an employee share scheme do not come within s 101(2) nor is the shareholder allotted bonus shares liable under s 101(3) and (4) unless he knew or ought to have known that they were issued in contravention of s 101(1).

---

[1] CA 1985, s 101.
[2] Ibid, s 101(3) and (4).
[3] Ibid, s 112(1).

Expert's report for non-cash consideration[1]

3.13 Payment for shares may be in cash or kind, i e money or money's worth.[2] Where a public company accepts payment for shares in kind it may not allot the shares unless the consideration for the allotment has been valued in the way specified in the Companies Act and a report on the value of the consideration has been made and a copy of that report has been sent to the allottee.[3] This protects the company from issuing its shares in return for overvalued consideration. The rule is limited to public companies although cases where there has been such a transaction have included private companies.[4]

Allotments in connection with take-over bids involving share exchanges and in connection with mergers are excluded from these provisions.[5]

---

[1] And see further para 4.08.
[2] CA 1985, s 99.
[3] Ibid, s 103. A similar requirement is imposed on public companies accepting non-cash assets from the subscribers to the memorandum.
[4] See, e g *Salomon v Salomon & Co Ltd* [1897] AC 22; *Re Wragg* [1897] 1 Ch 796.
[5] CA 1985, s 103(3) and (5) and see para 4.09.

PUBLIC ISSUES BY PUBLIC COMPANIES

Minimum subscription

3.14   The minimum subscription required by CA 1985, s 83 is only necessary on the *first* offer by prospectus of shares by a public company. It prevents a commitment to purchase shares in a company from arising where the response to the offer has been poor. In addition, a company may only make an allotment if the issue is subscribed for in full, or if it is only partially subscribed, if the offer has stated that allotment would be made anyway or on specified conditions.[1]

[1] CA 1985, s 84.

Stock Exchange listing

3.15   Where a public offer of shares is made prior to a listing on The Stock Exchange, and application has been made for listing, a prospectus must state that the listing is being sought. Special rules apply to such allotments.[1] In particular, any monies received from applicants must be placed in a separate bank account[2] and if permission is sought and refused or permission is not sought before the third day after the issue of the prospectus the allotment or sale is void and all money must be returned to the applicant.[3] If the money is not returned within eight days the directors are jointly and severally liable to repay the monies along with interest at five per cent. Any director who can show that the default was not due to his misconduct can escape liability.[4] This provision applies equally to shares to be issued as a result of an offer for sale.[5]

[1] CA 1985, ss 86 and 87.
[2] Ibid, s 86(6).
[3] Ibid, s 86(4).
[4] Ibid, s 86(5).
[5] Ibid, s 87.

No allotment within three days of prospectus

3.16   No allotment may be made by a company making a public offer of its shares until the third day after the issue of the prospectus.[1] This prevents speculators subscribing for all the shares before the general public have had an opportunity to assess the merits of the offer.

[1] CA 1985, s 82.

Return of allotments

3.17   Each time a company makes an allotment of shares it must within one month of the allotment make a return to the registrar of companies, stating the number and nominal amount of the shares allotted, the name and addresses of the allottees, whether the shares are paid up and if not, how much is outstanding.[1]

If shares have been issued for non-cash consideration the contract under which they were allotted or a memorandum of the terms of the agreement (where no written contract exists) must accompany the return.[2] All allotments must be duly stamped.

The court may extend the time for filing the return if it is satisfied that the omission was accidental or due to inadvertence or that it was just and equitable to grant relief.[3]

If default is made in complying with this section every officer who is in default is liable on conviction to a fine not exceeding the statutory maximum or after continued contravention to a default fine.[4]

In the financial year in which new shares are allotted or debentures issued the company must give details of the issue in its accounts.[5]

---

[1] CA 1985, s 88(2)(a).

[2] Ibid, s 88(2)(b). A public company which has issued shares for non-cash consideration must also file with the registrar a copy of the expert's report required by CA 1985, s. 103. See para 4.10.

[3] CA 1985, s 88(6).

[4] Ibid, s 88(5).

[5] Ibid, Sch 4, paras 39 and 41.

SHARE CAPITAL

Meaning

3.18 All companies limited by shares must include in their memorandum of association a statement of the share capital with which they are to be formed. This is known as the *authorised* or *nominal share capital* and must be divided into shares of different nominal amounts. Before the company can be formed it must have obtained binding promises from at least two persons[1] that they will on formation of the company subscribe for at least one share in the company. These persons, the subscribers, sign the memorandum recording their agreement. On formation these shares are deemed to have been issued.[2] There is however no requirement that the subscribers to the memorandum should take up the whole of the company's authorised share capital. The company must state in its memorandum the division of its capital into shares of different values, for example the capital may be £100,000, divided into 70,000 £1 ordinary shares and 30,000 £1 preference shares. The different value attached to the shares is called the *nominal* or *par value* of the share and the share capital rules refer generally to the nominal value of the share and not the *market value* of the share which differs commonly from the nominal value.

The authorised or nominal share capital is divided into the *issued* and *unissued share capital*. The issued share capital represents that part of the company's authorised share capital which has been subscribed for and allotted, the unissued being the difference between the authorised and issued share capital. The company may issue shares up to its authorised share capital but if it wishes to issue more it must alter the authorised share capital amount in its memorandum. Different procedures apply to an increase of the authorised share capital and an increase in the issued share capital. Increase of the authorised share capital[3] is the concern of the members only and they cannot delegate this function; a new issue of shares is primarily the function of the shareholders, but it may be delegated to the directors.[4]

The issued share capital may be further divided into the called-up and uncalled share capital. The called-up share capital means so much of the company's share capital as equals the aggregate amount of the calls made on its shares (whether or not those calls have been paid), together with any share capital paid up without being called and any share capital to be paid on a specified future date under the articles, the terms of allotment of the relevant shares or any other arrangements for payment of those shares.[5] Uncalled share capital is the difference between the issued share capital and the called-up share capital. While issued share capital not paid is a form of asset of the company, it is a liability to the shareholders concerned who are liable to pay up the amount outstanding on the shares according to the terms of their agreement with the company, though the uncalled liability must be paid at the latest when, and if, the company goes into liquidation. Where a company issues partly paid shares on terms that the outstanding amount will only be called if and when the company goes into liquidation, the uncalled capital is sometimes referred to as *reserve capital* though the term *reserve liability* is used by the Act.[6]

Only private companies may issue shares and postpone payment of the whole of the purchase price, a public company must receive at least one-quarter of the nominal value on its shares and the whole of any premium at the time of allotment.[7]

The difference between the company's unissued share capital and uncalled share capital is that as the unissued share capital has not yet been subscribed for or allotted, no-one is liable to pay for it, whereas the issued and allotted but uncalled share capital is a liability of the members and the company may call it up as specified.

Most of the rules relating to the raising and maintenance of share capital now refer to the issued (or allotted) share capital, rather than the nominal share capital which was the original yardstick. The Act prefers the word 'allotted' instead of 'issued'. The term 'allotted' is defined for the purposes of the Act, but 'issued' is not. Allotted is where a person acquires an unconditional right to be included in the company's register of members in respect of those shares.[8] It is thought that there is no substantive difference between the words issued and allotted.

---

[1] CA 1985, s 24. Prior to 1980 public companies needed seven subscribers to the memorandum.

[2] CA 1985, s 22.

[3] See para 3.27, below.

[4] CA 1985, s 80, see para 3.04, above.

[5] CA 1985, s 737; see e g s 264(1)(a) and Sch 4, Note 12 on balance sheet formats.

[6] CA 1985, s 120. As the 'reserve liability' is in fact an asset this term is misleading.

[7] CA 1985, s 101.

[8] Ibid, s 738.

Quasi-share capital

3.19 The phrase quasi-share capital is not a statutory term but is a useful abbreviation for the funds which, although not share capital, are required by law to be treated as if they were. The two funds usually dealt with under this heading are the *share premium account* and the *capital redemption reserve*. The reserve fund might also be a candidate for inclusion under the heading quasi-share capital.[1]

---

[1] See para 3.25, below.

Share premium account

3.20 A company must attach a nominal value to its shares but this is not necessarily the price at which they will be issued. The company may not issue its shares at less than the nominal value but may issue them for more, i e at a premium. Where shares are issued at a premium, the amount representing the premium must be put into a separate account, the *share premium account*. Prior to 1948 any share premium could be distributed to the shareholders by way of dividend, however as this was not trading profit it was thought that allowing the company to distribute it as dividend might mislead people regarding the profitability of the company. Since 1948 the company has had to treat the amount in its share premium account for most purposes as if it were share capital.[1]

The share premium account can be used only for specified purposes:

(a) in paying up unissued shares of the company to be allotted to members of the company as fully paid bonus shares; or

(b) in writing off preliminary expenses; or

(c) in writing off the expenses of, or commission or discount allowed on, any issue of shares or debentures of the company; or

(d) in providing for the premium payable on redemption of any debentures of the company;[2] or

(e) in providing for a premium on redeemable shares issued at a premium and redeemable at a premium where redemption is made out of the proceeds of a fresh issue of shares.[3]

Any other use of the share premium account is subject to the same procedure as a reduction of share capital under CA 1985, s 135.[4]

The obligation to transfer an amount equivalent to the share premium to a separate account applies whether or not the shares are issued for cash or non-cash consideration.[5] Where the issue is for cash, it is easy to work out the amount of the premium, but where the issue is for non-cash consideration there may be problems. If a public company issues its shares for non-cash consideration it must obtain a valuation of that consideration by an expert.[6] The expert's report must state how much of the consideration is attributable to the nominal value of the share and how much is attributable to the premium. The company must then transfer an amount equivalent to that assessment to the share premium account. In private companies the position is less clear though it was held that on a take-over where shares were issued for non-cash consideration and the parties knew that the consideration represented a premium, the company was obliged to transfer the difference between the nominal value and the price paid to the share premium account.[7] Where shares were exchanged for shares as part of a take-over this caused particular problems as funds which represented assets available for distribution in the target company on transfer would be treated as share premium and therefore no longer available for distribution in the hands of the acquiring company. As a direct result of the decision in *Shearer v Bercain Ltd*,[8] ss 36–41 of CA 1981[9] were introduced to provide relief from this rule in certain cases.

---

[1] CA 1985, s 130.
[2] Ibid, s 130(2).
[3] Ibid, s 160(2).
[4] CA 1985, s 130.
[5] *Henry Head Ltd v Ropner Holdings* [1952] Ch 124.
[6] CA 1985, s 103. See para 3.13, above.
[7] *Shearer v Bercain Ltd* [1980] 3 All ER 295.
[8] Ibid.
[9] Now CA 1985, ss 131–134.

Relief from CA 1985, s 130

3.21   The problem highlighted in *Shearer v Bercain* was that if the non-cash consideration was shares given in exchange for shares, the value of those shares would represent the acquired company's assets, i e capital *and profits* and on a transfer there might be an element of premium on the shares issued. If the whole of this amount were to be transferred to the nominal capital and share premium account that which in one company was distributable profit (and available for dividend payment) was turned into quasi-capital or undistributable profit and locked into the acquiring company. This might render the new shares less marketable, the availability of dividend distribution being reduced, and inhibit otherwise economically desirable mergers. To counter this, in cases of mergers and group reconstructions the s 130 rule may be relaxed as discussed below.

Merger relief: CA 1985, s 131

3.22   If the issuing company (Company A) has secured at least 90 per cent of the equity shares of another company (Company B) in pursuance of an arrangement providing for the allotment of Company A's equity shares in exchange for the issue or transfer of the equity shares of Company B or cancellation of any such shares, s 130 will not apply.[1] If the arrangement also provides for the allotment of shares in Company A for *non-equity shares* in Company B or the cancellation of such shares, s 130 will not apply.[2] The relief granted by s 131 only applies to the premium arising on shares issued as part of an arrangement which procures 90 per cent or more.

In determining the 90 per cent required for the operation of the relief Company A may take into account shares acquired or cancelled by virtue of the agreement, i e as if all the terms of the agreement had already been complied with and the company's purpose was to acquire at least 90 per cent of Company B's equity share capital. Equity shares has the same meaning as for CA 1985, s 736 (definition of holding and subsidiary companies), i e shares which carry participating rights either to dividend or capital or both.

If the equity share capital of Company B is divided into different classes of shares, relief will only be available if s 131 is satisfied in relation to each class.[3]

---

[1] CA 1985, s 131.
[2] Ibid, s 131(3).
[3] Ibid, s 131(5).

Group relief: CA 1985, s 132

3.23 Where the issuing company (Company A) is a wholly-owned subsidiary of another company (Company B) and allots shares to Company B or to another wholly-owned subsidiary of Company B (Company C) in consideration for the transfer to it of non-cash assets from any other company in the group and those shares are allotted at a premium, Company A need not transfer any more than the *minimum premium amount* to its share premium account.[1] The minimum premium amount is the amount by which the base value (i e the cost to the transferor or, if lower, the value at which they are carried in the transferor's books of the transferred assets at the time of transfer) exceeds the aggregate nominal value of the shares allotted. Thus distributable profits on the transferred shares need only be put into the share premium account if necessary to ensure that the nominal amount on the new shares is protected.[2]

For the purposes of both s 131 and s 132 the relief applies to any issue of shares within these provisions made on or after 4 February 1981 and so in some cases will be retrospective. These provisions effectively reversed the decisions in *Henry Head Ltd v Ropner*[3] and *Shearer v Bercain Ltd*,[4] though the general principle remains where these sections are not applicable.

The Secretary of State has power to relieve companies from the consequences of s 130 in relation to non-cash premiums or to restrict or otherwise modify any relief available under ss 130–133 by statutory instrument where it appears to him appropriate to do so.[5]

---

[1] CA 1985, s 132(1) and (2);
[2] CA 1985, s 132(2).
[3] [1952] Ch 124.
[4] [1980] 3 All ER 295.
[5] CA 1985, s 134.

Capital redemption reserve

3.24 Under the CA 1948 whenever a company wishes to redeem its redeemable preference shares, in order to preserve the total amount set aside for capital, an amount equal to the nominal value of the shares redeemed had to be placed to a capital redemption reserve fund.[1] This fund could only be used for specified purposes and otherwise was subject to the rules relating to raising and maintenance of share capital as if it were share capital.[2]

Where shares are redeemed or purchased out of profits by virtue of CA 1985, ss 159 and 162 and shares are cancelled as a result, it might look as if the company had increased its fund available for distribution by way of dividend even though the redemption or purchase was out of profits. Thus although stated to be a redemption, or purchase out of profits there would appear to be a reduction of capital (see Table 1 below). In order to protect the company's capital fund a company is required to transfer to a capital redemption reserve an amount equivalent to the redeemed or purchased capital[3] (see Table 2 below).

Table 1 *(Without s 170)*

		Share capital	Profits	Assets
Before purchase or redemption		30,000	200,000	230,000
Purchase or redemption of £10,000 shares out of profits	i) payment to shareholders		(10,000)	(10,000)
	ii) cancellation of shares	(10,000)	10,000	
After purchase or redemption		£20,000	200,000	220,000

The problem here is that the £10,000 share capital must be cancelled to reflect the cancellation of the shares redeemed or purchased, but the share capital representing the cancelled shares must go somewhere, it cannot stay in the share capital account and therefore must go to profit.

Table 2 *(With s 170)*

		Share capital	Quasi-capital including capital redemption reserve	Profits	Assets
Before purchase or redemption		30,000	—	200,000	230,000
Purchase or redemption of £10,000 shares out of profits	i) Payment to s/holders			(10,000)	(10,000)
	ii) Cancellation of shares	(10,000)		10,000	
	iii) Transfer to capital redemption reserve		10,000	(10,000)	
After purchase or redemption		£20,000	10,000	190,000	220,000

The aggregate amount in the share capital account and the quasi-share capital account, i e £30,000 equals the amount which prior to the redemption or purchase was in the share capital account.

The capital redemption reserve can be used by the company for the issue of paid-up bonus shares (in which case the quasi-capital become capital) or for the purchase or redemption of shares out of capital under CA 1985, s 171. This would reduce the share capital or quasi-share capital but it is subject to the safeguards in ss 171 and 172, and only private companies may make use of its provisions.[4]

[1] CA 1948, s 58 (now repealed).
[2] The word fund has now been dropped from the title of this account.
[3] CA 1985, s 170.
[4] See paras 4.32–4.41, below.

Reserve fund

3.25 Another candidate for inclusion in quasi-share capital is the reserve fund which a public company must establish in certain situations.

Companies are now empowered to purchase or redeem their shares in a variety of circumstances but always subject to safeguards designed to protect the capital fund for the creditors. A company may acquire its shares in ways other than purchase or redemption,[1] e g gift, acquisition by nominees, and such shares must either be disposed of within a specified period or cancelled. If cancelled, although the company has provided no consideration for these shares it will appear from the accounts that there has been a reduction of capital (see Table 3 below). A *public company* which shows its own shares as an asset is required to transfer an amount equivalent to the nominal value of the shares to a statutory reserve fund from the company's distributable profits (see Table 4 below).[2]

Table 3 *(Without s 148(4))*

	Share capital	Profits	Assets
Before gift of shares	100,000	200,000	300,000
After gift of 20,000 shares } Cancellation	(20,000)	20,000	
	£80,000	220,000	300,000

Table 4 *(With s 148(4))*

	Share capital	Reserve fund	Profits	Assets
Before gift of shares	100,000	—	200,000	300,000
After gift of 20,000 shares } i) Cancellation	(20,000)		20,000	
ii) Transfer		20,000	(20,000)	
	£80,000	20,000	200,000	300,000

Such a reserve fund is not available for distribution by way of dividend. No further mention is made of the use of this fund, thus it is assumed that for all other purposes it is to be treated as share capital, except that it may be available for the payment of an issue of bonus shares.

---

[1] See CA 1985, s 143(3).
[2] CA 1985, s 148(4).

Alterations of share capital

3.26   The company's memorandum must include a statement of the company's authorised share capital (unless it is an unlimited company). The clauses in the memorandum which were originally unalterable can now, subject to one exception,[1] be altered. The capital clause can be altered in four basic ways: the company may increase its authorised share capital, it may subdivide or consolidate its share capital, it may convert shares into stock or it may cancel unissued shares.

---

[1] I e the clause stating where the company's registered office is to be situated.

Increase

3.27   An increase of share capital far from being detrimental to the creditors would be advantageous, particularly if linked with an actual increase in the company's assets. An increase of share capital need only be empowered by the company's articles and a resolution of the company in general meeting.[1] Either a special or ordinary resolution will suffice and which one depends on the stipulation in the company's articles, if no mention is made Table A articles provide that an ordinary resolution will do.

---

[1] CA 1985, s 121.

Sub-division, consolidation, etc

3.28   The memorandum requires a statement of the authorised or nominal share capital plus the division of that capital into shares of varying amounts. A sub-division or consolidation is a process whereby the total amount of capital is not increased or reduced but the division of the shares is altered. A consolidation may be effected as part of an administrative tidying up exercise, e g where 1p shares were issued originally and the company wishes to convert them into £1 shares. A subdivision may be required when a company wishes to make its share more marketable by dividing them into smaller units, e g £10 shares divided into ten £1 shares.

As neither a subdivision nor a consolidation is intended to alter the overall capital amount, there is no threat to the creditor and the company can alter its share capital in this way by passing a resolution in general meeting,[1] which can be either an ordinary or special resolution but this depends on the company's articles.

---

[1] CA 1985, s 121.

Shares into stock

3.29 Stock has been described as 'a set of shares put together in a bundle'.[1] Stock cannot be issued directly by a company, but the company may issue shares which are subsequently converted into stock. Stock has the advantage over shares that it can be divided into any fraction and split, while a share cannot be subdivided by the shareholder. A company may convert its shares into stock if it has power in its articles and passes the requisite resolution,[2] but such a conversion can only be made where the shares are fully paid up. A conversion from shares to stock has no effect on the total amount of the capital.

[1] *Morris v Aylmer* (1875) LR 7 HL 717 at 725.
[2] CA 1985, s 121.

Cancellation of unissued shares

3.30 Creditors suffer no detriment if the authorised but unissued share capital is reduced, since unissued shares are represented by no asset of the company and could remain unissued indefinitely. S 121 empowers a company to cancel its unissued share capital by passing a resolution of the company in general meeting. Such action is usually referred to as a diminution of capital to distinguish the process from a reduction of capital.[1]

[1] See para 4.42, below.

4 Raising and maintenance of share capital

Sally A Jones

INTRODUCTION

4.01 The share capital of a company is seen as a fund to which the company's creditors can look for payment if the company fails to pay its debts. Certain rules have been developed, principally by the courts, in an attempt to preserve the share capital or the assets represented by this capital for the ultimate benefit of the creditors. Many of the rules are based on the idea that no capital should be returned to the shareholders as this would be reversing the normal hierarchy of recovery on a liquidation, i e creditors taking in priority to shareholders. The company, whilst a going concern, cannot do that which would defeat the priority of claims on a liquidation. Of course, the rules developed by the courts have taken account of the obvious, since legal rules in themselves cannot prevent a company from a physical loss of capital.[1] A company may lose money in its day to day business and no legal rules will prevent this.

In addition to protecting the share capital for the creditors the rules have also often protected shareholders from abuse by directors who, if they had unrestricted control over the company's share capital, might use their powers to their own advantage, e g controlling votes attached to shares in order to perpetuate their position as director, or selling or giving shares to themselves in order to keep control of the company.

The rules relating to the raising and maintenance of share capital fall into two clear categories, those designed to ensure that the company obtains some value for the issue of shares and those designed to protect the share capital in the hands of the company.

(a) Raising of share capital

The general rules are

    (1) The company must be paid for its shares.[2]
    (2) The company may not issue its shares at a discount.[3]

(b) Maintenance of share capital

The overriding principle is that a company may not reduce its share capital by an unauthorised distribution to the shareholders. The rules under this heading are merely examples of this wider rule.

    (3) Subject to certain exceptions a company cannot become a member of itself or it cannot purchase its own shares.[4]

(4) A company cannot provide financial assistance for the purchase of its own shares.[5]

(5) A company cannot pay a dividend except out of profits available for distribution as defined.[6]

The following paragraphs of this chapter deal with these rules and the exceptions to them in turn.

[1] But see para 4.49, below.
[2] See paras 4.03–4.11, below.
[3] See para 4.14, below.
[4] See paras 4.17–4.21, below.
[5] See paras 4.50–4.60, below.
[6] See paras 4.68–4.77, below.

Raising of share capital

4.02 A company must be paid for its shares and it must be paid at least the nominal value of the share. It is not necessary for the company to receive payment on issue as long as there is an outstanding liability to pay, which the company may call up according to the terms of its agreement with the shareholder, usually on the terms of the articles.

If the shares are very marketable, the company may be able to issue them at a premium, i e a price in excess of the nominal value, in which case the company is entitled to the nominal amount plus the premium, but company law only *obliges* the company to issue the shares for the nominal amount. Where the new issue of shares could be issued at a premium but the directors choose to issue them at par, there is no breach of capital rules but this may be evidence of a breach of director's duty.[1] Directors are obliged to obtain the best possible price for the company's shares, and issuing shares at par when they could have been issued at a premium may put them in breach of this duty. The exception to this is where a company makes a rights issue, where it is usual to give existing shareholders an opportunity to subscribe for new shares at a favourable price.

[1] *Henry Head Ltd v Ropner Holdings* [1952] Ch 124.

Payment for shares — general

4.03 Consideration required to support a contract for the purchase of shares is the same as any contractual consideration except that the nominal value of the share is regarded as the minimum consideration. Consideration may be in cash or kind, money or money's worth.[1] Money's worth includes goodwill and know-how.

Consideration in money or in kind less than the nominal amount will be an issue at a discount, which is prohibited.[2]

[1] CA 1985, s 99.
[2] Ibid, s 100; see para 4.14, below.

Payment for shares — private companies

4.04   Payment for shares may be money or money's worth and on an issue of shares in a private company the whole of the purchase price can be postponed. Little difficulty is experienced with payment for shares in cash, the rule is applied easily, but non-cash consideration is more problematic. The general contractual principle is that consideration must be sufficient, i e of some value, but need not be adequate,[1] i e equivalent. A company may agree to issue shares in exchange for inadequate consideration, as in *Salomon v Salomon & Co Ltd*.[2] The courts will only look at the adequacy of the consideration in cases of fraud or where the consideration is patently inadequate.[3] Where the company issues shares in exchange for over-valued consideration not only does this mean that the full nominal amount is never received by the company to the detriment of the creditors, but also the shareholder will have obtained his shares, and possibly a controlling interest, cheaply.

However, an issue of shares in these circumstances is not an issue at a discount as the courts held that the consideration is sufficient, thus for all intents and purposes the company has received the nominal value of its shares.

[1] E g *White v Bluett* (1853) 23 LJ Ex 36.
[2] [1897] AC 22.
[3] *Re Wragg Ltd* [1897] 1 Ch 796; *Re White Star Line* [1938] Ch 458.

Payment for shares — public companies

4.05   The basic principles outlined above apply to public companies, subject to some exceptions, in the same way as they apply to private companies.

A public company must receive payment for its shares and may postpone part but not the whole of the payment. At the time of issue the public company must receive one-quarter of the nominal value of its shares plus all of any premium.[1] This provides the company with some working capital at the outset. This rule applies to every issue of new shares by the company and not merely the first issue.

Whereas there is no statutory minimum amount of capital required to be issued by a private company, a public company must allot at least £50,000 of nominal share capital before it can commence business.[2] Thus, the public company must start life with at least £12,500 paid-up capital in its hands.

If a share is issued in contravention of s 101 the shareholder is liable to pay the difference between the required amount and the amount he has paid immediately along with interest at the appropriate rate. Bonus shares and shares subject to an employee share scheme are excluded from this provision.[3]

For the purpose of payment for shares in a public company the statutory definition of consideration differs from contractual consideration in three ways:

(1)   an agreement to provide work or services in exchange for shares is not good consideration;[4]

(2)   the performance of an undertaking is not good consideration if it is to be or may be performed more than five years after allotment;[5]

(3) non-cash consideration in exchange for shares is subject to valuation by an independent expert.[6]

[1] CA 1985, s 101.
[2] Ibid, s 117.
[3] Ibid, s 101(2) and (5).
[4] Ibid, s 99(2).
[5] Ibid, s 102(1).
[6] Ibid, s 103.

Provision of work or services: s 99(2)

4.06   In the past minority shareholders have suffered as a result of directors using the voting rights attached to shares to keep their position in the company. Prevention of such abuse lies behind the restrictions on companies buying their own shares and retaining voting rights which could then be used by the directors for their own benefit, e g keeping themselves in control. Moreover the provision of bogus consideration obviously affects the company's creditors who have a right to expect that the company has received value at least equivalent to the nominal value of the shares: CA 1985, s 99(2) attempts to limit the type of consideration acceptable to public companies. Such companies are not permitted to accept as payment for their shares an undertaking to do work or perform services for the company or any other person.

Although primarily aimed at directors and officers, the provision is not limited to directors, but to the provision of services by any person.

Any allottee who acts in breach of this section is liable to pay the company a sum equal to the nominal value of the share and the whole of any premium and interest at the appropriate rate.[1] So too is any holder of the shares who is not a bona fide purchaser for value of the shares or has derived title from a person who became a holder after the contravention and was not so liable.[2] Note that this liability arises whether or not the person in contravention of the section was ever a holder of the shares and covers an obvious method of avoiding the provision, e g where A promises to provide services to a public company in exchange for the allotment of shares to B.

S 99(2) does not prohibit a public company from allotting bonus shares or from paying-up, from available funds, any unpaid-up share capital.[3]

[1] CA 1985, s 99(3).
[2] Ibid, s 112.
[3] Ibid, s 99(4).

Deferred consideration: s 102

4.07   S 102 prohibits a public company from allotting shares as fully or partly paid-up if the consideration is or includes an undertaking which is to be or may be performed more than five years after the date of the allotment. This does not apply to shares allotted for cash, but note the minimum payment required by s 101.[1] Any variation of an agreement taking the performance of an undertaking outside the five year period is void.[2] If a company allots shares in contravention of the prohibition, the allottee is liable to pay the company the amount equal to the nominal value of the shares plus the whole of any premium with interest at the appropriate rate.[3]

Where a public company accepts the promise of an undertaking as consideration for its shares which is to be performed *within* five years, but that undertaking is not performed within five years, the allottee becomes liable as if the undertaking were to be performed outside of the five year period and is in contravention of s 102.[4] Any holder of the shares issued in breach is jointly and severally liable with any other person liable, unless he is a purchaser for value without notice or he derives his title from a person who became a holder after the contravention and was not liable.[5]

---

[1] See para 4.05, above.
[2] CA 1985, s 102(3).
[3] Ibid, s 102(2).
[4] Ibid, s 102(6).
[5] Ibid, s 112.

Independent expert's report: s 103

4.08　The problem of a company allotting shares for inadequate consideration by accepting over-valued assets has already been discussed.[1] Concern in this respect has led to the introduction of a requirement for an independent expert's report whenever a public company wishes to allot shares for non-cash consideration.[2] CA 1985, s 103 requires:

(a) the consideration to be valued in accordance with the provisions of the Act;
(b) a report in respect of the valuation to be prepared by a person qualified to be appointed or continue as auditor of the company, to be made not more than six months before the date of the allotment; and
(c) a copy of the report to be sent to the allottee.[3]

The report must state the nominal value of the relevant shares, the amount of any premium to be paid on those shares, the description of the consideration, the method used to value it and the date of valuation and the extent to which the shares are to be treated as paid up:

(i) by the consideration; and
(ii) in cash.[4]

The report must be made by an independent person, i e a person qualified to act as the company's auditor except that he may accept the valuation of another person as to the whole or part of the consideration, but only where this would be reasonable and that person has the requisite knowledge and experience to value the consideration and is not connected with the company. A person is connected with the company for these purposes if he is an officer or servant of the company or any other body corporate which is that company's subsidiary or holding company or a subsidiary of that company's holding company or a partner or employee of such an officer or servant.[5]

Where the independent expert makes use of another's valuation in accordance with s 108(2) he must state that fact in his report and give details of the person making the valuation and the consideration so valued and its method of valuation and date of such.[6]

The report of the independent expert must also contain, or be accompanied by, a note stating that it was reasonable to arrange for valuation by another person or to accept that valuation, where the expert has done so, and that whoever made the valuation the method used was reasonable in all the circumstances. Moreover, the expert must state that in his opinion there has been no material change in the value of the consideration since the valuation and that on the basis of the valuation, the consideration is not worth less than the aggregate of the nominal value and premium of the shares to be allotted in exchange.

Two safeguards are included in the provisions designed to prevent a company obtaining a valuation of non-cash consideration and keeping it 'on ice' until the time is right to issue shares in exchange for that consideration, these are:

(i) the report must not be more than six months old; and
(ii) since *the valuation* may take place more than six months before the allotment, the independent expert must state that there has been no material change in the value of the consideration since the valuation.

---

[1] See para 4.04, above.
[2] CA 1985, s 103.
[3] Ibid, s 103.
[4] Ibid, s 108(4).
[5] Ibid, s 108(2).
[6] Ibid, s 108(5).

Exceptions to s 103

4.09 CA 1985, s 103(1) must be complied with when a company is proposing to allot shares for non-cash consideration even though this is only part of the consideration from the allottee. Similarly, s 103(1) must be complied with when the company is proposing to allot shares and give either cash or other consideration to the shareholder in exchange for the non-cash consideration. CA 1985, s 108(7) provides that where the consideration is accepted partly in payment of the nominal value of the shares and any premium and partly for some other consideration given by the company, s 103(1) applies, as if references to the consideration accepted by the company included references to the proportion of that consideration which is properly attributable to the payment of that value and any premium.

In addition the independent person must carry out or arrange for such other valuations as will enable him to determine that proportion, and details of any valuations so made must be included in his report.[1] However, no valuation is required if a company issues new shares as bonus shares and appropriates its undistributed profits or its revenue or capital reserves in payment of the nominal value of the shares or any share premium on their issue.[2]

No expert's report is required if a public company is proposing to allot shares in connection with a transfer or cancellation of shares in another company, i e a take-over by way of exchange of shares followed by a cancellation, or a proposed merger of that company with another.[3] This relief is not granted where the take-over offer is not open to all the holders of the shares in the other company or where the arrangement is only in relation to a class of shares, i e the offer is not open to all the holders in that class.[4] The definition of both take-over and merger is narrow. A take-over will not come within the exception unless there is a general offer of the new shares to all the shareholders or the whole of a class of shareholders. A merger for these purposes does not include the acquisition of part of the assets or undertaking of the other company by the company issuing new shares, nor to the acquisition of the whole of the assets or undertaking in return for new shares and a cash or other payment.

[1] CA 1985, s 108(7).
[2] Ibid, s 103(2).
[3] Ibid, s 103(3).
[4] Ibid, s 103(4).

Expert's report — supplementary

4.10   The company is responsible for delivering a copy of any report required by s 103 to the registrar of companies for filing. This must accompany the return of allotments required under CA 1985, s 88 and the same penalties for breach that apply to s 88 apply to this requirement.[1]

To facilitate the expert's task in obtaining requisite information for the report, he is empowered to require from the officers of the company such information and explanation as he thinks necessary.[2]

[1] CA 1985, s 111(3).
[2] Ibid, s 110.

Consequences of breach of s 103

4.11   Breach of s 103 may take many forms, in particular,

(1) the company may fail to obtain the required independent valuation;
(2) the report may be based on or include incorrect information;
(3) the company may fail to file any report as required.

Where the company allots shares in breach of s 103(1) it appears that the allotment is valid, but if either the allottee has not received a report as required or there has been some contravention of the section which the allottee knew, or ought to have known, was a contravention the allottee himself is liable. It is assumed that the allottee knows that he is entitled to a report regarding non-cash consideration and he cannot escape liability by arguing that he has not received a copy of the report. The liability is to pay an amount equivalent to the nominal value of the shares plus the whole of any premium or such proportion of the amount as is treated as paid up by the consideration, and interest at the appropriate rate.[1]

Moreover, the provisions of s 112 apply to those people who have subsequently become holders of the shares, unless acquired for value at a time when he was ignorant of the contravention or from some person not liable for the contravention.

If directors allot shares in breach of s 103 both the company and any officer in default are guilty of a criminal offence and liable on conviction to a fine (no upper limit is specified where the conviction is on indictment.)[2]

Where the report is based on or includes incorrect information any person who knowingly or recklessly makes a misleading, false or deceptive statement which is material, is guilty of an offence.[3] This applies to any statement to a person carrying out a valuation or making the report, being a statement which conveys or purports to convey any information or explanation which that person requires, or is entitled to require, under s 110(1).

It is put beyond doubt that statements made which merely form the basis of the report though not directly incorporated into it will be within this section. The provisions of the Act do not exclude the operation of common law actions. Directors will also be liable to their companies for breach of duty and where an allotment made in contravention of s 103 causes loss to the company the directors will be liable.

Similarly, in addition to the particular offences created in the Act for misstatements, the independent expert or valuer (if another person) may be liable in negligence to the company if having made a negligent over-valuation, the company allots shares accordingly and suffers loss as a consequence.[4]

An expert will only be liable in negligence if the plaintiff can show that the expert owed him a duty of care. Whereas an expert owes a duty of care to the company in respect of work done on its behalf as a valuer, he owes no duty to the shareholders, even though as a result of his negligence the value of their shares may have fallen. In *Arenson v Casson Beckman Rutley & Co*[5] the court held the auditor liable to the vendor of shares because he knew that his valuation would be relied on as fixing the contract price. It is not thought that this case is authority for a general proposition that auditors owe a duty of care to all shareholders in respect of valuations.

---

[1] CA 1985, s 103(6).
[2] Ibid, s 114.
[3] Ibid, s 110(2).
[4] *Hedley Byrne & Co Ltd v Heller & Partners Ltd* [1964] AC 465.
[5] [1977] AC 405.

Acquisition from subscribers

4.12 On selling non-cash assets, e g a business to a company, an unscrupulous promoter may overvalue it and receive good consideration from the company in exchange. In order to prevent promoters or others selling worthless assets in this way CA 1985, s 104 provides that an expert's report is required where the company's consideration for the non-cash assets is one-tenth or more of the company's issued share capital. Like s 103 this requirement only applies to public companies and all the details required under s 103 apply to s 104. The transfer must be by a relevant person and this is limited to any subscriber to the memorandum and it must take place within the initial period, i e a two year period beginning with the date of the s 117 certificate. The major procedural difference between s 103 and s 104 is that in addition to an expert's report the company must authorise the particular transaction by ordinary resolution.

Note that to protect the company from issuing shares to a subscriber in exchange for overvalued consideration in a situation where there are no directors to arrange for a report, a public company is prohibited from allotting shares to a subscriber except for cash.[1]

---

[1] CA 1985, s 106.

Relief

4.13   Any person liable to a public company in respect of a contravention of ss 99, 102, 103 and 104 may be relieved of that liability by the court under CA 1985, s 113. The power to grant relief under this section only seems to avail the parties to the transactions in question and not others, e g directors or officers of the company in breach.[1] Relief is available where the person is liable in respect of any shares or payment for any shares or by virtue of an undertaking given to the company. The court may exempt such a person from liability in whole or in part where it is satisfied that it would be just and equitable to do so. In making its decision the court should have regard to any other liability in respect of those shares or the undertaking, whether any other person has paid or is likely to pay in respect of those shares and whether the applicant or any other person has performed or is likely to perform the undertaking or do any other thing in payment or part payment of the shares.[2] But relief is subject to two overriding principles: the court must be satisfied that the company has received money or money's worth in exchange for the issue of shares at least equal to the aggregate of the nominal value and the whole of any premium on the shares and where there is a choice of actions against a particular person, the company may decide which alternative remedy to pursue.[3]

The court's power to grant relief extends to any person who has been brought into the proceedings as a contributor for a contribution in respect of any liability to the company arising under ss 99, 102, 103 and 104 but the court also has the power to order that such a contributor is liable to make a larger contribution than he would otherwise be liable to make.[4]

Where a person has given an undertaking in or in connection with payment for shares, to do work or perform services or any other thing, he remains liable to perform in accordance with the agreement irrespective of contraventions of ss 99, 102, 103 and 104,[5] though presumably the agreement is unenforceable by the allottee himself. Where the allottee has performed the undertaking or provided the services, he will have a right against the company which can be set off against his statutory liability to pay for the shares, i e the nominal value plus all of any premium.

---

[1] Though the court may relieve them from liability for breaches of duty under its general power in CA 1985, s 727, where it is satisfied that the director has acted honestly and reasonably and ought fairly to be excused.

2 CA 1985, s 113(3).
3 Ibid, s 113(5).
4 Ibid, s 113(7).
5 Ibid, s 115.

A company may not issue its shares at a discount

4.14 In *Ooregum Gold Mining Co v Roper*[1] the court held that a company must receive at least the nominal value of its shares, a company may not give itself the power to issue its shares at a discount. This rule is now embodied in CA 1985, s 100. Until 1980 it was not clear whether a breach of this rule would render the issue void or would merely make the shares only partly paid up to the extent of the discount, thus the shareholder would be liable for the discount as if it were unpaid-up share capital.[2] The CA 1980 put it beyond doubt that the shares are valid and the shareholder is liable to pay an amount equal to the amount of the discount and interest on it at the appropriate rate. Any person who becomes a shareholder of shares issued in contravention of s 100 is liable to pay the difference unless he is a bona fide purchaser without notice exception or where the person becomes a holder after the contravention from a person who was not liable.[3]

Prior to 1980 there were two exceptions to this rule, a company could apply to the court under CA 1948, s 57 for power to issue shares at a discount and a company could issue shares to an underwriter up to a maximum commission of 10% of the nominal value of the shares, i e in effect an issue at a discount.[4] Only s 53 now CA 1985, s 97 remains. S 57 was used only rarely and has been repealed. An issue of shares in exchange for non-cash consideration may appear to be a disguised issue at a discount, but unless the issue can be challenged as an issue for patently inadequate consideration[5] or for non-compliance with s 103[6] (public companies only) this would not contravene s 100.

1 [1892] AC 125.
2 E g *Welton v Saffery* [1897] AC 299.
3 CA 1985, s 112.
4 CA 1948, s 53.
5 *Re Wragg* [1897] 1 Ch 796.
6 See para 4.08, above.

Summary — restrictions on issue and allotment

(a) All companies

4.15
(1) Authority to issue, implied if not expressly provided for in articles (para 3.04, above).
(2) Authority from shareholder to issue (CA 1985, s 80, para 3.04, above).
(3) Compliance with pre-emption rights (CA 1985, s 89, para 3.06, above).

(4) Issue must be bona fide for the benefit of the company and not for any collateral purpose (para 3.05, above).

(5) Return of allotments and where issue is for non-cash consideration a copy of the contract or a memorandum evidencing it (CA 1985, s 88, para 3.17).

(6) No issue at a discount and if shares are issued at a premium, the premium must be transferred to the quasi-share capital account, the share premium account (para 4.14, above).

(7) A company must be paid for its shares, payment may be in money or money's worth, CA 1985 s 99, (para 4.03, above).

(b) Public companies generally

(8) Must allot minimum share capital of £50,000 paid up to at least one-quarter of the nominal value plus all of any premium, before commencing business (para 3.11, above).

(9) On every issue of shares, not just those to comply with the minimum share capital requirement, the public company must receive at least one-quarter of the nominal value and all of any premium at the time of allotment (CA 1985, s 101, para 3.12, above).

(10) Subscribers' shares must be issued for cash as to nominal value and premium (CA 1985, s 106).

(11) Expert's report required on issue of shares for non-cash consideration except in take-overs (CA 1985 s 103, para 4.08, above).

(12) Non-cash consideration given in exchange for shares in a public company must not consist of an undertaking to do work or provide services (CA 1985, s 99(2), para 4.06, above).

(13) A public company may not allot shares in exchange for non-cash consideration which consists of an undertaking to be performed more than five years from the date of allotment (CA 1985, s 102, para 4.07, above).

(14) A public company may not acquire assets from a subscriber to the memorandum, whether in exchange for shares or other consideration without an expert's report on the value of the asset and authorisation by the shareholders (CA 1985, s 104, para 4.12, above).

(15) Copy of expert's report required under (CA 1985, s 103) filed with return of allotments (CA 1985, s 111, para 4.08, above).

(c) Public issue by public companies

(16) Compliance with rules relating to prospectuses (CA 1985, s 56, para 2.10, above).

(17) Company must state in prospectus the minimum share capital needed to commence business (CA 1985, s 83, para 3.14, above).

(18) No allotment may be made until three days have elapsed from the issue of the prospectus (CA 1985, s 82, para 3.15, above).

MAINTENANCE OF SHARE CAPITAL

A company may not reduce its share capital

4.16 Once the company has received payment for its shares it must attempt to keep the nominal share capital as a type of guarantee fund for the creditors in order to pay their debts if these cannot be paid otherwise. The rules relating to the maintenance of share capital stem from this principle and cover the more typical ways in which a company may give its capital away, e g to the shareholders. The ultra vires doctrine is another basic principle designed to protect the company's intra vires creditors. The company must not use any of its assets, including capital, in unauthorised activities. The traditional rules regarding the maintenance of capital usually also protect the company from abuses by the directors. They are:

(1) a company may not become a member of itself or purchase its own shares;

(2) a company may not provide financial assistance for the purchase of its own shares;

(3) a company cannot pay dividend except out of profits available for distribution.

A company may not become a member of itself

4.17 CA 1985, s 143 establishes the general rule that prohibits a company from acquiring its own shares, whether by purchase, subscription or otherwise. In *Trevor v Whitworth*[1] the court held that the company could not give itself the power to purchase its own shares and that such action is ultra vires and illegal. This common law principle was superseded by CA 1980, s 35.

The major reason for the prohibition on a company purchasing its own shares is that it would lead to a reduction of capital though this would only be the case if the purchase were made out of capital.[2] Other reasons put forward to justify the prohibition were:

(a) *trafficking*: this was never defined but seemed to mean that a company could possibly influence the market in its own shares by timely purchase or sale and false markets in its shares might be created;

(b) *abuses by directors*: votes attached to shares purchased by the company would be controlled and exercisable by the directors, and it was feared that they might use such votes for self-advancement or for excluding a minority shareholder from the company;

(c) *value of the shares*: if the company purchased its own shares and the price paid were too little, the value of the other shares would increase (see Figure 6, below), if the company purchased its own shares for a high price, the value of the other shares would be reduced (see Figure 7, below). Shareholders selling their shares would benefit in this case, but the remaining shareholders would have devalued shares.

Table 5

Company buys at under value

		Share capital and quasi-share capital	Profits	Value of each share
Before purchase net assets £30,000	£	10,000	20,000	$\dfrac{10{,}000 + 20{,}000}{10{,}000}$ = £3.00 each
		(£1 nominal value shares)		
		10,000	20,000	
After purchase of 4,000 shares at par net assets £26,000		10,000 (4,000)	20,000	$\dfrac{10{,}000 + 16{,}000}{6{,}000}$ = £4.33 each
		4,000	(4,000)	
		10,000	16,000	

Table 6

Company buys at over value

		Share capital and quasi-share capital	Profits	Value of each share
Before purchase net assets £30,000	£	10,000	20,000	$\dfrac{10{,}000 + 20{,}000}{10{,}000}$ = £3.00 each
		(£1 nominal value shares)		
		10,000	20,000	
After purchase of 4,000 shares at £5 each net assets £10,000		10,000 (4,000)	20,000 (16,000)	$\dfrac{10{,}000 + \text{nil}}{6{,}000}$ = £1.67 each
		4,000	(4,000)	
		10,000	—	

The provision in s 143 'No company limited by shares or limited by guarantee and having a share capital shall acquire its own shares,' is made subject to the exceptions listed in s 143 itself and this list is exhaustive. The prohibition relates to acquisitions of shares whether by purchase, subscription or otherwise but does not prohibit a company from acquiring its own fully paid up shares otherwise than for valuable consideration.[2] This confirms the pre-1980 cases[3] which permitted a company to accept a gift of its own shares as long as they were fully paid up. Although some of the objections raised in *Trevor v Whitworth* apply equally to a gift of shares at least the company is not reducing its capital, there is no outflow of funds and it has received full consideration for those shares.

Just as an acquisition by a company of its own shares might lead to a reduction of capital so too would a purchase by a subsidiary of its holding company shares, thus this is similarly prohibited.[4] Subject to the exceptions mentioned in s 23 a company may not become a member of its holding company and any such allotment or transfer is void. A subsidiary which was a member of its holding company on 1 July 1948 can continue to be a member.[5] S 23 has no application where the subsidiary is concerned only as personal representative or as a trustee.[6] S 23 does not appear to cover the case where a company holds shares in another company and it subsequently becomes that company's subsidiary. It can only be assumed that s 23 has no application to shares acquired before the relationship of holding and subsidiary arose, despite the wording of s 23 i e a company '*cannot*' be a member of its holding company.

---

[1] (1887) 12 App Cas 409.
[2] CA 1985, s 143(3).
[3] *Re Castiglione, Erskine & Co Ltd* [1958] 2 All ER 455; *Kirby v Wilkins* [1929] 2 Ch 444.
[4] CA 1985, s 23.
[5] Ibid, s 23(2).
[6] Ibid, s 23(4).

Nominee shareholdings

4.18　An easy way for a company to avoid the rule in *Trevor v Whitworth*[1] or in CA 1985, s 23 would be to acquire its own shares through a nominee who would hold the shares for the benefit of the company. Only the person whose name is on the share transfer is entitled to be registered as a member and the company cannot take notice of any trust, expressed, implied or constructive on the register.[2] A company may therefore hide behind this requirement and be beneficially entitled to its own shares. In such a case the person registered as a member is the only person liable on those shares to make any calls. In order to ensure that a company has no liability on partly paid-up shares acquired through a nominee, s 144 provides that where partly paid-up shares are issued to or acquired by a nominee of the company they are treated as being held by the nominee on his own account for all purposes and the company is regarded as having no beneficial interest in them.

The nominee is liable for calls on the shares and if he fails to pay any amount due on them within twenty-one days from being called on the directors of the company at the time of the acquisition become jointly and severally liable with the nominee, or if the nominee was a subscriber to the memorandum in respect of these shares the other subscribers are jointly and severally liable with him.[3]

CA 1985, s 144(1) and (2) does not apply if the company has no beneficial interest in the shares acquired by a nominee of the company, e g the company is acting as a trustee and the trust fund includes shares in that company, or to shares issued or acquired before the appointed day.[4]

Any subscriber or director liable as a result of s 144(3) may be relieved of liability by the court if it is satisfied that he has acted honestly and reasonably and having regard to all the circumstances of the case ought fairly to be excused. Relief may be of all or part of the liability on such terms as the court thinks fit.[5] The subscriber or director who may become liable under s 144 may apply for relief from liability in advance under s 144(4).

---

[1] (1887) 12 App Cas 409.
[2] CA 1985, s 360.
[3] Ibid, s 144(2).
[4] Ibid, s 145(2).
[5] Ibid, s 144(3).

Consequences of acquisition

4.19   The 1980 Act provided for the treatment of shares in itself acquired by or on behalf of a public company in various situations.[1] The provisions also extended to cover a private company which re-registered as a public company and would have come within s 146, and to a public company which is under an existing obligation by virtue of s 146 even though it re-registers as a private company. The treatment of their own shares acquired by public companies does not extend to private companies, except on re-registration as a public limited company.

S 146 applies:

(a) where shares are forfeited or surrendered for failure to pay any sums due in respect of those shares;

(b) where the company acquires shares other than by one of the exceptions in s 143(3) and the company has a beneficial interest in those shares, e g acquisition by way of gift;

(c) where a nominee acquires the company's shares and no financial assistance has been given directly or indirectly by the company and the company has a beneficial interest;

(d) where any person acquires shares in the company with financial assistance from the company and the company has a beneficial interest in those shares.[2]

In these circumstances, unless previously disposed of, the company must cancel the shares and diminish the value of its share capital accordingly and where the effect of cancelling the shares brings the company below the minimum share capital requirement, the company must apply for re-registration as a private company. In such a case the company does not need to comply with the statutory reduction procedure in CA 1985, ss 135 and 136 and the company may make such necessary alterations to the memorandum as are required in the circumstances.[3]

Neither the company, nor nominees nor the shareholder holding any shares which come within s 146(1) may exercise the votes attached to those shares and any purported exercise is void.[4]

Failure to cancel the shares or to re-register the company as required renders the company, and every officer of the company in default, liable to a fine. Failure to re-register as a private company as required means that the company remains a public company but is not one which can invite the public to subscribe for its shares, thus any attempt to make a new issue of shares available to the public will render the company and any officer in default liable on conviction to a fine. It is only for the purposes of CA 1985, s 81 that the public company is treated as a private company, in all other respects it is obliged to comply with public company rules until it has re-registered as a private company.[5]

Where shares are acquired by the company or a nominee of it and the company has no beneficial interest in them, s 146 does not apply. This pre-serves the right of companies acting as trustees or personal representatives to deal with such shares according to their trust and to retain any remuneration or expenses incurred in so acting. The exemption does not include the situation where the company has a beneficial interest in shares which have been acquired with financial assistance provided by the company. In this case, i e (d) above, the company must cancel the shares within one year of acquisition, whereas in cases (a), (b) and (c) above the company has three years to comply with the requirement of disposal or cancellation.

Finally, a public company which acquires its own shares otherwise than by purchase and cancels those shares, if those shares are shown in the company's balance sheet as an asset, must transfer an amount equal in value to the shares to a reserve fund from the company's distributable profits. This ensures that even where the company receives shares by way of gift, there is no reduction of share capital.[6]

---

[1] CA 1985, s 146. Those acquisitions permissible under CA 1985, s 143(3) are excluded from these provisions.
[2] CA 1985, s 146.
[3] Ibid, s 147.
[4] Ibid, s 146(4).
[5] Ibid, s 149.
[6] See para 3.24, above.

Breach of s 143

4.20 Not only do the officers of a company acting in contravention of s 143(1) commit an offence, but so too does the company itself, but whereas the officers of the company can be liable to a fine or imprisonment or both, a company may only be fined for its contravention of CA 1985, s 143(3).

In addition it is important to note that any purported acquisition in breach of s 143 is void,[1] this stresses the importance of the rule and if it were not so, the exhaustive list of exceptions to s 143 in s 143(3) would be meaningless. Where a company intends to acquire shares from X, a shareholder, the transaction to acquire the shares is void, X remains the holder of the shares and the company ceases to be liable to make the agreed payment, if any.

---

[1] CA 1985, s 143(2).

Exceptions to s 143(1)

4.21 The only permissible exceptions to s 143(1) are those listed in s 143(3):

'(a) The redemption or purchase of any shares in accordance with Chapter VII of this Part;

(b) the acquisition of any shares in a reduction of capital duly made;

(c) the purchase of any shares in pursuance of an order of the court under s 5,[1] s 54[2] or Part XVII;[3] or

(d) the forfeiture of any shares or the acceptance of any shares surrendered in lieu, in pursuance of the articles for failure to pay any sum payable in respect of those shares.'

Companies are permitted to redeem or purchase their own shares in the following situations:

(i)   redeemable shares out of profits;[4]

(ii) purchase of own shares out of profits;[5]

(iii) contingent purchase contracts for purchase of own shares out of profits;[6]

(iv) redemption or purchase of own shares out of capital (private companies only).[7]

These exceptions are dealt with below.[8] It is important to remember, however, that if a company cannot bring itself within one of the exceptions the general principle revives and the purported purchase or redemption is void.

---

[1] I e alteration of objects.

[2] Special resolutions resulting in company becoming private company, see para 4.47, below.

[3] Shareholder petition for unfairly prejudicial conduct, see para 4.47, below, and see chap . . . (minority shareholders' rights).

[4] CA 1985, s 159.

[5] Ibid, s 162.

[6] Ibid, s 165.

[7] Ibid, s 171.

[8] Paras 4.22 to 4.49.

REDEMPTION OR PURCHASE OF A COMPANY'S OWN SHARES

Redeemable shares

4.22 The concept of redeemable shares is not new. CA 1948, s 58[1] empowered companies to issue preference shares as redeemable. The new provision is not limited to preference shares. Any shares may now be issued as redeemable, though a company may not issue all its shares as redeemable otherwise on redemption of the last share the company would have no share capital. This would mean no members and the company would be in breach of CA 1985, s 24 requiring there to be at least two members. A company may not issue redeemable shares if the company does not have some non-redeemable shares.[2]

Any company wishing to issue redeemable shares must have power in its articles to do so. The company may insert such a clause in the same way as it effects any alteration of the articles, i e by special resolution under CA 1985, s 9. Apart from the provisions of the Act, the company may make its own rules regarding redemption which must also be included in the articles. S 159 empowers companies which have the requisite authority in their articles to issue redeemable shares.

Only fully paid shares can be redeemed otherwise there would be a cancellation of unpaid-up capital, which would amount to a reduction of capital. The shares must be issued as redeemable: it is not possible to convert shares into redeemable shares after issue. Shares may be issued either with a fixed date for redemption or be issued as redeemable at the option of the company or shareholder.[3]

---

[1] This section ceased to have effect by virtue of CA 1981, s 62.
[2] CA 1985, s 159(2).
[3] Ibid, s 159.

Payment for redemption

4.23 Payment for redeemable shares can only be made out of *distributable profits*[1] or out of the proceeds of a *fresh issue of shares* made for the purpose of redemption. Prior to CA 1981 all profits both distributable and undistributable could be used for a redemption. Moreover, payment of any premium on redemption must be paid out of distributable profits only.[2] This represents a considerable tightening of the pre-1981 position where premium could be paid either out of all profits (distributable or non-distributable) or the quasi-share capital, the share premium account.

Redemption is paid for either out of distributable profits or by the process of a new issue of shares which replaces the capital of those shares redeemed. The redeemed shares are treated as cancelled and the company's issued share capital diminished if necessary by the nominal value of those shares, but it is expressly stated that a redemption of shares under this section shall not be taken as reducing the company's authorised share capital. Thus, although the redeemed shares are not regarded as being available for re-issue,[3] the capital represented by those shares remains capable of being issued by the company up to the authorised share capital limit. In fact the company is empowered to issue shares up to the nominal amount of the shares redeemed as if those shares had never been issued and subject to certain requirements a new issue will not be a chargeable transaction under the Finance Act 1973. However, the exemption will not apply if the redeemable shares are not redeemed within one month of the issue of new shares.[4]

As a general rule premium due on redeemable shares is generally only payable out of the company's distributable profits, but where the company received a premium at the time of issue on the redeemable shares or there are funds in the company's share premium account, the company may pay any premium due on redemption out of the proceeds of a fresh issue as long as the amount does not exceed the premium received at the time of issue or the company's share premium account whichever is less. Where advantage is taken of this provision the amount of the company's share premium account shall be reduced by a sum corresponding to the premium payable on redemption.[5]

Table 7

	Share capital	Share premium account/capital redemption reserve	Profits	Assets
30,000 £1 nominal value non-redeemable shares	30,000			
10,000 £1 nominal value redeemable shares	10,000			
Premium of 50p on issue of non-redeemable shares		15,000		
Premium of £2 on issue of redeemable shares		20,000		
Before redemption	40,000	35,000	50,000	125,000

After redemption *Premium out of fresh issue* New issue of 20,000 £1 nominal value redeemable shares for £4	20,000	60,000		80,000
10,000 £1 nominal value redeemable shares redeemed at £3				
(i) Capital	(10,000)			(10,000)
(ii) transfer of capital				
(iii) premium				
(i e proceeds of new issue)	(20,000)			(20,000)
(iv) transfer of premium	20,000	(20,000)		
	50,000	75,000	50,000	175,000

---

[1] As defined in CA 1985, s 263; see para 4.68, below.
[2] CA 1985, s 143(2).
[3] But see below.
[4] CA 1985, s 161.
[5] CA 1985, s 160(2).

Capital redemption reserve

4.24 In all cases (whether purchase or redemption) where profits are used and the company's issued share capital is reduced on cancellation of the shares redeemed or purchased, the company must transfer to capital redemption reserve, an amount equal to the amount by which the company's capital has been reduced.[1]

Similarly, where a company redeems or purchases its own shares out of the proceeds of a fresh issue of shares, but the proceeds of the new issue is less than the nominal amount of the shares redeemed or purchased, an amount equivalent to the difference must be transferred to the capital redemption reserve, thus preserving the share capital. The capital redemption reserve is subject to the reduction of share capital rules as if it were paid-up share capital of the company.[2]

In certain circumstances a *private* company may redeem or purchase its shares out of capital.[3]

---

[1] CA 1985, s 170.

[2] CA 1985, s 170(4).

[3] See para 4.32, below.

Breach of contract to redeem or purchase shares

4.25   The redemption date for the redemption of redeemable shares will probably[1] be one of the terms of the contract between the company and the shareholder.[2] If the company refuses to pay on the due date, there will be a breach of contract. If the breach of contract causes greater loss than the redemption value of the shares to be redeemed, this difference, if paid by way of damages, might represent an unauthorised reduction of capital. This would certainly have the effect of giving a shareholder, with an action for damages against a company for failure to redeem or purchase his shares, priority over the company's creditors. It is therefore expressly provided that a company's failure to redeem or purchase shares will not make the company liable in damages.[3] Moreover, a court is not able to order specific performance of the contract for redemption or purchase if the company shows that it is unable to meet the cost out of its distributable profits. This relieves the company of liability to pay the redemption value or the agreed purchase price, i e the contract sum, if the company can show that it has not sufficient distributable profits. The creditors are protected against a return of capital even though the company would be in breach of contract not to make the payment.

Although the holder of redeemable shares or shares which the company has agreed to purchase may be at a disadvantage whilst the company is a going concern, if the redemption or purchase is not made on time, priority is given to such people if the company goes into liquidation. On liquidation where the shares have not been redeemed or purchased, the contract may be enforced against the company and the company, after paying off all the debts and liabilities and any preferred shares, must pay the amounts outstanding on redemption or purchase.[4]

Shareholders may enforce the contract against the company by virtue of these provisions only if the redemption or purchase was due before the commencement of the winding up, and if during the period between the due date for redemption or purchase and on the winding up, the company could lawfully have made a distribution equal to the value of the shares to be redeemed or purchased. In this way the holder of the redeemed shares gets no unfair priority over other shareholders.[5]

Any shares purchased or redeemed in priority on liquidation as a result of s 178(6) must be treated as cancelled by the company and are not available for re-issue.[6]

---

[1] Not necessarily though, as s 159 permits a company to issue shares as redeemable or liable to be redeemed at the option of the company or the shareholder.

[2] By virtue of the express contract entered into by the company and the shareholder, but more likely by virtue of CA 1985, s 14 which deems there to be a contract between the company and its members on the terms of the articles.

[3] CA 1985, s 178(2).

[4] Ibid, s 178(4)–(6).

[5] Ibid, s 178(5).

[6] Ibid, s 178(4).

Purchase of own shares

4.26   Following the publication of a Green Paper 'The Purchase by a Company of its own Shares' in 1980 the prohibition on the purchase of a company's own shares was relaxed by CA 1981. In particular, the relaxation was aimed at encouraging the expansion of small businesses, as investors were then able to subscribe money to companies on the basis that when (and if) the company's expansion was successful they might remove their capital. Share capital in the past has been regarded as an indefinite loan to the company[1] only repayable whilst the company is a going concern by using the CA 1985, s 135 procedure.[2] Although the power to issue redeemable preference shares has been available since 1929,[3] this lacks flexibility in that the date of redemption is not always the most opportune time for the company to repay the capital, yet redeemable shares must be *issued* as redeemable. The new power to purchase a company's own shares can be exercised at the most beneficial time to the company and its business needs, whilst incorporating necessary protections for the creditors and shareholders.

All companies having a share capital are empowered by CA 1985, s 162 to purchase their own shares (including redeemable shares) in accordance with the procedures laid down in CA 1985, Part V Chapter VII provided their articles authorise them to do so.

In order to take advantage of these provisions a company must be authorised to buy its own shares in its articles,[4] but a company may not purchase its own shares so as to leave only redeemable shares, whether or not the company is so authorised.[5] Neither, it is assumed, may a company purchase all its issued shares.

All the limitations imposed on a redemption of shares under s 160 are applied in the same manner to a purchase of shares by a company.[6] In particular, a public company[7] may only purchase its own shares out of the proceeds of a fresh issue made for the purpose or out of distributable profits, except that the terms and manner of purchase need not be determined by the articles as required by s 160(3). In addition, the rules governing compensating transfers, i e s 170,[8] apply equally to purchases.

---

[1] Compare with the usual nature of a debenture, see 4.83.

[2] I e Reduction of capital requiring court order, CA 1985 s 135, see para 4.42.

[3] CA 1929, s 46.

[4] CA 1985, s 162. The company could insert such a power by special resolution of the company under CA 1985, s 9.

[5] CA 1985, s 162(3).
[6] Ibid, s 162(2).
[7] See para 4.32, below.
[8] See paras 4.23 and 4.24, above.

Authority for off-market purchase and contingent purchase contracts

4.27 The power to purchase its own shares can only be implemented by employing one of the different procedures detailed in CA 1985, ss 163–166 as follows:

(i)   off-market purchases;
(ii) contingent purchase contracts;
(iii) market purchases.

An off-market purchase is not limited to those purchases of shares not listed on The Stock Exchange, but also includes those shares which are purchased on The Stock Exchange but which are not subject to a marketing arrangement on The Stock Exchange.[1] Any company which is listed on The Stock Exchange or any company which has been accorded unconditional facilities for dealing on The Stock Exchange will be a company subject to a marketing arrangement. The off-market procedure is for private companies (which cannot obtain a listing on The Stock Exchange) and those public companies which do not have a listing or only restricted access to The Stock Exchange.

A contingent purchase contract is a contract which although not a contract for the purchase of shares is one under which the company may become entitled or obliged to purchase shares, e g a contract to purchase an option. The contingent purchase is also subject to the requirements of s 165 and s 164(3)–(7).

This is a necessary anti-avoidance device and will prevent companies holding options on their own shares which they could take up at will, possibly creating false markets in the shares.

Any contract for an off-market purchase or contingent purchase contract must be approved in advance by special resolution of the company. Where a public company is proposing the purchase, the expiry date of the approval of the shareholders must be stated and in any case cannot extend for more than eighteen months after the date on which the resolution is passed.[2]

The authority for the proposed contract may be varied, revoked or from time to time renewed (subject to s 164(4)) but this can only be effected in the same way as the original authority, i e by special resolution.[3] But any resolution to confer, vary, revoke or renew authority for a proposed contract will not be effective if any member holding shares to which the resolution relates exercises voting rights attached to those shares in voting on the resolution and the resolution would not have been passed if he had not done so.[4] This proviso ensures that an interested shareholder is not in a position to influence the terms of his contract with the company, except that he may vote on the contract exercising voting rights attached to shares which are not the subject of the contract.

The resolution will not be effective if a copy of the contract or memorandum of its terms was not available for inspection by members both at the company's registered office for at least fifteen days prior to the meeting and at the meeting itself. The memorandum must contain the names of the shareholders whose shares are involved or where a contract is made available that contract must contain the relevant shareholders names or a memorandum be annexed to it that does include those names.[5]

A company wishing to vary the terms of an existing contract must obtain the approval of the shareholders by special resolution and subsections (3)–(6) of s 164 apply in the same way except that a copy of the original contract plus any previous memoranda of alteration must be available for inspection along with details of the revised contract.

The contingent purchase contract is subject to the same provisions relating to sanctions and most of the detailed rules also apply.[6]

---

[1] CA 1985, s 163(1).
[2] Ibid, s 164.
[3] Ibid, s 164(3).
[4] Ibid, s 164(5).
[5] Ibid, s 164(6).
[6] Ibid, s 165(2).

Authority for market purchases

4.28   A market purchase is any purchase made on The Stock Exchange, other than an off-market purchase as defined in s 163(1).[1] In order to make a market purchase of its own shares a company must first have been authorised by the company in general meeting.[2] No mention is made of the type of resolution required, thus it is assumed that unless the company's articles provide to the contrary, an ordinary resolution will suffice. The resolution is required to authorise the purchase and may confer general authority or authority limited to the purchase of shares of any particular class or description. Such authority as is conferred may be unconditional or subject to conditions, e. g valuation of shares by independent valuer.[3]

Unlike the authority for off-market purchases, the authority for market purchases is not for a particular contract, but certain details must be included in the authority. The authority must state the maximum number of shares to be acquired, the minimum and maximum prices which the company may pay for those shares and the date of expiry of the authority which in any case cannot be later than eighteen months after the resolution has been passed.[4] In order to comply with a statement of the minimum and maximum prices of the shares, it is sufficient if the company specifies a particular sum or provides a basis or formula for calculating the amount without reference to any person's discretion or opinion. Thus, a formula of five per cent above or below the prevailing market price would be acceptable but not 'at a price to be determined by the directors.'

If a company were to assign or relinquish its rights to contracts to purchase its own shares all the creditor and shareholder protections incorporated in the Act could be avoided, so a company is not permitted to assign its rights under a CA 1985, s 164 or s 165 contract or a contract for a purchase authorised under s 166. Similarly, any attempt by a company to release rights under contracts approved under s 164 or s 165 is void unless the release has been approved in advance by the company in accordance with the specified procedure. Any proposed release must be approved by a special resolution of the shareholders in general meeting and s 164(3)–(7) apply to a release as they apply to the authority for the purchase itself.[5]

[1] See para 4.27, above.
[2] CA 1985, s 166(1).
[3] Ibid, s 166(1).
[4] Ibid, s 166(3) and (4).
[5] Ibid, s 167.

Payment for purchase and other payments

4.29 As with redemption under s 159, consideration for the purchase by a company of its own shares must come out of the company's distributable profits or out of the proceeds of a fresh issue of shares made for the purpose. Any premium payable on purchase may only come out of the distributable profits.[1]

Other payments in connection with contracts for the purchase of a company's own shares must also come out of the company's distributable profits.[2] The other payments envisaged by the Act are payments in connection with:

(i)   rights acquired under an approved contingent purchase contract;
(ii)   variations of a s 164 or s 165 (off-market or contingent purchase) approved contract;
(iii) the release of the company's obligations under any contract approved under s 164 or s 165 or s 166 (market, off-market or contingent purchase).

Breach of s 168(1) has different consequences depending on the type of payment involved. If there is a breach in relation to (i) above, any purchase made in pursuance of such a contract is unlawful, i e of no effect. Where the breach is in connection with payments within (ii) above, any purchase following the variation is unlawful and breaches in connection with (iii) above, make the purported release void, the original contract is still in force and the parties liable on it accordingly.[3]

[1] CA 1985, s 162(2), applying s 160.
[2] Ibid, s 168.
[3] Ibid, s 168(1) and (2).

Registration of particulars

4.30 Registration requirements are two-fold, registration at Companies House and registration at the company's registered office. In respect of shares purchased by a company under s 162 the company must deliver to the registrar of companies a return in the prescribed form within 28 days of the purchase.[1] The form must state the number and nominal value of the shares purchased and the date on which they were delivered to the company. Where a public company has taken advantage of the power in s 162 to purchase its own shares, it must also state in the return the aggregate amount paid by the company for the shares and the maximum and minimum prices paid in respect of shares of each class purchased.[2] The company may make one return which deals with shares purchased under different contracts on different dates and reference to the aggregate amount above means the aggregate paid by the company for *all* the shares to which the return relates.

Failure to deliver a return as required by this section to the registrar is an offence and every officer in default is liable on conviction to a fine.[3]

A company entering into any contract approved under s 164 or s 165 or an approved purchase under s 166 must keep a copy of the relevant contract, or if the contract is not in writing a memorandum of that contract, at its registered office.[4]

The copy of the contract or the memorandum must be kept at the registered office from the conclusion of the contract and for ten years starting with the date on which all the purchases of shares included in the contract are concluded. During this period the memorandum and copy of the contract must be available for inspection by members of the company and if the company is a public company by any person during reasonable business hours and without charge.[5]

If the company fails to keep the details of the contracts and purchase authorisations at its registered office in accordance with s 169(4) or a company refuses to permit an eligible person to investigate those documents, the directors in default and the company are liable on conviction to a fine.[6] Moreover, the court has power to compel the company to permit a person immediate inspection of the copy or memorandum if the company has refused to do so.[7] Copies of all special resolutions must be filed with the registrar of companies within fifteen days of the passing of the resolution,[8] so the resolution approving an off-market purchase or a contingent purchase contract or variations thereof must be filed. The market purchase only requires an ordinary resolution but nevertheless is made subject to s 380.[9]

---

[1] CA 1985, s 169.
[2] Ibid, s 169(2).
[3] Ibid, s 169(6).
[4] Ibid, s 169(4).
[5] Ibid, s 169(5).
[6] Ibid, s 169(7).
[7] Ibid, s 169(8).

8 Ibid, s 380.
9 Ibid, s 380(4).

Effects of a purchase

4.31 When a public company acquires shares in the ways listed in s 146(1)[1] and cancellation of those shares reduces the company's share capital below the authorised minimum the company is required to re-register as a private company.

---

[1] See para 4.19, above.

Purchase or redemption of own shares: out of capital

4.32 In addition to empowering companies to redeem or purchase their own shares out of profits, CA 1985, Part V Chapter VII gives *private* companies a limited power to purchase or redeem their own shares out of capital. The power to purchase or redeem shares out of capital contained in s 171 is however subject to safeguards.

S 171 provides that a private limited company, if authorised by its articles, may make a payment in respect of a redemption or purchase under s 160 or s 162 otherwise than out of distributable profits of the company or the proceeds of a fresh issue i e out of capital. It seems likely that the authority in the articles would have to be precise and expressly provide for purchase or redemption *out of capital*.

Ss 171–177 lay down detailed rules to be complied with in order to give protection to both the shareholders and the creditors. The right to exercise the power granted by s 171 is dependent on agreement by shareholders who are not interested in the particular transaction and on the company having sufficient funds to pay its creditors in full. Subject to these safeguards there is no reason, particularly in a private company, to prohibit a return of capital to the members. S 171 gives the private company the power to reduce its capital without the necessity of complying with CA 1985, s 135,[1] which requires court sanction. However s 171 cannot be used in all the same circumstances as s 135 and as a general rule may be used only where the company has too much capital and the reduction would leave sufficient funds for payment of all debts and liabilities of the company.

---

[1] See para 4.42, below.

Permissible capital payment

4.33 The definition of capital for the purpose of s 171 is any fund other than distributable profits and proceeds of a fresh issue, whether or not this fund is technically capital.[1] For example undistributable profits would be 'capital' for this purpose. S 171 does not give private companies additional powers to make contracts for the purchase or redemption of shares, it merely extends the category of funds available for payment for a purchase or redemption. Thus, ss 159–166 must be complied with and if payment is to be out of capital ss 171–177 must be complied with in addition.

The right to make use of the company's capital for redemption or purchase is based on the idea that the company must first exhaust its distributable profits or any proceeds of a fresh issue. Only then can the company look to the capital, otherwise the company's capital could be handed back to shareholders, thus depleting the capital available for the creditors, even though other funds were available. These other funds could then be used for other purposes, e g a dividend distribution to shareholders thus reversing the normal priority given to creditors to the share capital.

The difference between the amount needed for the purchase or redemption and the amount available from distributable profits and proceeds of a fresh issue is known as the *permissible capital payment*.[2] In calculating the permissible capital payment the company is required to take into account the company's *available profits* and the proceeds of any fresh issue of shares, though it is not *required* to make a fresh issue. Available profits are distributable profits as defined in CA 1985, Part VIII but defined by reference to such accounts as are drawn up within three months of the directors' statutory declaration[3] and not the relevant accounts as defined in CA 1985, ss 270–275.[4] This is to ensure that companies do not use out of date accounts as the basis for determining what are available profits. Any lawful distributions made since that time from the distributable profits must be taken into account so as to reduce by that amount the profits now available.[5]

The permissible capital payment must be calculated on the basis of accounts as at a date within the three months ending with the date on which the directors made their statutory declaration.[6]

---

[1] CA 1985, s 171.
[2] Ibid, s 171(3).
[3] See para 4.37, below.
[4] CA 1985, s 172(1) and see para 4.76, below.
[5] CA 1985, s 172(4).
[6] Ibid, s 172(6).

Compensating transfers

4.34 Capital for the purposes of determining the permissible capital payment does not have the same meaning as share capital,[1] therefore it is essential to make special provision to prevent a distortion of the share capital account. If a company wishes to purchase or redeem its own shares, say for example it wishes to purchase 200 £1 nominal value shares at £1 each, and the permissible capital payment amounts to £150 (the remainder coming from other funds) the actual (non-distributable) capital is being reduced by only £150, not £200 but the number of shares reduced will be 200. Without some type of compensating transfer, it would appear in the company's books as if the whole £200 were coming out of capital.[2] S 171(4) provides that a compensating transfer of an amount equivalent to the difference between the nominal share capital and the permissible capital payment must be transferred to the capital redemption reserve. When the permissible capital payment is greater than the nominal value of the shares, i e where the shares are redeemed or purchased at a premium, s 171(5) permits the company to reduce its capital redemption reserve, share premium account or fully paid share capital and any. amount representing unrealised profits of the company[3] by a sum not exceeding the amount by which the permissible capital payment exceeds the nominal value of those shares.

Table 8

No compensating transfer

		Share capital	Quasi-share capital and undistributable profits	Distributable profits and proceeds of a fresh issue	Assets
Before purchase or redemption	(a)	600	100	50	750
After purchase or redemption of 200 £1 shares at £1	(b)	(200)			(200)
After purchase or redemption		400	100	50	550

Table 9

With compensating transfer — Permissible capital payment less than nominal value (s 171(4))

		Share capital	Quasi-share capital and undistributable profits	Distributable profits and proceeds of a fresh issue	Assets
Before purchase or redemption (As above)	(a)	600	100	50	750
After purchase or redemption of 200 £1 shares at £1	(b)	(200)			(200)
Transfer to capital redemption reserve	(c)		50	(50)	
After purchase or redemption		400	150	—	550

Table 10

With compensating transfer — Permissible capital payment greater than nominal value (s 171(5))

		Share capital	Quasi-share capital and undistributable profits	Distributable profits and proceeds of a fresh issue	Assets
Before purchase or redemption (As above)	(a)	600	100	50	750
After purchase or redemption of 200 £1 shares at £1.50	(b)	(200)	(100)		(300)
Transfer to capital redemption reserve*, etc.	(c)		50	(50)	
After purchase or redemption		400	50	—	450

* the amount by which permissible capital payment (£250) exceeds the nominal share capital (£200): i e £50.

Both of these provisions make certain that those amounts available for distribution are exhausted first and that the share capital is retained at the expense of the quasi-share capital funds. In calculating the amount of the permissible share capital payment the proceeds of any fresh issue of shares must be taken into account.

---

[1] See para 4.33, above.
[2] Table 10(b).
[3] Table 11(c).

Shareholder protection

4.35   As a general principle when a company purchases or redeems shares out of profits, shareholders are not prejudiced as a shareholder has no right to the company's profits only a hope of obtaining a satisfactory dividend. Whilst the company is a going concern it is up to the directors to decide whether to plough profits back into the business or distribute profits by way of dividend. Where, however, the company is proposing to use its capital for a purchase or redemption, shareholders have a justifiable interest to be protected, in particular, they may be concerned to ensure that there is no distortion of their priority rights to a return of capital on liquidation.

Three particular safeguards are provided. Ss 173–175 require consent to the payment by a special resolution of the general meeting, the directors must make a statutory declaration of solvency and dissenting shareholders have a right to apply to the court for the cancellation of the resolution.

(a) Special resolution

4.36   S 173 makes it clear that only resolutions approving payments out of capital in accordance with s 174 and s 175 are lawful. The words 'it is not

lawful' are similar to those used in s 151[1] (provision of financial assistan
and it is assumed that they have the same effect in s 173, i e not mer⸗⸗
making any payments void but also illegal. This has the consequence that if
the company has made a payment out of capital in breach of s 173 it would be
irrecoverable by the company, since in an illegal transaction the parties
cannot use the courts to recover any property transferred: loss lies where it
falls. This seems unfortunate when the safeguards attached to an exercise of
the power under s 171 are designed primarily to keep the company's capital
intact in so far as it is needed to satisfy the debts and liabilities due to its
creditors.

---

[1] And its predecessors: CA 1948, s 54, CA 1981, s 42. For a survey of the effects of these
words see para 4.50, below.

(b) Declaration of solvency

4.37 The directors are obliged to make a statutory declaration of solvency
under s 173(3). They must state that having made a full inquiry into the
company's affairs and prospects they have formed an opinion:

(a) that having made a payment out of capital there will be no reason why
the company is unable to pay its debts; and

(b) that having regard to their intentions for the next year with respect to
management and to the amount and character of financial resources,
in their view the company will be able to carry on business as a going
concern, and be able to pay its debts as they fall due, throughout that
year.

The statutory declaration must be in the prescribed form and contain
prescribed information. In particular, it must contain details of the permissible capital payment. In addition, the company's auditors must make a
report addressed to the directors which must be annexed to the declaration.[1]
This report must state that they have inquired into the company's affairs and
that the amount mentioned in the declaration as the permissible capital
payment is in their view properly determined in accordance with ss 171 and
172 and that they are not aware of anything which would indicate that the
opinion of the directors expressed in the declaration is unreasonable in all the
circumstances.

If the law did not prevent it a company wishing to make a purchase or
redemption out of capital in the future could obtain authority from the shareholders and a statutory declaration of solvency from the directors and keep
these in reserve until required. This would enable the company to defeat the
protection intended to be afforded by these safeguards. Elaborate rules are
included in the Act to prevent this, e g the use of available profits as opposed
to distributable profits for the purposes of s 171 and the time limit imposed
on the period for determining the permissible capital payment. It is also
provided that the resolution for payment out of capital must be passed on, or
within the week immediately following the date on which the directors make
their statutory declaration of solvency, and the payment itself must be made
not earlier than five weeks nor more than seven weeks after the date of the
resolution.[2] The prohibition on payment within the five weeks after the
resolution allows for members and creditors to exercise their right to object to
the payment under s 176.[3] The prohibition on payment after seven weeks

prevents the company from complying with all the requirements of s 171 but with no intention of paying the money immediately but holding back the payment until a time which may be favourable to particular shareholders, e g the directors.

The resolution authorising a payment out of capital will not be effective if either:

(i)   a shareholder interested in the purchase or redemption has exercised voting rights attached to those shares in voting on the resolution and the resolution would not have been passed but for his votes;[4] or

(ii) the statutory declaration or auditors' report was not available for inspection by members of the company at the meeting at which the resolution is passed.

The penalties imposed on directors for making a declaration of solvency without having reasonable ground for their opinions are severe leading on conviction to a fine or imprisonment for up to two years or both.

---

[1] CA 1985, s 173(5) and see paras 10.56 to 10.57, below.
[2] Ibid, s 174(1).
[3] See paras 4.38 and 4.40, below.
[4] Though an interested shareholder may use the votes attached to shares which are not the subject of the purchase to vote in favour of the resolution.

(c) Member's objection

4.38   S 176 gives any dissenting shareholder the right to apply to the court for cancellation of the resolution. Only shareholders who have not voted in favour of the resolution for the purchase out of capital may apply and must do so within five weeks following the date of the passing of the resolution. Where a member applies for cancellation under s 176 the company must give notice of that fact to the registrar of companies and within fifteen days of the court order, deliver a copy of that order to the registrar. This gives notice to any person searching the company's file at Companies House of the objection to the resolution and the confirmation or cancellation of that resolution as determined by the court.

The court can:

(i)   adjourn the proceedings so that satisfactory arrangements can be made for the purchase of dissentient members' interests;[1]
(ii)   confirm the resolution;
(iii) cancel the resolution on whatever terms and conditions it thinks fit.[2]

In particular the court has the power to alter or extend any date or period of time specified in the resolution or the provisions of Part V Chapter VII CA 1985, relating to redemption or purchase of shares.

---

[1] Such a purchase of a company's own shares comes within CA 1985, s 143(3)(a).
[2] CA 1985, s 177.

Creditor protection

4.39   This takes a number of forms:

(i)   Publicity of the proposed payments out of capital;[1]
(ii) declaration of solvency and auditors' report;[2]
(iii) objection to the court;[3]
(iv) extending liability of shareholders.[4]

---

[1] See para 4.40, below.
[2] See para 4.37, above.
[3] See para 4.40, below.
[4] See para 4.41, below.

Publicity and objection to the court

4.40 Consistent with the usual principle of protection of creditors in company law, protection is afforded by publicity. S 175 states that a company must cause to be published within one week of the passing of the resolution for the purchase out of capital a notice in the Gazette and either a notice in an appropriate national newspaper or individual written notice to all creditors.

The details to be included within this notice are statements that the company has approved payment out of capital, the date of the resolution and the permissible capital payment to be made. The notice must also state that the statutory declaration and the auditors' report are available for inspection at the company's registered office in accordance with s 173 and give creditors notice of their right to apply to the court to cancel the resolution, a creditor should therefore have a minimum of four weeks within which time he may exercise his right to object.

Creditors have a similar right to object to the resolution approving the payment out of capital as shareholders who did not vote in favour of the resolution. Any creditor may apply to the court and the court's powers are the same in respect of a creditor objection as with a member's objection, except that whereas the court may adjourn the proceedings and make satisfactory arrangements for the purchase of a dissentient member's interests, in the case of creditors, the court has the power to make arrangements for the *protection* of dissentient creditors, e g requiring the company to secure a previously unsecured debt.

Liability of past shareholders and directors

4.41 If the directors' statement regarding the solvency of the company in the year following the payment out of capital proves incorrect and the company goes into insolvent liquidation during that year, the shareholder whose shares were purchased or redeemed is liable to contribute to the company's assets up to an amount not exceeding the *relevant payment* made in respect of his shares. The relevant payment is the payment out of capital made in respect of the purchase or redemption. In these circumstances the directors who made the statutory declaration are jointly and severally liable with that person to contribute to the company's assets, though a director who can show that he had reasonable grounds for forming the opinion included in the declaration may be excused.

The liability of the former shareholder is similar to that of a former shareholder of an unlimited company which goes into insolvent liquidation. Share-holders may be unwilling to sell or redeem their shares if they might remain liable for one year after the payment, but there seems no reason why the shareholders should not at the time of purchase or redemption obtain an indemnity from the directors against having to contribute to the assets in this manner. Also, any person required to contribute as a result of this section may apply to the court for an order directing any other person jointly or severally liable in respect of that amount to make a contribution to him up to an amount which the court thinks just and equitable.[1] In this way the directors can be brought into the action. The former shareholder liable to contribute under this section is not to be regarded as a contributor for the purposes of the Companies Act generally nor the company's articles, unless the context otherwise requires. But such a contributor is given the right to apply for a winding up of the company on the grounds set out in s 517(1)(f) or s 517(1)(g), i e inability of the company to pay its debts and winding up on the just and equitable ground respectively, but may not petition qua-contributor in this section on any other ground.[2]

---

[1] CA 1985, s 504.
[2] Ibid, s 519(3).

Reduction of capital

4.42   Purchase and redemption of shares under CA 1985, Part V Chapter VII is the first exception listed in CA 1985, s 143(3),[1] reductions of capital duly made is the next category.[2] The fundamental principle is that a company may not reduce its capital because to do so would reduce the amount available to the creditors for payment of their debts. The powers included in CA 1985, whereby companies may purchase or redeem their own shares, are surrounded by safeguards for the protection of creditors, particularly when a purchase or redemption out of capital is proposed. In all these cases there must be sufficient funds for the payment of creditors. CA 1985, s 135 is a statutory procedure[3] involving court consent whereby a company may reduce its capital in any circumstances, even where there are insufficient funds for the creditors. The court's power to sanction a s 135 reduction is not circumscribed, any reduction may be sanctioned by the court.

A reduction of capital will sometimes involve a reduction in the nominal or authorised capital but there is no reduction proper unless issued share capital is reduced either by being paid back or written-off or where unpaid share capital is cancelled. There are three hurdles to be overcome in the procedure for reducing share capital: there must be authority in the articles or memorandum empowering the company to reduce its share capital, the company in general meeting must sanction the reduction by special resolution and court sanction must be obtained to confirm the proposed reduction. All these obstacles are designed to protect the interests of both creditors and shareholders.

---

[1] See para 4.21, above.
[2] CA 1985, s 143(3)(b).
[3] Reduction procedures should be distinguished from court orders for reduction which come within the third exception to s 143, s 143(3)(c), see para 4.47, below.

Types of reduction

4.43 It is important to stress that share capital can be reduced in any way under s 135, therefore purchases or redemptions outside of CA 1985, Part V, Chapter VII can be authorised by the court under s 135, e g s 135 could be used for a purchase or redemption of its own shares by a *public company* out of capital. S 135 cites three examples of the type of reduction a company may wish to use but expressly provides that these examples are not exhaustive and do not affect the generality of the section which provides for reductions in any way.

A company may wish to reduce its share capital by extinguishing or reducing the liability on unpaid-up shares, thus cancelling an existing liability of the shareholders to contribute the full nominal value of the shares. S 135 may be used as a tidying up exercise to bring the share capital into line with the company's actual assets, for example where the paid-up share capital is lost or unrepresented by available assets or where the company's share capital is in excess of its wants. Traditionally s 135 reductions of capital have been used either where the company has too much capital or where the company does not have enough capital. Since the introduction by CA 1981 of new powers for companies to purchase their own shares, s 135 will rarely be used in situations where the company has capital in excess of its needs. The new methods are simpler and probably cheaper as no application to court for sanction is required.

Where a company has suffered a loss of capital the existing creditors of the company have lost part of their protection and nothing can be done, but it would be misleading to allow the company to represent that it has more share capital than is shown by its assets, thus a reduction in these circumstances is favoured for the protection of potential investors and creditors. Such a reduction allows the company to write-off the loss and perhaps issue new shares. The court will need to be satisfied that the company has actually suffered a loss of capital and that such loss is not merely temporary.[1]

Table 11

	Share capital	Assets	Value of share
Before reduction			
120,000 £1 nominal value shares	£120,000	£90,000	$\frac{£90,000}{120,000} = 75p$
Capital reduction of £30,000	(30,000)		$\frac{£30,000}{120,000} = 25p$ per share
After reduction 120,000 75p nominal value shares	£90,000	£90,000	$\frac{£90,000}{120,000} = 75p$

---

[1] *City Property Investment Trust Corpn v Thorburn* 1896 23 (Ct of Sess) R 400.

Reduction practices

4.44   The major principle when making a reduction of capital on over-capitalisation under s 135 is that the usual priorities of repayment of capital on a liquidation will be followed.[1] Thus, if preference shares have priority to a return of capital they must be paid back first on a reduction.[2] The application of this principle has led to the decline in usefulness of the preference share. In *Re Saltdean*[3] the company applied for and was granted a reduction of capital in order to pay off all the preference shareholders at par in a situation where the company had funds in excess of its wants. The reduction meant that the preference shareholders were deprived of a sizeable dividend if the company were to distribute its excessive profits in that way. The court held that the reduction was not unfair because the preference shareholders had no right to the future profits and could have been paid off at par at any time.[4] The courts also expect that any reduction should apply equally to a particular class of shareholders or to all shareholders and cannot be used to buy out a difficult minority shareholder. Again this does not always work to the preference shareholders advantage, they may find that their shares are subject to a rateable reduction of capital along with the ordinary share-holders if they have no special priority as to capital. This may however affect their dividend entitlement if it is a fixed amount, because dividend entitle-ment is usually expressed as a percentage of the nominal capital value. Thus, a reduction of capital affecting both ordinary and preference shareholders may have disadvantageous consequences for the preference shareholder.[5]

For example, a company with 70,000 shares divided into 20,000 £3 nominal value preference shares with a fixed dividend of 10% and 50,000 £3 nominal value ordinary shares wishes to reduce its share capital by £70,000, i e to reduce the nominal value by £1 per share. If the preference shares have no priority to capital they must suffer a rateable reduction, i e to 20,000 £2 nominal value shares. The dividend entitlement will now be ten per cent of £2 whereas prior to the reduction the dividend would be ten per cent of £3. As long as these general principles of reduction are observed, despite the obvious hardship, the reduction will be sanctioned and no variation of class rights will have occurred so as to invoke the class rights procedure.[6]

However, where there are class rights attached to shares and a variation[7] is connected with a reduction of capital under s 135, class consent is required, i e consent by special resolution by the particular class affected or the holders of three-quarters of the nominal value of the issued shares of that class must consent in writing to the variation.[8] Variation means the same as before 1980 subject to one exception, an abrogation of rights may now amount to a varia-tion requiring class consent.[9] Otherwise, only a special resolution of all the company is required to authorise the reduction.

---

[1] E g *Prudential Assurance Co Ltd v Chatterley-Whitfield Collieries Ltd* [1969] AC 512.

[2] As in the *Prudential Assurance* case, above, see also *Re Saltdean Estate Ltd* [1968] 3 All ER 829.

[3] Ibid.

[4] In fact the company's proposal included a 25p premium per share, if the company had dis-tributed its profits as dividend, an entitlement of 1,625% would have been received.

[5] *Re Mackenzie & Co* [1916] 2 Ch 450.

[6] I e the procedure included in CA 1985, s 125, see paras 8.11 et seq (variation of class rights).

[7] For definition of variation see para 8.11.

[8] CA 1985, s 125(2) (introduced by CA 1980).

[9] See CA 1985, s 125(8).

Consideration by the court

4.45 The court has two functions, firstly to protect the creditors and secondly to consider the respective interests of the shareholders. Where the proposed reduction involves a repayment of capital to the shareholders or cancellation of unpaid-up share capital, the interests of creditors are jeopardised and their consent to the reduction is required,[1] unless the court exercises its discretion to dispense with the creditor's consent.[2] Where however the company is merely cancelling share capital to bring it into line with its assets and no money is to be repaid to the shareholders nor liability forgiven, the creditors have no right to consent or refuse consent to the reduction. Presumably, the reasoning is that it is too late, the money has been lost and no purpose would be served by giving creditors the right to object to the reduction. The court does have power to order an inquiry in such a case.[3]

The procedure to be followed when creditor consent is required is onerous, it is similar to that required for proof of debts on liquidation and in practice companies rely on the court exercising its power of dispensation under s 136(6). Alternatively, the company may secure the agreement of its creditors itself by guaranteeing their debts or paying them off. Where creditors have the right to consent and no general dispensation is granted, the court may dispense with the individual creditor's consent if the company secures payment of the debt.

Once the court is satisfied that either consent of the creditors is unnecessary or that consent has been granted or dispensed with the court may make an order confirming the reduction. Although no mention is made of considering shareholder interests at this stage,[4] the court may do so, even though the appropriate resolution has been passed and there is no relevant creditor objection, the court's confirmation is still discretionary. Moreover, the court may confirm the reduction on such terms and conditions as it thinks fit, in particular it may order the company to add the words 'and reduced' to its name for a specified period of time,[5] or the publication of the reasons for the reduction.[6] Where these orders are made, people dealing with the company will have notice of the reduction, however it is rare for the court to exercise its powers in this way.

[1] CA 1985, s 136(2) and (3).

[2] Ibid, s 136(6).

[3] Ibid, s 136(1).

[4] For example the court may look at the motives of the shareholders in passing the special resolution and is satisfied that the majority is acting for its own interests, the resolution will not be effective: *Re Holders Investment Trust Ltd* [1971] 2 All ER 289.

[5] CA 1985, s 137(1) and (2)(a).

[6] Ibid, s 137(2)(b).

Effects of reduction order

4.46 The reduction of capital is not effective until the court order and a minute recording the detailed confirmation of the company to the special resolution for reduction is registered with the registrar of companies.[1] The registration of the minute also effects any necessary alteration to the company's memorandum as if the order had originally been included in the memorandum.[2] Registration of the order and minute is conclusive evidence that all the requirements of the Act have been complied with, thus it would seem that shareholders could no longer obtain an injunction to prevent the reduction taking effect even though certain procedural requirements had not been complied with, e g the passing of a special resolution.[3]

The Act makes provision for a revival of a shareholder's liability on shares, where a reduction cancelled unpaid-up share capital or effected a return of capital, in cases where a creditor's name was not entered on the list of creditors entitled to object and who thus had no prior notice of the reduction. This only applies if the company itself is unable to pay the creditor's debt.[4]

S 135 procedure may be used by public or private companies and in the future may be more useful to public companies.[5] Where the reduction would reduce a public company's allotted share capital below the statutory minimum, the order and minute recording the reduction and the court's confirmation may not be registered by the registrar unless the court orders him to do so or the company re-registers as a private company.[6]

The procedure in ss 135–138 relates to reductions of share capital, but it should be remembered that the quasi-share capital funds (the share premium and the capital redemption reserve) are capital for the purpose of these provisions subject to the permitted exceptions. As far as the reserve fund[7] is concerned, the Act merely states that this cannot be distributed by way of dividend and it is not clear whether it can be reduced in other ways or whether it is subject to s 135.

---

[1] CA 1985, s 138(1) and (2).

[2] Ibid, s 138(5).

[3] *Ladies' Dress Association v Pulbrook* [1900] 2 QB 376.

[4] CA 1985, s 140.

[5] The EEC Second Directive has prevented the extension of all the powers of purchasing and providing financial assistance to public companies.

[6] CA 1985, s 139.

[7] Ibid, s 148(4). See para 3.25, above.

Reductions by court order

4.47　The third exception to the *Trevor v Whitworth* principle listed in s 143(3) is the purchase of any shares in pursuance of an order of the court under CA 1985, s 5, s 54 or Part XVII.

The court orders available under these sections unlike s 135 are regarded as remedies and not procedures where the main purpose is reduction. The power to order a reduction arises in those cases mentioned in s 143(3)(c) and it is assumed that these situations are exhaustive of the courts power to make such orders.

(a) Alteration of objects clause (CA 1985, s 5(5))

Ss 4 and 5 which provide for the method and details of alteration of objects gives the court power to provide for the purchase by the company of shares of any member of the company when making an order confirming the alteration, despite the objection of fifteen per cent of the company's shareholders.

(b) Old public companies becoming private companies (CA 1985, s 54)

When the new classification of public and private companies was introduced in 1980, certain transitional provisions were necessary. CA 1980, s 11[1] provided for application to the court to oppose a special resolution by an old public company to re-register as a private company. On such an application the court may confirm or cancel the resolution. The court may order the purchase of shares and make a corresponding reduction of capital in order to facilitate the acceptance of the order.[2] CA 1985, s 155[3] is also subject to the court's power in CA 1985, s 54 to order a reduction.

(c) Shareholder's petition for unfairly prejudicial conduct (CA 1985, Part XVII)

An order to reduce the company's share capital by a purchase of shares is just one of the many orders that the court may make where it is satisfied that a company's affairs have been conducted in a way which unfairly prejudices the shareholder making the application.

This is a particularly wide power as no minimum shareholding is required to bring it into play.

---

[1] Now CA 1985, s 54.
[2] CA 1985, s 54(6).
[3] See CA 1985, s 157(3).

Forfeiture or surrender of shares[1]

4.48 The final exception to s 143 is the forfeiture of any shares or the acceptance of any shares surrendered in lieu, in pursuance of the articles for failure to pay any sum payable in respect of those shares.[2] The company's articles usually provide the terms and conditions of forfeiture or surrender but in the case of public companies compliance must also be made with s 146, treatment of shares held by or on behalf of a public company.[3]

---

[1] See chap . . . (forfeiture and surrender).
[2] CA 1985, s 143(3)(d).
[3] See para 4.19, above.

Serious loss of capital

4.49   Where there is a serious loss of capital the directors of a public company are required to call an extraordinary general meeting of the company.[1] There will be a serious loss of capital if the company's net assets are half or less than the amount of its called-up share capital. Net assets are defined as the aggregate of the company's assets less the aggregate of its liabilities and called-up share capital is defined as the share capital equal to the aggregate amount of the calls made on its shares, plus any share capital paid-up without being called (e g by instalments) and any share capital to be paid on a specific future date under the articles. Note that the amount of calls made is included in called-up share capital even if the calls are unpaid.[2]

The directors must convene the meeting no later than 28 days after they have discovered this loss and the meeting must be held within 56 days of the obligation to convene the meeting arising. The obligation only arises when a director knows of the fact that the company's net assets are so reduced. It is not clear whether actual or constructive knowledge is required, but it may be assumed that where directors refuse to look at the company's accounts for fear that the assets will be found to be so reduced they cannot avoid the obligation by their refusal to look.

The purpose of the meeting is to discuss what measures should be taken to deal with the situation and no other matters may be discussed at the meeting unless the proper notice is given of these additional items.[3]

No mention is made of the type of measures that could be taken, but obvious ones are the removal and replacement of the directors, an agreement to put the company into liquidation or a reduction of capital under CA 1985, s 135.

Where a director knowingly and wilfully refuses to call a meeting or permits that failure or knowingly and wilfully authorises or permits that failure to continue after the expiry date for calling the meeting, he is liable on conviction to a fine not exceeding the statutory maximum.[4]

---

[1] CA 1985, s 142.
[2] Ibid, s 737.
[3] See chap 8.106 (notice of items for general meetings).
[4] At present, £2000; CA 1985, s 142(2).

FINANCIAL ASSISTANCE BY A COMPANY FOR ACQUISITION OF ITS OWN SHARES

Introduction

4.50   The obvious way to avoid the rule against a company purchasing its own shares in *Trevor v Whitworth* is for a company to lend or give its money to another person to enable that person to purchase the company's shares.[1]

Such a transaction might enable a person to purchase a company cheaply or for no outlay at all. In particular, this will occur if the company gives its money to another or where the contract of loan is illusory. This particular abuse was recognised early in the development of modern company law[2] and in 1929, s 45 made it unlawful for a company to provide financial assistance in connection with a purchase of its own shares, whether directly or indirectly and whether by means of a loan, guarantee, the provision of security or otherwise.

S 45 was amended and then replaced by CA 1948, s 54 which made it unlawful for a company to provide financial assistance for the purpose of a purchase or subscription of its own shares, whether directly or indirectly, and whether by means of a loan, guarantee, the provision of security or otherwise. It also prohibited the provision of financial assistance by a subsidiary company to anyone wishing to acquire or subscribe for shares in its holding company. CA 1948, s 54 caused many problems of interpretation e g there was no definition of the phrase 'financial assistance' and it was interpreted widely so that seemingly innocent transactions could be construed as illegal. The 1981 Act replaced s 54[3] but retained the phraseology and provided an exhaustive definition of the meaning of financial assistance and certain transactions were expressed to be outside its ambit.

It is clear that s 54 was often ignored[4] in practice and a number of cases have concerned breaches. There was pressure for relaxation and clarification of the rule, in particular the Jenkins Committee[5] recommended the provision of financial assistance in certain cases subject to safeguards.[6] CA 1981, s 43[7] introduced some relaxation of the basic prohibition but only for the benefit of private companies since the EEC Second Directive on Company Law prevents its extension to public companies.

---

[1] This differs from acquisition by nominees, see para 4.18, above.
[2] See Greene Committee Report on Company Law, (1926) Cmd 2657.
[3] Now CA 1985, s 151.
[4] Many company investigations have unearthed breaches of CA 1948, s 54.
[5] Jenkins Committee Report on Company Law, (1963) Cmnd 1749, paras 170–186.
[6] These are substantially the same as implemented in CA 1981.
[7] Now CA 1985, s 155.

Typical breaches

4.51 There are three principal recognisable breaches of the prohibition against the giving of financial assistance for acquisition of own shares though many variations on these basic forms have occurred.

(1) The most straightforward breach is where the company lends money to a person who uses the funds to purchase shares in the company. *Steen v Law*[1] is a typical example. Prior to 1981 a payment of dividend to a shareholder followed by a purchase by him of additional shares in the company could fall within the prohibition.[2]

(2) A second type of breach involves the giving of financial assistance by way of a security or repayment of a loan but after the acquisition has been completed. A person agrees to purchase the company's shares, that person has insufficient money and obtains a loan to pay for the shares if the company creates a charge over its assets to guarantee that loan or once the bidder is in control of the company's shares, directs the company to repay the loan on his behalf, financial assistance will have been provided.[3]

(3) The third type of breach involves indirect assistance, often of a complexity which may constitute an attempt to disguise a breach of the prohibition. The *Selangor United Rubber Estates Ltd v Cradock*[4] case is the best illustration of what might be called the circular cheque transaction.

Figure 1

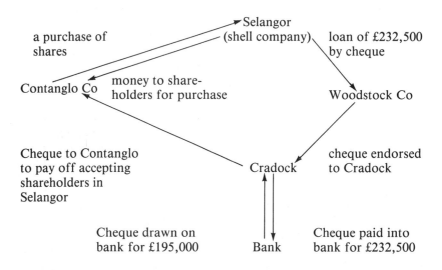

The company's money is lent to Woodstock Co which is controlled by Cradock and the cheque is handed over to Cradock. Meanwhile, Contanglo, acting on behalf of Cradock, makes an offer to the shareholders to purchase all the shares in Selangor. Seventy-nine per cent of the shareholders accept and Cradock uses most of the money lent to Woodstock to pay off the accepting shareholders. Woodstock makes no attempt to repay the 'loan' to Selangor, meanwhile Cradock has obtained seventy-nine per cent of the shares in the company and a profit of £37,500 (i e the difference between the loan and the amount paid to the accepting shareholders).

¹ [1964] AC 287.
² Now excluded by virtue of CA 1985, s 153(3)(a).
³ E g *Victor Battery Co Ltd v Curry's Ltd* [1946] Ch 242.
⁴ [1968] 2 All ER 1073

Prohibition of financial assistance

4.52 The amended prohibition operates in two situations. CA 1985, s 151(1) deals with financial assistance given before or at the time of the acquisition, e g (1) and (3), above and s 151(2) deals with financial assistance provided after the acquisition, e g (2), above.

CA 1985, s 151(1) provides that:

'. . . where a person is acquiring or is proposing to acquire shares in a company, it is not lawful for the company or any of its subsidiaries to give financial assistance directly or indirectly for the purpose of that acquisition before or at the time as the acquisition takes place'.

CA 1985, s 151(2) provides that:

'. . . where a person has acquired shares in a company and any liability has been incurred (by that or any other person) for the purpose of that acquisition, it is not lawful for the company or any of its subsidiaries to give financial assistance directly or indirectly for the purpose of reducing or discharging the liability so incurred.'

A few preliminary points of comparison with the old prohibition should be noted before turning to a more detailed discussion of the prohibition. In many respects the section is similar to s 54, in particular, the phrase, 'it shall not be lawful' (1948 Act) and 'it is not lawful' (1985 Act)[1] and both cover the provision of financial assistance whether direct or indirect. In some respects the new prohibition is wider, s 54 was limited to purchase or subscription, whereas s 151 covers all acquisitions, i e any method of acquiring shares including a transfer of shares. In some respects the new prohibition is narrower, e g s 54 prohibited financial assistance 'in connection with' etc, this is now replaced by the words 'for the purpose of' etc. Thus, provision of financial assistance followed by a purchase of shares only loosely connected will no longer be covered, unless the financial assistance was given for the purpose of the acquisition or, where the financial assistance is given after the acquisition of shares, it is for the purpose of reducing or discharging a liability (whether or not the liability was that of the acquirer or another person).

¹ Wording changed by CA 1985.

Financial assistance

4.53 Financial assistance is widely defined so as to catch those known cases of abuse and also those yet to be devised, but once established it may be possible to escape the prohibition by relying on the various exceptions (see para 4.54 below). Two general points should be emphasised at the outset. Where reference is made in CA 1985, s 151 to a person incurring any liability (e g s 151(2)), this includes his changing his financial position by making any agreement or arrangement or by any other means. It makes no difference that the agreement is unenforceable or that it is not made for the person concerned or is made jointly with another person.[1] In s 152(3)(b) it is provided that any reference in the Chapter to a person giving financial assistance for the purpose of reducing or discharging any liability incurred by any person for the purpose of the acquisition of shares includes giving financial assistance for the purpose of wholly or partly restoring his financial position to what it was before the acquisition took place.

Financial assistance in the context of s 151 means financial assistance given by way of gift, guarantee, indemnity, release or waiver of a right or obligation, or by way of a loan or any other agreement under which the obligations of the person giving the assistance are to be fulfilled at a time when any obligations of the other party remain unfulfilled, or by way of any other financial assistance which reduces the company's net assets to a material extent or which is given by a company which has no net assets. Note that indemnities in respect of the indemnifier's own neglect or default are not included, so where a company indemnifies an underwriter of shares against the company's own default or neglect this will not make the transaction unlawful within s 152(1)(a). The forms of financial assistance are various and release from a debt or postponement of a debt is as much financial assistance as a loan, so too is an agreement by a company to reduce the security for a debt. The situation where one party's obligations are fulfilled yet the other party's obligations are unfulfilled prevents a sham sale of assets to a company with an agreement to postpone the transfer of those assets or to repurchase them at a later date. The company would be obliged to perform its part of the agreement, paying the price, but the other party's obligations would be unfulfilled. This could on its face appear as a perfectly legitimate commercial transaction but in fact be a disguised provision of financial assistance.

S 152(1)(a)(iv) is intended to include all other types of financial assistance which should be prohibited, but by defining it by reference to the net assets being reduced, a gap may have opened up in the legislation. The wording of this subsection implies that only where the net assets are reduced or where the company has no net assets will there be any financial assistance. If, therefore, the particular assistance provided does not 'thereby reduce the net assets' it will not be financial assistance within s 151(1) or (2).

Net assets means the aggregate of its assets less the aggregate of its liabilities.[2]

The definition of financial assistance given in s 152(1) is exhaustive of the meaning of financial assistance for the purposes of s 151, thus any assistance outside of s 152(1) will not be prohibited. It is likely that all the cases within s 152(1) (and more) were caught by the old s 54 prohibition on financial assistance but as there was no statutory definition it was never absolutely clear what was included and what was excluded.

---

[1] CA 1985, s 152(3)(a).

[2] Ibid, s 152(2). This is the same definition used in relation to dividend distributions in CA 1985, s 264.

_____

Purpose exceptions

4.54 The definition of financial assistance within the old s 54 was wide and a number of innocent transactions were caught, e g in *South Western Mineral Water Co Ltd v Ashmore*[1] involving an agreement for the sale of a company after the death of the controller, it was only some time after the agreement was made that the parties realised that there was a breach of s 54, 'Poor Mr Ashmore did not know, of course, that by executing the debenture . . . he would be committing a criminal offence.'[2]

In *Belmont Finance Corpn v Williams Furniture Ltd (No 2)*[3] there was a bona fide commercial transaction, whereby G and his associates were to purchase Belmont in order to use its assets to finance the property development projects of other companies owned by them. It was held that even though the agreement for the purchase was a satisfactory commercial transaction, it nevertheless contravened CA 1948, s 54, as it was merely part of a scheme to enable G and his associates to acquire the company at no cash cost to themselves. In order to cover this situation CA 1985, s 153 provides that the provision of financial assistance will not be unlawful where the principal purpose of giving the assistance (or reducing or discharging a liability) is not for the purpose of acquisition or the financial assistance is but an incidental part of some larger purpose of the company. Foster J, at first instance in *Belmont*, found that the agreement was a bona fide commercial transaction, and therefore dismissed the action, i e such a transaction could not offend CA 1948, s 54. Buckley LJ suggested the following distinction. If a company (A Ltd) buys chattels from B Ltd which A Ltd genuinely wishes to acquire for its own purposes, the fact that B Ltd employs the proceeds in purchasing shares in A Ltd should not offend against the section. However, if A Ltd buys chattels from B Ltd in order to put B Ltd in funds to purchase shares in A Ltd, this is likely to offend against the section, as the sole purpose of the sale is to provide financial assistance and it is irrelevant that the contract was at a fair price.[4]

As the aim of the purpose exceptions is to solve the type of difficulty raised by Buckley LJ in *Belmont*, some idea of the meaning of principal purpose and larger purpose may be gleaned from this judgment.

Buckley LJ poses the problem of whether financial assistance is given in any case where the purchaser of shares is put in funds by the company selling shares. The court held in *Armour Hick Northern Ltd v Whitehouse*[5] that CA 1948, s 54 may be contravened if the vendor of shares is 'put in funds' in order to facilitate a sale of those shares. In this case a subsidiary company paid its parent company's debts owed to a third party, the third party having insisted on satisfaction of these debts before he was prepared to sell his shares to the directors of that company. These problems are partly remedied by the change of wording within s 151(1) and (2) itself, 'for the purpose of' instead of 'for the purpose or *in connection with*', but the purpose exceptions go further, since as noted the s 153(1) purpose exception applies to financial assistance given before or at the same time as the acquisition and s 153(2) applies to financial assistance following the acquisition of shares.

There are two particular exceptions:

(1) where the principal purpose of giving the financial assistance was not for the purpose of the acquisition and was given in good faith in the interests of the company; and
(2) where even if the principal purpose of giving the financial assistance was for the acquisition of shares it was an incidental part of some larger purpose and was given in good faith in the interests of the company.

It is likely that prior to CA 1981 if one of the purposes (albeit not the only or main purpose) of a transaction, was the provision of financial assistance it would be caught if the financial assistance were used to purchase the company's own shares. The change of emphasis by which the principal purpose of the provision of financial assistance must be the acquisition of the company's shares means the *Belmont* case would probably be decided differently now. In addition the giving of the assistance must be done in good faith. No help is given in defining principal purpose or larger purpose or good faith and it may be that the new section provides as much work for lawyers as the old s 54 has done in the past.

---

[1] [1967] 2 All ER 953.
[2] Per Cross J at 1120.
[3] [1980] 1 All ER 393.
[4] At 402.
[5] [1980] 3 All ER 833.

Authorised transactions

4.55　Not only is financial assistance exhaustively defined in CA 1985, s 152(1) but certain transactions are listed in s 153(3) which are not to be taken as prohibited transactions. Some of these may not have been caught by CA 1948, s 54 but there may have been some doubt and therefore for the avoidance of doubt it is provided that s 151 does not prohibit:

(a) any distribution of a company's assets by way of dividend lawfully made or any distribution made in the course of the winding up of the company;
(b) the allotment of bonus shares;
(c) a reduction of capital confirmed by the court under s 137;
(d) a redemption or purchase of any shares made in accordance with Part V, Chapter VII;
(e) anything done in pursuance of an order of the court made under s 425 (Compromises and arrangements with creditors and members);
(f) anything done under an arrangement made in pursuance of s 582 (power of liquidator to accept shares . . .);
(g) anything done under an arrangement made between a company and its creditors which is binding on the creditors by virtue of s 601.[1]

---

[1] CA 1985, s 153(3)(a)–(g).

Exempt transactions

4.56   In addition to the transactions mentioned in CA 1985, s 153 as not prohibited by s 151, there are three exceptions similar to those available in the former section. These are specifically exempted so as not to come within the prohibition.

(a) Where the lending of money is part of the ordinary business of the company and the lending is done in the ordinary course of business. Under the same exception in CA 1948, s 54 it was held that the company's main business had to be the lending of money to come within the exception and that the test was two-fold, i e that the lending of money had to be part of the company's ordinary business and that the particular loan must have been granted in the ordinary course of business, e g on usual commercial terms.[1] This exception would appear to protect lending institutions which have full knowledge of the purpose of the loan and that it is to be used to invest in themselves. The exception is thought necessary to protect such lending and finance companies from having to make full inquiry as to the use of all loans made, but will not protect them if the loan is not a usual commercial one, i e on lower rates than usual.

(b) Employee share schemes. If a company provides financial assistance for the acquisition of fully paid shares for employee share schemes, as defined in CA 1985, s 743, such assistance will be permissible. Pre-1981 trustees were required to hold shares on trust for the employees so the current exception is slightly wider. Directors who are also employees are people who may take advantage of the employee share scheme. It is thought that the share scheme set up will protect the company from abuses by the directors in this connection, but it would not appear to prevent the particular abuse which occurred in *Hogg v Cramphorn*.[2] In this case the directors set up an employee trust of which they were trustees, and to ward off a take-over bid the directors issued additional shares for the employee trust, the votes of which they controlled as trustees and which were sufficient to defeat the take-over bid.

(c) Loans to employees. A company may make loans to its employees with a view to enabling them to acquire fully paid up shares in the company to be held by themselves by way of beneficial ownership.

This exception differs from the old s 54 exception in that the company must have employed the person to whom it is making the loan in good faith. The company cannot make a sham appointment in order to lend a person money to buy its own shares. For the purposes of this subsection 'employees' does not include directors who may be employees. It is thought that a direct loan to a director may be too much of a temptation whereas loans to purchase shares for an employee share scheme of which the directors are members are indirect. Moreover, the tight control over loans to directors could be avoided by use of such an exception.[3] For the purposes of (b) and (c) the shares to be acquired must be fully paid.[4]

Under the old s 54 it seemed that if the company came within the exceptions there was no breach, but an additional requirement was added in 1981. A public company may only give financial assistance for one of the excluded categories if the company does not reduce its net assets or to the extent that those net assets are reduced, the financial assistance is provided out of distributable profits. Net assets for this section means the amount by which the aggregate amount of the company's assets exceeds the aggregate amount of its liabilities taking the amount of both assets and liabilities as stated in the company's financial accounts immediately prior to the financial assistance.[5] This differs from the definition of net assets for the purpose of s 152(1)(a)(iv) which provides that net assets is the same as for dividend distributions in s 263. The difference is that the s 154(2) definition of net assets is up to the date of the financial assistance whereas net assets for s 152(1)(a)(iv) are those net assets in accordance with the latest accounts.

---

[1] *Steen v Law* [1964] AC 287.
[2] [1967] Ch 254.
[3] See chap 6 (prohibition on loans to directors).
[4] CA 1985, s 153(4).
[5] Ibid, s 154(2).

Consequences of a breach of s 151

4.57 Controversy surrounded the original prohibition on financial assistance in relation to sanctions. In CA 1948, s 54 circumstances it was unlawful for a company to provide financial assistance and the section provided for a penalty of a fine up to a maximum of £100. Until 1980 when the CA revised many of the penalties within the Companies Acts generally, the £100 fine was the main penalty. In 1980 imprisonment was introduced for officers in default of CA 1948, s 54 for up to two years and the maximum fine was increased to £1000. The company is also liable to a fine up to the statutory maximum for breach of CA 1948, s 54.[1] As the prohibition on financial assistance was designed to protect a company's capital it seems ironical that the company itself could be liable thus reducing its capital even further.

At one time it was thought that this fine was the only consequence of a breach of CA 1948, s 54 and as Jenkins[2] pointed out, the maximum fine was hardly a deterrent when breaches of CA 1948, s 54 often involved thousands of pounds. Perhaps because of the inadequacy of the sanctions within the section the courts became particularly innovative in finding civil law sanctions, though obviously they could not create further criminal sanctions than those in the section itself.

Civil remedies

(a) Directors and constructive trustees. Directors owe fiduciary duties to their company,[3] thus, if they commit their company to a s 151 transaction they will be in breach of their duty to the company and liable to it in damages. In *Selangor*,[4] the directors were held liable for breach of their fiduciary duty but had insufficient funds to reimburse the company for its loss.

Directors may also be liable under s 631 (delinquent directors) if the company goes into liquidation.

Directors of other companies involved in s 151 breaches or non-officers of the company owe no duties to the company. In *Selangor*, the directors of Woodstock and Contanglo were in this position, and Cradock who was able to manipulate the directors of Selangor and Woodstock was not an officer of any company and therefore owed no fiduciary duty as a director.

In *Selangor* the court held that Woodstock Ltd, its directors, Contanglo Ltd and its directors were all liable as constructive trustees, i e on the basis that they had been entrusted with another's property and had taken advantage of that trust, in the words of Ungoed-Thomas J they had 'participated with knowledge in a dishonest and fraudulent design', and were liable to account as if they were trustees. Again, these parties had insufficient funds and attention turned to the one party in the case with money, the bank. The bank, which held both the company's and Cradock's account was held liable as a constructive trustee either on the basis that having received funds belonging to the company and thus being in a position of trust, it had knowledge, actual or constructive of the directors' breach or that whether or not it had actually received funds, the bank itself had participated in the dishonest and fraudulent design with knowledge. In *Selangor*, the bank had received the funds, as Cradock paid the company's cheque into his account with it, thus there was no need to distinguish these two situations; in any case the bank was already held liable in contract for the loss to the company. However, the Court of Appeal considered this question in *Karak Rubber Co v Burden*[5] and felt that a higher standard of knowledge was required to make a person liable as a constructive trustee when he had never had actual possession or control over the company's funds used in breach of s 151.

---

[1] Now CA 1985, s 151.
[2] Cmnd 1749.
[3] *Percival v Wright* [1902] 2 Ch 421.
[4] [1968] 2 All ER 1073.
[5] [1972] 1 All ER 1210.

4.58 (b) Liability in contract and tort. The bank in *Selangor* could have been liable on three distinct grounds, as constructive trustee,[1] in contract and in tort. Every bank owes a duty of care to its customers not to pay out on cheques which could be regarded suspiciously, it is for this reason that banks do not usually pay out on cheques which have been in circulation for more than six months. The bank, it was decided, did not know of the breach of s 151 but ought to have realised that there was something underhand and should have made some enquiries. Cradock's account at the bank had been in 'negligible credit', he then paid in a cheque for a large amount, drawn on a company (amounting in fact to most of its assets) and almost immediately drew a cheque on that account for the bulk of the money. It was on this ground that liability of the bank rested.

The bank was also held to be in breach of the duty of care owed to customers in tort, on the grounds that the bank had been negligent in failing to make enquiries regarding the payments to Cradock and the exhaustion of the company's funds.

A further basis of liability was suggested in *Belmont Finance Corpn v Williams Furniture Ltd (No 2)*,[2] of tort of conspiracy. For such an action to be successful the company would have to show that the defendants had combined to participate in a *common intention* to enter into the agreement to effect an unlawful purpose and that the company had suffered loss as a result. The advantage of suing under this head is that liability is not limited to a particular group of offenders, but any person, even the company, could be liable for the tort of conspiracy.

---

[1] See above.
[2] [1980] 1 All ER 393.

4.59   (c) Shareholder's actions. Where there is a breach of CA 1985, s 151, shareholders may have a right to sue in two circumstances, one in a derivative capacity, i e on behalf of the company and the other in a personal capacity, i e on their own behalf.

(i) Shareholder's derivative action. As a general rule a shareholder cannot sue in order to remedy a wrong done to the company, only the company can sue, i e the company is the only proper plaintiff.[1] However, where the company is controlled by those at fault the courts might exceptionally recognise a right of action by a minority shareholder.[2] A shareholder must show that a wrong has been done to the company and that that wrong would go unremedied if the shareholder were not allowed to sue.[3] Where directors have committed their company to a transaction in breach of s 151 and used their position in the company to protect themselves from legal action, either by exercising voting control or actual executive control,[4] a shareholder might be able to sue and, if he was successful, the court would order the wrongdoers to compensate the company to the extent of the company's loss. Note that in a derivative action, although a shareholder is suing, it is in truth the company's action and the company is entitled to the remedy.

The shareholder's statutory right to petition under CA 1985, s 459[5] might also be used in these circumstances. This petition may be used where the affairs of the company are being conducted in an unfairly prejudicial manner. CA 1980, s 75[6] which replaced CA 1948, s 210 puts it beyond doubt that an isolated act may constitute unfairly prejudicial conduct. If the shareholder is successful under this section the court may make any order it thinks fit, the 'remedy' may benefit the particular shareholder or it may benefit the company itself.

(ii) Shareholder's personal action. A company is obliged to act within its objects as stated in the memorandum and also it must act legally. If it does not do so a shareholder may complain to the court and request an injunction from the court to order the company to refrain from the proposed ultra vires or illegal conduct.[7] A breach of s 151 would be both ultra vires and illegal.

It has also been suggested that a shareholder could bring an action for tort of conspiracy for a breach of s 151.[8]

---

[1] Rule in *Foss v Harbottle* (1843) 2 Hare 461.
[2] See chap 8 (minority shareholder's action).
[3] E g *Menier v Hooper's Telegraph Works Ltd* (1874) 9 Ch App 350.
[4] See *Prudential Assurance Co Ltd v Newman Industries Ltd (No 2)* [1981] Ch 257.

5 See chap 8 (minority shareholder's action).
6 Now CA 1985, s 459.
7 *East Anglian Rly Co v Eastern Counties Rly Co* (1851) 11 CB 775.
8 In *Belmont Finance Corpn v Williams Furniture Ltd (No 2)* [1980] 1 All ER 393.

Validity of transactions

4.60 In practice the greatest problem with the prohibition on financial assistance is its effect on the various transactions involved. Most of these problems stem from the words, 'it shall not be lawful . . .' now 'it is not lawful'. The general principle is that an unlawful transaction is not merely void but void and illegal, and no property or rights are transferred under such an agreement. Thus, if a company 'lends' money to another to enable that person to purchase the company's shares, the money will still belong to the company, i e it will not have transferred to the purchaser — but the court will not order recovery of property transferred, under the doctrine that loss lies where it falls. The effect is that the company will not be able to enforce recovery of the loan. Thus the prohibition designed to protect companies also prevents them recovering any money handed out. In *Selangor*, the company had given most of its funds to Woodstock Ltd, and although it was never intended that the loan should be repaid, the court held it illegal anyway and refused to order repayment. The obvious way for the company to recover its money was closed. Circumstances may be complicated if a company has been given a security in exchange for such a loan.

Figure 2

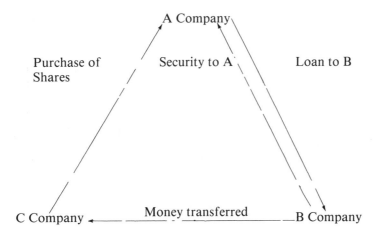

The common law position is that any transaction which depends for its validity on an illegal transaction is tainted with illegality and is itself void. Thus any security given in exchange for an illegal loan would appear to be void also, but Roxburgh J in *Victor Battery Co Ltd v Curry's Ltd*[1] held that such a security was valid even though the loan was void. This view was criticised in *Selangor*[2] albeit obiter; in *Heald v O'Connor*[3] the court held that a security would be invalid if given in return for a loan providing financial assistance.

Finally, the implications for the share purchase itself must be considered. The decided cases devote little time to this point.[4] In *Selangor*, Cradock became the owner of seventy-nine per cent of Selangor's shares but this was not considered any further. The courts (and legislature) are usually reluctant to hold contracts for the purchase of shares void as this might threaten the integrity of the share market and there is some suggestion that contracts for the purchase of shares will be valid if the parties could have purchased them without a breach of s 151.[5] On the other hand shares purchased by a company in breach of s 143 (purchase of own shares) renders the purchase contract void — the company does not become a member of itself and the shares still belong to the vendor. Bearing in mind that s 151 was introduced to protect companies from the consequences of a breach of the *Trevor v Whitworth* rule, it would seem strange if they have different consequences.

---

[1] [1946] Ch 242.
[2] Above.
[3] [1971] 2 All ER 1105.
[4] Only two cases appear to have discussed this point in detail, *South Western Mineral Water v Ashmore* [1967] 2 All ER 953 and *Lawlor v Gray* (1980) 130 NLJ 317.
[5] *South Western Mineral Water v Ashmore*, above.

Relaxation of s 151 for private companies (s 155)

4.61   The relaxation of the prohibition on giving financial assistance for the acquisition of a company's own shares was introduced in the CA 1981 and because of the numerous breaches of CA 1948, s 54 in the past, this relaxation is surrounded by many safeguards for the protection of the company's creditors and shareholders. The relaxation is only available to private companies and only if the set procedure is complied with according to an elaborate timetable.[1] These provisions only apply to those cases of giving financial assistance which but for the exceptional procedure would be breaches of s 151. The relaxation was introduced as one of the special exemptions designed to help small companies raise capital for the purpose of expansion.

Any company wishing to make use of s 155 is also subject to the general requirement that the proposed assistance must not reduce its net assets or if the net assets are reduced, the financial assistance must be provided out of the company's distributable profits.[2] In order to limit the relaxation to private companies, a private company subsidiary is not permitted to use s 155 to provide financial assistance to its public holding company, nor may a private company subsidiary (B Company below) give financial assistance to its holding company (A Company below) if the subsidiary is also a subsidiary of another holding company (C Company below) which is public and is in turn a subsidiary of the holding company.

Figure 3

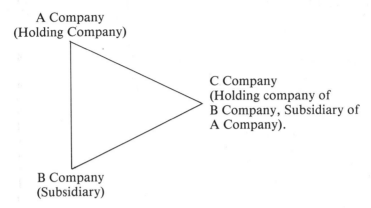

A Company
(Holding Company)

C Company
(Holding company of
B Company, Subsidiary of
A Company).

B Company
(Subsidiary)

B Company is prohibited from giving financial assistance to A Company, even though both companies are private companies, if C Company is a public company.[3]

---

[1] See para 4.66, below.
[2] CA 1985, s 155(2).
[3] Ibid, s 155(3).

Safeguards

4.62 S 155 provides three major safeguards:

(1) special resolution by shareholders;
(2) declaration of solvency in the prescribed form;
(3) member's right of objection.

In addition to these specific safeguards, the procedural timetable is strict and ensures that the fortunes of the company have not changed too dramatically between the authorisation of the financial assistance and the exercise of that authority. The exemption is only available if both the substantive requirements and the procedural requirements of ss 155–158 are complied with.

(1) Special resolution

4.63 The shareholders in general meeting must approve the giving of financial assistance by a special resolution, unless the company proposing to give the assistance is a wholly-owned subsidiary.[1] Where a company (Company B) is proposing to assist the acquisition of shares in its own holding company (Company A) the approval of the holding company's shareholders is required. A special resolution authorising financial assistance must also be passed by the shareholders of any company (Company C) which is the holding company of Company B and a subsidiary of Company A, unless it is a wholly-owned subsidiary, where the requirement would be unnecessary.

Even though the appropriate special resolutions have been passed, a company may not proceed to give the financial assistance until four weeks have elapsed since the date of the resolution or where there is more than one resolution, the date of the last one, unless there has been unanimous agreement to the resolutions. Nor may financial assistance be provided more than eight weeks *after* the directors' statutory declaration of solvency or after the last declaration where a number are required.[2] The company cannot pay the financial assistance out until all members having a right to object have had an opportunity to object[3] nor may it pay out after more than eight weeks, unless the court otherwise orders following rejection of an objection by minority shareholders. Of course, the company may not provide financial assistance during the hearing by the court of a valid application for cancellation of the resolution, unless the court itself orders.[4]

The special resolutions required must be passed by the company on the day or within seven days of the making of the directors' declaration of solvency.[5] Any special resolution authorising the provision of financial assistance under s 155 is ineffective if either the directors' declaration of solvency or the auditors' report are not available for inspection by members at the meeting at which the resolution is passed or if the court exercises its power to cancel the resolution.[6]

---

[1] CA 1985, s 155(4).
[2] Ibid, s 158.
[3] See para 4.65, below.
[4] Ibid, s 158(3).
[5] Ibid, s 157(1).
[6] Ibid, s 157(4); see para 4.65, below.

---

(2) Declaration of solvency

4.64   The directors of the company proposing to make the financial assistance and the directors of companies in the position of Company A and Company C above must make a declaration of solvency in the prescribed form.[1] This declaration must contain particulars of the assistance and of the business of the company and must identify the person to whom assistance is to be given. The directors must state that they have formed the opinion that there will be no ground on which the company could be found unable to pay its debts having regard to the situation prevailing on the day immediately following the date of giving the assistance and either that if the company is to be wound up within twelve months it will be able to pay its debts in full within twelve months of the commencement of the winding up or that in any other case it will be able to pay its debts as they fall due during the year following the date on which the financial assistance was given.[2]

Like the statutory declaration required under s 171, it must be supported by an auditors' report addressed to the directors.[3] This must state that the auditors have inquired into the company's affairs and are not aware that the directors' opinions are unreasonable in all the circumstances.

The statutory declaration of solvency and the auditors' report, in addition to being available at the meeting at which the resolution is proposed, must be delivered to the registrar of companies, along with a copy of the special resolution, if any, passed by the company, within fifteen days after the making of the declaration.[4] Failure to file the necessary documents with the registrar renders the company and every officer in default liable to a fine or on continued contravention to a default fine.[5]

Any director making a statement in the statutory declaration which he does not have reasonable grounds for making is liable on conviction to a fine or up to two years imprisonment or both.[6]

---

[1] CA 1985, s 155(6).
[2] Ibid, s 156(2).
[3] Ibid, s 156(4) and see paras 10.54 and 10.55, below.
[4] Ibid, s 156(5).
[5] Ibid, s 156(6).
[6] Ibid, s 156(7).

---

(3) Member's right of objection

4.65-4.67 The declaration of solvency is supposed to give adequate protection to the creditors, thus the right of objection to the special resolution authorising financial assistance does not extend to creditors. Only the holders of ten per cent or more of the nominal value of the company's issued shares or ten per cent of any class of shares or where the company is not limited by shares, ten per cent of the company's members may apply to the court for cancellation of the special resolution authorising financial assistance. Only those members who have not consented or voted in favour of the resolution may apply.[1] The rules regarding the application are the same as those under CA 1985, s 54 (special resolution resulting in a company becoming a private company),[2] in particular the court must either confirm or cancel the resolution and has power to make provision for the company to purchase the shares of *any member*, i e not just a dissenting member, of the company.

---

[1] CA 1985, s 157(2).
[2] Ibid, s 157(3).

Table 12: Procedural timetable (CA 1985, ss 155–158)

Day 1	Directors' declaration and auditors' report
Day 7 at latest	Shareholders meeting to approve by special resolution the provision of financial assistance
Day 22 at latest	Registration of directors' declaration, auditors' report and special resolution with Registrar of Companies
Day 35 at latest	Minority shareholders last day to object to the resolution

	No minority objection	*Minority objection*
Day 36	Company may commence payments under s 158	Notice to Registrar of minority's application to court
Day of hearing		Hearing
15 days after court hearing		Copy of court order delivered to Registrar: If application cancelled company may commence payments If application confirmed no provision can be made under s 155

Day 56 at latest	Last day on which company may provide financial assistance under s 155 unless court order to extend period of payment following hearing of minority objection

RESTRICTIONS ON DISTRIBUTION OF PROFITS AND ASSETS

Dividends generally

4.68   The right to receive a dividend is regarded as an important shareholder right. However despite provision in the articles for distribution of dividend, a shareholder is not actually entitled to a dividend until and unless the directors so determine.[1] The company is not required to pay any dividend in a given year even if one class of shareholders has a fixed dividend entitlement, e g the preference shareholders, and it cannot pay a dividend except out of the funds available for distribution by way of dividend.

Dividend is usually determined by reference to the nominal value of the share and may be expressed as a fixed percentage. This is most common with preference shares. Ordinary shares do not usually carry fixed dividend entitlement and a company may if it wishes make any dividend distribution to them out of its available funds. Dividends of one hundred per cent may occur. Where shares are only partly-paid, the articles may provide for dividend to be distributed by reference to the amount paid up on the share.[1]

Shareholders are entitled, in the absence of anything to the contrary in the articles, to their dividend in cash, and the company cannot insist that they accept any other form of payment, e g shares or debentures.[2]

---

[1] See Table A, art 104.
[2] *Wood v Odessa Waterworks Co* (1889) 42 Ch D 636.

Dividend rule

4.69   An easy way of reversing the priority to be accorded creditors regarding repayment of their debts would be to return money by way of dividend to the shareholders. The basic capital maintenance rule attempts to preserve the capital for the creditors by providing that companies may only pay dividends out of profits and may not make distributions out of capital. Prior to CA 1980 no definition was given as to the meaning of profits and it was generally thought that that which was not capital or quasi-capital was available for distribution by way of dividend.

There were two major criticisms of this common law rule:

(1)   a company could make a dividend distribution if it made a profit in any given year, i e irrespective of its past performance;

(2)   a company could, it seems, make a dividend distribution even out of its unrealised profits,[1] even unrealised capital profits.[2]

The new rules answer these criticisms.

---

[1] See *Dimbula Valley (Ceylon) Tea Co Ltd v Laurie* [1961] Ch 353.
[2] Though many companies include provision in their articles restricting dividend distributions to trading profits.

Distributions

4.70   Before turning to the new rules in detail it should be noted that the rules apply to all distributions made by the company, otherwise a disguised dividend could be granted and defeat the purpose of the prohibition.

Distribution means every description of distribution of the company's assets to members of the company whether in cash or otherwise except:

- (i) a bonus issue of shares, fully or partly paid;
- (ii) redemption or purchase of the company's shares out of capital or unrealised profit in accordance with CA 1985, Part IV, Chapter VII;
- (iii) reduction of share capital by extinguishing or reducing liability of a shareholder on any share in respect of unpaid up share capital or in paying off paid up share capital;
- (iv) distribution of assets on liquidation.[1]

The provisions of this part of the Act are without prejudice to any enactment or rule of law or any provision of a company's memorandum or articles restricting the sums out of which or the cases in which a distribution may be made.[2] S 263(2) does not purport to extend the categories of distributions or the sums available for distribution, it merely excludes particular situations from the definition of distribution. The company's own articles may further limit the company's ability to make certain distributions.

---

[1] CA 1985, s 263(2).
[2] Ibid, s 281.

Basic rule

4.71   Companies may only make distributions out of profits available for that purpose.[1] The profits which are available for distribution are the company's 'accumulated realised profits . . . less accumulated realised losses'.[2] The definition relies on the difference between realised profits and realised losses and no attempt is made to distinguish capital and income profits. Subject to the articles, so long as capital profits are realised a company may distribute them to the shareholders.

These rules introduced by CA 1980 as amended[3] apply to all distributions.[4] Until 1980 the common law left the determination of profits to the companies themselves and various different methods could be adopted in determining the profits available for distribution, e g:

- (1) *current earnings method*, actual receipts or gross earnings less expenses incurred in obtaining those receipts and earnings;
- (2) *earned surplus method*, like the method in (1) except that losses are brought forward and set-off against current earnings;
- (3) *balance sheet surplus method*, surplus of the company's assets over its liabilities, share capital and capital reserves for the accounting period.

The approach adopted by the CA 1980 was the balance sheet surplus method.

It should be noted that s 263 does not extend a company's power to make distributions, and the company may still restrict distributions, e g make them payable only out of certain funds.[5]

---

[1] CA 1985, s 263. Table A articles have also been amended to prohibit the payment of dividend or interim dividend except in accordance with CA 1980 Part III, see art 6 CA 1980, Sch 3, para 36(7).

[2] CA 1985, s 263(3). See also para 9.84, below.

[3] Some of these were necessary pursuant to the new accounting requirements of the Fourth Directive on Company Law which was implemented by CA 1981.

[4] See para 4.70, above.

[5] Cf definition of undistributable reserves, CA 1985, s 264(3) and para 4.75, below.

Accumulated realised profits

4.72 The basic provision, s 263(3), states that

'. . . a company's profits available for distribution are its accumulated realised profits, so far as not previously utilised by distribution or capitalisation, less its accumulated realised losses, so far as not previously written off in a reduction or reorganisation of capital duly made.'

References to profits and losses are references to revenue and capital profits and revenue and capital losses respectively, unless the context otherwise requires.[1] References to capitalisation in relation to the profits of the company means:

(1) applying the profits (including the share premium account[2]) in paying in whole or part unissued shares issued to the members as bonus shares;

(2) transferring profits to the capital redemption reserve.[3]

The use of the word accumulated means that a company can no longer look at the accounts of a particular year in isolation to determine whether it has profits available for distribution, the losses or profits of previous years must be brought into account.

Realised profits are all the company's profits, both capital and income, that have been earned by the company. Unrealised profits are those book profits which arise on an upward revaluation of the company's fixed assets. Unrealised profits are no longer available for distribution,[4] and the company cannot apply unrealised profit in paying up debentures or any amounts unpaid on any of its issued shares.[5] Unrealised profits arising upon revaluation of fixed assets are not generally available for dividend, but there are two exceptions.

(1) *CA 1985, s 276* provides that where a company makes a distribution of, or which includes, a non-cash asset and any part of the amount at which the asset is stated in the relevant accounts is represented as unrealised profit, this may be treated as realised profit for the purpose of calculating the amount available for distribution. This amendment to the original rules is designed to encourage or at least not restrict sales of the company's undertaking and demergers.

(2) *CA 1985, s 275(2)* provides that where an unrealised profit arises on a revaluation of a fixed asset and this is followed by the writing off or retention of a sum for depreciation by reference to the revalued amount, there will be a

deemed realised profit of the amount by which the amount written off or retained exceeds the amount which would have been written off or retained if the revaluation had not been made.

	Asset Value £	*Provision for depreciation at 10%* £
1980	5,000	500
1981	5,000	500
1982 (revaluation)	7,000	700
1983	7,000	700
1984	7,000	700

If the company had not revalued in 1982, the provision for depreciation would have continued at £500 per year but because of the revaluation the depreciation percentage (if it remains static) will result in an increase of £200 each year. This £200 may be treated as a realised profit and therefore available for distribution.

The Act also gives some guidance as to the meaning of realised profits in situations where there might be difficulty in distinguishing between realised and unrealised profits of items prior to the new rules when no such distinction was necessary.

(1) No records (s 275(3))

In order to smooth the transition from the old rules to the new rules, provision is made for those companies which have no record of the original cost of acquisitions. S 275(3) provides that the asset's cost is taken to be the value at which it was first recorded in the company's accounts. This also applies to cases where the records are not lost but the cost could only be obtained with unreasonable expense or delay.

(2) Distinction unclear (s 263(5))

It might also be difficult for the company to determine what prior to CA 1980 was a realised or unrealised profit, as no distinction was previously necessary. Provided the directors have made reasonable enquiries in order to determine whether they were realised or unrealised they may treat the profits as realised,[6] i e a presumption in favour of their being realised and thus available for distribution.

---

[1] CA 1985, s 280(3).
[2] I e for this purpose the share premium account is profit, CA 1985, s 130(3).
[3] CA 1985, s 280(2).
[4] As in *Dimbula*, above.
[5] CA 1985, s 263(4).
[6] Ibid, s 263(5).

Accumulated realised losses

4.73   The accumulated realised losses must be set against the accumulated realised profits in determining the legality of a distribution under CA 1985, s 263. The new rule makes two major alterations to the pre-1980 common law position; not only does it require the company to bring forward losses from previous accounting periods, but also requires the company to take into account any reduction of capital under s 135 by which the company was permitted to write off lost assets.

All losses are to be regarded as realised except those arising in respect of a diminution in value of a fixed asset appearing on a revaluation of all the fixed assets (or all the fixed assets excluding goodwill).[1] A realised loss is any amount written off or retained either as a depreciation, renewal or diminution allowance or provision for unknown liabilities which cannot be determined with substantial accuracy.[2] It seems that directors may revalue only one asset and revalue it down if required, rather than undertake a general revaluation. Revaluation for the purposes of s 275(1) includes any consideration by the directors of a company of the value at any particular time of any fixed asset of the company.[3]

Where directors are relying on s 275(4) and no actual valuation has taken place a note to the accounts must state:

(1) that the directors have considered the value of any fixed assets without actually revaluing them; and

(2) that they are satisfied that the aggregate value of those assets is or was not less than the aggregate amount at which they are or were stated in the company's accounts; and

(3) that the relevant items affected are accordingly stated in the relevant accounts on the basis that a revaluation of the company's fixed assets took place at that time.[4]

Development costs shown as an asset in the accounts must be regarded as a realised loss,[5] except so far as any part of that amount represents an unrealised profit made on a revaluation. This does not apply provided there are special circumstances justifying the directors' decision not to treat it as a realised loss and the directors explain their conduct in a note to the accounts.[6]

S 275(3), i e where there is no record of original cost, applies to a loss on an item as it applies to a profit and the value ascribed to the asset is the value as contained in the earliest available record.[7] S 263(5), i e inability to determine whether realised or unrealised losses, also applies to the determination of realised and unrealised profits, but whereas inability to determine whether profit is realised or unrealised enables the company to treat the profit as *realised*, inability to determine whether losses are realised or unrealised renders the losses *unrealised*. This gives the widest interpretation to profits available to be distributed.

---

[1] CA 1985, s 275(1).
[2] Ibid, s 275(1).
[3] Ibid, s 275(4).
[4] Ibid, s 275(6).
[5] Ibid, s 269(1) and (2).
[6] Ibid, s 269.
[7] Ibid, s 263(5).

Fixed and circulating assets

4.74 Provision for depreciation of fixed assets must be treated as a realised loss.[1] The Act defines fixed assets as assets of a company intended for use on a continuing basis in the company's activities and any assets not intended for such use shall be taken to be current assets.[2]

---

[1] CA 1985, s 275.
[2] CA 1985, Sch 4, para 77.

Additional rules for public companies

4.75 S 263 applies to both public and private companies and lays down the basic test for defining distributable profits as 'the accumulated realised profits less accumulated realised losses'. But public companies are subject to an additional rule. Even though the company has profits available for distribution according to s 263, it is still prohibited from making a distribution unless its net assets are at least equal to the aggregate of its called-up share capital and its undistributable reserves and it can only make a distribution if it does not reduce the company's net assets below its called-up share capital and undistributable reserves.[1] A company's net assets for the purposes of the Act are the aggregate of its assets less the aggregate of its liabilities.[2] The company's called-up share capital is the same as for s 142,[3] and includes those amounts called-up but not paid.

The company's undistributable reserves are:

(a) the share premium account;
(b) the capital redemption reserve;
(c) the amount by which the company's accumulated unrealised profits so far as not previously utilised by capitalisation exceeds its accumulated unrealised losses (so far as not previously written off in a reduction or reorganisation of capital);[4] and
(d) any other amounts which the company is prohibited from distributing either by law or according to its own memorandum or articles, e g prohibited by law, for instance the reserve fund established when a company acquires its shares in s 146 circumstances,[5] or prohibited by the memorandum or articles, i e companies sometimes include a clause limiting dividend payment to trading profits of a particular year.

The purpose of this provision is to ensure that a public company does not pay out a dividend if it has insufficient assets to cover its liabilities and the whole of its issued share capital; it effectively means that a public company must make up any unrealised losses before it pays anything to its shareholders.

The Act also deals with distributions by investment companies[6] and defines realised profits for insurance companies with long term business.[7] [An investment company may make a distribution at any time out of any undistributed excess of realised revenue profits over realised revenue losses provided this does not reduce its assets to an amount below one and a half times its aggregate liabilities. An insurance company must treat as a realised profit or loss:

(a) any amount properly transferred to its profit and loss account from a surplus in its long-term business funds and

(b) any deficit in those funds, as shown by an actuarial investigation.

Ed.]

---

[1] CA 1985, s 264(1).

[2] Ibid, s 264(2).

[3] See para 4.49, above.

[4] Capitalisation for s 264(3)(c) applies to every capitalisation except a transfer of profits to capital redemption reserve on or after 22 December 1980, CA 1985, s 264(3).

[5] See para 3.25, above.

[6] CA 1985, s 265 and see para 1.14, above.

[7] Ibid, s 268.

Relevant accounts

4.76   As a basic rule, whether the company has distributable profits available for dividend is determined by reference to the company's relevant accounts which are the latest set of audited accounts laid before members.[2]

S 270(3) and (4) states that a company's relevant accounts are:

(a) the last *annual accounts* made in accordance with Part VII and prepared for the company's last accounting reference period (these will usually be the accounts referred to); or

(b) *interim accounts*, which are required only where a distribution by reference to the annual accounts as in (a) would be a contravention of the basic rule regarding distributions, so that interim accounts are necessary to enable a reasonable judgment to be made of the amounts of any relevant item;[3]

(c) *initial accounts*, where a company has not yet had to produce annual accounts but wishes to declare a dividend within its first accounting reference period, initial accounts may be used as necessary.[4]

---

[1] CA 1985, s 270.

[2] And see chap 9 (accounting requirements).

[3] Relevant items include e g profits, losses, assets and liabilities: s 270(2). Ed.

[4] For *public* companies initial and interim accounts must give a true and fair view, be properly prepared and filed with the Registrar. Initial accounts of public companies must be audited. Ed.

Consequences of unlawful distribution

4.77   There was some doubt prior to CA 1980 as to the consequences of making an unlawful distribution. It seems that directors in breach were liable for the amount by which the company had paid a dividend out of capital.[1] Moreover, a public accountant responsible for preparing the company's accounts on which directors based their dividend entitlement has been held liable to the company to the extent of the unlawful overpayment.[2] Whether shareholders were liable to pay back the amount paid out of capital was unclear.

A member is liable to repay an unlawful distribution to the company if at the time of the distribution he knows or has reasonable grounds for believing that it is made in breach. Where the distribution is in kind, he is liable to repay an amount equivalent to the value of the distribution.[3] This liability is without prejudice to any other obligation imposed on a member to repay a distribution unlawfully made, e g a company may include provision for repayment of unlawful distribution in its articles and the member would be bound by this.[4]

No provision imposing liability on the company's officers is made for contravention of the dividend rules, but it can be assumed that directors will remain liable to repay the amounts overpaid on the basis of breach of fiduciary duty to the company as above. Moreover, if directors intend to produce a false market in the shares by granting a dividend out of capital they may be criminally liable for conspiracy,[5] or the tort of conspiracy.

---

[1] *Re Exchange Banking Co, Flitcroft's case* (1882) 21 Ch D 519.
[2] *Leeds Estate Building and Investment Co v Shepherd* (1887) 36 Ch D 787.
[3] CA 1985, s 277(1).
[4] Ibid, s 277(2).
[5] *Burnes v Pennell* (1849) 2 HLC 497.

DEBENTURES

Introduction

4.78   Comprehensive treatment of debentures is worth a book of its own. This work considers the major features of debentures and those rules which are unique to the debenture in company law. The major remedy available to a debenture holder in the event of default is to appoint a receiver.[1]

Companies can raise capital in the same ways as an individual, by loan, overdraft, mortgage etc, but there are two methods of raising capital that are unique to companies: shares and the floating charge. The floating charge is a type of debenture. The word debenture is not defined in companies legislation, it is a term applied to any document evidencing a loan. In company law the word debenture is usually reserved for secured loans and a floating charge is a type of secured loan.

The traditional company debentures fall into two categories of secured loans, the loan secured by way of a fixed charge and the loan secured by way of a floating charge.

---

[1] See chap 11.

Fixed charge

4.79 This covers any loan which is secured over a fixed asset or a group of fixed assets belonging to the company. Fixed assets in this context must be contrasted with circulating assets; an individual cannot create a fixed charge over assets which are constantly changing or being used and replaced. Such charges are prohibited by the Bills of Sale Acts 1882–90 if created by individuals, companies are excluded from the provisions of those Acts. Companies must however comply with the registration requirements of the Companies Act and charges created or acquired by a company must be registered at the company's registered office[1] and notice of most charges must also be given to the registrar of companies at Companies House.[2]

A fixed charge provides the best security for a creditor since he may enforce the security on liquidation in satisfaction of his debt and is unaffected by the insolvency of the company. A fixed charge may be either legal or equitable. In any conflict between a legal or equitable charge the legal one prevails.

---

[1] CA 1985, s 407.
[2] Ibid, s 395.

Floating charge

4.80 The floating charge is a creation of company law, in fact the combination of the prohibition on the creation of chattel mortgages without registration and the inability to register goods which are not specific, which applies to all persons other than companies[1] means that the floating charge does not exist outside company law. A floating charge is defined by Romer LJ in his classic statement in *Re Yorkshire Woolcombers' Association Ltd*:[2]

'(a) if it is a charge on a class of assets of a company present and future;
(b) if that class is one which, in the ordinary course of the business of the company, would be changing from time to time; and
(c) if you find that by the charge it is contemplated that until some future step is taken by or on behalf of those interested in the charge the company may carry on its business in the ordinary way as far as concerns the particular class of assets I am dealing with.'

The major advantage of the floating charge is that a company may deal with its goods even though subject to a charge, the charge does not prevent the company dealing with the goods as it does not attach to any specific goods until 'crystallisation'. Crystallisation occurs on the happening of certain events, usually specified in the deed of charge, e g appointment of a receiver or the company going into liquidation. The creditor takes the risk that the company may not replace the type of goods covered by the charge or may not replace them at a constant rate.

A floating charge may be a general charge, i e over the company's undertaking or on all its property both present and future, or the charge may be created over a part of the company's property, e g the stock in trade or over one particular business of the company. A floating charge is by its nature equitable, it cannot be legal, therefore in any conflict between legal and equitable charges, the legal charge has priority.

On liquidation the holders of the floating charge are treated as any other secured creditors and may choose to enforce their security or claim as unsecured creditors for the debt. But whereas the holder of the fixed charge is not subject to any limitation on his ability to enforce the security, the holder of the floating charge is subject to CA 1985, s 614(2)(b). This section provides that the preferential debts[3] may be paid out of the assets subject to a floating charge if the company has insufficient other assets to pay those debts in full. This makes the floating charge more vulnerable than the fixed charge.

In a winding up the liquidator may be able to avoid certain payments and securities. In particular the rules relating to fraudulent preferences in bankruptcy[4] are applied to companies. Where a company makes any payment or disposition of property to a creditor within six months of the commencement of the winding up with a view to giving such creditor preference over other creditors it shall be deemed fraudulent and void.[5] This would apply to all charges created within six months of the liquidation. CA 1985, s 617 provides that any floating charge created by the company within twelve months of the commencement of winding up is invalid. In this situation no fraud or intention to prefer is required. Such a floating charge may be valid if the holder can show that it secured a cash payment or that the company was solvent immediately after the creation of the charge.[6]

A failed *Romalpa* clause will often be treated by the courts[7] as an attempt to create charge over the goods to the extent of the price, such a charge would by its nature be a floating charge.[8]

---

[1] See para 4.79, above.
[2] [1903] 2 Ch 284 at 295.
[3] An exhaustive list of those claims ranking as preferential is given in Sch 19, see chap 11.
[4] See Bankruptcy Act 1914, s 44(1) (as amended by CA 1947, s 115).
[5] CA 1984, s 615.
[6] Ibid, s 617(1).
[7] E g *Re Bond Worth Ltd* [1980] Ch 228; *Borden (UK) Ltd v Scottish Timber Products Ltd* [1981] Ch 25.
[8] See generally para 4.81, below.

Retention of title clauses

4.81   The fixed and floating charges are interests in the property of another person, i e the company. The company creating the charge is the owner of property which is made subject to the charge. The secured creditor is therefore only a person with rights against the company's property and his rights might be defeated if the company chooses to sell, give away or deal with its property or by defective or non-registration of the charge as required.[1] Moreover, the trade creditors of a company are usually unsecured creditors and on a liquidation of the company would take after the secured creditors and preferential claims. In recent years, trade creditors have felt increasingly vulnerable, companies have more of their assets subject to charges and there has been an increase in insolvent liquidations. The suppliers of aluminium foil hit upon the idea of inserting a clause in their contract of sale which reserved the rights of ownership in *their* goods until the buyer had paid for them. The buyer company went into liquidation before payment was made and the seller claimed his goods back. The court held that it was possible for the seller to have the goods back as he was still the owner of them.[2] The effect of this was to upgrade the trade creditor from his usual position of an unsecured creditor in the liquidation of his customer to the best position of security, i e as owner of the goods.[3] The goods could not then form part of the buyer company's assets for distribution on liquidation. The *Romalpa*[4] case was quickly followed by other cases where the courts seemed determined to reduce the effectiveness of such clauses. In *Re Bond Worth Ltd*,[5] a clause purporting to retain 'equitable and beneficial ownership' was held only to be effective as a floating charge and void against the liquidator for non-registration. In *Borden (UK) Ltd v Scottish Timber Products Ltd*[6] the court held that the purchaser had to receive the goods either as bailee or a fiduciary of the seller to render the reservation of title effective, as the purchaser in the case did not act in either of these capacities, the seller ceased to be the owner of the goods. As a result of these cases and others, it seemed almost impossible to devise a reservation of title clause which would give effect to the seller's intention. This was confirmed by the first instance decision in *Clough Mill Ltd v Martin*,[7] but the Court of Appeal has made it clear that a seller may effectively reserve title to his property even though the buyer has certain rights over it, e g to deal with it, and that such an attempt will not necessarily be seen as an attempt to create a security over the goods which would require registration to be valid against the liquidator.

---

[1] According to CA 1985, s 395.
[2] *Aluminium Industrie Vaassen BV v Romalpa Aluminium Ltd* [1976] 2 All ER 552.
[3] And therefore entitled to rely on proprietary rights rather than personal rights against the buyer.
[4] Above.
[5] [1980] Ch 228.
[6] [1981] Ch 25.
[7] [1984] 1 All ER 721.
[8] *Clough Mill Ltd v Martin* [1984] 3 All ER 982.

Debentures and shares — similarities

4.82 Debentures and shares are two methods of raising capital used by companies and although they are different in a number of respects, treatment of them in company law is often similar. In particular, formalities relating to prospectuses, issue, allotment, transfer and transmission are very similar. The requirements of The Stock Exchange apply equally to debentures and shares, no distinction is made on the Stock Market regarding the nature of the particular corporate investment. The rules regarding transfer are identical, even to the extent that the same form is used, a stock transfer form.[1]

Both debentures and shares are choses in action, i e giving the holders rights against the company, but whereas debentures are normally secured and therefore give the holder proprietary rights, the share is never secured and a shareholder only has his personal rights against the company in respect of the debt evidenced by the share.

---

[1] See Stock Transfer Act 1963.

Debentures and shares — dissimilarities

4.83 Most of the similarities between shares and debentures relate to formalities and technical rules, but shares and debentures are essentially different in substance. A debentureholder is never more than a creditor (secured or unsecured) of the company, the shareholder is a member of the company and is given certain rights by company law and by the company itself, to act. In particular, the shareholder may attend and vote at general meetings (if, as is usual, his shares have voting rights attached) and certain actions cannot be taken by the company unless and until the shareholders have made a decision by resolution in a general meeting, e g alteration of articles.

A debentureholder's rights are embodied in his contract with the company, in this contract he may be granted special rights, e g to appoint a director, but if these rights are inconsistent with the rights of the shareholder, the company will have to act in breach of contract. A company cannot take away the shareholder's right to dismiss a director, therefore if a debentureholder is given a right to appoint a director, the shareholders may immediately dismiss him, even though this would constitute a breach of contract between the debentureholder and the company and possibly also a breach of contract between the director and the company.

The interest payable on a debenture is often equated with the dividend paid on shares. There are, however, many differences. The debentureholder is only entitled to the amount stated in his debenture as interest and cannot obtain more, the shareholder, at least the equity shareholder, is entitled to the amount which the directors declare as dividend and which is available for distribution by way of dividend, this is not limited to a fixed percentage. Similarly, on liquidation the debentureholder is only entitled to a return of his capital plus any interest in arrears, the ordinary shareholder is entitled to participate in all the assets remaining to the company after its debts have been paid, this amount is not limited, the shareholders are entitled to all the company's 'equity'.

It is only the company's share capital which is thought to need protection for the benefit of the company's creditors, thus the rules relating to raising and maintenance of share capital only apply to share capital and not loan stock. A debenture may be issued at a discount,[1] a company may purchase or redeem its own debentures without condition, a company may provide financial assistance for the purchase of its own debentures and a company may pay interest on a debenture out of capital. Moreover, interest payable on a debenture is paid out of pre-tax assets whilst dividend on a share can only be paid out of post-tax profits.[2]

The remedies of a debentureholder differ from those of a shareholder. The debentureholder has contractual, i e personal rights, against the company and may sue to enforce these, and where necessary claim damages from the company in a debentureholders' action. A shareholder, although in a contractual relationship with the company,[3] has never been allowed to sue the company and claim damages for a breach of contract.[4] The debentureholder's rights to a return of capital and to receive interest on that capital are actionable if the due date for payment has passed. A share is an indefinitely postponed debt and the shareholder has no right to recover it (unless the shares are issued as redeemable[5]) until the company is in liquidation and all the creditors have been paid off in full. As far as dividend is concerned, a shareholder is not entitled to dividend unless and until it is declared by the directors, though even if declared before a company goes into liquidation the shareholder will only have the status of a deferred creditor[6] in the company's liquidation regarding the arrears of dividend declared.

The typical company debenture is secured and the debentureholder's position is strengthened by the remedies available to him to enforce the security.

The main remedy which is usually included in the debenture document is the right to appoint a receiver. Even where the debenture is silent on this matter, the court has power to appoint a receiver in certain circumstances.[7]

A debentureholder may also take the unusual step of asking a court to foreclose on the security, i e a request to the court to take possession of the security and realise it for the satisfaction of the creditors' debts.

Both shareholders and debentureholders have a right to petition for the winding up of a company: the ultimate sanction against the company, but the grounds on which they may petition differ. In particular, creditors may petition for a winding-up order where the company is unable to pay its debts,[8] whereas a shareholder's usual ground for petitioning is the 'just and equitable' ground.[9] In order to succeed on the just and equitable ground the shareholder must show that he has a tangible interest in the liquidation,[10] this usually means a financial interest and if the company is insolvent the shareholder will be unable to show that he has such an interest. It is assumed that a debentureholder has a financial interest.

---

[1] Though a company may not issue a debenture at a discount with an immediate right to convert it into a share. To permit this would effectively sanction an issue of shares at a discount: *Moseley v Koffyfontein Mines Ltd* [1911] 1 Ch 73.

[2] Corporation tax is payable on a company's profits, in calculating profits for this purpose dividend distribution cannot be excluded.

[3] By virtue of CA 1985, s 14.

[4] It is thought that such a claim has never been permitted because it might destroy a creditor's priority to payment of debts in advance of shareholders. Support for this view can now be obtained from CA 1985, s 178(3) which prohibits the court from making an order for specific performance of the contract to purchase or redeem shares if the company has insufficient assets to cover its liabilities, and from CA 1985, s 178(2) which provides that a company shall not be liable in damages for failure to redeem or purchase its own shares.

[5] But see n 4, above.

[6] I e he takes after the company's creditors but before the company's shareholders.

[7] This remedy is dealt with further in chap 8.

[8] CA 1985, s 517(f).

9 Ibid, s 517(g).
10 E g *Re Othery Construction Ltd* [1966] 1 All ER 145.

5　Transfer and transmission of shares

Sally A Jones

Transfer and transmission of shares — meaning

(a) Issue and transfer

5.01　An issue of shares is where the company and the shareholders are the parties to the transaction, while a transfer of shares is the method by which the property in the shares moves from one shareholder to another. An issue of shares must constitute a contract between the company and the member, because a company cannot give its shares away, the member must pay for them. A transfer on the other hand need not be contractual, i e for consideration, a shareholder may give his shares away.

(b) Transfer and transmission

A transfer is effected by the act of the parties to the agreement, i e the transferor shareholder and transferee shareholder. Transmission is the term reserved for the case where the property in shares moves from one person to another by operation of law, e g on bankruptcy, or on death, by will or intestacy.

(c) Transfer and Registration

CA 1985, s 14 deems a contract to exist between the company and every member of the company, the terms of which are the memorandum and articles of the company.[1] The s 14 contract is dependent on registration. A shareholder taking shares from another shareholder has no contract with the company unless and until he is registered as a member. Registration is essential to give effect to a transfer of shares.

(d) Transfer and assignment

Technically a transfer of shares, because of s 14 has the effect of an assignment, i e it affects a third party's interest and the transferee is able to enforce rights against this party, i e the company. A transferee has an automatic right to be registered as a member unless the company has reserved the right to refuse. Shares sold on The Stock Exchange may not have any restriction on their transfer, this would restrict the free transfer of shares on the market.[2]

[1] See chap 1.
[2] Rules of Stock Exchange, Appendix 34, Sch VII.

Transfer of shares — generally

5.02   One of the fundamental concepts of the new company limited by shares was the free, i e unrestricted, transferability of shares. Subject to the company's articles, a shareholder may transfer his shares to whoever he likes and the transferee has a right to be registered as a member.[1] Note that a company is assumed to have the power to allow transfer of its shares and there is no need to include such a fundamental right in the company's objects clause or its articles. A shareholder is bound to observe any restrictions on transfer in the articles because the s 14 contract is binding on him in the same way as it is binding on the company.

Two common restrictions included in a private company's articles are:

(1)   pre-emption rights,[2] i e on a sale of shares, a shareholder must offer them first to the existing shareholders;

(2)   a right of refusal to register members within the discretion of the directors. In fact until 1980 the definition of a private company[3] required some restriction on the transfer of a private company's shares and these were the common restrictions. This requirement has now been repealed but many private companies will have retained this form of restriction in their articles and thus it is still of importance.

Public companies may if they wish include restrictions on transfer in their articles, however any public company wishing to obtain or retain a listing on The Stock Exchange must not include any restriction on the free transfer of shares.[4] This is essential to the smooth running of the Stock Market.

[1] *Re Discoverer's Finance Corpn Ltd, Lindlar's Case* [1910] 1 Ch 312, CA, though not if the company has since gone into liquidation.
[2] These must be distinguished from pre-emption rights *on issue*, see para 3.06, above, and see chap 8 further.
[3] CA 1948, s 28 repealed by CA 1980, Sch 4.
[4] Requirements for Admission to listing, Stock Exchange Regulations, Sch VII, Part A, para A2.

Form of transfer

5.03   It is unlawful for a company to register a transfer of shares unless a 'proper instrument of transfer' is delivered to the company.[1] The main purpose of this section was to ensure that the correct stamp duty was paid and attempts to avoid a transfer by deeming shares to pass from A to B may be declared invalid as an attempt to avoid stamp duty.[2]

Three possible forms are acceptable for the purpose of s 183:

(1)   a form complying with the Stock Transfer Act 1963 (which applies to debentures as well as shares);

(2)   a form complying with the terms of the company's articles so long as

the requirements of the Stock Transfer Act 1963 are complied with, this is used for fully or partly paid shares;

(3) The Stock Exchange form of transfer, but only for transfers of shares on The Stock Exchange.[3]

S 183 does not apply to a transmission of shares.

The 1963 Stock Transfers Act introduced a simplified form of transfer, which only needs to be executed by the transferor and does not need to be attested.[4] However, this Act only has application to fully paid up shares and where shares are partly paid up the form is the one specified in the articles. The articles usually provide, see Table A, article 23 (as amended by CA 1967), for transfer in any *'usual or common form'*. Common form may it seems mean the form required by the Stock Transfer Act, Sch 1.

---

[1] CA 1985, s 183.
[2] *Re Greene* [1949] Ch 333.
[3] See The Stock Exchange (Completion of Bargains) Act 1976.
[4] Stock Transfer Act 1963, s 1.

Procedure on transfer

5.04   The procedure, apart from the special procedure for securities sold on The Stock Exchange,[1] to be used for a transfer depends on whether the transferor shareholder is transferring his entire shareholding or only a part of it.

(i) *Entire shareholding*

A single transfer document is required in this situation, the transferor (having received the price of the shares if it is a transfer by way of sale) delivers a signed transfer to the transferee along with the share certificate. The signed transfer must be a proper instrument in accordance with CA 1985, s 183. The transferee is then obliged to have the transfer duly stamped and he must deliver the stamped transfer and share certificate and the registration fee, if required, to the company. The company is obliged to register the transfer within two months after it is lodged with the company.[2] The new member's name is entered on the register, the company cancels the old share certificate and issues the transferee with a new one. If the company does not wish to register the transfer, it must within two months of lodgement inform the transferee of the decision to refuse to register.[3] The company does not have to give notice of refusal to register to the transferor shareholder, who is technically still a member.[4]

(ii) *Part shareholding*

If the transferor shareholder is intending to keep part of his shareholding, he will be reluctant to part with the share certificate to a transferee, which evidences the entire shareholding. The transferor therefore sends the completed transfer and his share certificate to the company. The company then endorses the transfer with a statement that the share certificate has been lodged with it and sends the transfer only to the transferor. The transferor then sends the transfer to the transferee, in return for payment, if any.

The transferee executes the transfer stamps it and returns it with any registration fee to the company, the company (as with the procedure for transfer of the entire shareholding) registers the transfer or gives due notice of refusal to register the transfer. The company must then cancel the original share certificate and issue new ones to the parties according to their entitlement.

The certificate by the company of lodgement of the shares only represents to the transferee that a certificate has been received by the company, it does not represent that the transferor has title to the shares evidenced by the certificate. If the company makes a fraudulent or negligent certification, the company is liable in damages to any person who acts in good faith to his detriment in reliance on that false certification.[5]

The company is under a duty to the transferee to cancel the original share certificate, therefore if the company negligently returns the original certificate to the transferor shareholder and loss is caused to a third party, i e the transferor purports to transfer all his shares to a third party which transfer would be ineffective as part of the share will have already been transferred to the transferee, the company is not liable for the loss caused to that third party.[6] That person's loss has been caused by the transferor's fraud and not the company's negligence.

---

[1] See para 5.05, below.

[2] 14 days if listed securities are involved, Rules of The Stock Exchange, Appendix 34, Sch VIII, Part A.

[3] CA 1985, s 183.

[4] The transferor would have been entitled to notice of the company's refusal to register a transfer if the Jenkins' Committee recommendations had been implemented.

[5] CA 1985, s 184(2).

[6] *Longman v Bath Electric Tramways Ltd* [1905] 1 Ch 646.

The Stock Exchange (Completion of Bargains) Act 1976

5.05   Detailed consideration of The Stock Exchange procedures are beyond the scope of this work, but brief reference should be made to the TALISMAN[1] system introduced in 1976. The Stock Exchange (Completion of Bargains) Act 1976 facilitated the introduction of this new computerised system.

The main changes introduced by this Act were:

(1) a company is exempt from CA 1985, s 185, i e to prepare share or stock certificates in respect of securities allotted or transferred to the Stock Exchange nominee, SEPON Ltd;

(2) a company was empowered to have an official seal for the sealing of shares or stock certificates;

(3) companies could keep registers and records required by CA 1985, s 722 otherwise than in legible form as long as the method of recording the details were capable of being reproduced in legible form;

(4) new transfer forms under The Stock Transfer Act 1963 can be approved by the Treasury.[2]

¹ TALISMAN stands for Transfer Accounting, Lodgement for Investors and Stock Management for Jobbers.
² This power has now been exercised by The Stock Exchange (Addition of Forms) Order 1979.

Restrictions on transfer

5.06 The general rule is that shares are transferable without restriction except those restrictions imposed by law or the company's articles of association.¹

(a) Legal restrictions

A company must refuse to register a transfer unless it is correctly stamped.² The legal requirements imposed on private companies to restrict the transfer of shares have now been removed.³ Transfers of shares (but not debentures) are avoided if the company is in compulsory liquidation or under supervision, but the court has power to permit a transfer.

¹ See, e g Table A, Art 23.
² Stamp Act 1891, s 1 and Sch 1, Finance Act 1963, s 55 and Sch 2.
³ CA 1948, s 28 repealed by CA 1980, Sch 4 but see para 5.07(b), below.

(b) Restrictions in the articles

5.07 Articles giving directors a right to refuse to register a transfer have been subject to much discussion and many cases. Though the significance is less now that such a clause is no longer a legal requirement, the construction of such articles which will continue to be used in companies' articles is still important. A restriction on transfer is necessary in those companies where it is hoped to keep control in the hands of a small group, such a clause can also be used to prevent the dissemination of information to competitors who might purchase shares in a company to obtain an unfair advantage.

If the company's articles grant the directors the right to refuse to register a transferee's shares the courts are loath to interfere with the director's exercise of discretion and will only do so if there is evidence of impropriety.¹ The power to refuse to register may be absolute or limited to certain grounds and in the latter case the directors may only refuse to register on those specified grounds. However, they do not need to give reasons for their refusal and a transferee will only be able to challenge the exercise of their discretion if he can discover their reasons.² If the directors do give reasons for their exercise of discretion, the court can decide whether they are sufficient to justify the refusal and the courts can order the company to register the transfer³ or the court can rectify the register by substituting the name of the transferee for the name of the transferor under CA 1985, s 359.

An improper exercise of their right to refuse to register a transfer is a breach of fiduciary duty owed to the company, but the company is the only person who may sue for breach of this duty and the transferee has no locus standi to sue.[4] If the right to register a transfer is not exercised properly or in time the right to have the transfer registered revives and the transferee's usual right is to apply to the court for rectification of the company's register.

---

[1] E g *Stewart v James Keiller & Son Ltd* (1902) 4 F 657.

[2] *Re Coalport China Co* [1895] 2 Ch 404.

[3] *Re Bede Steam Shipping Co Ltd* [1917] 1 Ch 123, CA.

[4] The transferee might be able to bring a derivative action for fraud on the minority or pursue a remedy under CA 1985, s 459.

Rights of purchaser and vendor

5.08   All rights between the purchaser and vendor depend on the terms of their contract. However, certain terms may be implied. The transferor undertakes by that contract to hand over a genuine instrument of transfer and the share certificate (or an instrument of transfer stamped 'certificate lodged' or similar in the case of a partial transfer) and that he will not do anything to impede the registration of the transfer. The transferee undertakes to pay the price and will indemnify the transferor from any calls or other liability which may arise in relation to the shares.

These terms will be implied into the contract, if not expressly provided, unless expressly excluded by the parties or by a provision inconsistent with them. The transferee may not sue the transferor where the directors refuse to register a transfer under any power given to them in the company's articles, this is a risk the transferee takes, though he may sue the transferor if the contract 'guarantees registration'.[1] Of course where there is no contract of sale between the transferor and transferee, the transferee will have no rights against the transferor nor against the company until registered as a member, the transferor would remain entitled to dividend and to vote and would still be recognised as the member.

---

[1] *London Founders Association Ltd and Palmer v Clarke* (1888) 20 QBD 576, CA.

Priorities — competing claims

5.09   The rules are complex when two parties claim to be entitled to the same shares. Three basic principles emerge from the cases:

(1) *Forgeries*

A forgery is a complete nullity and of no effect, with the consequence that any person relying on a forged instrument of transfer or forged share certificate has no rights on it. Moreover, if a company has relied on a forgery, it will still be liable to the true owner and the company can be compelled to restore his name to the register if it has removed it.[1]

Companies usually suffer as a result of any forgery and thus it has become common for them to write to the transferor informing him of any transfer being lodged with the company for registration, giving him an opportunity to object. Failure to reply to the company's notice does not estop the true owner claiming entitlement to the shares at a later date despite the forgery.[2] It is therefore usual for companies to insure against the use of forged transfers. Companies are also empowered to make payments to those parties who have suffered as a result of a forged instrument, even though the company has no legal obligation to pay,[3] Forged Transfers Act 1891 and 1892.

(2) *First to register prevails*

Where there are two competing claims to shares by innocent parties the person who is registered as member and therefore has legal title to the shares has priority. This does not mean that he cannot hold the shares beneficially for another, and this will be the situation where there is a contract of transfer but the company has yet to register the transferee as member. The transferor, whose name is still on the register, is the legal owner of the shares but holds them on trust for the transferee.

(3) *First in time prevails*

Where none of the parties have been registered as members and both are innocent parties, priority goes to the person whose equitable title arose first.

---

[1] *Barton v North Staffordshire Rly Co* (1888) 38 Ch D 458.
[2] *Re Bahia and San Francisco Rly Co* (1868) LR 3QB 584.
[3] Such an express power would be needed otherwise shareholders may challenge such ex gratia payments as ultra vires the company and therefore void. Without the right to grant such compensation the company's credibility on the Stock Market and its reputation generally might be seriously impaired.

Share certificates

5.10 Share certificates must be completed and ready for delivery within two months after allotment or lodgement of a transfer,[1] except where a company is exempt under the Stock Exchange (Completion of Bargains) Act 1976.[2] Share certificates do not themselves represent the share, i e they are not a chose in action, but they are prima facie evidence of title under s 186.

A share certificate issued by a company is 'a declaration by the company to all the world that the person in whose name the certificate is made out and to whom it is given, is a shareholder in the company, and it is given by the company with the intention that it should be so used by the person to whom it is given, and acted upon in the sale and transfer of shares'.[3] The company will be estopped from denying the representation made by the certificate against any person relying on it[4] but the company will not be estopped when the certificate is a forgery[5] and a certificate has been held to be forgery when signed by the relevant officers but without authority.[6]

The share certificate usually records two representations:

(1) who is the owner of the shares; and
(2) how much is outstanding on the shares.

The principles of estoppel appear to be the same as for any estoppel, the person with authority (i e the company or the board on behalf of the company) makes a representation to another person, that person relies on the representation to enter into a contract. The share certificate represents the shareholder as the owner of the shares and the amount outstanding on those shares, if a person[7] relies on those representations and suffers loss as a result, the company will be estopped from denying the truth of the representation. A forged certificate not made with the authority of the company cannot be used as the basis of an estoppel.

---

1 CA 1985, s 185.
2 See para 5.05, above.
3 *Re Bahia etc* (above) per Cockburn CJ at 595.
4 *Pickard v Sears* (1837) 6 Ad & El 469.
5 *Ruben v Great Fingall Consolidated Co* [1906] AC 439.
6 *Mahony v East Holyford Mining Co* (1875) LR 7 HL 869.
7 E g a purchaser of the shares, *Burkinshaw v Nicholls* (1878) 3 App Cas 1004 or a mortgagee, *Bloomenthal v Ford* [1897] AC 156.

Bearer shares

5.11   Although CA 1985, s 188 provides for the issue of share warrants made payable to bearer in respect of fully paid shares, such shares are not common in the UK. Until 1979 the Exchange Control Act 1947 limited the usefulness of these shares as shares warrants required Treasury consent. These restrictions have been suspended[1] and this may lead to some increase in the number issued.

A company must also be empowered by its articles to issue share warrants as opposed to shares payable to an individual. A share warrant once issued is made payable to bearer and the bearer (holder) of it is absolutely entitled to the shares named in it, transfer is effected by mere delivery, thus no fees are payable on transfer, though stamp duty is payable on issue at the rate of three times the usual amount.[2]

The bearer of a share warrant is not usually entitled to vote unless he had lodged his warrant with the company prior to the meeting, this prevents any disputes regarding entitlement to the shares arising at the meeting itself.

---

1 Exchange Control (Securities etc) Exemption Order SI 1979/1333.
2 Finance Act 1963, s 59(1).

Mortgaging of shares

5.12   A share is a piece of property albeit an intangible one. A share certificate records the debt owed by the company to the holder and is the best
evidence of this indebtedness. A shareholder may wish to raise money on the
security of this property but without selling the shares, he may do this either
by creating a legal mortgage or an equitable mortgage over the shares. A legal
mortgage gives the lender the best security as, during the currency of the loan,
becomes the member and is entitled to exercise the usual membership rights.
The lender and the shareholder agree between themselves that once the loan
has been repaid in full the shares will be transferred to the original shareholder. This method is rather cumbersome as two transfers are necessary and
two lots of stamp duty. Moreover, such security is inappropriate where the
shares are only partly-paid as the lender would become liable for the outstanding calls, a risk he would understandably be reluctant to accept.

Equitable mortgage of shares

5.13   The equitable mortgage of shares is a more popular method of
securing a loan as it avoids the transfer procedures of a legal mortgage. The
shareholder remains legal owner of the shares but holds them on trust for the
benefit of the lender, who thus has an equitable interest. The major risk here
to the lender is that the shareholder's control over the shares is unrestricted
and he could give good title to the shares to a bona fide purchaser, the
lender's equitable interest would be defeated as long as the bona fide
purchaser had no notice of the lender's interest. In order to prevent this
happening it is usual to deposit the share certificate (still in the shareholder's
name) with the lender, in this way the shareholder is prevented from
physically dealing with the shares because he does not have the main evidence
of title. The lender may still be at risk, however, as the shareholder may
persuade the company that he has lost his share certificate and that they
should issue a new one, the shareholder could then give a good legal title to a
bona fide purchaser who did not have notice of the lender's interest. The
equitable mortgagee can take steps to reduce this risk by serving a 'stop
notice' on the company.[1] This stop notice is an instruction to the company
not to register a transfer or pay a dividend in respect of those shares without
giving notice within eight days to the issuer of the stop notice. The issuer must
then take appropriate action to enforce his rights.

When an equitable mortgage is created by the deposit of a share certificate
it is common for it to be accompanied by a blank transfer signed by the shareholder. The agreement between the shareholder and lender will provide for
the completion of the transfer by the lender in certain cases of default, e g
arrears in paying interest on the loan or arrears in repayment of capital.

The equitable mortgage will take priority over a charging order made after
the creation of the mortgage. A charging order can be made by a court at the
instance of a judgment creditor of the shareholder. The charging order

attaches to the shares for the benefit of the judgment creditor but only to the same extent as the shareholder's interest, i e subject to the mortgage.

---

[1] Charging Orders Act 1979 and Rules of the Supreme Court 1965, Ord 50, rr 11–15.

Appendix[1]

COMPANIES ACT 1985, SCH 3

MANDATORY CONTENTS OF PROSPECTUS

PART I

MATTERS TO BE STATED

*The company's proprietorship, management
and its capital requirement*

1.—(1) The prospectus must state—

   (*a*) the number of founders or management or deferred shares (if any) and the nature and extent of the interest of the holders in the property and profits of the company;

   (*b*) the number of shares (if any) fixed by the company's articles as the qualification of a director, and any provision in the articles as to the remuneration of directors; and

   (*c*) the names, descriptions and addresses of the directors or proposed directors.

(2) As this paragraph applies for the purposes of section 72(3), sub-paragraph (1)(*b*) is to be read with the substitution for the reference to the company's articles of a reference to its constitution.

(3) Sub-paragraphs (1)(*b*) and (1)(*c*) do not apply in the case of a prospectus issued more than 2 years after the date at which the company is entitled to commence business.

---

[1] See para 2.11, above.

---

2. Where shares are offered to the public for subscription, the prospectus must give particular as to—

   (*a*) the minimum amount which, in the opinion of the directors, must be raised by the issue of those shares in order to provide the sums (or, if any part of them is to be defrayed in any other manner, the balance of the sums) required to be provided in respect of each of the following—

(i) the purchase price of any property purchased or to be purchased which is to be defrayed in whole or in part out of the proceeds of the issue,

(ii) any preliminary expenses payable by the company, and any commission so payable to any person in consideration of his agreeing to subscribe for, or of his procuring or agreeing to procure subscriptions for, any shares in the company,

(iii) the repayment of any money borrowed by the company in respect of any of the foregoing matters,

(iv) working capital, and

(*b*) the amounts to be provided in respect of the matters above mentioned otherwise than out of the proceeds of the issue and the sources out of which those amounts are to be provided.

Details relating to the offer

3.—(1) The prospectus must state—

(*a*) the time of the opening of the subscription lists, and

(*b*) the amount payable on application and allotment on each share (including the amount, if any, payable by way of premium).

(2) In the case of a second or subsequent offer of shares, there must also be stated the amount offered for subscription on each previous allotment made within the 2 preceding years, the amount actually allotted and the amount (if any) paid on the shares so allotted, including the amount (if any) by way of premium.

4.—(1) There must be stated the number, description and amount of any shares in or debentures of the company which any person has, or is entitled to be given, an option to subscribe for.

(2) The following particulars of the option must be given—

(*a*) the period during which it is exercisable,

(*b*) the price to be paid for shares or debentures subscribed for under it,

(*c*) the consideration (if any) given or to be given for it or the right to it,

(*d*) the names and addresses of the persons to whom it or the right to it was given or, if given to existing shareholders or debenture holders as such, the relevant shares or debentures.

(3) References in this paragraph to subscribing for shares or debentures include acquiring them from a person to whom they have been allotted or agreed to be allotted with a view to his offering them for sale.

5. The prospectus must state the number and amount of shares and debentures which within the 2 preceding years have been issued, or agreed to be issued, as fully or partly paid up otherwise than in cash; and—

(*a*) in the latter case the extent to which they are so paid up, and

(*b*) in either case the consideration for which those shares or debentures have been issued or are proposed or intended to be issued.

Property acquired or to be acquired by the company

6.—(1) For purposes of the following two paragraphs, 'relevant property' is property purchased or acquired by the company, or proposed so to be purchased or acquired,

   (*a*) which is to be paid for wholly or partly out of the proceeds of the issue offered for subscription by the prospectus, or

   (*b*) the purchase or acquisition of which has not been completed at the date of the issue of the prospectus.

(2) But those two paragraphs do not apply to property—

   (*a*) the contract for whose purchase or acquisition was entered into in the ordinary course of the company's business, the contract not being made in contemplation of the issue nor the issue in consequence of the contract, or

   (*b*) as respects which the amount of the purchase money is not material.

7. As respects any relevant property, the prospectus must state—

   (*a*) the names and addresses of the vendors,

   (*b*) the amount payable in cash, shares or debentures to the vendor and, where there is more than one separate vendor, or the company is a sub-purchaser, the amount so payable to each vendor.

   (*c*) short particulars of any transaction relating to the property completed within the 2 preceding years in which any vendor of the property to the company or any person who is, or was at the time of the transaction, a promoter or a director or proposed director of the company had any interest direct or indirect.

8. There must be stated the amount (if any) paid or payable as purchase money in cash, shares or debentures for any relevant property, specifying the amount (if any) payable for goodwill.

9.—(1) The following applies for the interpretation of paragraphs 6, 7 and 8.

(2) Every person is deemed a vendor who has entered into any contract (absolute or conditional) for the sale or purchase, or for any option of purchase, of any property to be acquired by the company, in any case where—

   (*a*) the purchase money is not fully paid at the date of the issue of the prospectus.

   (*b*) the purchase money is to be paid or satisfied wholly or in part out of the proceeds of the issue offered for subscription by the prospectus,

   (*c*) the contract depends for its validity or fulfilment on the result of that issue.

(3) Where any property to be acquired by the company is to be taken on lease, paragraphs 6, 7 and 8 apply as if 'vendor' included the lessor, 'purchase

money' included the consideration for the lease, and 'sub-purchaser' included a sub-lessee.

(4) For purposes of paragraph 7, where the vendors or any of them are a firm, the members of the firm are not to be treated as separate vendors.

Commissions, preliminary expenses, etc

10.—(1) The prospectus must state—

> (*a*) the amount (if any) paid within the 2 preceding years, or payable, as commission (but not including commission to sub-underwriters) for subscribing or agreeing to subscribe, or procuring or agreeing to procure subscriptions, for any share in or debentures of the company, or the rate of any such commission,
>
> (*b*) the amount or estimated amount of any preliminary expenses and the persons by whom any of those expenses have been paid or are payable, and the amount or estimated amount of the expenses of the issue and the persons by whom any of those expenses have been paid or are payable.
>
> (*c*) any amount or benefit paid or given within the 2 preceding years or intended to be paid or given to any promoter, and the consideration for the payment or the giving of the benefit.

(2) Sub-paragraph (1)(*b*) above, so far as it relates to preliminary expenses, does not apply in the case of a prospectus issued more than 2 years after the date at which the company is entitled to commence business.

Contracts

11.—(1) The prospectus must give the dates of, parties to and general nature of every material contract.

(2) This does not apply to a contract entered into in the ordinary course of the business carried on or intended to be carried on by the company, or a contract entered into more than 2 years before the date of issue of the prospectus.

Auditors

12. The prospectus must state the names and addresses of the company's auditors (if any).

Interests of directors

13.—(1) The prospectus must give full particulars of—

> (*a*) the nature and extent of the interest (if any) of every director in the promotion of, or in the property proposed to be acquired by, the company, or
>
> (*b*) where the interest of such a director consists in being a partner in a firm, the nature and extent of the interest of the firm.

(2) With the particulars under sub-paragraph (1)(*b*) must be provided a statement of all sums paid or agreed to be paid to the director or the firm in cash or shares or otherwise by any person either to induce him to become, or to qualify him as, a director, or otherwise for services rendered by him or the firm in connection with the promotion or formation of the company.

(3) This paragraph does not apply in the case of a prospectus issued more than 2 years after the date at which the company is entitled to commence business.

Other matters

14. If the prospectus invites the public to subscribe for shares in the company and the company's share capital is divided into different classes of shares, the prospectus must state the right of voting at meetings of the company conferred by, and the rights in respect of capital and dividends attached to, the several classes of shares respectively.

15. In the case of a company which has been carrying on business, or of a business which has been carried on for less than 3 years, the prospectus must state the length of time during which the business of the company (or the business to be acquired, as the case may be) has been carried on.

PART II

AUDITORS' AND ACCOUNTANTS' REPORTS TO BE SET OUT IN PROSPECTUS

Auditors' report

16.—(1) The prospectus shall set out a report by the company's auditors with respect to—

(*a*) profits and losses and assets and liabilities, in accordance with sub-paragraphs (2) and (3) below, as the case requires, and

(*b*) the rates of the dividends (if any) paid by the company in respect of each class of shares in respect of each of the 5 financial years immediately preceding the issue of the prospectus, giving particulars of each such class of shares on which such dividends have been paid and particulars of the cases in which no dividends have been paid in respect of any class of shares in respect of any of those years.

If no accounts have been made up in respect of any part of the 5 years ending on a date 3 months before the issue of the prospectus, the report shall contain a statement of that fact.

(2) If the company has no subsidiaries, the report shall—

(*a*) deal with profits and losses of the company in respect of each of the 5 financial years immediately preceding the issue of the prospectus, and

(*b*) deal with the assets and liabilities of the company at the last date to which the company's accounts were made up.

(3) If the company has subsidiaries, the report shall—

(*a*) deal separately with the company's profits or losses as provided by sub-paragraph (2), and in addition deal either—

(i) as a whole with the combined profits or losses of its sub-sidiaries, so far as they concern members of the company, or
(ii) individually with the profits or losses of each subsidiary, so far as they concern members of the company,

or, instead of dealing separately with the company's profits or losses, deal as a whole with the profits or losses of the company and (so far as they concern members of the company) with the combined profits and losses of its subsidiaries; and

(*b*) deal separately with the company's assets and liabilities as provided by sub-paragraph (2), and in addition deal either—

(i) as a whole with the combined assets and liabilities of its sub-sidiaries, with or without the company's assets and liabilities, or
(ii) individually with the assets and liabilities of each subsidiary.

indicating, as respects the assets and liabilities of the subsidiaries, the allowance to be made for persons other than members of the company.

Accountant's reports

17. If the proceeds of the issue of the shares or debentures are to be applied directly or indirectly in the purchase of any business, or any part of the proceeds of the issue is to be so applied, there shall be set out in the prospectus a report made by accountants upon—

(*a*) the profits or losses of the business in respect of each of the 5 financial years immediately preceding the issue of the prospectus, and

(*b*) the assets and liabilities of the business at the last date to which the accounts of the business were made up.

18.—(1) The following applies if—

(*a*) the proceeds of the issue are to be applied directly or indirectly in any manner resulting in the acquisition by the company of shares in any other body corporate, or any part of the proceeds is to be so applied, and

(*b*) by reason of that acquisition or anything to be done in consequence of or in connection with it, that body corporate will become a sub-sidiary of the company.

(2) There shall be set out in the prospectus a report made by accountants upon—

(*a*) the profits or losses of the other body corporate in respect of each of the 5 financial years immediately preceding the issue of the prospectus, and (*b*) the assets and liabilities of the other body corporate at the last date to which its accounts were made up.

(3) The accountants' report required by this paragraph shall—

(*a*) indicate how the profits or losses of the other body corporate dealt with the report would, in respect of the shares to be acquired, have concerned members of the company and what allowance would have fallen to be made, in relation to assets and liabilities so dealt with, for holders of other shares, if the company had at all material times held the shares to be acquired, and

(*b*) where the other body corporate has subsidiaries, deal with the profits or losses and the assets and liabilities of the body corporate and its subsidiaries in the manner provided by paragraph 16(3) above in relation to the company and its subsidiaries.

Provisions interpreting preceding paragraphs, and modifying them in certain cases

19. If in the case of a company which has been carrying on business, or of a business which has been carried on for less than 5 years, the accounts of the company or business have only been made up in respect of 4 years, 3 years, 2 years or one year, the preceding paragraphs of this Part have effect as if references to 4 years, 3 years, 2 years or one year (as the case may be) were substituted for references to 5 years.

20. The expression 'financial year' in this Part means the year in respect of which the accounts of the company or of the business (as the case may be) are made up; and where by reason of any alteration of the date on which the financial year of the company or business terminates the accounts have been made up for a period greater or less than one year, that greater or less period is for purposes of this Part deemed to be a financial year.

21. Any report required by this Part shall either indicate by way of note any adjustments as respects the figures of any profits or losses or assets and liabilities dealt with by the report which appear to the persons making the report necessary, or shall make those adjustments and indicate that adjustments have been made.

22.—(1) A report required by paragraph 17 or 18 shall be made by accountants qualified under this Act for appointment as auditors of a company.

(2) Such a report shall not be made by any accountant who is an officer or servant, or a partner of or in the employment of an officer or servant, of the company or the company's subsidiary or holding company or of a subsidiary of the company's holding company.

In this paragraph, 'officer' includes a proposed director, but not an auditor.

(3) The accountants making any report required for purposes of paragraph 17 or 18 shall be named in the prospectus.

Table 13

REDEMPTION OUT OF PROFITS — CHECKLIST[1]

(1) Authority in the articles, alteration of articles by special resolution if necessary, CA 1985, s 159, and s 9.
(2) Shares fully paid, CA 1985, s 159(3).
(3) Shares *issued* as redeemable, CA 1985, s 159(1).
(4) After redemption must be at least two shareholders and at least one shareholder must hold non-redeemable shares, CA 1985, s 24 and s 159(2).
(5) Terms of redemption provided for in articles, CA 1985, s 160(3).
(6) Payment out of distributable profits or proceeds of a fresh issue, CA 1985, s 160.
(7) Payment of any premium out of distributable profits or from proceeds of fresh issue if premium paid on issue, CA 1985, s 160(2).
(8) Shares treated as cancelled, CA 1985, s 160(4).
(9) Relevant compensating transfer to capital redemption reserve to maintain share capital, CA 1985, s 170.

---

[1] See paras 4.22–4.25, above.

Table 14

PURCHASE OF OWN SHARES OUT OF PROFITS — CHECKLIST[1]

(1) Authority in the articles, alteration of articles by special resolution if necessary, CA 1985, s 162 and s 9.
(2) Shares must be fully paid, CA 1985, s 162(2).
(3) Members must not be less than two and at least one shareholder must hold non-redeemable shares, CA 1985, s 24, s 1 and s 162(3).
(4) Terms of purchase must provide for payment at time of purchase of shares, CA 1985, s 162(2).
(5) If market transaction (public companies only), ordinary resolution required granting authority to purchase, CA 1985, s 166(1).
(6) If off-market transaction (public or private companies) or contingent purchase contracts, special resolution required to approve particular purchase, CA 1985, s 164(2), s 165(2).
(7) If off-market or contingent purchase contract, copy of contract must be available for inspection fifteen days before the meeting and at the meeting itself, CA 1985, s 164(6) and s 165(2).
(8) Authority for off-market transaction of a public company not to exceed eighteen months, CA 1985, s 164(4).
(9) Payment out of distributable profits or proceeds of fresh issue, CA 1985, s 160(1).
(10) Payment of any premium out of distributable profits or from proceeds of fresh issue if premium paid on issue, CA 1985, s 160(2).
(11) Shares treated as cancelled, CA 1985, s 160(4).
(12) Relevant compensating transfer to capital redemption reserve to maintain share capital, CA 1985, s 170.
(13) Copy of any purchase contract to be available at registered office for inspection for ten years, CA 1985, s 169(4).
(14) Return relating to shares purchase to be filed with registrar of companies within twenty-eight days of purchase, CA 1985, s 169(1).
(15) Copy of resolution approving purchase sent to registrar of companies within fifteen days, CA 1985, s 380.
(16) Quaere, if public company is there a need to re-register as private because share capital reduced below minimum?

---

[1] See paras 4.26–4.31, above.

Table 15

PURCHASE OR REDEMPTION OUT OF CAPITAL — CHECKLIST

In addition to the procedural requirements listed in Table 13 (redemption) or Table 14 (purchase), the *private* company may redeem or purchase its shares out of capital if it complies with the following:

(1) authority in the articles which must be applicable to purchases or redemption out of *capital*, alteration of articles by special resolution if necessary, CA 1985, s 171 and s 9;

(2) payment must not exceed the permissible capital payment, CA 1985, s 171(3);

(3) relevant compensating transfer, CA 1985, s 171(4) and (5);

(4) special resolution of shareholders approving payment out of capital, CA 1985, s 173(2);

(5) declaration of solvency by directors in prescribed form, CA 1985, s 173(3);

(6) accounts specially prepared for the purpose, CA 1985, s 172(3);

(7) auditors' report addressed to the directors annexed to the declaration of solvency, CA 1985, s 173(5);

(8) special resolution above (4) must be passed on or within one week of directors' statutory declaration, CA 1985, s 174(1);

(9) the company may not make any payment out of capital within five weeks of the resolution or after seven weeks, CA 1985, s 174(1);

(10) members and creditors must be given an opportunity to object to the court for cancellation of the resolution approving payment, CA 1985, s 176;

(11) special resolution must be filed with registrar of companies within fifteen days of passing it, CA 1985, s 380;

(12) publication of notice of resolution in Gazette. and either a national newspaper or written notice to all creditors within one week of the resolution, CA 1985, s 175;

(13) statutory declaration and auditors' report must be available for inspection by members at meeting proposing the resolution, CA 1985, s 174(4), and available for inspection by creditors up to five weeks after the date of the resolution, CA 1985, s 175(6);

(14) copy of directors' declaration and auditors' report must be filed at Companies House not later than the first notice date (i e date of publication in Gazette or notification to creditor whichever is earlier), CA 1985, s 175(5);

Table 169

(15) if member or creditor objects, copy of objection to registrar of companies and within fifteen days of court order, a copy of the order, CA 1985, s 176(3).

6 Management, directors and secretary

Peter Castle

Introduction

6.01 A company requires a constitutional body to direct and manage its business or activities from day to day. This body of persons by whatever name called is in fact its legal directors. With regard to a company it is this body which is given the function by the owners of the shares to utilize its property for its purposes and obtain, in a commercial company, a return on its investment.

As such the directors are not employees (in legal terminology called servants) of the company. They may be in another capacity employees and in fact very often are employees. As such they are executive or managing directors: in other words, 'working directors'.

Every company, subject to its articles, can have as many directors as it desires, but must have at least one director or two if public and formed after November 1929.[1]

---

[1] CA 1985, s 282.

Appointment

6.02 The first directors are appointed on incorporation by a statement signed by or on behalf of the subscribers containing a signed consent by each of the persons named as a director therein.[1] On registration of the memorandum and articles the statement signed by the subscribers setting out the particulars of the directors and including a signed consent by each of the directors to act must be delivered to the registrar.[2]

Subsequent directors of a public company must be appointed by individual separate resolutions unless a composite resolution has been unanimously agreed to by the shareholders.[3] The articles of association may give power to an outsider to appoint qne or more directors. Such a right is enforceable by an order of the court though it would seem that a person who is 'personally objectionable' will not be appointed.[4]

Power to appoint additional directors is frequently conferred on the directors by the Articles. However, in cases of difficulty where agreement cannot be reached the general meeting will usually retain a residual power.[5]

Casual vacancies are normally filled by the directors. Such vacancies occur when a previous directorship determines prior to its allotted time, e g by death.[6]

Alternate Directors may be appointed to act for a director if the articles so provide. Such a director has the full status of a director while his appointor is absent. He is not entitled, however, to remuneration from the company.[7]

Managing Directors are usually appointed (if power to so do is given in the articles) by the Directors and have, as their name implies, some powers to manage the whole or part of the business. This depends upon the particular articles.[8]

[1] CA 1985, s 13(5) Form 10.
[2] Ibid, ss 10, 12.
[3] Ibid, s 292.
[4] *British Murac Syndication Ltd v Alperton Rubber Co Ltd* [1915] 2 Ch 186.
[5] *Worcester Corsetry Ltd v Witting* [1936] Ch 640.
[6] *Munster v Cammell Co* (1882) 21 Ch 183.
[7] Table A regs 65–69. Companies (Tables A–F) Regulations 1985.
[8] Table A regs 71–72.

Qualifications

6.03 Directors of public companies (or their subsidiaries) must be under 70 years of age before appointment and must retire at the next general meeting after attaining the age of 70 years unless the general meeting after special notice appoints the director having been given notice of his age.[1] The age limit does not have effect if the articles of a company registered after the beginning of 1947 (or amended articles adopted after the beginning of 1947) provide otherwise.[2]

The articles may provide that the director must buy shares in the company or be of a certain nationality. In practice the tendency today is not to require share qualifications.

[1] CA 1985, s 293(1)–(6).
[2] Ibid, s 293(7).

Disqualification

6.04 The following persons may not be directors:

(i) a person against whom a disqualification order is made in circumstances where he has committed an indictable offence in connection with the promotion, formation, management or liquidation of a company or with the receivership or management of the company's property;[1]
(ii) undischarged bankrupts;[2]
(iii) a person against whom a disqualification order is made where he has been guilty of fraudulent trading or he has been persistently in default in making returns and filing accounts and other documents pursuant to the Companies Act;[3]
(iv) a person against whom a disqualification order is made where:
    (a) he has been a director of an insolvent company which has at that time gone into liquidation;
    (b) he has been within five years of the liquidation of the above

company a director of another liquidated insolvent company;
  (c)   his conduct has in the opinion of the court made him unfit to manage a company.[4]

A public register is maintained of disqualification orders.[5]

The Articles often provide that a director vacates his office if he becomes of unsound mind, or ceases to hold qualification shares. The effect is usually (dependent on the construction of the articles) automatic.[6]

---

[1] CA 1985, s 296.
[2] Ibid, s 302.
[3] Ibid, ss 297, 298.
[4] Ibid, s 300.
[5] Ibid, s 301.
[6] Table A reg 81 (Tables A–F) Regs 1985.

Irregular appointments

6.05   The effect of the provisions of the Companies Acts is that the acts of a person who appears to be duly appointed and qualified as a director are valid despite any defects in his appointment.[1]

However, a person who knows of the defect in appointment is not protected and this extends to knowledge of a probable defect.[2] Further, all persons taking an interest through or under such a person are in no better position.[3]

Strictly a director who is invalidly appointed cannot claim his fees, but if he has worked he may be able to obtain a quantum meruit for his services.[4]

An informally appointed director who acts may be estopped from alleging his invalidity.[5]

A director remains such until a change is notified to the Registrar and published in the Gazette (or the change can be shown to be otherwise known to the person dealing with the company).[6]

An irregular appointment coupled with the director being held out as such by the rest of the board and shareholders may make the company liable for his acts.

---

[1] *Morris v Kanssen* [1946] AC 459; CA 1985, s 285.
[2] *Morris v Kanssen* (above).
[3] *Morris v Kanssen* (above).
[4] *Craven-Ellis v Canons Ltd* [1936] 2 KB 403.
[5] *Faure v Phillipart* (1888) 58 LT 525 at 527.
[6] CA 1985, ss 42, 711 Form 288.

RETIREMENT, RESIGNATION, REMOVAL

6.06   Generally speaking one third of the directors retire each year though the Articles can provide otherwise.[1]

If only two are left, neither need retire.[2] Reg 75 of Table A provides that upon retirement a director is deemed to be re-elected unless the general meeting expressly resolves not to fill the office or a resolution for re-election is put to the meeting and lost.

It has been held in Scotland[3] that not holding a meeting when the articles provided that all the directors should retire at the general meeting resulted in the directors retiring automatically — a decision which might be considered somewhat illogical in that ex hypothesis there was no general meeting to retire at.

A director can resign at any time on communication whether oral or in writing save that if the terms of his appointment provide a particular body to which resignations should be addressed, notices or resignation sent to any other body of the company are ineffective.[4]

Notwithstanding anything in the articles or in any agreement the general meeting may by ordinary resolution requiring special notice remove a director.[5]

This can be done in breach of contract and in effect prevents security of office being given.[6]

What cannot be achieved directly may be achieved indirectly by conferring weighted voting rights on the director in the event of a resolution to remove him. Such an article has been accepted by the House of Lords,[7] but has been criticised. Further it has been suggested that if it prevents the articles being altered by special resolution it deprives the company of a fundamental right to alter its articles.[8] The answer to this may be that it does not in law prevent the articles being altered. It merely prevents the other shareholders from procuring a sufficient majority to outvote the director. Of course, if it is used in such a way as to be oppressive, a petition under s 459 may be appropiate.

Where a resolution is proposed under CA 1985, s 303 the director has an opportunity to make representations to shareholders before he is removed from office.[9] When the notice is given he can request the company to send his written representations to the shareholders. If the written representations are received in time they must be sent out.[10] If not, the director may require them to be read out.[11] The company (or another interested person) can object if the representations give needless publicity to defamatory matter.[12] The director is entitled to be heard at the meeting.[13]

A director who is removed retains his rights to damages or compensation (if any).[14]

The removal of a director in a small domestic or quasi-partnership company may be a ground for seeking to wind up on the ground that it is just and equitable to do so.[15]

---

[1] Table A reg 73, 1985 Regs.
[2] *Re Moseley & Sons Ltd* [1939] Ch 719.
[3] *Alexander Ward & Co Ltd v Samyang Navigation Co Ltd* 1973 SLT (Notes) 80 see [1975] 2 All ER 424.
[4] *Latchford Premier Cinema Ltd v Ennion* [1931] 2 Ch 409.
[5] CA 1985, s 303(1)(2).
[6] Ibid, s 303(5).
[7] *Bushell v Faith* [1970] AC 1099.
[8] (1970) JBL 1.
[9] CA 1985, s 304(1).
[10] Ibid, s 304(2).
[11] Ibid, s 304(3).
[12] Ibid, s 304(4).
[13] Ibid, s 304(1).
[14] Ibid, s 303(5).
[15] *Ebrahimi v Westbourne Galleries Ltd* [1973] AC 360.

Remuneration

6.07   In the absence of provision in the articles directors cannot claim remuneration.[1] In practice, the articles invariably provide for remuneration and it is then a matter for the directors.[2] Accrued remuneration is a debt in respect of which time runs under the Limitation Acts and the accounts duly signed (except where signed by himself) may be an acknowledgement and constitute a new accrual of the cause of action.[3]

There is no contractual claim by virtue of the articles as such,[4] but usually a director will have impliedly contracted on the terms in the articles when he accepted appointment.[5]

Usually remuneration is (or ought to be) voted in general meeting (though it depends on the articles). If it is not voted but all the shareholders approved it, then it takes effect as a resolution.[6]

If the articles provide for extra remuneration for specific services then usually it is unenforceable unless and until the directors have resolved as to the method of calculation and the amount to be paid.[7]

Directors who incur liabilities in carrying out their function are entitled, like trustees, to an indemnity.[8] In the absence of express provision this does not extend to expenses for travelling to and from board meetings.[9] However, all other expenses incurred incidental to being a director are recoverable. If a director receives more than his entitlement in remuneration, it is repayable by him as on a breach of trust.[10]

All payments which are made as remuneration must be paid subject to income tax, i e they may not be paid free of tax and if expressed to be so must be grossed up at the appropriate rate.[11]

The accounts must show the directors' remuneration and other emoluments.[12]

Where a director ceases to be such during a period for which remuneration is to be paid, unless the remuneration provision is so worded as to require a lump sum payable on completion of the period, the director will (subject to what is said below) be entitled to a proportionate part of his remuneration.[13] The point is uncertain because while the Court of Appeal in 1889 had decided that a director was entitled to a proportionate part of his remuneration, later judges[14] at first instance came to the opposite conclusion, apparently failing to appreciate the effect of the decision or to take account of the Apportionment Act 1870. Accordingly, the law is somewhat obscure.

[1] *Hutton v West Cork Rly* (1883) 23 Ch D 654.   [2] Table A reg 82 (1985 Regs).
[3] *Orton v Cleveland etc Co* (1865) 3 H & C 868.
[4] *Re Richmond Gate Property Co Ltd* [1965] 1 WLR 33.
[5] *Re Peruvian Guano Co* [1894] 3 Ch 690.
[6] *Re Duomatic Ltd* [1969] 2 Ch 365; *Cane v Jones* [1981] 1 All ER 533; *Re Halt Garage Ltd* 1982 3 All ER 1016, [1982] 1 Ch 478 at 490, 509.
[7] *Nelberg v Woking Shipping Co Ltd* [1958] 2 Lloyd's Rep 560; see now [1982] 3 All ER 1016.
[8] *Re German Mining Co* (1853) 4 De G M & G 19.
[9] *Young v Naval, Military and Civil Service Co-op Society of South Africa* [1905] 1 KB 687.
[10] *Leeds Estate etc Co v Shepherd* (1887) 36 Ch D 787.
[11] CA 1985, s 311. Companies Consolidation (Consequential Provisions) Act 1985, s 15.
[12] CA 1985, s 231, Sch 5, para 22.
[13] *Swabey v Port Darwin Gold Mining Co Ltd* (1889) 1 Meg 385.
[14] See the judgment of the Divisional Court over-ruled by the Court of Appeal on grounds not affecting the validity of this point in *Moriarty v Regent's Garage etc Co* [1921] 1 KB 423.

PROCEEDINGS OF DIRECTORS

6.08   The directors generally act and can only act as such collectively. The articles or, if empowered by the memorandum and articles, the directors collectively, may direct otherwise.[1]

---

[1] See e g *Re Portuguese Copper Mines* (1889) 42 Ch D 160 at 167.

Directors' meetings

6.09   Generally speaking the directors have control over how they will regulate their meetings except that each director is entitled to take his part and exercise his vote. The directors act by majority and the chairman normally has a second vote as a tie breaker.[1]

Usually some form of quorum provision will be present which will be expressed not to apply to filling vacancies if the total number of directors falls below the quorum.[2] A quorum does not include directors disabled from voting because of personal interest.[3]

Directors meetings are held as frequently as necessary and in established companies, generally, at regular intervals. Valid decisions are not confined to formal meetings: whenever and wherever the directors collectively take a decision, in effect, a meeting will have been held.

Generally meetings can be summoned either by a director or the secretary at fixed times or upon proper notice.[4] If all the directors agree to take a decision and hold a meeting without notice, the meeting is effective.[5] Notice need only be given to directors within the UK or who can be easily contacted.[6]

An irregular meeting will be effective so far as persons dealing with a company are concerned.[7] However, the decision of the meeting relied on must purport to be a decision of the directors. Such an irregularity as on its face precludes a collective decision cannot amount to a decision of the directors on which an outsider could rely as he would not be 'in good faith'.[8]

---

[1] Table A, reg 88 (1985 Regs).
[2] Table A, regs 89, 90 (1985 Regs).
[3] *Re North Eastern Insurance Co* [1919] 1 Ch 198.
[4] Table A, reg 88 (1985 Regs).
[5] *Barron v Potter* [1914] 1 Ch 895.
[6] *Halifax Sugar Co Ltd v Francklyn* (1890) 59 LJ Ch 591.
[7] *Royal British Bank v Turquand* (1856) 6 E & B 327.
[8] CA 1985, s 35.

Resolutions

6.10   The decisions of the directors are normally expressed as resolutions which are recorded by the Secretary. These records form the minute book which must be kept of all directors' proceedings. Decisions can in fact be extremely informal and it is the secretary's function to ensure proper records are kept of proceedings.[1]

The wording of resolutions can be crucial since unless, where appropriate, it clearly covers all the subsequent acts necessary to complete any transaction, the matter may have to be considered by the board upon successive occasions thereby diverting time from more pressing matters.

---

[1] CA 1985, s 382.

Delegation

6.11   If the articles permit, the directors can delegate their activities to committees or managing directors or any other person or persons permitted.[1]

The articles generally govern what may be delegated and to whom. However, it must be appreciated that if pursuant to the Articles the directors hold out to the world that a committee or a person has executive powers (e g a managing director) the company will generally be bound by the activities of such executive within the field covered by the expressed function or position.

---

[1] Table A, reg 72.

Managing director

6.12   Remuneration of a managing director is generally fixed by the directors.[1] As a director, he is not an employee, but usually a managing director will be expressly or impliedly engaged as such, i e he will be an employee with a contract of employment (in writing or oral). This of course does not necessarily follow in small family companies where in effect the rest of the family has merely acquiesced in giving the executive director plenipotentiary powers. As such (in the absence of other specific arrangements) his position will be no more than general agent and not employee.

---

[1] Table A, reg 84.

6.13   The termination of a managing director's employment will entitle him to damages if:

(1)   he has a contract (express or implied) with the company;
(2)   the directors have power on the wording of the articles to contract for an unfettered period;
(3)   the contract in fact entered into does not expressly include a power of revocation or is totally inconsistent with any power in the articles to revoke so that it does not impliedly include such a power.[1]

---

[1] *Shindler v Northern Raincoat Co Ltd* [1960] 2 All ER 239.

DIRECTORS' FIDUCIARY DUTIES

Introduction

6.14 A director of a·company is said to owe fiduciary duties. By this is meant that the director is in a position of trust so that a court of equity will, on behalf of those to whom that 'trust' is owed, ensure by its orders that the director acts fairly and does not abuse his position.

Generally speaking it is the company on whose behalf the court acts,[1] but, of course, where the director in any particular case holds himself out as acting for others (such as individual shareholders) his duties of trust will likewise be owed to them and the court will equally act on their behalf.[2] Similarly, by virtue of the relationships of the directors to the shareholders in particular companies, such as family companies, particular duties may be held to arise either merely not to act negligently[3] (tort) or to act subject to the duties implied in equity as a fiduciary.[4] As is apparent from the above these duties are imposed by the courts, but in many cases the Companies Act supplements and regulates the position.

---

[1] *Percival v Wright* [1902] 2 Ch 421.
[2] *Allen v Hyatt* (1914) 30 TLR 444.
[3] *Prudential Assurance Co Ltd v Newman Industries Ltd (No 2)* See at first instance [1981] Ch 257 at 302 varied on appeal at [1982] Ch 204.
[4] *Coleman v Myers* [1977] 2 NZLR 225; *Gething v Kilner* [1972] All ER 1166.

Objects of the duty

6.15 The basic duty established by the court is one owed to the company as a whole. The interests of a particular section or sections of the company are not the same as the company. Indeed, the width of the interest has been recognised by Megarry J in the phrase 'present and future members of the company, as a whole'.[1] To 'members' has been added 'creditors' as being persons to whom the duties are owed where a company is no longer solvent.[2] This, however, is probably not strictly accurate since an insolvent company ought to be wound up or refinanced under some formal or informal scheme of arrangement. Accordingly, creditors are merely objects in the sense that they have a right upon winding up through the liquidator to investigate and ensure that the company's property was not mis-applied. Prior to insolvency their interest, legal as well as commercial, is to be paid.

In addition to the members, CA 1985, s 309 (originally CA 1980, s 46) extends the duty to include the 'interests of the employees in general' as well as the interests of its members. This section does not make it clear as to how to act if the interests of members and employees are irreconcilable. To leave the question to the business judgment of directors will result probably in little change from the position prior to 1980, at least so far as the company is a going concern. The management of a company without taking into account the interests of the employees will probably lead to a disruptive workforce (or at least an uncommitted, unenthusiastic workforce) so that prior to 1980 their interests were included, a contented workforce being beneficial to the company.[3] With regard to a company which is about to cease being a going concern, the position is most uncertain, but it is suggested that in an insolvent company the exercise of director's powers to vote 'senior' employees large benefits would not be upheld by the courts at least so far as there was the slightest risk of the directors obtaining a personal advantage. The section may well however have enabled a solvent company to make provision for their employees generally despite its being wound up.[4]

[1] *Gaiman v National Association for Mental Health* [1971] Ch 317.
[2] *Multinational v Multinational Services* [1983] 1 Ch 258 at 288 Eg; *Walker v Wimborne* (1976) 50 ALJR 446; note also CA 1985, s 390(2)(a) whereunder a resigning auditor must in his resignation give a statement concerning any circumstances connected with the resignation which ought to be brought to the notice of the members or creditors.
[3] *Hutton v West Cork Rly Co* (1883) 23 Ch D 654.
[4] Thereby reversing *Parke v Daily News* [1962] Ch 927; CA 1985, ss 659 and 719.

Bona fides

6.16   The directors must act 'bona fide in what they consider — not what a court may consider — is in the interests of the company.'[1] The courts will only interfere where it is considered that no reasonable director could possibly have concluded that what was proposed was in the interests of the company, or presumably, its employees.[2] This can, of course, occur not merely by dishonesty or positive mistake, but also by inadvertence or plain ignorance.[3] Further, the interests of the 'group' of which the company is a member can be taken into account so long as the interests of the group are not in conflict with the interests of the company.[4]

[1] *Re Smith and Fawcett Ltd* [1942] Ch 304.
[2] *Heron International Ltd v Lord Grade and Associated Communications Corporation plc* [1983] BCLC 244 CA.
[3] *Re W & M Roith Ltd* [1967] 1 All ER 427.
[4] *Charterbridge Corporation v Lloyds Bank Ltd* [1970] Ch 62.

Purpose of power

6.17   The powers of the directors must be exercised for the purpose for which they were conferred. Thus, the power of issuing shares must not be used purely to confer on the board control of the general meeting no matter how much the directors bona fide believe they are acting in the interests of the company, e g in defeating an unwanted takeover bid.[1] On the other hand while interference in the balance of power in the shareholders' meeting is not allowed in this way it would seem that in domestic family companies the power to refuse to register transfers can be used to prevent an outsider obtaining a voice at meetings or even control.[2] The same position appears to prevail in quasi-partnerships and non-commercial companies formed to promote certain views where some members hold irreconcilably opposite views.[3] Accordingly, each case has to be approached on the merits of the particular exercise of power proposed or carried out. The court will then decide, having taken into account the views of the directors, whether what is proposed is proper. If it is not proper,[4] then so long as the question is not ultra vires the general meeting, the court may adjourn for the meeting to decide.[5]

1 *Hogg v Cramphorn Ltd* [1967] Ch 254.
2 *Re Smith & Fawcett Ltd* [1942] Ch 304.
3 *Gaiman v National Association for Mental Health* [1971] Ch 317.
4 *Howard Smith Ltd v Ampol Petroleum Ltd* [1974] AC 821.
5 *Bamford v Bamford* [1970] Ch 212.

Conflict of interest and duty

6.18 The directors must not put themselves in a position where their personal interests conflict with their duties.

Duty of disclosure

6.19 A director may not enter into a contract with his company (except in certain very limited cases) unless he makes full disclosure of all material facts to the company's members who then approve the contract.[1] This is notwithstanding that the contract is fair and beneficial.

If this rule is breached, subject to the articles, any sale of property belonging to the company can be set aside or, in the alternative the directors can be made liable in damages for any loss caused by the non-disclosure.[2]

A director is interested whether he acts personally with his company or through a third party or has a shareholding in another company which is conducting business with the first-named company.[3] If, however, he is a shareholder he can use his votes to approve his acts unless by so doing it amounts to oppression or fraud on a minority.[4]

1 *Aberdeen Rly v Blaikie* (1854) 1 Macq 461.
2 *Re Cape Breton Co* (1885) 29 Ch D 795.
3 *Transvaal Lands Co v New Belgium etc Co* [1914] 2 Ch 488.
4 *Cook v Deeks* [1916] 1 AC 554.

Waiver by the articles or statute

6.20 A director who is in any way, whether directly or indirectly, interested in a contract or proposed contract with the company must declare the nature of his interest at a meeting of the directors.[1] This cannot be watered down by the Articles.[2] However, while as a general rule a director cannot vote on such matters in which he is interested, the exceptions (whereby a director can vote where the contract or arrangement is with another company in which the director is only interested as an officer or holder of shares or other securities) are so wide that the general rule is almost nullified in most practical situations.[3] It is also provided that the directors can vote in respect of each other's service contracts[4] and in private companies complete relaxation of the rule is permitted if the shareholders resolve.[5] Further, such contracts (being offices or places of profit) in which a director is interested, as are discussed above, are not liable to avoidance and the directors are excused liability for an account of profits where the 'mere' connection which is alleged is their position as a director.[6]

Provision in the articles or any contracts cannot give a director an indemnity for liability for negligence, default, breach of duty or breach of trust except in relation to the successful defence of such claims or where the court gives relief where a director is honest and reasonable under s 727.[7]

---

[1] Table A, regs 85, 94 (1985 Regs); CA 1985, s 317.

[2] CA 1985, s 317.

[3] Table A, reg 94 (1985 Regs); *Prudential Assurance Co Ltd v Newman Industries Ltd (No 2)* [1982] Ch 204.

[4] Table A, reg 97 (1985 Regs).

[5] Table A, reg 96 (1985 Regs), but quoted or listed companies are not permitted this laxity without Stock Exchange approval.

[6] Table A, reg 85 (1985 Regs).

[7] CA 1985, s 310.

Extent of disclosure provisions

6.21   The provisions as to disclosure extend beyond the interests of the director himself to persons upon whose 'directions or instructions the directors are accustomed to act' ('shadow directors').[1] Disclosure must be to the board of the fact of the interest and as to its nature.[2] This can be done by a general notice that a director is interested in contracts in respect of a specific company so long as he takes reasonable steps to ensure the matter is brought up and considered at the next board meeting.[3] Disclosure to the board while relieving the director from criminal liability to pay a fine does not in itself overcome any rule of law restricting directors from having an interest in contracts with the company.[4]

---

[1] CA 1985, s 317(8).

[2] Ibid, s 317(1).

[3] Ibid, s 317(3)(4).

[4] Ibid, s 317(9).

Special contracts regulated or prohibited: enforcement of fair dealing by directors[1]

6.22   (a) Directors service contracts (copies) must be available for inspection by members and directors' emoluments must be disclosed in the annual accounts.[2] Such contracts, if exceeding a period of five years must be approved in general meeting.[3] The provisions apply to service contracts and to contracts of service.[4] Further, they apply to contracts whether the company is disabled from serving a notice of termination for five years or is disabled from so serving a notice except in specified circumstances.[5] Further, they apply to options to renew and also where more than six months before expiration a further term is given in substitution, which, together with the unexpired portion of the old contract, amounts to more than five years.[6] A memorandum of such contracts must be made available at the company's registered office fifteen days before the relevant meeting and at the meeting for inspection.[7] Non-compliance with the provisions makes any term contravening the section void and the agreement terminable on reasonable notice by the company.[8]

(b) Loans to directors, guarantees and other securities for such loans in excess of £2,500 may not be made by a company to its directors or the directors of its holding company.[9]

Further, a wider restriction is imposed on public companies relating to every company within the group of which such a company forms part ('relevant company').[10] Such loans cannot be made to the director or any person 'connected with him', i e spouse, infant children, step-children, company with which the director is associated, a trustee of a trust (except a pension scheme or employee share scheme) of which he or his said family or associated company are beneficiaries, and a partner of the director or his said family or associated company.[11]

A director is associated with a company if he (or persons connected with him) controls one-fifth of the votes at a general meeting.[12] The provisions do not apply to companies merely belonging to the same group as the associated company.[13] There are exceptions for moneylending companies and banks.[14] Further, loans (in respect of relevant companies) not exceeding £10,000 may be made to directors to pay for expenditure incurred for the purposes of the company.[15] Similar provisions and controls exist in respect of 'quasi loans' and relevant companies where third parties are paid directly so that the director becomes liable to the company.[16]

(c) Similar controls exist with regard to 'credit transactions' and relevant companies as defined.[17]

(d) The provisions also prevent assignments to or assumptions of rights, obligations or liabilities by companies which would have contravened the provisions if the company had originally entered into them.[18]

(e) Criminal liability is imposed on directors of 'relevant companies' (public companies) who permit prohibited transactions.[19] Civil liability is imposed in respect of all companies in effect making the transaction voidable in analogous circumstances to rescission in equity and further making the director or connected person accountable for profits and liable to indemnify the company for losses.[20]

(f) Transfers of property to his company by a director or acquisitions of directors of his company's property valued in excess of £50,000 or ten per cent of the company's net assets (unless less than £1,000) must be approved or ratified within a reasonable period.[21] There are certain exceptions and contravention results in the transaction being voidable and the director, person connected with him and any other director authorising the transaction becomes accountable for profits and liable to indemnify losses.[22]

(g) Payments for compensation for loss of office and in connection with a takeover bid or such other company undertaking must be approved in general meeting in advance.[23]

---

[1] CA 1985, Part X.
[2] Ibid, ss 318, 231, 237, Sch 5, Part V.
[3] Ibid, s 319.
[4] Ibid, s 319(7).
[5] Ibid, s 319(1).
[6] Ibid, s 319(2).
[7] Ibid, s 319(5).
[8] Ibid, s 319(6).
[9] Ibid, ss 330(2), 334.
[10] Ibid, ss 330(3)(4), 331(6).
[11] Ibid, s 346.

12 Ibid, s 346(4).
13 Ibid, s 333.
14 Ibid, s 338.
15 Ibid, s 337(1)(2)(3).
16 Ibid, ss 330(3), 331(3).
17 Ibid, s 330(4), 331(7).
18 Ibid, s 330(6).
19 Ibid, s 342.
20 Ibid, s 341.
21 Ibid, ss 320, 321, 322.
22 Ibid, s 322(3).
23 Ibid, ss 312, 313, 314 and 316.

Duty not to use company property for own benefit without proper authority

6.23   A director, unless duly authorised, may not make a profit for himself from the use of company assets, information and opportunities. If he does he is accountable for any profit made.[1] It would seem that in some circumstances the director will be entitled in calculating profits to an allowance for his time and trouble.[2] Further, in some circumstances the consent or ratification of the activities of the director by the company will be effective to entitle the director to keep his profit.[3] The cases do not seem to elucidate the principles clearly as to when an allowance will be made and as to when consent or ratification will be effective.

So far as the former question is concerned an allowance would not be made if the case concerned an appropriation by the director of profits made in dealing with assets which had been used without the knowledge of the shareholders or the other directors in circumstances where it was known by the director that those others would not have consented. Similarly, the procurement of a consent by the exercise of majority voting power would not be effective to preclude the company obtaining an account[4] of profits nor would it seem to permit the director obtaining an allowance. Where however the asset of the company is not being appropriated but is being used for the benefit of the company in circumstances where an incidental profit is procured for the director, it would seem that the director ought on principle to be allowed an amount for his time and trouble.[5] Further if an independent board or the other shareholders consented to or ratified such profit being kept by the director there would then be, it would seem, a valid bar preventing such persons (or purchasers of the company) turning round and recovering the profit in an action for an account.[6] Of course, one problem in the *Regal* case is that it would appear that the accountable directors could have obtained consent or ratification. Accordingly, it raises the question as to whether if all the shareholders and directors know of a breach of trust and acquiesce, tacitly consenting, but in fact by oversight no formal resolution is passed, can purchasers from those shareholders use the company to recover the profit? *Regal* would appear to answer the question in the affirmative. The result, however, would appear to be inequitable and to ignore the possibility of the court holding there to have been an implied agreement amounting in effect to a resolution duly performed between all the shareholders and directors.[7]

1 *Cook v Deeks* [1916] 1 AC 554; *Regal (Hastings) Ltd v Gulliver* [1942] 1 All ER 378.
2 *Boardman v Phipps* [1967] 2 AC 46 (see first instance and CA).

3 *Regal (Hastings) Ltd v Gulliver* [1967] 2 AC 134 at 152–153.
4 *Cook v Deeks* [1916] 1 AC 554.
5 *Boardman v Phipps* [1967] 2 AC 46 at 104, 112.
6 *Regal (Hastings) Ltd v Gulliver* [1967] 2 AC 134 at 140, 152–153.
7 See *Re Duomatic Ltd* [1969] 2 Ch 365. *Re Halt Garage (1964) Ltd* [1982] 3 All ER 1016; *Rolled Steel Ltd v British Steel Corpn* [1982] Ch 478 at 490, reversed in part on appeal not affecting this point [1985] 2 WLR 908.

Relief from liability

6.24 (a) In any proceedings against a director for negligence, default, breach of duty or breach of trust the court can wholly or partly relieve him from liability if it considers he acted honestly and reasonably and, having regard to all the circumstances of the case, he ought fairly to be excused.[1]

(b) Proceedings against directors for negligence or breach of trust or any breach of duty must be commenced within six years of the wrongful act or omission.[2]
The period of limitation does not apply to fraud or a fraudulent breach of trust;[3] nor does it apply to a director who retains the company's property or converts it to his own use.[4]

(c) Directors who are liable to pay compensation in respect of any damage suffered by another person may recover contribution from any other person liable in respect of the same damage.[5] There is a similar right in equity where two or more persons are liable to the same demand.[6]

(d) Directors can recover money wrongly paid to shareholders where the recipient knew that the payment should not have been made.[7]

1 CA 1985, s 727; *Customs & Excise Comrs v Hedon Alpha Ltd* [1981] QB 818.
2 Limitation Act 1980, s 21.
3 Ibid, s 21(1).
4 Ibid, s 21(2).
5 Civil Liability (Contribution) Act 1978.
6 *Dering v Earl of Winchelsea* (1787) 1 Cox Eq Cas 318.
7 *Moxham v Grant* [1900] 1 QB 88.

Criminal liability

6.25 (a) A director or other company officer is guilty of an offence[1] and liable to imprisonment for a term not exceeding seven years if:

(i) with intent to deceive members or creditors about the affairs of the company
(ii) he publishes or concurs in publishing
(iii) a written statement or account
(iv) which to his knowledge is or may be misleading, false or deceptive
(v) in a material particular.[2]

(b) In the case of winding-up by or under the supervision of the court, the court may require the liquidator to refer any officer prima facie criminally liable to the prosecuting authority, and in the case of voluntary liquidations, liquidators are required to initiate steps to lead to the prosecution of directors where they appear to be criminally liable.[3]

(c) A person issuing a prospectus including an untrue statement is liable to imprisonment or a fine or both unless he proves the statement was immaterial or he had reasonable grounds to believe and did believe the statement.[4]

(d) The Companies Acts provide in numerous cases for fines when an officer is in default in carrying out his duties.[5]

In a winding-up the Companies Act provides further penalties of fine and imprisonment for making false statements in Company books and documents or for destroying, altering, mutilating etc company documents.[6]

---

[1] Theft Act 1968, s 19.

[2] *R v Kylsant* [1932] 1 KB 442.

[3] CA 1985, s 632.

[4] Ibid, s 70.

[5] Ibid, s 730 and Sch 24.

[6] Ibid, s 627; Prevention of Fraud (Investments) Act 1958, ss 13, 14 (as amended by the 1985 legislation). See chap 11, below.

DIRECTORS' LIABILITY TO OUTSIDERS

Contracts

6.26   Directors are not personally liable on contracts made by them for and on behalf of their company. They are mere agents. They can make themselves liable by contracting without authority or by contracting personally without disclosing the fact of agency or without purporting to bind the company.

Statutory liability

6.27   Directors may be liable:

(1) to subscribers for shares or debentures for loss or damage caused by a mis-statement in a prospectus;[1]
(2) to an allottee of shares for loss and damage caused by an irregular allotment;[2]
(3) to a subscriber for failure to repay application monies for shares where the minimum subscription has not been reached or, in the case of shares to be dealt with on a stock exchange, an application to deal on the Stock Exchange is not made or is refused;[3]
(4) when the company is found to have been fraudulently trading or there is fraud or deception etc during or prior to winding up;[4]
(5) to parties to transactions where a company commences business without a minimum requirement certificate;[5]
(6) to an existing shareholder who suffers loss on failure to comply with pre-emption requirements.

---

[1] CA 1985, s 67.

[2] Ibid, s 85(2).

3 Ibid, ss 83(4), 86(4).
4 Ibid, ss 458, 624, 625, 626, 627, 628, 629, 630 and 631.
5 Ibid, s 117(8).

Tort

6.28 A director who is party to a fraud or to the commission of any other tort is personally liable to the injured party. This may particularly be important in small companies where a director or shareholder tries to avoid personal liability for negligence where his company is not worth powder and shot.[1]

However, a director is not liable for the torts of his co-directors unless he has expressly or impliedly authorised them.[2]

1 *C Evans and Sons Ltd v Spritebrand Ltd CA* [1985] 2 All ER 415.
2 See *British Thomson-Houston v Sterling* [1924] 2 Ch 33 at 38–39; *Rainham v Belvedere* [1921] 2 AC 465 at 475; *Cargill v Bower* (1878) 10 Ch D 502; *Selangor United Rubber Estates Ltd v Cradock (No 3)* [1968] 2 All ER 1073.

Directors' duties to the company as its agent, servant or trustee

6.29 Directors are agents of the company when it acts through them.[1] Further, as referred to above, their position as directors put them in a position of trust and the courts have always tended to treat them as holding positions analogous to trustees.[2] The true position however, is that their powers are conferred on them by statute or by the constitution of the company for the purposes of the company and therefore they cannot use these powers for ulterior purposes and, by virtue of their special position as directors, they are under an obligation to execute the office faithfully which they have undertaken.[3]

Accordingly, they are liable as 'fiduciaries' to carry out their functions honestly in good faith for the proper purposes of the company. The fiduciary duties are dealt with above. The duty to carry out their functions is dealt with here.

The duty to carry out their functions is clear. It is a duty to exercise care, diligence and skill. The question of breach of such duty depends upon the degree of care, diligence and skill required in each case.[4] Directors traditionally were not intended to be experts but honest amateurs in managing the business of a company.[5]

Such directors accordingly are not expected to act with any more care than is reasonably to be expected from them having regard to their knowledge and experience. Further, such directors are not liable for errors of judgment and are exonerated if they act honestly for the benefit of the company.[6] They are also entitled to receive at face value (in the absence of suspicious circumstances) reports of experts and of other officers and managers of the company.[7] In addition they are entitled to give only intermittent attention to company business and need not attend every board meeting.[8]

Outside the area of the honest amateur the degree of care, skill and diligence can be much greater, depending upon the particular company, director and surrounding circumstances. Thus an expert appointed as such may well reasonably be expected from his greater knowledge and experience to have a greater degree of skill.[9] Directors with service contracts who are paid as executive directors for their professionalism or for their work for the company in some area or department or otherwise will reasonably be expected to be diligent in attendance at Board Meetings, skilful and careful in carrying out their work.[10] Such directors are still entitled however to delegate to servants or other directors without risk, though clearly, from his knowledge and experience such a person should be more astute in discovering inadequacy and fraud.[11]

---

[1] *Ferguson v Wilson* (1866) 2 Ch App 77.
[2] *Re Lands Allotment Co* [1894] 1 Ch 616.
[3] *Re City Equitable Fire Insurance Co* [1925] 1 Ch 407.
[4] *Re City Equitable Fire Insurance Co*, (above).
[5] *Re Brazilian Rubber Plantations & Estates Ltd* [1911] 1 Ch 425.
[6] *Lagunas Nitrate Co v Lagunas Syndicate* [1899] 2 Ch 392.
[7] *Dovey v Cory* [1901] AC 477.
[8] *Re Denham & Co* [1883] 25 Ch D 752.
[9] *Re Brazilian Rubber Plantations & Estates Ltd* [1911] 1 Ch 425.
[10] *Harmer v Cornelius* (1858) 5 CB (NS) 236.
[11] *Re City Equitable Fire Insurance Co* (above); *Dorchester Finance Co Ltd v Stebbing* (22 July 1977 (unreported)) Foster J.

INFORMATION RELATING TO DIRECTORS

Register of directors and secretaries

6.30 The register records present and former names of directors and secretaries, usual address (residential), age (where age limit applies), nationality, business occupation, directorships held in last five years (other than certain subsidiaries or parent companies), and if director of a corporation, its name and registered office.[1]

The register is open to inspection by the public. It must be amended as required and notification sent to the Registrar.[2]

---

[1] CA 1985, ss 288, 289, 290. See also para 7.13.
[2] Ibid, s 288(2) and (3).

Register of directors' interests in shares and debentures

6.31 The register must record directors' interests giving the number and amount of shares or debentures of each class.[1]

The obligations as to notification by a director are as follows:

(a) at time of appointment;[2] and, on subsequently becoming or ceasing to be interested, contracting to sell, assigning right to subscribe, or being granted or exercising or assigning a right to so subscribe by a related company[3] (hereinafter called 'relevant events');

(b) in writing expressly pursuant to CA 1985, s 324 stating any price or consideration to be paid, the relevant event and the registered names;[4]

(c) within five days following the director's appointment or the relevant subsequent event or, if he is not aware of the interest, within five days following that on which he becomes aware;[5]

(d) of all interests including:
  (i) trust interests as beneficiary
  (ii) interests held by companies which act on his instructions or of which the director controls one-third or more of the voting power;
  (iii) interests held under or acquired by contract;
  (iv) interests which he is entitled to call for;
  (v) interests in respect of shares or debentures where any right thereunder is controlled by the director (except as proxy);
  (vi) joint interests.[6]

The exemptions of notification are as follows:

(1) interests in reversion or remainder where director has life interest;
(2) interests held as bare or custodian trustee;
(3) certain interests in unit trusts and statutory schemes;
(4) any interests excepted by regulations made by the Secretary of State. These have included: co-trustees of Public Trustee;
(5) pre-emption right in shares of private company conferred by memorandum or articles;
(6) interests in industrial and providential societies.
(7) interests in certain pension schemes;
(8) interests of director in wholly owned subsidiary where the holding company maintains a register and the director is director of holding company;
(9) interests of director of wholly owned subsidiary where holding company or related company incorporated outside Great Britain.[7]

Notification includes interests of spouse and infant children.[8]

Failure to notify is punishable on summary conviction or on conviction on indictment with imprisonment or a fine.[9]

The company must keep a register of the above information and also of the grant or exercise of the right to subscribe for shares or debentures in itself at the registered office or where the register of members is kept so long as notice of the place of the register is given to the Registrar.[10]

The company must notify the relevant stock exchange of information disclosed to it under the above provisions.[11]

The register must have an index.

Inspection by members and other persons must be permitted.

The register must be available for inspection at general meeting.[12]

There are penalties for non-compliance.[13] Notification is not notice of a trust.[14]

---

1 CA 1985, ss 324, 325, 326. See also para 7.14.

2 Ibid, s 324(1).

3 Ibid, s 324(2).

4 Ibid, s 324(2)(3)(c), Sch 13, Part III.

5 Ibid, s 324(3), Sch 13, Part II.

6 Ibid, s 324, Sch 13, Part I.

7 Ibid, s 324, Sch 13, Part I, paras 9–12, Companies (Disclosure of Directors' Interests) (Exceptions) Regulations 1985 (SI 1985/802).

8 Ibid, ss 327, 328.

9 Ibid, s 324(7).

10 Ibid, s 325, Sch 13, paras 25–27.

11 Ibid, s 329.
12 Ibid, s 325(5), Sch 13, Part IV, para 29.
13 Ibid, s 326(2).
14 Ibid, Sch 13, Part IV, para 24.

Record for inspection of directors' service contracts

6.32   Companies must permit members to inspect the terms of directors' service contracts having more than twelve months to run either by keeping a copy or recording a written memorandum.[1]

The documents might be kept at the registered office or the place where the register of members is kept or the principal place of business situated in the part of Great Britain in which the company is registered.

Inspection may be carried out only by members. There are penalties for disobedience.

1 CA 1985, s 318.

Business letters

6.33   Where a business letter indicates the company's name and names one director — all directors must be named.[1]

1 CA 1985, s 305. See para 7.04.

Listed companies

6.34   The Stock Exchange must be notified of interests of directors and others in shares and debentures listed on a recognised stock exchange notified to a company and of any changes in those interests.[1]

1 CA 1985, s 329.

Acquisitions

6.35   Take-over offers must disclose benefits to be given to directors and any arrangements with them.[1]

1 CA 1985, s 314.

SECRETARY

6.36   Every company must have a secretary, who may not also be the sole director. The secretary has specific statutory duties and has to ensure that the carrying out of the administration of the company itself, in particular the activities of the board of directors, is recorded properly.[1]

1 *Panorama Developments (Guildford) Ltd v Fidelis Furnishing Fabrics Ltd* [1971] 2 QB 711.

Appointment

6.37 The secretary is (or the secretaries are) normally appointed by the directors (depending on the articles). In one man companies he cannot be the same person as the only director.[1]

The directors of a public company have a duty to ensure that the secretary is sufficiently experienced to carry out his duties. Persons qualified are experienced secretaries who have been secretaries for three out of the previous five years other than in a private company, chartered or certified accountants, chartered secretaries, cost and management accountants, public finance accountants, barristers, solicitors, advocates or other persons who the directors are satisfied are capable of carrying out the functions by reason of being a member of some other similar body.[2]

The register of directors must include the secretaries in the same way giving the same information as the directors.[3]

If the secretary cannot act then his deputy or other officer *duly* authorised by the board can deputize.[4]

[1] CA 1985, s 283.
[2] Ibid, s 286.
[3] Ibid, s 288.
[4] Ibid, s 283(3).

Powers

6.38 The secretary has ostensible authority to contract with regard to *administrative matters*.[1] Otherwise he has *no* authority except that which is conferred by the Articles or the Companies Act or specifically authorised by the directors.

[1] *Panorama Developments (Guildford) Ltd v Fidelis Furnishing Fabrics Ltd* [1971] 2 QB 711.

Duties

6.39 The secretary *customarily* has the following duties:

(1) to be present at meetings of the company (shareholders and directors);
(2) to issue all notices;
(3) to look after the company books and documents;
(4) to give information to members, directors and others entitled;
(5) to keep the official records, minutes, registers etc;
(6) to certify the transfers of shares (if duly authorised);
(7) to make returns to the registrar of companies.

The Act includes the secretary as having the following duties:

(1) to sign the annual return;[1]
(2) to verify the statement to the official receiver on winding up by the court and to the receiver when one is appointed of substantially the whole of the assets;[2]

(3) to sign the form of application to change a company from limited to unlimited or vice versa;[3]

(4) to sign the statutory statement to enable the Registrar to issue the certificates so that a public company can do business;[4]

(5) to sign the application required to change from private to public status.[5]

In addition to the above duties there are a number of general duties conferred upon the officers of the company which clearly fall within the ambit of administration matters and which, if not carried out, will result in the secretary being liable.

Examples of these matters are the numerous registers of directors and their interests, the registers of charges, the returns to the registrar of allotments and of purchases by the company of its own shares. Liability is generally only imposed where the secretary is in default, i e where he knowingly and wilfully authorises or permits the default. Generally speaking where the directors have appointed a qualified secretary there can be no excuse for such a person to allow a default to continue as soon as he knows of the default. Further there can be little excuse for such a person if he allows himself to remain ignorant in an attempt to avoid liability.

---

[1] CA 1985, s 365.
[2] Ibid, ss 496(2), 528(3).
[3] Ibid, ss 49(4), 51(4).
[4] Ibid, s 117.
[5] Ibid, ss 43(3), 685(4)(c).

Relationship with company

6.40   A secretary, if he has a contract with the company, will be entitled to his rights under that. This will usually put him in the position of a servant or employee.[1] If the secretary is a body corporate the contract is more likely to be a contract for services rather than a contract of service.

Where a secretary is an employee he has, in addition to his contractual rights, the statutory rights all employees have. These rights are modified upon winding up or upon appointment of a Receiver. Readers should refer to the standard works on employment law for these matters.

A secretary both as an employee and as an office holder cannot make a profit from company property or from his position and keep it.[2] He is accordingly accountable as a fiduciary,[3] is subject to the fraudulent trading and misfeasance jurisdiction under CA 1985, ss 458, 630, 631 and, subject to any relevant period of limitation, can be forced to pay over to the company improper gains or profits made.[4]

---

[1] *Eley v Positive Government Security Life Assurance Co Ltd* (1876) 1 Ex D 88, CA.
[2] *Reading v A-G* [1951] AC 507.
[3] *Regal (Hastings) v Gulliver* [1942] 1 All ER 378.
[4] *Selangor v Cradock* (No 3) [1968] 2 All ER 1073.

INSIDER DEALING

Introduction

6.41 In addition to the rules precluding fiduciaries using the company's assets, opportunities and information for their own benefit, it is a criminal offence for certain persons having access to inside information to deal with securities relating to the company in respect of which such information is possessed. The sections however depend on carefully drawn definitions and only affect certain specific classes of persons. The effect of the sections, beyond purely imposing criminal liability, is debatable. While misuse of information by a fiduciary may well entitle the company to compensation, use of insider information in circumstances where before insider dealing was legislated against the user would have been lawfully entitled to keep the benefit cannot, it is thought, confer of itself any new right on the company to an account nor will it entitle any company to a criminal compensation order since it will not have suffered any loss.

Persons prohibited from dealing as insiders

6.42 Dealing on recognised stock exchanges and off-market dealing is prohibited.[1]

(i)   by a connected person;
(ii)   a Crown servant;
(iii)   a take-over bidder;
(iv)   a person obtaining information from the above.

The above persons (i)–(iii) are 'insider dealers'.

---
[1] Companies Securities (Insider Dealing) Act 1985.

A connected person

6.43 In order to be 'connected' a person must be:

(a)   a director or other officer of the company (or its subsidiaries or holding company or other subsidiaries of the holding company, in the Act called 'a related company'); an employee of the company or related company; an individual in any professional or business relationship with the company or related company (or whose employer or company of which he is a director is in any such relationship),[1] and,

(b)   (except in the case of a director) in such a position as may reasonably be expected to give him access to 'unpublished, price sensitive information which it would be reasonable to expect him not to disclose except in the proper performance of his functions'.

---
[1] Companies Securities (Insider Dealing) Act 1985, s 9.

6.44 An individual who is or has been in the preceding six months knowingly a connected person:

(a) may not deal in securities of the company if he has information which he knows is unpublished, price sensitive information which he holds by virtue of being connected with the company and which it would be reasonable to expect him, by virtue of his position, not to disclose except in the proper performance of his function;[1] and,

(b) may not deal in securities of any other company if he has information which he knows is unpublished, price sensitive information in relation to the other company which he holds by virtue of being connected with his own company, and which it would be reasonable to expect him, by virtue of his position, not to disclose except in the proper performance of his functions and the information relates to an actual or contemplated transaction involving both companies or one of the companies and securities of the other or relates to the fact that such a transaction is no longer contemplated.[2]

In order to be 'unpublished price sensitive information' it must be information not generally known to those accustomed or likely to deal in securities which would materially affect the price and which relates to specific matters of concern to the company (rather than matters of a general nature).[3]

---

[1] Companies Securities (Insider Dealing) Act 1985.

[2] Ibid, s 1(2).

[3] Ibid, s 10.

6.45   A recognised stock exchange for the above purposes includes an investment exchange.[1]

Off-market dealing is any dealing (other than through a recognised stock exchange) in listed securities (or securities in respect of which price information has been published within the previous six months) through an off-market dealer (or his officer, servant or agent) who is making a market where the connected person knows that the securities are listed or otherwise advertised (as above), the dealer is an off-market dealer and that the dealer is making a market, (i e letting prospective vendors and purchasers know he is willing to deal in the shares).[2]

There are certain exemptions from liability in respect of the issue managers of off-market dealers dealing in international bonds designed to ensure that the penalization of off-market traders does not kill certain markets, e g the Eurobond market.[3] If these relaxations were not allowed, off-market dealers would be discouraged from legitimate trading by virtue of the risk that their special knowledge gained in individual deals might be 'unpublished price sensitive information'.

---

[1] [i e an organisation maintaining a system for communicating confirming security offers and deals amongst subscribers, e g an electronic system such as Ariel. Ed.] Companies Securities (Insider Dealing) Act 1985, ss 13, 16.

[2] Ibid, s 4.

[3] Ibid, s 6.

Crown servants

6.46   A present or former Crown servant who holds unpublished, price sensitive information, relating to the securities of any company, which has been obtained by virtue of his position as a Crown servant and which it would be reasonable to expect him not to disclose except in the proper performance of his functions, is barred from dealing on a recognised stock exchange or engaging in off-market dealing in those securities, to the same extent as connected persons.[1]

---

[1] Companies Securities (Insider Dealing) Act 1985, ss 2 and 3.

Take-over bidders

6.47   Take-over bidders are not prohibited from proceeding with their bids as such. They are, however, prohibited from dealing (whether 'on' or off-market) in any other capacity where their knowledge that they contemplate bidding (or no longer contemplate bidding) is unpublished price sensitive information in relation to the securities.[1]

---

[1] Companies Securities (Insider Dealing) Act 1985, s 1(5).

Third parties obtaining information from 'insider dealers'

6.48   Any individual who knows or has reasonable cause to believe that he has obtained information from an insider which constituted unpublished, price sensitive information in the hands of the insider is prohibited from dealing 'on' or off-market to the same extent as the insider dealer.[1]

---

[1] Companies Securities (Insider Dealing) Act 1985, s 1(3).

Counsellors, procurers and communicators

6.49   Individuals who are or would be insider dealers or who have obtained their information from such persons in circumstances where they also are prohibited from dealing, may not counsel or procure other persons to deal in those securities.

Those who may not counsel or procure also may not communicate the information to others if they know or have reasonable cause to believe that the information will be used for insider dealing or for counselling or procuring insider dealing.[1]

The prohibition on counselling and procuring extends to dealing on stock exchanges outside Great Britain (other than recognised stock exchanges) where the person counselling or procuring knows or has reasonable cause to believe the other person will so deal.[2]

---

[1] Companies Securities (Insider Dealing) Act 1985, s 1(7)(8).
[2] Ibid, s 5.

Permitted insider dealing

6.50   The following persons and individuals are permitted to do certain acts within limitations which would otherwise constitute 'insider dealing':

(a) international bond dealing by issue managers' (above);
(b) dealing by individuals acting otherwise than with a view to the making of a profit or the avoidance of a loss;[1]
(c) trustees or personal representatives (despite having inside information) dealing or counselling or procuring another to deal in securities if they act on the advice of a person who appeared to the trustee or personal representative to be the appropriate person from whom to seek advice and who did not appear himself to be prohibited from dealing;[2]
(d) liquidators, receivers, trustees in bankruptcy entering in transactions in the course of the exercise in good faith of their functions as such;[3]
(e) dealing by individuals using information obtained in the course of a business as a jobber being of the type it would be reasonable to expect a jobber to obtain in the ordinary course of his business and if he acts in good faith in the course of that business;[4]
(f) individuals merely completing or carrying out a transaction where otherwise they would be liable by reason of information relating to that transaction.[5]

---

[1] Companies Securities (Insider Dealing) Act 1985, s 3.
[2] Ibid, s 7.
[3] Ibid, s 3(1)(b).
[4] Ibid, s 3(1)(c).
[5] Ibid, s 3(2).

Liabilities

6.51 Contravention of the prohibition against insider dealing give rise to the following liabilities and penalties.

Criminal

On indictment: two years or unlimited fine or both.
On summary conviction: six months or fine up to £1,000 or both.
Where a person has suffered loss:

(i) a compensation order in favour of the person suffering loss;
(ii) in the Crown Court, a criminal bankruptcy order.

Civil

None, though the proceedings may disclose information giving rise to proceedings for breach of trust, confidence, contract etc.[1]

---

[1] Companies Securities (Insider Dealing) Act 1985, s 8(3).

Directors' option dealing

6.52 It is an offence for a director in respect of the company of which he is a director or its related companies:

(i) to buy the right to call for the delivery of a specified number or amount of quoted shares or debentures at a specified price and within a specified time ('call' option);[1]

(ii) to buy the right to make delivery of a specified number or amount of quoted shares or debentures at a specified price and within a specified time ('put' option);[2]

(iii) to buy the right (at the election of the director) to call for or make delivery of a specified number or amount of quoted shares or debentures at a specified price and within a specified time.[3]

The prohibition extends to the director, spouse and minor children.
The prohibition does not extend to:

(i) private companies;[4]

(ii) unquoted securities;[5]

(iii) rights to subscribe for shares;[6]

(iv) purchase of debentures carrying the right to subscribe for shares or to be converted into shares.[7]

Dealings by a spouse or children are not penalized if they can prove they had no reason to believe their spouse or parent was a director of the company.[8]

---

[1] CA 1985, s 323(1)(a).
[2] Ibid, s 323(1)(b).
[3] Ibid, s 323(1)(c).
[4] Ibid, s 323(3).
[5] Ibid, s 323(3).
[6] Ibid, s 323(5).
[7] Ibid, s 323(5).
[8] Ibid, s 327.

Liabilities

6.53 Contravention of the prohibition against option dealing gives rise to the following liabilities and penalties.

Criminal

On indictment: two years or unlimited fine or both.
On summary conviction: six months or fine not exceeding £1,000 or both.

Civil

None, save that contracts made for an illegal purpose or tainted with illegality are void.

Further insider control

6.54 The City Code on Take-Overs and Mergers includes rules intended to prevent the abuse of inside information; The Stock Exchange requires listed companies to adopt rules controlling directors of listed companies regarding dealing in their securities in terms consistent with the Model Code issued by the Stock Exchange.

7 Administration, registers and returns

Keith Walmsley

STATUTORY BOOKS AND REGISTERS

7.01 The companies legislation requires a number of statutory books and registers to be maintained with respect to every registered company. In some cases, these are an important part of a company's original records, e g the Register of Members or minute book, evidencing entitlements or interests of members or others. In most cases, however, the prime purpose is to make information regarding the affairs of the company publicly available and the register is not of material evidential significance regarding the matters recorded in it.

The following table, Table 1, lists the registers and books required to be maintained and indicates where they must be kept and whether they are available for public inspection.

Statutory registers (including minute books and accounting records) may be kept either in the form of bound books or by recording the relevant matters in any other manner; in the latter case adequate precautions must be taken for guarding against falsification and facilitating its discovery.[3] The registers may be kept otherwise than in a legible form (e g on a computer) so long as the recording is capable of being reproduced in a legible form.[4]

Registers of debenture holders are not included in the table 1, opposite as there is no statutory requirement to keep such registers.[5] Where, however, such a register is kept, similar provisions apply with respect to location of register (and notification of location to the Registrar) and rights of inspection of the register as apply to the register of members.[6]

It should be noted that where a requirement is imposed to keep a statutory register, this requirement is not excused if no entries yet need to be made in the register. It may still be informative for a person inspecting a register to find no entries in the register (e g the register of charges) as this may amount to a confirmation that no registrable matters exist.

---

[1] Unless the register of members has at all times been kept at the registered office, notice of the place at which it is kept and of any change of location, must be given to the Registrar (on form 353). (s 353(2)); similar provisions apply in the case of the register of directors' interests (form 325 being applicable) (s 325; Sch 13 Part IV).

[2] The register must be open to the inspection of any member of the company without charge (and of any other person on payment of a fee not exceeding 5p, no fee being payable by any creditor of the company in relation to the register of charges or by any person in relation to the register of interests in shares) during business hours for at least 2 hours each day. Any person may also require the company to provide (within 10 days from the date of the request for same) a copy of the register of members, register of directors' interests or register of interests in shares, or

TABLE 1

Register or book	Where to be kept	Whether available for public inspection	CA 1985 section imposing requirement	Cross reference in this guide
Register of members	Registered office or some other place (within the jurisdiction) notified to the Registrar	Yes[2]	ss 352, 353	7.9
Register of directors and secretaries	Registered office	Yes[2]	ss 288–290	7.13
Register of directors' interests in shares and debentures	Registered office or same place as register of members[1]		s 325	7.14
Register of interests in shares (applicable only to public companies)	Same place as register of directors' interests	Yes[2]	s 211	7.15
Register of charges (applicable only to limited companies) and copies of instruments creating charges	Registered office	Yes[2]	ss 406, 407	7.17
Minute books of general meetings and board meetings	Registered office (minutes of general meetings); board minutes may be kept where directors determine	No (but members of the company may inspect minutes of general meetings)	ss 382, 383	8.133–8.134
Directors' service contracts (copies or memoranda of terms)	Registered office, place where register of members kept or principal place of business (if within the jurisdiction)	No (but members of the company may inspect)	s 318	6.22, 6.32
Accounting records	Where directors determine	No	ss 221, 222	

any part, for a fee not exceeding 10p per 100 words copied. Copies of instruments creating charges are only open to the inspection of members and creditors of the company.

  [3] CA 1985, s 722.

  [4] Ibid, s 723; see also the Companies (Registers and other Records) Regulations 1985, SI 1985/724.

  [5] There may be an obligation to keep a register under the terms of the debentures.

  [6] CA 1985, ss 190 and 191.

RETURNS AND FORMS

7.02 It will be seen that most of the books and registers listed in table 1 are available for public inspection. Accessibility of these for scrutiny at the registered office (or other permitted location) is accordingly one of the more important ways provided in the companies legislation for the publication of information regarding a company's affairs.

The other most important way in which such information is made public is by requiring particulars to be filed at the Companies Registry of important changes in a company's constitution or affairs and by requiring certain information regarding a company's affairs to be filed on a regular periodic basis. In most cases the information is filed on companies forms (available from the Companies Registry or from law stationers) prescribed by statutory instrument.

Table 2 lists the main events requiring the filing of information at the Companies Registry.

The information filed is available for inspection on microfiche at the Companies Registry and includes, for the sake of completeness, particulars of the location of the company's books and registers open to public inspection if they are not located at the registered office.

OFFICIAL NOTIFICATION

7.03 If the companies legislation requires a prescribed form or other document to be filed with the Registrar, this obligation is generally backed by provision for default fines or other penalties.[1] The principle of 'official notification' adds a further, possibly more serious, consequence of default. The Registrar is required to publish in the Gazette notice of the issue or receipt by him of specified forms and documents (e g relating to changes of directors or registered office, changes to memorandum or articles, allotments of shares, special resolutions or winding-up resolutions).[2] A company is not entitled to rely, against other persons, on the following events:

(a) the making of a winding-up order (or the appointment of a liquidator in a voluntary winding up),

(b) alteration of the memorandum or articles of association,

(c) change of directors, or

(d) (as regards service of any document on the company) change of registered office

unless the event had been notified at the material time (or is shown by the company to have been known at that time to the person concerned).[3] If the material time falls on or before the fifteenth day after the date of official noti-

TABLE 2

Event requiring filing of information at Companies Registry	Forms or documents to be filed	CA 1985 section imposing requirement	Cross reference in this guide
Formation of company	Memorandum and articles of association, forms 10, 12 and PUC 1 (and possibly form 224 re accounting reference date)	ss 10, 12, 13, 224	1.17–1.23
Change of registered office	Form 287	s 287	7.8
Change of directors or secretary or in their particulars	Form 288	ss 288–290	7.13
Increase of nominal capital or other change in capital structure	Form 123 (with copy of resolution) or form 122 or various forms re reduction or repayment of shares or changes of class rights	ss 121–141	Chap 4
Allotment of new shares	Relevant form PUC or form 88(2) (and if consideration other than cash, form 88(3) or copy of contract for allotment)	s 88 and Finance Act 1973 Part V	
Passing of special or extraordinary resolution of members	Copy of resolution	s 380	
Alterations to memorandum or articles of association	Copy of relevant resolution and reprint of memorandum or articles, as altered	ss 4–6, 9, 16–18	
Change of name of company	Copy of relevant resolution (and fee of £40)	s 28	77
Resignation or removal of auditor	Copy of notice of resignation or, if auditor removed, form 386	ss 386, 390	10.13, 10.17
Change of accounting reference date	Form 225(1) or 225(2)	ss 225, 226	7.18
Registration of a charge created by the company	Form 395 (or 397, 398, 400)	Part XII	7.19
Annual return	Form 363 (and fee of £20) — copy of accounts also requires to be filed	ss 241, 363–365	
Appointment of receiver to, or winding-up of, company	Various	Parts XIX and XX	11.33

fication, the company is precluded from relying on the happening of the event only if it is shown that the person concerned was unavoidably prevented from knowing of the event at that time.

---

1 See CA 1985, Sch 24.

2 Ibid, s 711.

3 Ibid, s 42; however, publication under s 711 of a company's liquidation does not give the company's landlord constructive notice of the liquidation: *Official Custodian for Charities v Parway Estates Developments Ltd* [1985] Ch 151, CA.

HEADED STATIONERY

7.04   A further way in which information regarding a company is required to be made public is by certain information having to be shown in legible characters on headed stationery and on certain other business documentation. The full name of a company must be shown on all its business letters and in all notices and other official publications of the company and in all bills of exchange, promissory notes, endorsements, cheques and orders for money or goods purporting to be signed by or on behalf of the company and on all bills or parcels, invoices, receipts and letters of credit of the company.[1]

The following information must be shown on all business letters and order forms[2] of a company:

(a)   the place of registration of the company[3] and its registration number

(b)   the address of its registered office[4]

(c)   if the company is an investment company within the meaning of CA 1985, s 266, the fact that it is such a company

(d)   if the company is a limited company exempt from the obligation to use the word 'limited' as part of its name, the fact that it is a limited company.[5]

There is no obligation to give details of share capital on business letters and order forms, but if any reference is made this must be to paid-up share capital.[6]

There is no requirement to state the names of all directors on headed stationery. If, however, the name of any director is shown (otherwise than in the text or as a signatory), the names of all the directors must be given[7] including Christian names or initials.

---

1 CA 1985, s 349.

2 In the view of the Department of Trade and Industry, 'order forms' means forms which a company makes available for other persons to order goods and services from the company including coupons in newspapers which the public fill in asking for goods to be supplied; it is submitted that the expression could also cover forms used by the company itself to order goods or services from others.

3 I e 'England and Wales', 'Cardiff', 'Wales', 'Scotland' or 'Edinburgh'; the Registrar has stated that companies using the terms 'England' or 'London' for this purpose were not required to change their letterheads as a result of the move of the Companies Registry to Cardiff.

4 Even if the only address shown is the registered office, in the view of the Department of Trade and Industry, the fact that it is the registered office must be stated.

5 CA 1985, s 351, as the section is intended to give effect to the First Company Law Directive (68/151/EEC), which relates only to limited companies, its provisions would not appear to apply to unlimited companies.

6 Ibid.

7 CA 1985, s 305; this provision does not apply to companies registered before 23 November 1916.

COMPANY SEAL

7.05 Reference has already been made to the need for a company to execute certain documents under seal.[1] Every incorporated company is required to have its name engraved in legible characters on its seal.[2]

The articles of association usually contain provisions regulating the affixing of the seal and the attestation of the use of the seal.[3] If a sealed document is on the face of it properly executed (e g in accordance with the articles of association of the company), persons dealing with the company are entitled to presume that the document is validly sealed.[4] Further, regardless of the provision of the articles of the company concerned, in favour of a purchaser[5] a deed is deemed duly executed if the seal of the company is affixed to the deed in the presence of and attested by its clerk, secretary or other permanent officer or his deputy and one member of the board of directors, council or other governing body (for this purpose it is sufficient if a seal purporting to be the company's seal has been affixed to the deed and for the sealing to have been attested by persons purporting to hold any of the specified offices).[6]

A company may have, for use for sealing securities issued by the company and for sealing documents creating or evidencing securities so issued, an official seal which is a facsimile of the company's common seal with the addition on its face of the word 'Securities'.[7] The use of such a seal will be found convenient to enable a service registrar located away from the company's premises to seal share certificates issued by the registrar on behalf of the company.

A company which transacts business abroad may, if authorised by its articles, have an official seal for use in an overseas territory and may by writing under its common seal authorise a person in the territory to affix the official seal to any deed or document to which the company is a party. The official seal will be a facsimile of the company's common seal with the addition to its face of the name of every territory, district or place where it is to be used.[8]

1 E g deeds (see para 1.74, above) or share certificates (see para 5.10, above).

2 CA 1985, s 350.

3 See Table A, reg 101.

4 See CA 1985, s 35 and *Gloucester County Bank v Rudry etc Co* [1895] 1 Ch 629 but cp *Ruben v Great Fingall Consolidated* [1906] AC 439; *Clarke v Imperial Gas etc Co* (1832) 4 B & Ad 315 and *Hill v Manchester etc Co* (1833) 5 B & Ad 866 as regards the circumstances in which the presumption of validity may be rebutted.

5 But not in favour of the company itself.

6 Law of Property Act 1925, s 74.

7 CA 1985, s 40 (see CC(CP)A 1985, s 11 as regards companies incorporated before 12 February 1979).

8 CA 1985, s 39.

COMPANY NAMES — PUBLICATION

7.06   The name of a company must be kept painted or affixed on the outside of the office of the company or place of its business in a conspicuous place and in legible letters. The name must also be engraved in legible characters on the company's seal.[1] Further, as already mentioned,[2] the name must be shown on various types of business documents issued by a company.

Breach of these requirements renders the company and any offices in default liable to a fine. More seriously, if any officer of a company or any person on its behalf signs or authorises the signature on behalf of a company of any bill of exchange, promissory note, endorsement, cheque or order for money or goods in which the name of the company is not stated as required, he is personally liable to the holder of the bill of exchange, etc for the amount thereof unless it is duly paid by the company.[3] Mis-statement of the name of a company in such a document (even of a minor nature such as omission of an ampersand)[4] may result in personal liability even if the holder has not been misled thereby.[5] The use of conventional abbreviations for corporate status such as 'Ltd', 'PLC' or 'Co' are not, however, treated as being mis-statements for this purpose.[6]

---

[1] CA 1985, ss 348 and 350; see para. 7.05, above.
[2] See para 7.4, above.
[3] CA 1985, s 349(4).
[4] *Hendon v Adelman* (1973) 117 Sol Jo 631.
[5] *Durham Fancy Goods Ltd v Michael Jackson (Fancy Goods Ltd* [1968] 2 QB 839 at 846.
[6] *Banque de L'Indochine et de Suez SA v Euroseas Group Finance Co Ltd* [1981] 3 All ER 198; see also CA 1985, s 27.

CHANGE OF COMPANY NAME

7.07   A company name may be changed by special resolution passed in general meeting.[1] The new name takes effect from the date on which the Registrar issues an altered certificate of incorporation showing the new name.[2] The new name must be acceptable for registration under the control of company names provisions[3] and it is also desirable that the chosen name should not be such as to render the company liable to a 'passing off' action.[4] A change of name does not affect any rights or obligations of the company or render defective any legal proceedings commenced in the old name prior to the change of name which may be continued under the new name.[5]

In certain cases the Secretary of State has power to direct a company to change its name from an undesirable name; this applies to names adopted on a voluntary change of name as well as to names adopted on original incorporation.[6]

---

[1] CA 1985, s 28(1); a fee of £40 is payable when a print of the special resolution is filed with the Registrar.
[2] Ibid, s 28(1) and (6).
[3] See para 1.25, above; in particular the name must not be 'too like' or 'the same as' a name already on the Registrar's index or be otherwise prohibited and if specified 'restricted' words are included in the name the necessary consents must first be obtained.
[4] See para 1.25, above.

5 CA 1985, s 28(7).
6 See para 1.27, above, CA 1985, ss 28(2) and (3) and 32.

CHANGE OF REGISTERED OFFICE

7.08 Any change in the situation of the registered office of a company[1] (which must be situated in England, Wales or Scotland)[2] must be notified to the Registrar within 14 days of the change.[3] Changes of registered office are required to be 'officially notified' by the Registrar,[4] by publication in the Gazette. The new registered office must be situated within the part of Great Britain specified for this purpose in the memorandum of association of the company.[5] All communications and notices may be addressed to a company at its registered office[6] and legal process and other documents may be served on a company by leaving it at or sending it by post to its registered office.[7] The location of the registered office is also of importance as the place at which certain statutory books and registers of the company are required to be kept.[8]

1 The change is usually authorised by a resolution of the board of directors.
2 CA 1985, s 2(1)(b); see n. 5, below.
3 Ibid, s 287(2); form 287 is required to be used for this purposes. See para 7.4, above regarding the requirement to state registered office on headed stationery.
4 See para 7.3, above; the company may accordingly not be able to rely on the change until its official notification is complete.
5 See para 1.17, above; thus a company registered in England and Wales cannot change its registered office to an address situated in Scotland.
6 CA 1985, s 287(1).
7 Ibid, s 725(1).
8 See para 7.1, above.

REGISTER OF MEMBERS

7.09 Every company is required to keep a register of its members containing the following particulars:

(a) the names and addresses of all members and (if applicable) a statement of the shares (or stock) held by each member distinguishing each share by its number (if any) and class (if applicable) and of the amount paid or credited as paid on the shares of each member and, in any other case where the company has more than one class of members, the class to which each member belongs
(b) the date on which each person was registered as a member
(c) the date at which any person ceased to be a member.[1]

The entry in the register relating to a former member may be removed from the register 20 years after the date on which he ceased to be a member.[2]

The register should be kept up to date to reflect any changes in particulars of registered members whether resulting from legal transfers or transmissions of shares or from changes of name or address of existing shareholders, satisfactory evidence of the change having been produced to the company. It has been questioned whether a secretary may give effect to such alterations of the register without express authorisation by the board of directors.[3] In a voluntary winding-up the register may be altered by the liquidator to give effect to transfers sanctioned by him.[4]

If a company has more than 50 members it must, unless the register is itself alphabetical, also keep an index of members' names. This must be kept with the register and is open to inspection in the same way as the register; the index must be altered to reflect any changes in the register within fourteen days of the change.[5]

The register of members is prima facie[6] evidence of any matters directed or authorised by the Act to be inserted in it.[7]

A company may close the register, on giving notice by advertisement in a newspaper circulating in the district in which its registered office is situated, for a period or periods not exceeding in total 30 days in each year.[8]

---

[1] CA 1985, s 352; see para 7.1, above regarding the form, location and inspection of statutory registers.

[2] Ibid, s 352(6) and (7).

[3] *Matlock Old Bath Hydropathic Co Ltd, Wheatcroft's Case* (1873) 29 LT 324 at 326; *Chida Mines Ltd v Anderson* (1905) 22 TLR 27: these longstanding authorities are now rather out of line with current commercial practice particularly having regard to the extent to which the areas of ostensible authority of the secretary have increased since the early part of this century.

[4] CA 1985, s 576; *National Bank of Wales, Re Taylor, Phillips and Rickard's Case* [1897] 1 Ch 298.

[5] CA 1985, s 354.

[6] But not conclusive evidence, e g if a person has been placed on the register without his consent he may enforce removal of his name (*Reese River etc Co v Smith* (1869) LR 4 HL 64), though such a person should act without delay when the matter comes to his notice or he may become subject to the liabilities of membership by being 'held out' as a member (*Re Scottish Petroleum Co* (1883) 23 ChD 413 at 434). See generally para 7.11, below regarding rectification of the register.

[7] CA 1985, s 361.

[8] Ibid, s 358; in practice this provision is little used, companies generally instead fixing a 'record date' for striking members' entitlements (e g on declaration of a dividend).

NOTICES OF TRUST NOT TO BE ENTERED ON THE REGISTER OF MEMBERS

7.10 In the case of companies registered in England and Wales, no notice of any trust, expressed, implied or constructive may be entered on the register of members.[1] The company is accordingly only concerned with the registered members who will be solely liable to the company for any calls[2] and conversely beneficiaries under a trust affecting shares in the company have, as such, no direct rights against the company. There is no objection to registered shareholdings being divided into designated accounts bearing distinctive references after the name of the member (e g 'A' a/c, 'B' a/c, etc) provided the reference is not in a form which indicates or implies the existence of a trust.

---

[1] CA 1985, s 360; the disclosure obligations regarding directors' interests and the keeping of a register of these interests (see para 7.14, below) are not in conflict with this provision (Sch 13, para 24).

[2] In *Re Perkins, ex p Mexican Santa Barbara Mining Co* (1890) 24 QBD 613 it was held that a company had no lien upon certain of its shares for a debt due to it by the beneficiary of a trust to which the shares were subject.

RECTIFICATION OF REGISTER OF MEMBERS

7.11 Errors or mis-statements[1] in the register of members may not be corrected without the authority of the court.[2] S 359 provides a summary procedure for applying to the court for an order for rectification of the register in the following cases:

(a) if the name of any person is, without sufficient cause; entered in or omitted from the register, or
(b) if default is made or unnecessary delay takes place in entering on the register the fact of any person having ceased to be a member.

The application to the court may be made by the person aggrieved, any member of the company or the company itself. The jurisdiction to make a rectification order is not affected by the liquidation of the company.[3] If appropriate, the court may appoint the applicant or some other person to make the necessary correcting entry in the register.[4]

---

[1] See para 7.9, n 6, above.
[2] *Gardiner v Victoria Estates Co Ltd* 1885 12 R 1356, (Ct of Sess); in modern practice minor clerical slips are, however, commonly corrected without recourse to the Court, the company requiring in appropriate cases a no sub-sale/no change of beneficial ownership declaration from the person who lodged the transfer or other instrument giving rise to an incorrect entry.
[3] *Re Sussex Brick Co* [1904] 1 Ch 598.
[4] *Reese River etc Co v Smith* (1869) LR 4 HL 64 at 80.

OVERSEAS BRANCH REGISTERS

7.12 A company having a share capital whose objects comprise the transaction of business in certain prescribed overseas countries or territories[1] may keep in any of those countries or territories in which it transacts business a branch register of members resident there.[2]

Notice must be given to the Registrar (on form 362), within fourteen days of the relevant event, of the situation of the office where the register is kept and of any change in its situation or of its discontinuance.[3] The register may be rectified by any competent court in the country or territory concerned[4] and forms part of the main register of members,[5] (shares registered in an overseas branch register being accordingly not separately included in the main register kept in Great Britain).[6] The company must transmit to its registered office a copy of every entry in an overseas branch register as soon as may be after the making of the entry and the company must keep duly entered up a duplicate of each overseas branch register (the duplicate to be kept with the main register of members).[7]

---

[1] The countries or territories include Northern Ireland; any part of Her Majesty's dominions outside the United Kingdom, the Channel Islands or the Isle of Man; and the countries listed in Sch 14, Part I.
[2] CA 1985, s 362; the description 'overseas branch register' supersedes the earlier expressions 'dominion register' or 'colonial register' appearing in earlier enactments or instruments (see s 362(2)).
[3] CA 1985, Sch 14, Part II, para 1.
[4] Ibid, para 3.

REGISTER OF DIRECTORS AND SECRETARIES

7.13 Every company is required to keep a register of its directors and secretaries.[1]

The register must contain the following particulars in respect of each director:[2]

(a) in the case of an individual
- (i) his present Christian name (or forename) and surname,[3]
- (ii) any former[4] Christian name (or forename) or surname,[3]
- (iii) his usual residential address,
- (iv) his nationality,
- (v) his business occupation (if any),
- (vi) any other directorships which are held by him or which have been held by him at any time during the previous five years,[5]
- (vii) if the company is subject to CA 1985, s 293 (age limit for directors), the date of his birth,

(b) in the case of a corporation
- (i) its corporate name,
- (ii) its registered or principal office.

The register must contain the following particulars in respect of the secretary (or in respect of each joint secretary):[6]

(a) in the case of an individual
- (i) his present Christian name (or forename) and surname,[3]
- (ii) any former[4] Christian name (or forename) and surname,[3]
- (iii) his usual residential address;

(b) in the case of a corporation (or Scottish firm)
- (i) its corporate or firm name,
- (ii) its registered or principal office.

Any change among the directors or secretary or in their particulars must be notified to the Registrar within fourteen days of the change;[7,8] it is, of course, also necessary to update the register to reflect the change.

---

1 CA 1985, s 288; see para 7.1, regarding the form, location and inspection of statutory registers and para 7.4, above regarding the possible need to give the names of directors on company stationery.

2 CA 1985, s 289; for this purpose, 'director' includes a shadow director (i e a person in accordance with whose directions or instructions the directors are accustomed to act, but excluding such acting only on advice given in a professional capacity — s 741).

3 In the case of a peer or person usually known by a title different from his surname, that title is treated as being his surname (s 289(2)(b)).

4 References to a former name do not include
- (a) in the case of a peer or person known by a British title different from his surname, the name by which he was known prior to adoption of or succession to the title; or
- (b) a former Christian name or surname disused or changed before the person concerned attained the age of 18, or which has been changed or disused for at least 20 years.
- (c) the name by which a married woman was known prior to marriage (s 289(2)(c)).

⁵ It is not necessary to include particulars of a directorship not held at any time during the preceding five years, or a directorship held in a dormant company (as defined in CA 1985, s 252(5)) or in a company which is a wholly owned member of the same group of companies as the company keeping the register; 'company' for this purpose includes any body corporate incorporated in Great Britain (s 289(3) and (4)).

⁶ CA 1985, s 290; where all the partners in a firm are joint secretaries, the name and principal office of the firm may be stated instead of the particulars listed below.

⁷ CA 1985, s 288(2); the prescribed form 288 contains provision, where used to notify the appointment of a new director or secretary, for a consent to act in that capacity to be signed by the appointee.

⁸ See para 7.3, above regarding the requirement for the Registrar to give official notification of the change.

REGISTER OF DIRECTORS' INTERESTS IN SHARES AND DEBENTURES

7.14   Every company is required to keep a register of directors' interests in the shares and debentures of the company.¹ Any information disclosed to the company by a director² under s 324 (duty of disclosure re interests in shares or debentures of the company)³ must be entered in the register against the director's name with the date of the entry.⁴ The company is also required, on its own initiative, to enter in the register details of the grant to a director of any right to subscribe for shares or debentures of the company or of the exercise of such right.⁵ Entries must be made within three business days of the obligation to make the entry arising.⁶

The register must be produced at the commencement of the company's annual general meeting and remain open and accessible during the meeting to any person attending the meeting.⁷

---

¹ CA 1985, s 325; see para 7.1, above regarding the form, location and inspection of statutory registers (Sch 13, Part IV lays down detailed requirements regarding the manner of keeping the register). See also para 6.31.

² For this purpose a shadow director is treated as a director (CA 1985, s 325(6)).

³ See para 6.19.

⁴ CA 1985, s 325(2); if the shares or debentures concerned are listed on The Stock Exchange the company must notify The Stock Exchange of the information received, by the next business day (s 329).

⁵ CA 1985, s 325(3) and (4).

⁶ Ibid, Sch 13, para 22.

⁷ Ibid, Sch 13, para 29.

REGISTER OF INTERESTS IN SHARES

7.15   Every public company is required to keep a register of interests in shares. Any information disclosed to the company by any person under Part VI of CA 1985 (disclosure of interests in shares) must be entered in the register against the name of that person with the date of the entry.¹ Entries must be made within three business days of the obligation to make the entry arising.²

A person is liable to make disclosure to a public company if he knowingly becomes interested (or becomes aware that he is interested) in five per cent or more of any class of its voting share capital, if he ceases to be so interested or if there is a one percentage point change in an already notified interest.[3] For this purpose the interests of a person's spouse and minor children or any body corporate of which he has control of the board or one third shareholding control are aggregated with his own interests.[4] Interests are widely defined as including an interest of any kind whatsoever, e g interests under a trust, under a purchase contract, rights to call for delivery of shares and 'put' or 'call' options.[5] Certain interests are, however, disregarded including discretionary interests under a trust, interests as bare trustee and interests held by way of security as part of a banking transaction.[6]

The required notification must be given to the company in writing within five business days of the obligation to notify arising and must include the name and address of the person giving the notification and the following information:

(a)   the share capital to which it relates
(b)   the number of shares in which the person knows he is interested (or that the person no longer has a notifiable interest, in which case (c) below will not be relevant)
(c)   the identity of each registered holder of shares to which the notification relates and the number of shares held by that holder (so far as known to the person notifying)
(d)   if the person is a director of the company, that the notification is given in fulfilment of a specified provision of Part VI of CA 1985.[7]

Where persons are acting 'in concert' together in relation to acquisitions of shares in a public company, they will each be regarded as interested for the above purposes in any shares covered by the arrangement and may accordingly each be under an obligation to make notification to the company and to keep the other 'concert parties' informed of any acquisitions or disposals of shares under the arrangement.[8] This provision applies where the persons concerned knowingly enter into an agreement or arrangement including provision for the acquisition by any of them of interests in voting shares of the company if this also includes provisions imposing obligations or restrictions on any party with respect to the use, retention or disposal of any interests acquired under it and an interest in the shares of the company is in fact acquired under the agreement or arrangement.[9] The provision does not apply to an agreement which is not legally binding (unless it involves mutuality in the undertakings expectations or understandings of the parties) or to bona fide underwriting or sub-underwriting agreements.[10]

Where a person authorises an agent to acquire or dispose of shares on his behalf, he must secure that the agent notifies him of any transactions effected by the agent which may give rise to disclosure obligations under the above provisions.[11]

---

[1] CA 1985, s 211; see para 7.1, above regarding the form, location and inspection of statutory registers (ss 211 and 217–219 lay down detailed requirements regarding the manner of keeping the register).
[2] CA 1985, ss 211(3) and 220(2).
[3] Ibid, ss 198–201.
[4] Ibid, ss 203 and 207.
[5] Ibid, s 208.
[6] Ibid, s 209.

[7] Ibid, ss 202 and 210(2).
[8] Ibid, ss 204–206.
[9] Ibid, s 204.
[10] Ibid, s 204(6).
[11] Ibid, s 210(1).

COMPANY INVESTIGATIONS OF INTERESTS IN ITS SHARES

7.16 A public company may require any person whom the company knows or has reasonable cause to believe to be interested (or to have been interested within the previous three years) in voting shares of the company to confirm whether or not this is the case and if the confirmation is in the affirmative to give, if required, the following information to the company:

(a) particulars of his own present interest in voting shares of the company (or interests held within the previous three years);
(b) where any other interest in the shares subsists (or subsisted within the previous three years), such particulars of that interest as the company may require (so far as lies within his knowledge);
(c) where his interest is a past interest, particulars of the identity of the person who held the interest immediately upon his ceasing to hold it (so far as lies within his knowledge).[1]

Any requirements imposed on a person under this provision must be the subject of a notice in writing to the person concerned giving him a reasonable time in which to comply.[2] Any information received by the company in response to a requirement imposed by it must be entered in a separate part of its register of interests in shares[3] against the name of the registered holder of the shares, the entry to indicate the fact that the requirement was imposed and the date on which it was imposed.[4]

If a person fails to comply with a requirement imposed under the above provisions, the company may apply to the court for an order that the shares in question be subject to restrictions under Part XV of CA 1985.[5] The Secretary of State may (if there are special reasons) grant exemption from complying with requirements imposed under the provision.[6]

A company may be required to exercise its powers under these provisions on the requisition of the holders of one-tenth of the paid up voting share capital of the company; the requisition(s) must state the manner in which the powers are to be exercised and give reasonable grounds for requiring the company to exercise those powers in the manner specified.[7]

On conclusion of a requisitioned investigation the company must cause a report of the information received thereunder to be prepared, the report to be available for inspection at the registered office. If the investigation is not concluded within three months, interim reports must be prepared and made available at three-monthly intervals.[8]

[1] CA 1985, s 212.
[2] Ibid, s 212(4).
[3] See para 7.15, above.
[4] CA 1985, s 213(1).
[5] Ibid, s 216(1); the articles of association of the company may also provide for these or other forms of disenfranchisement of the shares in question.

[6] Ibid, s 216(5).
[7] Ibid, s 214.
[8] Ibid, ss 215 and 219.

REGISTER OF CHARGES

7.17   Every limited company is required to keep a register of charges and to enter in the register all charges specifically affecting property of the company and all floating charges on the company's undertaking or any of its property.[1] Each entry must give:

(i)   a short description of the property charged;
(ii)   the amount of the charge;
(iii)   the names of the persons entitled to the charge (unless a security to bearer).[2]

Failure to enter a charge in the register does not affect the validity of the security[3] and errors on the register do not affect priorities[4] (but failure to file particulars with the Registrar as required may affect priorities).[5] Every company (whether or not limited) must cause a copy of every instrument creating a charge requiring registration under Part XII of CA 1985 to be kept at its registered office.[6]

[1] CA 1985, s 407; see para 7.1, above regarding the form, location and inspection of statutory registers.
[2] Ibid, s 407(2).
[3] *Wright v Horton* (1887) 12 App Cas 371, HL.
[4] *Re General South American Co* (1876) 2 ChD 337, CA.
[5] See para 7.18, below.
[6] Ibid, s 406; see para 7.1, n 2, above regarding inspection of such copies.

REGISTRATION OF CHARGES AT THE COMPANIES REGISTRY

7.18   In addition to the requirement mentioned in para 7.17, above which applies to all charges, a further formality is required for certain categories of charges. Prescribed particulars of these (together with any instrument creating the charge) must be filed with the Registrar for registration within 21 days after the date of the charge's creation, failing which the charge will be void against the liquidator and any creditor of the company.[1]

The categories of charges[2] affected are as follows:

(a)   charge to secure an issue of debentures;
(b)   charge on uncalled share capital;
(c)   charge created or evidenced by an instrument which, if executed by an individual, would be registrable as a bill of sale,
(d)   charge on land (wherever situated) or any interested in it, but not including a charge for any rent or other periodical sum issuing out of the land;
(e)   charge on book debts;
(f)   floating charge on the company's undertaking or property;[3]

(g) charge on calls made but not paid;
(h) charge on a ship or aircraft, or any share in a ship;
(i) charge on goodwill, on a patent or licence under a patent, on a trademark or on a copyright or a licence under a copyright.

Only charges created by a company are registrable. Charges arising by operation of law are not registrable.[4] However, an equitable charge which arises in law on a deposit of title deeds is regarded as being created by agreement and thus as requiring registration.[5]

Charges not registered within 21 days of creation are void only as against the creditors and a liquidator — they are valid as against the company or a receiver. Should a charge become void in this way this does not affect the validity of the liability intended to be secured which thus ranks instead as an unsecured liability — indeed when the charge becomes void the money secured by it immediately becomes payable.[6] Non-registration is also likely to prejudice the priority of ranking of a security.

The company is required to effect registration of registrable charges created by it though it is open to any person interested in a charge to effect registration.[7] On registration of a charge the Registrar issues a certificate of registration, a copy of which must be endorsed on every debenture or debenture stock certificate the payment of which is secured by the charge concerned.[8] Where property ceases to be subject to a registered charge, the Registrar may on receipt of a statutory declaration in the prescribed form, enter a memorandum of satisfaction in the Registrar's register of charges to record this.[9]

Should registration not be effected within the time limit of 21 days or a registration be subject to an error, the court has jurisdiction to extend the time allowed for registration or to rectify the registered particulars. The jurisdiction is exercisable where the non-registration or error was accidental or due to inadvertence or to some other sufficient cause or is not of a nature to prejudice the position of creditors or shareholders or on other grounds it is just and equitable to grant relief.[10] If late registration is permitted this would usually be without prejudice to the rights of parties acquired during the period between the date of creation of the charge and the date of its actual registration.[11] An order for extension of time would be granted only in exceptional cases if a winding up has commenced.[12]

The registration provisions extend to charges on property in England and Wales which are created, and to charges on property in England and Wales which is acquired, by a body corporate incorporated outside Great Britain which has an established place of business in England and Wales.[13]

---

[1] CA 1985, s 396; registration is also required when a company acquires property subject to an existing charge in which event time limits run from the date of acquisition.

[2] For this purpose the expression 'charge' includes a mortgage (CA 1985, s 396(4)).

[3] Certain forms of 'retention of title' clauses may require registration under this head (*Re Bond Worth Ltd* [1980] Ch 228 but cp *Clough Mill Ltd v Martin* [1984] 3 All ER 982).

[4] E g a solicitor's lien or an unpaid vendor's lien on sale of land to the company (*London and Cheshire Insurance Co Ltd v Laplagrene Property Co Ltd* [1971] Ch 499, but cf *Burston Finance v Speirway Ltd* [1974] 3 All ER 735). There is also no requirement for registration of charging orders on the land of a company in favour of a judgment creditor (*Re Overseas Aviation Engineering (GB) Ltd* [1963] Ch 24).

[5] *Re Wallis and Simmonds (Builders) Ltd* [1974] 1 All ER 561.

[6] CA 1985, s 395(2).

[7] Ibid, s 399.

[8] Ibid, s 402; under s 401 such a certificate is conclusive evidence that the requirements as to registration have been satisfied (see *R v Registrar of Companies, ex p Central Bank of India* (1985) Times, 2 August, CA); however, if the particulars filed in the registry are incorrect or incomplete and are not corrected within the 21-day period the registration may be rejected by the Registrar, it is therefore of considerable importance that the particulars filed with the Registrar are correct and complete in all respects.

[9] Ibid, s 403.

[10] Ibid, s 404.

[11] See *Watson v Duff Morgan and Vermont (Holdings) Ltd* [1974] 1 All ER 794.

[12] *Re Mechanisations (Eaglescliffe) Ltd* [1966] Ch 20.

[13] CA 1985, s 409; this applies even if the company has failed to *register* a place of business in England and Wales (*Slavenburg's Bank NV v Intercontinental Natural Resources Ltd* [1980] 1 All ER 955).

ANNUAL RETURN

7.19   Every company having a share capital is required at least once in each year to make a return to the Registrar in the prescribed form of various details relating to the company.[1] The return need not be made in the year of incorporation of the company or, if it is not required to hold an annual general meeting during the following year, in that year.[2] The return must be completed within 42 days after the annual general meeting for the year and a copy must then be forwarded forthwith to the Registrar signed by a director and the secretary of the company.[3]

Companies not having a share capital are also subject to similar requirements.[4]

[1] CA 1985, s 363; Sch 15 — the prescribed form is form 363 (the matters covered include the registered office, location of registers of members and debenture holders, shares and debentures, indebtedness, past and present members and directors and secretary).

[2] CA 1985, s 363(3).

[3] Ibid, s 365.

[4] Ibid, s 364 — the prescribed form is form 363.

8 Shareholder rights, company meetings and investigations

Professor L H Leigh

SHAREHOLDERS AND SHAREHOLDERS' RIGHTS

8.01 In general, the shareholders are the members of the company, but it is possible for a member not to be a shareholder, as where the company has no share capital. A person may become a member of a company by subscribing to the memorandum, by applying for an allotment of shares, by taking a transfer of shares (including those who take on the death or bankruptcy of a member) and by taking up qualification shares (in the case of a director). The subscribers to the memorandum are deemed to have agreed to become members of the company and are entered in its register of members on incorporation; other persons become members when their name is entered on the register of members.[1] A company may become a member of another.[2]

---

[1] CA 1985, s 22(1) and (2).
[2] Ibid, s 375.

8.02 A subscriber to the memorandum must take and pay for his shares from the company. In the case of a private company he may pay in money or money's worth.[1] In the case of a public company, he must provide the money, but this obligation only applies to the case where shares are taken pursuant to an undertaking given by the subscriber in the memorandum. It does not affect any other agreement by a subscriber to the memorandum to take shares.[2] Where a subscriber is entitled to have shares allotted to him as fully or partly paid up otherwise than in cash, under a contract with the company under which property has been transferred or services rendered, he need not pay cash, but will come under obligations concerning the performance of undertakings and valuations.[3]

---

[1] *Re Baglan Hall Colliery Co* (1870) 5 Ch App 346.
[2] CA 1985, s 106 formerly CA 1980, s 29; see also V Joffe and A Hochhauser, *The Companies Act 1980: A Practical Guide* (1980) para 4.113.
[3] CA 1985, ss 99–102 and 112 (consequential liability).

8.03 A minor may become a member of a company unless the articles forbid it.[1] The directors may, if the articles so provide, refuse to accept the minor as a member. A member who is a minor may repudiate his liability as a member during minority or within a reasonable time of attaining majority. Unless he repudiates he will be liable to pay calls made on his shares. In general, he will be unable to recover moneys paid in respect of his shares since reocvery will only be possible if there has been a total failure of consideration.[2] He may refuse to pay calls, but he cannot then retain his shares.[3] He may contract to sell his shares, but any such contract is voidable. If shares are transferred to a minor whose name is placed on the register in ignorance of the fact of minority, the company may seek rectification of the register in which case the transferor's name may be ordered to be put back on the register.[4]

[1] The age of majority is now 18; see Family Law Reform Act 1969, s 1.

[2] *Steinberg v Scala (Leeds) Ltd* [1923] 2 Ch 452; see further *Cheshire and Fifoot's Law of Contract* (10th edn, M Furmston, 1981) pp 388–390.

[3] See Table A, arts 18 and 19.

[4] *Re Asiatic Banking Corpn, Symon's Case* (1870) 5 Ch App 298; on rectification generally, see CA 1985, s 359.

8.04   A person ceases to be a member on the following events; on·the transfer of his shares, but he remains liable as a contributory if winding up commences within one year;[1] on the forfeiture of the shares;[2] when the company has been wound up; on sale by the company under its lien;[3] on death, but his estate continues to be liable; on the rescission of his contract to take the shares; and on the repayment of the capital represented by his shares.

[1] CA 1985, ss 502 and 503.

[2] If forfeiture is provided for by the articles; see Table A, regs 18–22; on consequent reduction of capital in the case of a public company, see CA 1985, ss 146–149 and discussion at paras 8.33–8.35 infra.

[3] Table A, regs 8–11. Under art 8, the lien extends to dividends payable on such shares.

8.05   Power is commonly given in the articles to issue different classes of shares. If Table A articles are used, the conditions upon which shares are issued are determined by the company in general meeting and very wide latitude is given.[1] The presumption of equality as between shareholders, of equal rights and equal liability,[2] may be and usually is rebutted by the terms of issue which will give in clear language special rights to a class or classes of shareholders. The terms of issue may distinguish as between classes of shareholders as to rights to dividend, to return of capital, or to voting at meetings of the company. Furthermore, the power to issue different classes of shares, ranking in preference to those already issued may be taken by alteration of the articles.[3]

[1] Table A, reg 2.

[2] *Birch v Cropper* (1889) 14 App Cas 525.

[3] *Andrews v Gas Meter Co* [1897] 1 Ch 361.

8.06   Where a company which does not have a share capital creates a class of members with rights which are not stated in the memorandum or articles or in a registrable resolution, the company must, within one month from the date of creation of the class deliver a statement containing particulars of the rights attached to that class.[1]

[1] CA 1985, s 129; The section contains ancillary provisions as well, in respect of the registration of variations (forms 129(1), (2) and (3)).

8.07 A similar period applies to variations of such rights[1] and to the assignment of a new name or new name or designation to any class of members.[2]

---

[1] CA 1985, s 129(2).

[2] Ibid, s 129(3); provision for delivery of a statement is made where the company has such a class on the day when the provision comes into force (ibid, s 129(4)).

Preference shares

8.08 For the purposes of variation of rights, the class of shares most commonly considered is the preference share.[1] In contrast to ordinary shares, preference shares ordinarily entitle the holder to payment of dividends in priority to other classes, or to a preference in repayment of capital, or both. The precise preference given will depend upon the terms of issue in respect of which it is difficult to generalise.[2] The entitlement to a preferential dividend may be expressed as cumulative or non-cumulative. If the preference shares are cumulative, the holders will be entitled to have the deficiencies made up from the profits of subsequent years before anything is distributed to other shareholders, but not otherwise.[3]

---

[1] Other classes include ordinary shares (with full voting rights), ordinary shares without voting rights, deferred or founders shares, and these latter may carry, for example, weighted voting rights.

[2] See *Re Walter Symons Ltd* [1934] Ch 308 at 311–312 per Maugham J.

[3] In *Staples v Eastman Photographic Materials Co* [1896] 2 Ch 303 there is said to be a general prima facie rule of construction in favour of treating preference shares as cumulative.

8.09 In almost every case preference shares will carry the right to a preferential dividend while the company is a going concern, and the right to repayment of capital (not necessarily in priority) if there are sufficient assets available in a winding up. Difficult problems can arise in a winding up, however. If the company is solvent, a question concerning the payment of arrears of dividend may arise.[1] There is a prima facie presumption that dividends and arrears thereof are only payable while the company is a going concern, and are therefore no longer payable once winding up has begun. That inference is rebuttable where there are express words in the terms of issue to the contrary, or a definition in the right to dividend which is inconsistent with it.[2] The leading cases turn on the terms of issue and the distinctions made are often tortuous.[3] The terms of issue may, again, give to preference shareholders a right to the repayment of capital before the other shareholders, but the right must be conferred in clear terms since, otherwise, the general principle is that all shareholders share equally in a winding up.[4] Again, the terms of issue may enable preference shareholders to share in surplus assets with the other shareholders after their capital had been repaid. It is upon preference shareholders to show that they are entitled to share in this way.[5]

---

[1] CA 1985, s 502(1)(b) which provides that sums due to a member by way of a dividend are not debts due to the member, by the company, in any case of competition between the company and a member.

[2] *Re E W Savory Ltd* [1951] 2 All ER 1036; *Re Walter Symons Ltd*, above.

³ *Re E W Savory Ltd*, above; *Re Wharfedale Brewery Co Ltd* [1952] Ch 913, [1952] 2 All ER 635.
⁴ *Birch v Cropper* (1889) 14 App Cas 528 at 543; *Re National Telephone Co* [1914] 1 Ch 755 at 774.
⁵ *Scottish Insurance Corpn Ltd v Wilsons and Clyde Coal Co Ltd* [1949] AC 462; *Re Isle of Thanet Electric Supply Co Ltd* [1950] Ch 161.

Redeemable shares

8.10   Both private and public companies may issue redeemable shares of any class, including preference and equity shares and deal in their own shares, subject to safeguards in the interests of capital maintenance.[1] A company limited by shares or by guarantee and having a share capital may issue shares which are to be redeemed or which are liable at the option of the shareholder or the company to be redeemed.[2] The company must be authorised by its articles to issue such shares, and redemption must be effected on the terms specified by the articles.[3] No redeemable shares may be issued at any time when there are no issued shares of the company which are non-redeemable.[4] Redeemable shares may not be redeemed unless they are fully paid, and the terms of redemption must provide for payment on redemption.[5]

[1] See L H Leigh and H C Edey, *The Companies Act 1981, Text and Commentary* (1981) paras 242–284A.
[2] CA 1985, s 159(1).
[3] Ibid, s 159(1) and s 160(3).
[4] Ibid, s 159(2).
[5] Ibid, s 159(3).

Variation of class rights

8.11   This topic is usually dealt with in the articles; if it is not, then the rules concerning the availability of, and procedure for, variation are contained in the CA 1985, which applies also to the abrogation of such rights[1] and to the alteration or insertion into the articles of provisions relating to the variation of class rights.[2] S 125 by its plain terms applies to a company whose shares are divided into different classes. Where the company's capital consists of shares of one class only, the rights attaching to such shares may be varied by special resolution altering the articles.[3]

[1] CA 1985, s 125.
[2] Ibid, s 125(7).
[3] CA 1985, s 9; see V Joffe and A Hochhauser, *The Companies Act 1980, A Practical Guide* (1980) para 5.101.

8.12   Where the rights are attached to a class of shares by the memorandum, and the memorandum and articles are silent as to variation, then the rights may only be varied by unanimous agreement of all members of the *company* (not the class).[1] This result could also be achieved by a scheme of arrangement.[2] It is not possible to circumvent the procedure by first inserting and then exercising a variation of rights clause.[3]

[1] CA 1985, s 125(5).
[2] Under CA 1985, ss 425 or 427.
[3] Such a course may have been possible at common law; see *Re National Dwellings Society* (1898) 78 LT 144.

8.13 Where rights are attached to a class of shares otherwise than by the memorandum (for example by the terms of issue) and the articles do not contain provision for the variation of rights, then those rights may be varied if either the holders of three quarters in nominal value of the issued shares in that class give written consent to the variation or the variation is approved by an extraordinary resolution passed at a class meeting, together with any further requirement relating to such variation, however imposed.[1] These provisions are mandatory and override anything which may be inserted in the articles.

[1] CA 1985, s 125(2).

8.14 Where rights are attached to shares, whether by the memorandum or otherwise, and the memorandum or articles do contain provision for variation, and the variation of those rights is connected with the giving, variation, revocation or renewal of an authority for the purpose of an allotment of securities by the directors, or with a reduction of share capital, then the same majority consents as mentioned in the preceding paragraph must be obtained, and any further requirements must also be satisfied.[1] Again, these are overriding requirements.

[1] CA 1985, s 125(3).

8.15 The provisions of the articles alone will govern variation in the following cases. The first is where rights are attached to shares by the memorandum or otherwise, and the articles contain provision for their variation and have done so from the time of original incorporation. The second is where rights are conferred otherwise than by the memorandum and the articles provide for the variation of rights, whenever that provision was first included. Then, provided further that the variation does not relate to authority given, etc, in relation to an allotment by directors and is not related to a reduction of capital, rights may be varied in accordance with the articles.[1]

[1] CA 1985, s 125(4).

8.16 There can, therefore, be no variation of rights unless the statutory criteria are satisfied, and, where a power is found in the articles, any additional requirements contained in them. Furthermore, any alteration of a variation of rights provision in the articles, or for inserting such a provision in the articles is itself treated as a variation of rights and subject to the same stringent conditions as a variation itself.[1]

[1] CA 1985, s 125(7).

8.17   The general provisions of the Companies Acts and the provisions of the articles relating to general meetings apply so far as applicable to meetings of shareholders, whether required by the Acts or the articles, called to consider a variation of rights.[1] The necessary quorum (save at an adjourned meeting) is two persons holding or representing by proxy at least one-third in nominal value of the issued shares of the class.[2] Any holder of shares of the class present in person or by proxy may demand a poll.[3]

---

[1] CA 1985, s 125(6); the references are to ss 369, 370, 376, and 377.
[2] Ibid, s 125(6)(a); note that for an adjourned meeting, the quorum is one person holding shares of the class or his proxy.
[3] Ibid, s 125(6)(b).

8.18   If at a class meeting a resolution is duly passed varying class rights, the holders of not less in the aggregate than fifteen per cent of the issued shares of that class may, provided that they did not consent to or vote for the variation, apply to the court to have the variation cancelled. Such an application has a suspensory effect; the variation is not then to take effect until it has been affirmed by the court.[1] An application must be made within 21 days after the date on which the consent was given or the resolution passed.[2] The court on hearing the application may, if it is satisfied, having regard to all the circumstances of the case, that the variation would unfairly prejudice the stockholders of the class represented by the applicant, disallow the variation. Otherwise, it shall allow it.[3]

---

[1] CA 1985, s 127(2).
[2] Ibid, s 127(3).
[3] Ibid, s 127(4).

8.19   CA 1985, ss 425 and 427 concerning the court's powers to approve a compromise with creditors and members by means of a scheme of arrangement, or a reconstruction or amalgamation of a company remains relevant in this connection.

8.20   The courts have approached the question of what constitutes a variation of class rights in a cautious and very formal way. The courts have distinguished between the rights attaching to each share, and the conditions necessary for the full enjoyment of those rights. Thus an increase in capitalisation which by increasing the number of both preference and ordinary shares would dilute the control of the existing preference shareholders, was held not to be a variation. There is, Lord Evershed MR remarked, in *White v Bristol Aeroplane Co Ltd*,[1] '. . . a . . . sensible distinction between an affecting of the rights and an affecting of the enjoyment of the rights, or of the stockholders' capacity to turn them to account.' Thus, where voting rights attaching to each share are unaffected, in the sense that they are not being modified, dealt with or abrogated, there will be no variation.[2] Indeed, a rateable reduction of capital which affected the dividend rights of preference shareholders because it reduced the number of shares on which dividends might be paid was held not to be a variation of class rights because the proposal did not affect the rate of preference dividend to be paid on each share.[3] A reduction of capital which is in accord with the rights attached to the shares of the company is, again, not a variation of class rights.[4] Where, however, a proposed reduction is not in accordance with class rights, the company must show either that the reduction was sanctioned by the votes of those holding a sufficient majority of the shares of that class, voting 'in the bona fide belief that they are acting in the interests of the general body of members of that class',[5] in which case the court will approve the reduction unless the objectors can show that it is unfair, or otherwise that it is affirmatively shown to be fair by the proposers. It should, however, be borne in mind that shareholders (and debenture holders) may vote to protect their own interests, restrained only by fraud,[6] In *Re Holders Investment Trust Ltd*,[7] the court held that preference shareholders who, because they were also holders of a majority of ordinary shares stood to gain substantially from a proposed reduction which involved the cancellation of redeemable preference shares, failed to consider the interests of the class. This case seems to be an exception to that general rule. It may be, however, that the case is explicable on the footing that the interests of the class were not simply inadequately considered, but never considered at all, and that something approaching fraud is shown where the shareholders supporting the reduction stand to gain in another and inimical capacity. In such a case the situation approaches that of expropriation.[8]

---

[1] [1953] Ch 65 at 75.

[2] *Re John Smith's Tadcaster Brewery* [1953] Ch 308.

[3] *Re MacKenzie & Co Ltd* [1916] 2 Ch 450.

[4] *Re Saltdean Estate Co Ltd* [1968] 1 WLR 1844; [1968] 3 All ER 829.

[5] *Re Holders Investment Trust Ltd* [1971] 1 WLR 583 at 589, [1971] 2 All ER 289 at 294.

[6] *British America Nickel Corp v O'Brien* [1927] AC 369; *Re Hellenic and General Trust Ltd* [1976] 1 WLR 123; [1975] 3 All ER 382.

[7] At note 5, above.

[8] In some circumstances, as e g where the company is owed money by a member and the articles so provide, appropriation may be proper, but that is a special case, see *Allen v Gold Reefs of West Africa, Ltd*, [1900] 1 Ch 656.

Pre-emption

8.21 It has always been possible for members of a company to enjoy pre-emption rights where these were provided for in the memorandum or articles or by contract. Such provision was commonly made in the articles of private companies. Under the CA 1985 statutory rights of pre-emption are given, as are rights to amend or dispense with such rights.[1]

---

[1] For further details, see V Joffe and A Hochauser, op cit paras 3.201–3.222.

8.22 We commence with the statutory provisions. CA 1985, s 89(1) applies both to private and public companies in respect of equity shares allotted wholly for cash.[1] 'Equity security' means a share which does not enjoy only limited rights in respect of dividends *and* capital in a distribution.[2] It also excludes shares held in right of an employees' share scheme, but the definition of these is such as to give their holder rights in respect of the pre-emptive scheme also.[3] The terms also comprehends a right to subscribe for or to convert any securities of the company into equity securities. Furthermore, references to the allotment of such securities include references to the right to subscribe for or convert shares into equity securities.[4] Shares comprehended within the pre-emptive scheme are known as 'relevant shares'.[5]

---

[1] CA 1985, ss 86(1) and 94(2).

[2] CA 1985, s 94(2) and (5).

[3] Ibid, note that these shares participate only if the sole reason why they would otherwise be excluded is that they are held by a person for an employees' share scheme.

[4] CA 1985, s 94(2).

[5] Note that the term does not comprehend a share shown in the memorandum to have been taken by a subscriber thereto, or a bonus share.

8.23   The basic scheme of the section is to provide that a company proposing to allot equity securities shall not allot any of these securities on any terms to any person unless it has made an offer to each holder of the shares to allot him on the same or more favourable terms a proportion of those shares pro rata to his original holding, and unless the period for acceptance of the offer has expired.[1] It is, however, more complicated in its details. Although rights to subscribe for or convert shares into equity securities are equity securities so that they must be offered pro rata to existing shareholders, a holder of a right to subscribe or convert is not himself a person holding relevant shares. He need not, therefore, be offered any right of pre-emption. Secondly, as a result of the rather complex set of definitions in s 94, shares to be held for employees' share schemes are not relevant shares and therefore not equity securities. It follows that a company can allot shares for an employees' share scheme without having to make a pro rata offer to other shareholders. Furthermore, the holder of relevant employee shares may renounce or assign shares which the company allots to him pursuant to the scheme without forcing the company to offer shares pro rata to other shareholders.[2] Finally, the pre-emption provisions do not apply where a company is, by any enactment, prohibited, whether generally or in special circumstances, from offering or allotting equity securities to any person.[3] In such case, his shares are disregarded and the pre-emption scheme applies to other shareholders only.

---

[1] CA 1985, s 89(1), note that the holder must have held his shares for a period of 28 days ending with the day immediately preceding the offer.

[2] Ibid, s 89(5), read with s 94.

[3] Ibid, s 93.

8.24   S 89 may be excluded by the provisions of the memorandum and articles when dealing with rights of preemption applying to any particular class of equity securities. The company must be required to offer shares of that class which it proposes to allot, pro rata to existing holders of such shares.[1] If then the company offers to allot shares to such a holder, and he or anyone in whose favour he has renounced his right accepts the offer, the company may allot the shares without making an offer to all shareholders, which it would otherwise have to do under s 89(1).[2] The general statutory right of pre-emption will, however, still apply to shares which have not been taken up pursuant to the offer. Such shares will have to be offered pro rata to existing holders of relevant shares or relevant employee shares.[3]

1 CA 1985, s 89(2); it is to be noted that the offer will have to be on the same terms as those which apply under s 89(1), and that employees' share scheme shares are also comprehended.

2 By ibid, s 96(4) a company other than a public company registered as such on original incorporation which is subject to such a requirement contained other than in the memorandum and articles is treated as though the restriction were contained therein.

3 This will include a holder who has previously refused to take up the share under such an offer; see Joffe and Hochhauser, op cit, para 3.212.

8.25 The provisions of s 89(2) and (3), excluding the statutory scheme, are cast in limited terms. In particular, s 89(3) only applies where the offer has been accepted. It would not, of itself, enable the company to exclude the statutory scheme in respect of shares which have been offered and declined. Pre-emption rights can be provided for by the memorandum or articles and are commonly provided for in the articles of private companies, and these will prevail over the statutory scheme, excluding the latter expressly or by implication.[1] In the case of a public company, the statutory scheme can be excluded by virtue of the provisions of s 95.

1 CA 1985, s 91.

8.26 An offer required by s 89 may be notified to any person by serving it upon him personally or by post in the manner specified in Table A.[1] Where he holds a share warrant, or would not be entitled to receive notice of general meetings, the offer or a notice thereof may be made by publishing it in the Gazette. Where the provisions of ss 89(1), 90(1)–(5), or 96 or a provision to which s 89(3) applies are contravened, the company and its culpable officers are liable to compensate a person to whom an offer should have been made for his losses.[2]

1 See Table A, regs 111, 112 and 113; this will apply even though the company's articles are not cast in Table A form.

2 CA 1985, s 92.

8.27 The directors of a company may be authorised to allot equity securities without reference to the scheme of s 89. Two cases are envisaged. The first is where the directors are generally authorised to allot equity securities; the second is where they are given a general or limited authority to issue such securities and a specified allotment is in contemplation.[1] In the first case, that of general authority involving the allotment of equity securities in general, the directors may be given power to disregard s 89 in whole or in part, either by the articles or by a special resolution. In the second case, such authority may be given in respect of a specified allotment, by special resolution. In this latter case, the special resolution, or a special resolution to renew such a resolution, must be recommended by the directors, and a statement must be circulated with the notice of the meeting, setting out the directors' reasons for making such a recommendation, the amount to be paid to the company in respect of the equity securities to be allotted, and the directors justification of that amount.[2] It is an offence knowingly to authorise or permit the dissemination of misleading, false or deceptive information.[3] A power, whether conferred under the articles or by special resolution, ceases to have effect when revoked, or when it would expire if not renewed. It may be renewed by special resolution.[4] Where an offer or agreement to offer securities is made at a time when the authority subsists, the allotment may take place even though it will do so after the expiration of the power.[5]

---

[1] CA 1985, s 95(1) and (2); note the reference to the directors' power to allot shares under s 80.
[2] Ibid, s 95, sub-s (5).
[3] Ibid, sub-s (6).
[4] Ibid, sub-s (3).
[5] Ibid, sub-s (4).

8.28   Transitional provisions relating to share allotments are contained in s 96, the most significant parts of which have been mentioned.

8.29   As noted, statutory rights of pre-emption are commonly modified or excluded in relation to pre-emptive rights provisions which are contained in the articles of private companies and which, by restricting transfer to outsiders, help to perpetuate close control. These provisions may impose restrictions on transfer, or they may provide for the compulsory acquisition of shares. For example, there may be an agreement between a company's employee or officer and the company that, on leaving the company, he will sell and transfer his shares to the company's controllers at a price to be fixed by a suitable formula.[1] The former, relatively common type of restriction on transfer, is a clause in the articles giving pre-emptive rights to other members to acquire shares of a member who desires to sell all or part of his holdings. Such restrictions are perfectly lawful.[2] Indeed, such a clause has been upheld where only one member remained to buy the shares.[3] The courts will apply such provisions in strict conformity with their terms. Thus where certain registered holders of shares entered into a contract with another, binding themselves to put him as fully into control of the company as they could without registering a transfer, the company was held entitled to a declaration that the shareholders in question were bound to follow the pre-emption procedure, and could only escape offering their shares to the existing shareholders by annulling their bargain.[4] A registered shareholder who holds shares as a bare trustee for beneficiaries, e g a bank which holds shares as personal representative of a deceased member, on trust for his beneficiaries, need not, where it does not propose to transfer the shares to the beneficiaries, comply with the pre-emptive provisions and offer them to existing members. It would only be obliged to do so if it proposed to transfer them to the beneficiaries, or was required by the beneficiaries so to do. If neither of these conditions applies, the trustee is not a proposing transferor within the meaning of the article.[5]

---

[1] For an example, see *Langen and Wind Ltd v Bell* [1972] Ch 685, [1972] 1 All ER 296. The court there was concerned to safeguard the unpaid vendor's lien on shares.
[2] *Borland's Trustee v Steel Bros & Co Ltd* [1901] 1 Ch 279.
[3] *Jervis Motors (Harrow) Ltd v Carabott* [1964] 3 All ER 89, [1964] 1 WLR 1101.
[4] *Lyle and Scott v Scott's Trustees and British Investment Trust Ltd* [1959] AC 763, [1959] 2 All ER 661.
[5] *Safeguard Industrial Investments Ltd v National Westminster Bank, Ltd* [1980] 3 All ER 849; affd [1982] 1 All ER 449.

8.30 In general, a sale to a third person in violation of the articles gives no right to that person to be entered on the register as a member, but it is not wholly devoid of effect. Where the sale is made to other members, failure to follow a pre-emptive provision in the articles is said not so to vitiate the transaction as to give rise to a total failure of consideration. Instead, the sale operates to pass a beneficial interest to the purchaser.[1] This curious result is difficult to justify since it could deprive other members of their right to force compliance with the articles and so deprive them of their right to purchase. It hardly seems consistent with the notion that where a member contracts as in the *Lyle and Scott* case to put another as effectively as may be in control of the company without transferring shares, that member must offer the shares in accordance with the pre-emptive provision.[2] For, the above proposition hardly seems consistent with the notion that an equitable interest has passed, unless the articles also serve in some way, in respect of someone not a party to them, as a source of power to expropriate. Nor is it consistent with the notion that the articles provide the only means by which a member of a company can form an agreement for the sale of his shares.[3] There are, thus, obscurities of doctrine which are as yet unresolved.

[1] *Hawks v McArthur* [1951] 1 All ER 22.
[2] Para 8.29, above.
[3] *Hunter v Hunter* [1936] AC 222.

8.31 In cases involving the enforcement of pre-emptive rights, a member may enforce the articles directly against another member who is obliged by them to purchase his shares.[1] The member need not, it would seem, join the company in the action.[2]

[1] *Rayfield v Hands* [1960] Ch 1, [1958] 2 All ER 194.
[2] Cf *Welton v Saffery* [1897] AC 299.

8.32 The articles frequently provide for sale at a fair value to be determined by the auditor. The auditor's valuation can only be challenged by showing that he made a mistake of a substantial character or materially misdirected himself in the course of his valuation, as by committing a serious arithmetical error. Where the company is in a perilous condition, he may rightly value the shares having regard to the break-up value of the company. Furthermore, even though the shares constitute a controlling block, the valuation need not be enhanced by reference to that consideration, at least where there is no reason to suppose that the shares will be purchased en bloc.[1]

[1] *Dean v Prince* [1954] Ch 409; *M Jones v R R Jones* [1971] 2 All ER 676, [1971] 1 WLR 840. Note that an auditor or other expert valuing shares pursuant to an article giving pre-emptive rights in respect of retiring members' shares may be sued where he has acted negligently; *Arenson v Casson Beckman, Rutley & Co* [1977] AC 405; *Leigh v English Property Corpn Ltd* [1976] 2 Lloyd's Rep 298.

Forfeiture and surrender

8.33 Provision for the forfeiture and surrender of shares is commonly made in the articles.[1] In the case of a public company, the procedure is regulated by statute.[2] In brief, unless the shares once forfeited or surrendered are disposed of within three years, the company must cancel them and diminish the amount of share capital by their nominal value.[3] Where the effect of cancellation is to bring the nominal value below that of the authorised minimum, the company must apply for re-registration as a private company.[4] A company could, it seems, sell forfeited shares at a discount, since the prohibitions against discounting shares apply only to allotment.[5] The purchaser of forfeited shares is, however, liable to pay amounts unpaid on forfeiture and is usually not entitled to vote until arrears are paid.[6]

[1] E g, Table A, regs 18–22.
[2] CA 1985, s 146; the provision also applies to a private company which forfeits shares and then, within three years, converts to a public company; ibid, s 148.
[3] Ibid, s 146(2) and (3); by s 37(4), neither the company nor its nominee may exercise voting rights in the shares.
[4] Ibid, s 146(2)(b); note that no special resolution is required for reducing share capital, and a company which fails to re-register is treated as a public company but may not offer its shares to the public, s 149.
[5] Cf ibid, s 100.
[6] If Table A articles are employed, the problem would be obviated by not registering a transfer until payment is made. The previous member's liability continues until the company receives payment in full for the forfeited shares; Table A, art 21.

8.34   The directors must exercise the power of forfeiture bona fide for the benefit of the company. Directors may not, e g, decide to forfeit their own shares so as to escape liability on them; the forfeiture will be void and the liability remains.[1] The court may grant relief to a member whose shares have been forfeited if the forfeiture has been irregular.[2]

[1] *Re Esparto Trading Co* (1879) 12 Ch D 191.
[2] *Garden Gully United Quartz Mining Co v McLister*, (1875) 1 App Cas 39.

8.35   The surrender of non-fully paid up shares may be accepted only when forfeiture is justified. Even if a surrender of shares not fully paid up is made for the benefit of the company, it will be void unless forfeiture is justified. For example, a surrender of shares by directors to offset a loss made by the company was void.[1] At common law a company could accept a surrender of fully paid shares where this did not involve a reduction of capital.[2] This does not seem to have been altered by statute.[3]

[1] *Bellerby v Rowland and Marwood's Steamship Co Ltd* [1902] 2 Ch 14.
[2] *Bellerby's* case, above; see also *Eichbaum v City of Chicago Grain Elevators Ltd* [1891] 3 Ch 459; *Rowell v John Rowell & Sons Ltd* [1912] 2 Ch 609.
[3] CA 1985, s 143(3) which enables a company to acquire any of its own fully paid up shares for other than valuable consideration, and s 146(1)(b); thereafter they are dealt with in the same manner as forfeited shares.

Lien

8.36   The general rule is that a company may not take a lien or charge on its own shares, and any such charge is void.[1] There is an exception however; under the articles the company is usually given a lien on every share not fully paid up for all moneys called or payable to the company, and such lien, as noted, usually extends to dividends payable on the shares.[1] The lien is usually enforceable by a power of sale. Any surplus on sale is payable to the member.[2]

[1] See e g Table A, arts 8–11.
[2] This facility is preserved by CA 1985, s 150 and see CC(CP)A 1985, s 6. On the wider aspects, see V Joffe and A Hochhauser, op cit, para 6.501.

DIRECTORS' DUTIES AND MINORITY SHAREHOLDERS' RIGHTS

8.37 A breach of directors' duties of care and skill or of good faith may result in injury to the company, to the interests of shareholders, or both. Accordingly, a cause of action may lie at the instance of the company or of its shareholders where they are injured in their personal capacity.

8.38 It is a fundamental rule of company law that where a wrong has been done to a company, it is the company itself which must sue.[1] If articles in the form of Table A are employed, the right to bring an action will vest in the directors as an incident of their general power to manage the affairs of the company.[2] No single shareholder or minority of shareholders can force the company to bring action or bring action on behalf of the company, provided that the directors' action is ratifiable by the company in general meeting and provided that the company's controllers are not using their position to shield themselves from liability for a wrong or wrongs which they have perpetrated. This is known as the rule in *Foss v Harbottle*,[3] and it applies to all cases in which the complaining members have the means of procuring a suit to be brought by the company.[4] The rule is justified on several bases. It is considered desirable that matters internal to a company should be settled within the company. The court will not substitute its business judgment for that of the controllers. It is also justified as preventing futile litigation[5] and as preventing a company from tearing itself to pieces.[6] It must be borne in mind that an unwanted action may, even though resulting in an award of damages to the company, also subject it to disproportionate harm.[7]

[1] *Burland v Earle* [1902] AC 83.
[2] Table A, reg 70 and see *Shaw (John) & Sons (Salford) Ltd v Shaw* [1935] 2 KB 113.
[3] (1843) 2 Hare 461.
[4] *Mozley v Alston* (1847) 16 LJ Ch 217.
[5] *Cotter v National Union of Seamen* [1929] 2 Ch 58.
[6] *Compagnie de Mayville v Whitley* [1896] 1 Ch 788 at 807.
[7] Remarks of the Court of Appeal in *Prudential Assurance Co Ltd v Newman Industries Ltd (No 2)* [1982] 1 All ER 354 at 364.

8.39 The rule barring minority actions is not, however, given an inflexible application. Certain matters fall outside the principle of majority rule. Ultra vires acts cannot, for example, be ratified by the company, and this rule is not affected by s 9 of the European Communities Act 1972 now CA 1985, s 35 which only relaxes the ultra vires rule in respect of dealings with third parties. Matters requiring a special resolution are not made subject to ratification by a simple majority in general meeting since this would subvert the protection accorded by the requirement. Shareholders' personal rights cannot be abrogated by a majority of other shareholders. Finally, and most troublesome, are the cases where the alleged wrongdoers are in control of the company and will not allow action to be brought in its name. Justice requires an exception in such a case if wrongdoers are not to escape with impunity.

8.40   Accordingly, in *Edwards v Halliwell*[1] the rule and its exceptions are stated as follows. First, where a wrong is allegedly done to a company, the proper plaintiff is the company itself. Secondly, where the wrong is ratifiable by a simple majority of the company, no individual member can be allowed to bring action on its behalf. To this rule, there are the following exceptions:

(1) where the activity is ultra vires, any individual member may sue (usually for an injunction);

(2) where the matter is one which must be decided by special resolution;

(3) where the action represents an infringement of the personal rights of shareholders;

(4) where the activity falls within that class of cases which are compendiously termed a fraud on the minority;

(5) perhaps, but this is very doubtful, in any other case where the interests of justice require that an exception to the rule should be made;

(6) where, in a case where the interests of some part of the members have been unfairly prejudiced, the Court makes an order pursuant to s 75(4)(c) of the Companies Act 1980, authorising civil proceedings to be brought on behalf of the company.

---

[1] [1950] 2 All ER 1064 at 1066–67 per Jenkins LJ.

8.41   Actions falling under the above exceptions may be personal, representative, or derivative. Where a shareholder brings action in respect of an ultra vires act, or an infringement of his personal rights, he may sue in his personal capacity. A shareholder who brings action not only in respect of his personal rights but in respect of the personal rights of a group of members (such as a class of shareholders) may sue in a representative capacity on behalf of himself and all other shareholders whose rights are the same as his own, and the controllers are made defendants.[1] Where, however, the action is brought essentially to vindicate the company's rights, the action is derivative i e it derives from the company's own powers to sue in character and may be brought by the shareholder in a representative capacity on behalf of himself and all other shareholders except the controllers, who are made defendants. The company is added as a party defendant so that it may be bound by and take the benefit of any judgment.[2] It is not designated as a plaintiff simply because the essence of the action is that the directors will not allow action to be brought in its name.

---

[1] RSC, Ord 15, r 12.
[2] *Wallersteiner v Moir (No 2)* [1975] QB 373.

8.42   Where action has been brought by a minority shareholder in the company's name the court may strike it out, if there appears to be a majority in the company disfavouring action, thus subjecting the shareholder to liability in costs.[1] There have also been instances, apparently proper, where a shareholder has been allowed to bring a derivative action in his own name, without recourse to class action procedure.[2] Costs are a troublesome element in derivative suits. In *Wallersteiner v Moir*[3] the Court of Appeal intimated that as a derivative suit is brought to benefit the company and not the named plaintiff, the trial court should order that the company pay the plaintiff's costs down to judgment, whether the action succeeds or not, provided that it was reasonable and prudent in the company's interests to bring the action and that it was brought in good faith. The plaintiff should apply at the commencement of the action for authority to proceed on this basis.

---

[1] *Silber Light Company v Silber* (1879) 12 Ch D 717; note that this case precedes the modern Art 80 and assumes, as do others, that the general meeting has a competence in respect of the decision to commence an action. See also *Marshall's Valve Gear Co Ltd v Manning, Wardle & Co Ltd* [1909] 1 Ch 267.
[2] *Wallersteiner v Moir (No 2)* [1975] 1 All ER 849; *Daniels v Daniels* [1978] Ch 406.
[3] [1975] 1 All ER 849.

8.43 Where on the facts there appear to be causes of action both on behalf of the company and of shareholders in a personal or representative capacity, both sets of claims may be vindicated in the same action. It is not, however, possible to use the shareholder's personal action as a vehicle for recovering damages on the part of the company.[1]

---

[1] *Prudential Assurance Co Ltd v Newman Industries Ltd (No 2)* [1982] Ch 204.

8.44 *The ultra vires exception.* This exception refers to acts which are ultra vires the company, rather than acts which are simply beyond the powers of directors. The former class of acts is not ratifiable, whereas the latter is.[1] Each member has the right to ensure that the company's funds are applied to its proper objects.[2] Where ultra vires is in issue, the court looks only to see whether the activity is ultra vires, and not to its character and whether it is meritorious or otherwise.[3] An individual shareholder may also maintain an action where the activity is illegal,[4] and he may sue to restrain the company from an ultra vires or illegal act even though he has in the past been a party to misconduct of the type complained of.[5]

---

[1] *Normandy v Ind Coope & Co Ltd* [1908] 1 Ch 84.
[2] *Simpson v Westminster Palace Hotel Co* (1860) 8 HL Cas 712.
[3] *Yorkshire Miners Association v Howden* [1905] AC 256.
[4] *Powell v Kempton Park Racecourse Ltd* [1899] AC 143.
[5] *Moseley v Koffyfontein Mines Ltd* [1911] 1 Ch 73; but he may not sue in respect of such acts in which he participated: *Towers v African Tug Co* [1904] 1 Ch 558.

8.45 *Exemption based on special resolution.* The proposition that a member may sue where the controllers have improperly caused that to be done which could only be properly done by a special resolution is illustrated by *Baillie v Oriental Telephone & Electric Co Ltd.*[1] Special resolutions concerning the directors' remuneration were passed by a general meeting, with the requisite majority, but the resolutions were fatally flawed because the notice of the meeting did not give adequate disclosure to shareholders of the facts on which they were asked to vote. The fact that such a resolution was within the powers of the company to pass, did not bar the plaintiff share-holder's action. Shareholders have a right to ensure that special procedures of this sort are followed.

---

[1] [1915] 1 Ch 503; see also *Cotter v National Union of Seamen* [1929] 2 Ch 58; *Edwards v Halliwell* [1950] 2 All ER 1064.

8.46   *Fraud on the minority.* Actions brought under this head are derivative in character, and brought to vindicate the company's rights. A resolution of the general meeting cannot authorise or validate a fraud upon the company. If action were not permitted then, as Page-Wood VC noted in *Atwool v Merryweather*,[1] it would be impossible to set aside a fraud committed by a director who controlled the votes of the company. Similarly, the general meeting cannot ratify a breach of directors' duties where the directors have misappropriated property of the company or where, in a case where they have taken unto themselves a corporate opportunity, the court imposes a trust on the benefits thereof in favour of the company.[2] Nor are directors or controlling shareholders allowed so to dispose of the company's property as to benefit a majority of the members at the expense of a minority.[3]

---

[1] (1867) LR 5 Eq 464.
[2] *Cook v Deeks* [1916] 1 AC 554; note that the ratification was procured with the assistance of the directors' voting powers.
[3] *Menier v Hooper's Telegraph Works* (1874) 9 Ch App 350; *Alexander v Automatic Telephone Company* [1900] 2 Ch 56.

8.47   Where it is desired to commence a derivative action, the minority shareholder must allege both that a fraud was perpetrated on the company, and that the wrongdoers are in control and will not lend the company's name to the proceedings. A derivative action is inappropriate where the wrong is to the plaintiff in another capacity, for example that of director.[1] These issues are to be dealt with before any of the substantive issues are tried. To allow the case to be tried before deciding whether the plaintiffs are entitled to bring the action would subvert the very purpose of the general rule against such suit. On the hearing of the preliminary issue, the court, for the same reason, cannot proceed upon the assumption that the allegations in the pleadings are true; equally it cannot reasonably expect the plaintiff to prove them at the preliminary stage. The obligation upon the plaintiff is therefore to establish a prima facie case in respect both of the allegations of fraud and control. The trial judge may find it right to grant an adjournment to enable a meeting of shareholders to be convened so that he can reach a conclusion in the light of proceedings at that meeting.[2]

---

[1] *Lee v Chou Wen Hsien* [1984] 1 WLR 1202.
[2] *Prudential Assurance Co Ltd v Newman Industries Ltd (No 2)* [1982] 1 All ER 354 at 366.

8.48   The plaintiff must show that he or she is a proper person to bring the action. A defendant in a minority shareholder's action may set up against the plaintiff any defence which he could set up had the action been brought by the plaintiff personally. This will be of importance where the company is closely held, essentially an emanation of the defendant, and where the plaintiff seeks via a derivative action to secure relief which could be had, or was already obtained, in an action against the defendant personally.[1]

---

[1] *Nurcombe v Nurcombe* [1985] 1 All ER 65.

8.49 There is no close definition of control. Of course, where the wrong-doers hold more than fifty per cent of the shares in general meeting, they plainly have control, and this is so whether they hold the shares in their own name or through nominees. In a proper case the court will no doubt be willing to go behind the register of shares in order to determine who is beneficially interested,[1] and this task should be facilitated in future by the provisions of the Companies Act 1985 concerning the disclosure of beneficial interests in shares.[2] Academic studies have demonstrated clearly that a company can be controlled even though the controllers hold less than fifty per cent of the shares,[3] and this truth has been recognised by the courts. In the *Prudential Assurance* case, Vinelott J at trial, in a statement of principle from which the Court of Appeal did not dissent, stated that control can comprehend the case where the alleged wrongdoers control, by their influence, the board of directors and, directly or indirectly (through the use of proxy votes) the votes capable of being cast in general meeting.[4] The Court of Appeal itself noted that control embraces a broad spectrum extending from an overall absolute majority of votes at one end, to a minority of votes at the other end made up of those likely to be cast by the delinquent himself, plus those voting with him as a result of influence or apathy.[5] It seems clear that there is no inflexible standard of control, and that the enquiry is largely factual.

---

[1] *Pavlides v Jensen* [1956] Ch 565, [1956] 2 All ER 518.
[2] See at para 8.155, infra.
[3] E g M Pickering, 'Shareholder Voting Rights and Company Control', (1965) 81 LQR 278.
[4] [1980] 2 All ER 841 at 872-3.
[5] [1982] 1 All ER 354 at 364.

8.50 It may be noted here that the rule in *Foss v Harbottle* has no application if an action has been allowed to proceed and has resulted in a judgment for the benefit of the company. In particular, it does not require the plaintiff to obtain leave to bring an action for the company which would, formally, be a totally different litigation. If at the end of the day fraud is proved, the company will not be capable of condoning it if the fraud will only be confirmed by a majority with the use of the directors' own voting power.[1]

---

[1] *Prudential Assurance Co Ltd v Newman Industries Ltd (No 2)* [1982] Ch 204 CA.

8.51 The plaintiff must also show that the controllers' actions amounted to a fraud on the company. This term is by no means closely defined. Furthermore, some actions which amount to wrongs against individual shareholders, also amount to wrongs done to the company. A leading authority categorises those actions which amount to frauds against the minority as follows:[1]

(a) expropriation of the property of the company or, in some cases, that of the minority;
(b) breach of directors' duties of good faith; and,
(c) voting for company resolutions not bona fide and in the interests of the company as a whole.

On the other hand, directors' actions in respect of a take-over which have the direct effect of depreciating the value of individual share holdings amount to injuries personal to members and fall entirely outside the rule in *Foss v Harbottle*.

---

[1] Gower's *Principles of Modern Company Law* (4th edn, 1979), p 649.

8.52   These three categories no doubt merge into each other. They have, nonetheless, at least a descriptive value. The first is evidenced by *Cook v Deeks*,[1] where directors of a company to which a lucrative railway contract had been offered, on the basis of the company's past performance, diverted the contract to another company in which they were interested without disclosing the fact to a third director or obtaining the approval of shareholders. They were held liable, on a derivative action, to disgorge profits to the benefit of the first company. Similarly, in *Menier v Hooper's Telegraph Works*[2] James LJ states that although shareholders of a company may vote their shares for the purposes of their own interests:

'. . . yet that the majority of shareholders cannot sell the assets of the company and keep the consideration, but must allow the minority to have their share of any consideration which may come to them.'

Again, in the *Prudential Assurance* case, allegations which clearly would support a derivative suit if made out were that the directors by means of false and tricky statements procured the company to purchase on behalf of the wronged company, at an overvalue, the assets of another company which they desired to rescue and for the purpose of doing so.[3]

---

[1] [1916] 1 AC 554.
[2] (1874) 9 Ch App 350 at 354.
[3] [1982] Ch 204, CA; *Atwool v Merryweather* (1867) LR 5 Eq 464 is also of this type.

8.53   Cases of the second type are considered further in relation to the personal action, but they also amount to corporate wrongs. A company can sue, as against its members, to enforce and restrain breaches of its regulations.[1] Difficult problems arise, however, concerning whether particular breaches are capable of being ratified by a majority in general meeting, or not.

---

[1] *Hickman v Kent or Romney Marsh Sheep-Breeders Association* [1915] 1 Ch 881.

8.54   An example of the third category, but one which as will be seen can also be classified as a wrong done to the company is afforded by cases concerning or involving improper share allotments, where these are made by directors with a view to preserving their control. This is not a proper purpose and amounts to a wrong done to the company as well as to individual members.[1] It is, however, capable of ratification.

---

[1] *Hogg v Cramphorn Ltd* [1967] Ch 254; *Bamford v Bamford* [1970] Ch 212.

8.55   The cases noted above all involve either misappropriation of property or some element of fraud in the sense of improper motive.[1] It is clear that no minority shareholder action lies in respect of simple negligence on the part of directors. Thus in *Pavlides v Jensen*,[2] the authority of which was subsequently upheld in the Court of Appeal,[3] pleadings which alleged that the directors of a company sold a mine belonging to it at a considerable undervalue, and that they were therefore grossly negligent, were held not to disclose a cause of action at the instance of minority shareholders. The wrong was capable of ratification.

---

[1] *Heyting v Dupont* [1964] 2 All ER 273.
[2] [1956] Ch 565.
[3] *Multinational Gas and Petrochemical Co v Multinational Gas and Petrochemical Services Ltd* [1983] 3 WLR 492 at 520, per Dillon J.

8.56   A derivative action may, however, lie where the directors in parting with the company's property do so in a grossly negligent fashion. In such a case a resolution of shareholders may not be enough to shield directors. This suggestion has, however, been advanced only tentatively. At most, it would give relief only in cases approaching recklessness and fraud.[1]

---

[1] *Multinational Gas and Petrochemical Co v Multinational Gas and Petrochemical Services Ltd*, above.

8.57   A derivative action does lie where directors who part with the company's property in such a fashion, obtain a personal benefit thereby. In *Daniels v Daniels*,[1] a case where fraud was not pleaded, two directors of the company procured the company to transfer land to one of the directors who was the wife of the other, at a gross undervalue. Templeman J held that in a case where directors act without fraud, but in breach of their duty of care, and as a result not only harm the company but obtain a benefit for themselves, a minority shareholder may sue. It would be monstrous, given the difficulty of proving fraud, if the *Foss v Harbottle* exception were so narrowly drawn that directors could make a profit from their own negligence. It has further been suggested that action ought to lie where the result of the directors' actions is not to benefit themselves, but some associated person, for example the wife of an associate.[2] It is, however, far from clear how far the *Daniels v Daniels* principle extends. A learned author submits, understandably but wrongly, that the ratio of the case turns on the point that the benefit obtained by the directors was an acquisition and disposal of the company's assets and, therefore, a misappropriation of advantages, and that the action was derivative though not cast in representative form.[3] It is apparent that the authorities upon which Templeman J relies do concern breaches of fiduciary duty where fraud need not be alleged in order to obtain recovery.[4] It is also probable that the principle in *Daniels v Daniels* is most likely to apply in the context of acquisitions and dispositions of corporate property. Furthermore, the case has been cited in a later judgment as an example of fraud upon a power.[5] Nonetheless, no court has sought to characterise the case definitively as pertaining to breach of fiduciary duty. The question concerning fraud in an extended sense is dealt with below.

---

[1] [1978] Ch 406.
[2] *Prudential Assurance Co Ltd v Newman Industries Ltd (No 2)* [1980] 2 All ER 841 at 864, per Vinelott J; the issues are not discussed in the Court of Appeal.
[3] Lord Wedderburn in (1978) 41 MLR 569.
[4] *Alexander v Automatic Telephone Co* [1900] 2 Ch 56; *Cook v Deeks* [1916] 1 AC 554.
[5] *Estmanco (Kilner House) Ltd v Greater London Council* [1982] 1 All ER 437.

8.58   The ambit of 'fraud' is thus uncertain, and it is likely to remain so as courts strive to fit an increasing number of difficult cases within it. The supposed fifth exception to the rule in *Foss v Harbottle* which would permit an action wherever the interests of justice require it is not given much significance as a residual head of power. Instead, there is a tendency to widen the scope of fraud. In *Estmanco (Kilner House) Ltd v Greater London Council*,[1] Megarry V-C holds that injustice is a reason for making an exception from the rule in *Foss v Harbottle*, but it is not the rule itself. It is too variable to be so. The jurisprudence of exceptions continues to develop, however. His Lordship suggests, tentatively, that:[2]

'It may be that the test may come to be whether an ordinary resolution of the shareholders could validly carry out or ratify the act in question . . .'

This formula is, however, circular.[3] Nor is it helpful to explain recent decisions on the footing simply of fraud on a power, for that would leave inexplicable cases like *Regal (Hastings) Ltd v Gulliver*[4] where the misuse of power was treated as ratifiable. In the *Prudential Assurance* case, Vinelott J strove to find an intermediate category between fraud and simple negligence such as would justify an action, but, references to *Daniels v Daniels* apart, it cannot be said to have resulted in any settled principle and the outer boundaries of the 'fraud' exception to *Foss v Harbottle* remain undefined.

---

[1] [1982] 1 All ER 437.
[2] Ibid, at 444.
[3] See per Vinelott J in *Prudential Assurance Co Ltd v Newman Industries Ltd (No 2)* [1980] 2 All ER 841 at 859–60.
[4] [1942] 1 All ER 378.

8.59   Actions brought to enforce management in accordance with the articles are both derivative and personal. They do not, however, give rise to relief in damages. The relief sought is most commonly an injunction or an order setting aside a transaction. If directors propose to take action in breach of the articles, they may be restrained by injunction.[1] Similarly, if action is proposed to be taken in respect of a resolution passed in an irregular fashion, the directors may be restrained from doing so.[2] Where, however, an irregularity has occurred, the question whether an action lies will again involve consideration of the exceptions to *Foss v Harbottle*.

---

[1] In general, see RJ Smith, 'Minority Shareholders and Corporate Irregularities', (1978) 41 MLR 147; *Wood v Odessa Waterworks Co* (1889) 42 Ch D 636.

[2] *Hutton v West Cork Rly* (1883) 23 Ch D 654.

8.60 It is clear that a shareholder has a right to exercise the rights which appertain to his shareholding. If his rights are infringed on a matter of substance he has an unqualified right to vindicate them.[1] The leading case is *Pender v Lushington*[2] in which the right of the plaintiff to vote his shares was wrongly disallowed. Jessel MR held, however, that his right to vote shares was a right of property which the company could not deny him. Where, however, the complaint refers only to what the courts characterise as a mere matter of procedure, any action may be defeated by ratification.[3] In such a case, where the complaint is usually put as being that the plaintiff asserts a right to have the company managed in accordance with its articles, a right which also pertains to the company,[4] the court will disallow the action unless there is something illegal, oppressive or fraudulent in the case. Thus, for example, while the courts will intervene to prevent the dissipation of the company's funds by payments made on the basis of inaccurate accounts, they will not allow a shareholder to complain of the manner in which a company's accounts were prepared, this being a matter of business judgment.[5] The boundaries between ratifiable and unratifiable breach are obscure and there is no agreement on the underlying theory according to which such cases are classified.[6]

---

[1] *Edwards v Halliwell* [1950] 2 All ER 1064.

[2] (1877) 6 Ch D 70.

[3] *MacDougall v Gardiner* (1875) 1 Ch D 13; *Bentley-Stevens v Jones* [1974] 2 All ER 653, [1974] 1 WLR 638.

[4] *Hickman v Kent or Romney Marsh Sheep-Breeders Association* [1915] 1 Ch 881.

[5] *Devlin v Slough Estates Ltd* [1983] BCLC 497, no question of formats was involved.

[6] See RJ Smith at para 8.59, above; cf C Baxter, 'The Role of the Judge in Enforcing Shareholder Rights' [1983] CLJ 96.

8.61 Apart from the case where it is sought to exclude a shareholder's right to vote, clear cases where the action cannot be defeated by ratification include: those where directors seek to subvert provisions in the articles which require the concurrence of all directors in certain types of activity,[1] or which restrict the class of persons who may be appointed or act as directors,[2] or where directors seek to exclude one of their number from board meetings.[3] On the other hand, a shareholder cannot sue to test the issue whether a person is validly holding office as a director since any defect in appointment can be put right by the general meeting.[4] While he can sue to restrain the implementation of resolutions at a general meeting which was never validly constituted,[5] he cannot complain of mere irregularities at a general meeting[6] and though he might have had a complaint as shareholder or director of irregularities at a meeting of directors, he cannot complain where those matters are later ratified by a general meeting.[7] In short, where the wrong is dual in character, personal to the plaintiff but also amounting to a wrong against the company, and it does not take the form of an appropriation of corporate property or advantages or property in which other shareholders are entitled to share, and is not an infringement of personal rights of property, but is rather an infringement of what might be thought of as the company's constitution, it will be ratifiable and shareholder action will be subject to the rule in *Foss v Harbottle*.[8]

---

[1] *Salmon v Quin & Axtens Ltd* [1909] 1 Ch 311.
[2] *Kraus v JG Lloyd Pty Ltd* [1965] VR 232.
[3] *Pulbrook v Richmond Consolidated Mining Co* (1878) 9 Ch D 610.
[4] *Kraus v JG Lloyd Pty Ltd*, above.
[5] *Musselwhite v CH Musselwhite & Son Ltd* [1962] Ch 964 where no one even sought to take a *Foss v Harbottle* point.
[6] *Cotter v National Union of Seamen* [1929] 2 Ch 58.
[7] *Browne v La Trinidad* (1887) 37 Ch D 1.
[8] See also *Foster v Foster* [1916] 1 Ch 532 (contracting with the company and voting as director in defiance of articles); *Hodgson v NALGO* [1972] 1 All ER 15.

8.62   The question arises whether the action can be defeated by the possibility of ratification or only by ratification itself. Prima facie the answer ought to be the former, since the rule forbids the ventilation of internal disputes in the absence of fraud, oppression or illegality.[1] Nonetheless, exceptions to the rule have been suggested. The first concerns the case where threatened action is too imminent to admit of a general meeting being held before the action complained of is taken. In such cases it has been intimated that the court ought to allow a minority shareholder action.[2] Doubtless it will be convenient in many of these cases to award an interim injunction (where this is possible), leaving it to a general meeting to determine whether the proposal complained of should be ratified.

---

[1] *MacDougall v Gardiner* (1875) 1 Ch D 13.
[2] *Hodgson v NALGO*, above at 140.

8.63   A second purported exception derives from two decisions on the personal action.[1] These are *Hogg v Cramphorn Ltd*[2] and *Bamford v Bamford*.[3] The former case involved an alleged improper allotment of shares made in order to block a take-over bid. This allotment was not made bona fide and in the best interests of the company, since a company's controllers cannot issue shares merely to maintain control, whatever their view of the coming controllers.[4] The court allowed the action to proceed even though the directors' action was held, ultimately, to be ratifiable. It should however be noted that two of the allegations were of unratifiable breaches, while it had not been clear, before this case, that improper allotments of shares could be ratified. The latter case, where the wrong was allegedly ratifiable, turned on a preliminary point, whether the directors' actions could be and had been, ratified by a general meeting. The Court of Appeal held that it was ratifiable and that ratification could bar an action provided that the directors did not act fraudulently or dishonestly. It is submitted that where the directors' actions are capable of ratification by the general meeting, the action cannot proceed.

---

[1] Wedderburn, (1968) 31 MLR 668; RJ Smith in (1978) 41 MLR 147 argues that the rule in *Foss v Harbottle* does not apply to the personal action. Sed quaere.

2 [1967] Ch 254.

3 [1970] Ch 212.

4 On the wider question of the purposes for which allotments may be made, see *Mutual Life Insurance Co of New York v The Rank Organisation Ltd* [1985] BCLC 11.

8.64 In the preceding two cases, the wrong was as much done to the company as to individual members who, after all, were suing to ensure that the company was managed in accordance with the articles. Given the very formal reasoning in the cases on the alteration of class rights concerning what are rights attaching to shares,[1] it could hardly be said that the same issues were involved as those which arise when it is contended that a right of property attaching to shares has been denied, as where at a meeting the right to vote shares is refused.[2] It is submitted that where the personal right urged is one to have the company managed in accordance with the articles, the breach complained of is not vital to the company's constitution, and no proprietary right of another character is urged, the shareholder action can be defeated by the possibility of ratification. In other words, the shareholder action in this context stands on the same footing as an action which is allegedly wholly derivative. Where the action is personal in the sense of affecting property rights attaching to shares, ratification has no application.[3] In the former class of action it would seem that the court will not allow the controllers to vote their shares in order to procure ratification of the act or acts complained of.

1 E g *White v Bristol Aeroplane Company Ltd* [1953] Ch 65; *Re John Smith's Tadcaster Brewery* [1953] Ch 308.

2 *Pender v Lushington* (1877) 6 Ch D 70.

3 *Devlin v Slough Estates Ltd* [1983] BCLC 497. There is no shortage of competing theories; see for example, RJ Smith (1978) 41 MLR 147; cf C Baxter, [1983] CLJ 96 (whose use of the authorities is sometimes rather startling). There is little agreement among the textbook writers either.

8.65 *Relief from liability.* Under s 310 of the CA 1985 a director cannot shield himself from liability by means of an indemnity clause in the articles. Any provision in the articles or in a contract exempting a director or other officer, including an auditor from, or indemnifying him against a liability that would otherwise attach to him in respect of any negligence, breach of duty or breach of trust of which he is guilty is void. By a proviso, a company may, however, in pursuance of any such provision, indemnify such a person against any liability involved in his successful defence of civil or criminal proceedings involving a wrong to the company, or in connection with a successful application for relief from liability under CA 1985, s 727, or, s 144(3).[1] Where Table A articles are used, such an exempting provision will be found in reg 118.

1 CA 1985, s 144 refers to the liability of a subscriber or nominee to pay up shares issued to him. Sub-s (3) allows the court in a proper case, to excuse him from liability in whole or in part.

8.66 Under CA 1985, s 727, if the court is satisfied that the officer has acted honestly and reasonably and ought fairly to be excused, the court may relieve him from his liability, either in whole or in part. The director can discharge his obligation to act reasonably by showing that he had done everything which a normal man would do in the conduct of his own affairs.[1] This may, in some cases, include the obligation to take professional advice such as that of a solicitor before committing the company to a particular course of action.[2] The court may even relieve the director from liability for an ultra vires act. In one such case, the directors had adverted to the ultra vires question, and had then proceeded on the basis of counsel's advice.[3] The courts will not, however, relieve against liability where directors fail to exercise a discretion of their own and simply follow the instructions of a controller who procured their place on the board; puppets act at their own risk.[4]

[1] *Re City of London Insurance Co Ltd* (1925) 41 TLR 521.
[2] *Re Duomatic Ltd* [1969] 2 Ch 365, [1969] 1 All ER 161.
[3] *Re Claridge's Patent Asphalte Co Ltd* [1921] 1 Ch 543.
[4] *Selangor United Rubber Estates Ltd v Cradock (No 3)* [1968] 2 All ER 1073, [1968] 1 WLR 1055, and see *S v Shaban* 1965 (4) SA 646.

8.67   The court may exercise its powers to grant relief either in connection with proceedings which have commenced or which the director believes may be commenced. The court will have regard to the view which shareholders take in connection with the matter, but their view is not decisive.[1]

[1] *Re Gilt Edge Safety Glass Ltd* [1940] Ch 495, [1940] 2 All ER 237, qualifying the remarks of Maugham J (as he then was) in *Re Barry and Staines Linoleum Ltd* [1934] Ch 227.

8.68   S 727 is limited in an important respect. The only proceedings where relief may be claimed under it are those brought against the director for breach of his duties towards the company or its shareholders or for breach of his duties under the Companies Acts, and even then it is only applicable where the company as opposed to a third party brings the proceedings in question.[1] By parity of reasoning the same principle ought to apply where the director seeks relief in respect of any apprehended claim. He should only be able to claim relief in respect of breach of duty to the company or its shareholders or under the Companies Acts in circumstances where the company might seek redress from him.

[1] *Customs & Excise Commrs v Hedor Alpha Ltd* [1981] QB 818, [1981] 2 All ER 697.

8.69   *Statutory protection.* The restrictive character of the rule in *Foss v Harbottle* has led to the creation of statutory remedies for minority shareholders. These, though independent, are related in scope and so are considered together. The first is the remedy of a winding up order on the just and equitable ground; the second is the power in the court under CA 1985, s 459 to make orders remedying a situation which is unfairly prejudicial to the interests of the members of the company or some part of them.

8.70   *The winding up order.* Under CA 1985, s 517(g), a court may grant an application to wind up a company if it is of opinion that it is just and equitable to do so. It is obliged to grant the order if it is of opinion that the petitioners are entitled to relief either by winding up or by some other means, and that in the absence of any other remedy it would be just and equitable to order a winding up unless it is also of opinion, both that some other remedy is available to the petitioners and that they are acting unreasonably in seeking to have the company wound up rather than pursuing that other remedy.[1] The conditions are thus conjunctive. On the hearing of such a petition, the petitioner must show that the continuance of the company would be unjust to the petitioner and that that injustice cannot be remedied by any other step reasonably open to him.[2] The remedy under CA 1985, s 459 is in many instances an alternative to that contained in CA 1985, s 517(g), and the reasonableness of the petitioner in seeking a winding up rather than the alternative remedy is a relevant matter for the court to take into consideration.[3]

---

[1] CA 1985, s 520(2).
[2] In *Re A Company (No 002567 of 1982)* [1983] 1 WLR 927.
[3] *Gammack, Petitioner* 1983 SLT 246.

8.71 It has been held that in determing the issue of reasonableness, the court must look at the situation when the petition is being heard and not merely as it was when the petition was being presented. It must assume that all the averments in the petition will be proven at the hearing and, where the majority have made offers to terminate the situation complained of, in particular offers to purchase the minority's shares, it must have regard to the terms of such offers.[1]

---

[1] In *Re A Company (No 002567 of 1982)* [1983] 1 WLR 927; *Bryanston Finance Ltd v De Vries (No 2)* [1976] Ch 63 at 77 per Buckley J.

8.72 In order to obtain the remedy, a shareholder (or his personal representative) must show that he has a tangible interest in a winding up; that is, that there would be assets available for distribution if a winding up were ordered.[1] He may not bring the petition for an ulterior purpose such as that of forcing the repayment of a loan,[2] or attempting to force the directors to register a transfer of shares which it is within their powers to refuse.[3] Where, however, the petitioner seeks a winding up order for the benefit of a class of creditors of which he is a member, the fact that he acts from motives of malice will not result in rejection of the petition.[4] On the other hand, where the petitioner relies on oppressive conduct, he need not show that he is being oppressed qua member; it is enough if he is a member and the oppression relates to him in some other corporate capacity such as that of director.[5]

---

[1] *Re Expanded Plugs Ltd* [1966] 1 All ER 877, [1966] 1 WLR 514; *Re Othery Construction Ltd* [1966] 1 All ER 145, [1966] 1 WLR 69.
[2] *Re Bellador Silk Ltd* [1965] 1 All ER 667.
[3] *Charles Forte Investments Ltd v Amanda* [1964] Ch 240, [1963] 2 All ER 940; note, however, that where grounds for a winding up order exist, a bankrupt member may petition as a contributory at the instance of his trustee in bankruptcy; *Re K/9 Meat Supplies (Guildford) Ltd* [1966] 3 All ER 320, [1966] 1 WLR 1112.
[4] In *Re A Company (No 001573 of 1983)* (1983) 4 Co L 163; *Bryanston Finance Ltd v De Vries*, above.
[5] *Ebrahimi v Westbourne Galleries Ltd* [1973] AC 360.

8.73   The most obvious case where relief is given is where the petitioner alleges that he was 'squeezed out' or frozen out from his rightful share in the management of the company. This may well be coupled with a refusal to allow the member to sell his shares freely. In these circumstances, the courts operate flexible doctrines of fairness and good faith.

8.74   The leading case, the facts of which are by no means unusual, is *Ebrahimi v Westbourne Galleries Ltd.*[1] The company was formed in 1958 to take over an existing carpet business founded by Nazar, the second respondent. The signatories to the memorandum were Nazar and the appellant who became the first directors of the company and who were allotted 500 shares each. Soon after formation, the third respondent, Nazar's son, was made a director, and each of the existing directors transferred 100 shares to him. As a result, the Nazars had, between them, a majority of the votes at general meeting. Until disputes arose, all three remained directors. Company profits were distributed entirely as directors' remuneration. No dividends were ever paid, although, before the courts, in the instant case, the Nazars undertook to make provision for the future payment of dividends. Lord Wilberforce inferred that the appellant who had long been in partnership with Nazar with equal rights of management joined in the formation of the company on the basis that the character of the association 'would as a matter of personal relation and good faith, remain the same'.[2] Disputes arose, as a result of which the appellant was excluded from management; their details need not concern us here.

---

[1] [1973] AC 360, [1972] 2 WLR 1289; the facts are similar to those in *Re A Company (No 002567 of 1982)* [1983] 1 WLR 927.

[2] [1973] AC at 380, [1972] 2 WLR 1289 at 1299.

8.75   The respondents caused the company to pass an ordinary resolution removing the appellant from office as director. This action was effective in law.[1] The appellant brought a petition for relief under both CA 1948, s 210, and s 222(f).[2] Their Lordships accepted that the appellant's conduct was not such as to justify his exclusion from management.

---

[1] See CA 1948, s 184.

[2] CA 1948, s 210 was the forerunner of CA 1985, s 459; CA 1948, s 222(f) is now CA 1985, s 517(g).

8.76   The roots of s 517(g) lie in the law of partnership. The courts do not, however, apply in an unadulterated form, considerations which apply to the dissolution of partnerships.[1] The courts must, in each case, examine the relationship between the members and their rights and obligations towards each other, in order to ascertain whether, in all the circumstances, grounds exist which make it just and equitable that the company should be wound up. The importance of the origins of the provision in partnership law lies in the application of the conceptions of probity, good faith and mutual confidence which were developed in that law. These considerations make it inequitable that a company should be permitted to disregard the obligations, rights and expectations held by persons who enter a company. The point is particularly strong where persons, formerly partners, incorporate their business subject to understandings concerning, inter alia, the right to manage which underlay the partnership. The point is not, however, restricted to such cases. It could apply generally to companies formed by persons on the footing of specific mutual understandings concerning such matters. It seems clear that, so far as these provisions apply and enable the court to override provisions of the memorandum and articles by which members would ordinarily be bound, they are most likely to be applied in the case of the closely-held company, often converted from the partnership form, since it is in this sort of company that such understandings are most likely to be found to exist.

¹ In addition to the instant case, see also *Re K/9 Meat Supplies (Guildford) Ltd*, above.

8.77 Before controllers of closely-held companies can exclude persons from management who had legitimate expectations to the enjoyment of managerial rights from a share in management, they will have to show that there was a valid business reason for exclusion; it will not be enough simply to show that there is a legal provision permitting exclusion.¹ Among valid reasons for exclusion are, it is submitted, deadlock attributable to the fault of the person excluded, incompatibility among the members as a result of which others find it impossible to work with that person, incompatibility of temperament, lack of probity,² incapacity to manage and the legitimate fear that a member also engaged in a competing business might betray its trade secrets.³ The controllers cannot, however, simply exclude a member because they feel that they, or the company would be better off without him. The injured member needs to discharge the onus of showing that his exclusion was not bona fide in the interests of the case since that could become little more than an alibi for a refusal to examine the merits of the case.⁴

¹ *Ebrahimi v Westbourne Galleries Ltd*, above.
² This is a general ground for allowing the petition; see *Loch v John Blackwood Ltd* [1924] AC 783, PC.
³ Competing directorships are not, of course, disallowed as such; *Bell v Lever Bros Ltd* [1932] AC 161.
⁴ *Ebrahimi v Westbourne Galleries Ltd* [1972] 2 WLR 1289 at 1300, per Lord Wilberforce.

8.78 The provision also protects rights of membership. The just and equitable clause is not to be limited by reference to the contractual force of the articles if the result is to defeat reasonable expectations to membership, for example of persons whose claims arise from devolution of shares in a family company from a deceased parent.¹

¹ *Ebrahimi v Westbourne Galleries Ltd*, above, disapproving remarks of Simonds J (as he then was) in *Re Cuthbert Cooper & Sons Ltd* [1937] Ch 392.

8.79 S 517(g) will not, however, always override the provisions of the memorandum and articles. Its operation is based upon the existence of understandings among the members appropriate to qualify the effect of the provisions of the memorandum and articles. A member cannot thus claim a share in management where such claim runs counter to understandings accepted by the members.[1] Nor will it avail a member whose exclusion was attributable to his own fault.[2] Furthermore, there may well be cases where the equities favour some remedy other than a winding up. In such a case the court may either prefer to proceed under another provision, perhaps CA 1985, s 459, or stand the petition over with a view to a settlement.[3]

---

[1] *Re Fildes Bros Ltd* [1970] 1 All ER 923.
[2] *Re Leadenhall General Hardware Stores Ltd* (1971) 115 Sol Jo 202.
[3] In *Re A Company (No 002567 of 1982)* [1983] 1 WLR 927.

8.80   There are, of course, other grounds upon which a court may determine to wind up a company on the just and equitable ground. An example is where the substratum of the company has gone, today a rather rare occurrence.[1] The remedy may also be granted in a case of deadlock, particularly where the company is controlled by a small number of persons.[2] Want of probity on the part of the controllers is a further ground which may be particularly helpful where directors who hold a controlling shareholding fail to hold meetings, submit accounts or declare dividends giving rise to a suspicion that they wish to acquire the shares of the company at an undervalue.[3]

---

[1] *Re German Date Coffee Co* (1882) 20 Ch D 169; for further details see *Buckley On The Companies Acts* (14 edn, 1982) Vol 1, pp 528–9.
[2] *Re Yenidje Tobacco Co Ltd* [1916] 2 Ch 426.
[3] *Loch v John Blackwood Ltd*, above.

8.81   A petition under CA 1985, s 517(g) is sometimes brought, not because the petitioner wants a winding up order, but because he hopes to provoke a settlement on equitable terms. While the remedy under CA 1985, s 459 may be more appropriate where the petitioner claims in respect of injury done to him as a member, it may well not apply where the injury complained of is exclusion from management since that is not a complaint qua member.[1] The courts have sometimes asserted a very broad equitable jurisdiction to deal with situations of this nature. It will of course only be exercised where the grievance subsists at the time of hearing.[2]

---

[1] On the other hand, a failure by a dominant member as director properly to inform members who are director of the company's affairs will found a petition under ss 459–461 of the Companies Consolidation Act 1905. See *Re Bird Precision Bellows Ltd* [1984] BCLC 195.
[2] In *Re A Company (No 002567 of 1982)*, above; *Re Fildes Bros Ltd* [1970] 1 All ER 923.

8.82   An example of the discretion claimed by courts is provided by a case involving a freeze out from management.[1] The court accepted that the petitioners had been given adequate financial information by the controllers to enable them to assess accurately the fairness of offers made to buy out their shares, and accepted that the petitioners had acted unreasonably in refusing to accept the controllers' ultimate offer. In particular the Judge, Vinelott J, was at pains to point out that a minority shareholder, unlike a partner, has no right to have the assets of the company sold in the open market so that he can be sure that fair value is being obtained for them, nor can he insist that the controllers buy his shares at his own valuation or face a winding up. Nevertheless, rather than dismiss the petition which a strict application of principle would seem to have required, the learned judge stood the petition over pending a settlement, and further intimated that the share valuation should be at the lower, current valuation (the shares having declined in value over the period since negotiations started) because the petitioner had been unreasonable in declining earlier offers. Nor could the petitioner complain of not sharing in profits during the freeze out and seek to have a lost entitlement taken into account in the valuation since his loss was the result of his earlier unreasonable attitude. He was in addition assessed to costs. It is submitted that the course of action taken by the court, though doubtless convenient, is not justified by CA 1985, s 520 simply because the court is required to determine whether the petitioner is entitled to relief by way of winding up, which was not the case, or to some other relief, an issue discussed but not decided in the case.

---

[1] In *Re A Company (No 002567 of 1982)*, above.

8.83 The last point is of general importance. The court has a wide discretion under CA 1985, s 520. It may on the hearing of such a petition dismiss it, or adjourn the hearing conditionally or unconditionally, or make any interim order, or any other order that it thinks fit.[1] In order, however, to make a winding up order the court must conclude in favour of the petitioner's entitlement to relief, as noted, and that in the absence of any other remedy it would be just and equitable to wind up the company. Those conditions define the jurisdiction of the court. If by his own wilful refusal to reach a proper compromise the petitioner has helped to create a situation adverse to his own interests, he should not be entitled to have the company wound up. On the other hand, his petition will not necessarily be barred simply because he has acted culpably. The petitioner may succeed though he has behaved badly provided that it is the respondents' conduct which was the substantial cause of the destruction of mutual confidence between the parties.[2]

---

[1] *Re A Company (No 002567 of 1982)* [1983] 2 All ER 854.
[2] *Re RA Noble (Clothing) Ltd* [1983] BCLC 273.

8.84 The petitioner is limited in arguing his petition to the heads of complaint set forth in it. He cannot refer to any new head not covered in it. In deciding the petition, the court has regard to the facts as they exist at the time of hearing; not to past abuses.[1]

---

[1] *Re Fildes Bros Ltd* [1970] 1 All ER 923.

8.85 *The section 459 remedy.* This is an entirely independent alternative to a winding up order under s 517(g) of the CA 1985. Any member of a company may apply to the court by petition for an order under s 459 on the ground that the affairs of the company are being or have been conducted in a manner which is unfairly prejudicial to the interests of some part of the members including at least himself, or that any actual or proposed act or omission (including an act or omission on its behalf) is or would be so prejudicial.[1] A similar power to petition in the case of unfairly prejudicial conduct ensures to the benefit of the Department of Trade and Industry on receipt of a report under s 437 or an exercise of its powers under ss 447 or 448 or in respect of certain reports into insurance companies.[2] The court if it thinks the petition well founded may make such order as it thinks fit for giving relief in respect of the matters complained of. An individual petitioner need not come into court with clean hands, but his prior misconduct may render the other side's conduct not unfair, albeit prejudicial, or it may affect the relief which the court is minded to give.[3]

---

[1] CA 1985, s 459(1); by sub-s (2) this includes a person who is not a member but a person to whom shares have been transferred or transmitted by operation of law.
[2] Ibid, s 460.
[3] *In Re London School of Electronics* [1985] 3 WLR 474.

8.86   It is not clear whether a member who petitions under CA 1985, s 459 must allege unfair prejudice to his interests as member, or whether he may, as in the case of a just and equitable winding up, allege unfair prejudice to a wider range of interests, as for example those arising under any under-standings concerning the right to manage. Under this provision's pre-decessor, s 210 of the CA 1948, the petitioner was obliged to allege conduct which injured him as member. The present provision speaks, not as its pre-decessor did of injury to some part of the members, but of unfair prejudice to their interests.[1] Commentators assumed that in this respect the law remains unchanged[2] and that view has been upheld in at least one reported case.[3] On the other hand, Vinelott J has suggested that the change in wording was intended to bring a case such as *Ebrahimi's* case within the section.[4] So too has Nourse J.[5] The matter remains doubtful; the wording may have been altered simply in the interests of elegance; after all, it was the interests of the members which were being injured before, as now but the better view seems to be that the wider connotation was intended.

---

[1] *Elder v Elder & Watson Ltd* 1952 SC 49.
[2] E g V Joffe and A Hochhauser, *The Companies Act 1980: A Practical Guide* (1980) para 12.203.
[3] In *Re A Company (No 004475 of 1982)* [1983] Ch 178.
[4] In *Re A Company (No 002567 of 1982)* [1983] 2 All ER 854.
[5] In *Re A Company (No 003420 of 1981)* (1983) Times, 4 November.

8.87   Section 459 requires that the conduct complained of was unfairly pre-judicial to some part of the members. At least one decision seems to suggest that where the conduct adversely affects the interests of all shareholders alike, it may not be made the subject of a s 459 petition.[1] This, if so, looks decidedly odd, but it may be premised on the view that the normal machinery of the general meeting affords a sufficient vehicle for redress and, with respect to contrary views, the conclusion is consonant with the principles of majority rule and judicial abstention from interference with the internal affairs of companies, which s 459 may not have been intended to disturb. Its function may be to provide a wider range of procedures and ampler remedies.

---

[1] *Re Carrington Viyella plc* (1983) 4 Co Law 164 and note by Sealey.

8.88   S 459 is cast in terms of unfairly prejudicial conduct. This must refer to a subsisting interest. A member cannot, for example, complain of the directors' refusal to propound a scheme of arrangement or purchase which might benefit him.[1] Otherwise, the phrase is a wide one, presumably much wider than the test which formerly applied (under CA 1948) of burdensome, harsh or wrongful.[2] A shareholder can bring himself within the provision by showing that the value of his shareholding has been seriously diminished or jeopardised by the unfair conduct of the company's controller. The reach of the section is, however, wider, and extends to cases where the reasonable by-stander would regard the petitioner as having been unfairly prejudiced. The petitioner need not show that the controller acted in bad faith or with a conscious intent to prejudice him.[3] It seems clear that at least some invasions of the shareholders' right to have the constitution observed will not be taken as unfairly prejudicial.[4] A member must, however, show not only prejudice, but also an element of unfairness. He cannot, therefore, complain of pre-judicial conduct where the company can show that it acted fairly in the interests of the general body of shareholders.[5] Nor can he complain of exclusion from management where his own conduct is the substantial cause of the destruction of mutual competence between the parties in a company which is a quasi-partnership.[6]

---

[1] In *Re A Company (No 002567 of 1982)* [1983] 2 All ER 854.
[2] *Scottish Co-operative Wholesale Society v Meyer* [1959] AC 324.
[3] *Re RA Noble (Clothing) Ltd* [1983] BCLC 273.
[4] *Re Carrington Viyella plc* (1983) Co Law 164.
[5] Cf *Re Jermyn Street Turkish Baths Ltd* [1971] 3 All ER 184.
[6] *Re RA Noble (Clothing) Ltd*, above.

8.89   Under s 459 the court may make an order where the act or omission complained of or anticipated is a single instance; the court's powers are not restricted to the case where there has been an unfairly prejudicial course of conduct.

8.90   As noted, the court may, on a petition under s 459, make any order it thinks fit. S 461 lists, by way of example, the following types of orders:[1]

(a) regulating the conduct of the company's affairs in future;
(b) requiring the company to refrain from doing or continuing to do an act complained of or to do an act which it has failed to do;
(c) authorising civil proceedings to be brought in the name and on behalf of the company; and
(d) providing for the purchase of the petitioner's and other shares in the company by other members or by the company, and in the latter case making provision for the reduction of capital accordingly.

---

[1] CA 1985, s 461(2).

8.91   While there has as yet been little case law on these provisions, an example of the first type of order can be seen in *Re HR Harmer Ltd*,[1] a case under the former s 210 where a tyrannical father who held a majority of votes in the company by virtue of a weighted shareholding, exercised his control irregularly without regard to the wishes of the board. The court upheld an

order that the father be retained as a consultant, but that he not further interfere with the management of the company, but enjoy the office of life
president without duties, rights or powers. In short, the power is a wide one,
to restructure management.

---

[1] [1958] 3 All ER 689.

8.92   The order most commonly applied for is one which directs the
majority of the company to purchase the petitioner's shares. Here, there have
been helpful statements on the issue of share valuations, always a difficult
problem where the shares are not listed on The Stock Exchange or commonly
dealt with. There is no categoric rule concerning the time at which shares are
to be valued. If, for example, the petitioner acted unreasonably in refusing
offers made for his shares, and the company's business deteriorates in the
period preceding the petition, the shares may be properly valued in
accordance with the company's state of affairs at the time of hearing.[1] This
may well not apply, however, where the respondent's misconduct, rather
than general economic conditions, caused the diminution in value. Where the
respondents refuse to make a fair offer and the company's business declines,
the fair rule may be to order a valuation at the date of the matters complained
of. In some cases it may, in valuing shares, be right to take into account the
fact that the petitioner was frozen out of all benefits in the company.[2]

---

[1] In *Re A Company (No 002567 of 1982)* [1983] 1 WLR 927.
[2] In *Re A Company (No 002567 of 1982)* [1983] 2 All ER 854.

8.93   In several recent cases the courts have ventured some general guidance
in matters of share valuation. The existence of any general rule concerning
valuation has been denied.[1] Where the petitioner acquired shares on the
formation of a company formed to take over an existing business or to start a
new one on what was essentially a quasi-partnership basis, the valuation
adopted cannot properly be discounted on the footing that the shares represent a minority holding. The petitioner, after all, seeks an order because of
unfair prejudice by the controllers making it intolerable for him to remain a
member. His shares should be valued pro rata according to the value of the
company's shares as a whole. If the order provides for the purchase of a
delinquent majority, it would not be fair to give them a price which involved
an element of premium. A discounted valuation might be proper where the
petitioner deserved to be excluded. Such a basis might well be proper also
where the petitioner acquired his shares originally on a discounted basis. In
general, however, the pro rata basis for valuation appears to be that which
the courts favour in the absence of circumstances pointing to another basis as
more just in the given case. Prima facie, an interest in going concern ought to
be valued as at the date of the order for purchase.[2] As in the normal s 459 case
there will have been no agreement for the purchase of shares, there can be no
power in the court to award interest on the purchase price in respect of any
period before judgment.[3]

---

[1] *Re Bird Precision Bellows Ltd* [1984] BCLC 195; *Re A Company, No 003420 of 1981*, The
Times Law Report, 4 November, 1983; In *Re London School of Electronics* [1985] 3 WLR 474.

2 In *Re London School of Electronics* (1985) The Times Law Report, 9 April.
3 *Re Bird Precision Bellows Ltd*, above.

MEETINGS AND PROCEEDINGS

General meetings

8.94 While the articles usually confer general authority on the directors to carry on the company's business, ultimate control over it is vested in the shareholders in general meeting.[1] The articles will provide for the calling each year of an annual general meeting and for extraordinary meetings to be called when necessary.[2] All general meetings other than the annual general meeting are called extraordinary general meetings.[3]

1 *Barron v Potter* [1914] 1 Ch 895; *Bamford v Bamford* [1970] Ch 212; *Marshall's Valve Gear Co Ltd v Manning Wardle & Co Ltd* [1909] 1 Ch 267.
2 Table A, reg 37.
3 Ibid, reg 36.

8.95 An annual general meeting must be held in each calendar year and not more than fifteen months may elapse since the preceding annual general meeting. Notices calling the meeting must specify that it is the annual general meeting.[1] So long as the company holds its first annual general meeting within eighteen months of incorporation, it need not hold another meeting in the year of its incorporation or in the following year.[2] A company which makes default in holding an annual general meeting may be directed to do so by the Department of Trade and Industry acting on the application of any member. The Department of Trade and Industry has power to give such directions for the calling and conduct of the meeting as it thinks fit and may direct that one member of the company present in person or by proxy shall constitute a meeting.[3] If there is default in holding a meeting the company and every officer of the company who is in default shall be liable to a fine, the amount of which will depend upon whether the matter is prosecuted summarily or on indictment.[4]

1 CA 1985, s 366, and see Table A, reg 38.
2 Ibid, s 366(2).
3 Ibid, s 367.
4 Ibid, ss 366(4) and 367(2).

8.96 The Act does not specify what matters must be transacted at the annual general meeting. However, the appointment of an auditor,[1] the adoption of accounts,[2] the receipt of the directors' report[3] and the election and remuneration of directors are matters for the annual general meeting.[4]

1 Strictly, the CA 1985, s 384 concerning the appointment of auditors refers back to s 227 thereof, and refers to a general meeting following the accounting reference period, but this will almost inevitably be the agm provided that the company is functioning normally.
2 CA 1985, s 241.
3 Ibid, s 235.

4 Table A, art 82 simply provides that the remuneration of directors shall be determined by the general meeting.

8.97   An extraordinary general meeting may be convened by the directors of their own volition on the requisition of members holding one-tenth of the voting power at a general meeting.[1] The requisition must state the objects of the meeting to be called, be signed by the requisitionists, and deposited at the registered office of the company.[2] If the directors fail to proceed to convene a meeting within 21 days of the requisition, the persons making the requisition may do so. The obligation of the directors is, however, to convene the meeting within 21 days of the requisition; it is not an obligation to hold the meeting within that period.[3] The reasonable expenses which requisitionists incur are payable by the company which is itself indemnified by withholding the sum from the directors' remuneration.[4]

1 CA 1985, s 368(1) and Table A, reg 37.
2 Ibid, s 368(2) and (3).
3 Ibid, s 368(4) and see *Re Windward Islands Enterprises (UK)* [1982] CLY 306.
4 Ibid, s 368(6).

8.98   Under certain circumstances, the company's auditor may by requisition require the directors forthwith to convene an extraordinary general meeting of the company. This power arises where the auditor has resigned, and his notice of resignation contains a statement that there are circumstances which he considers should be brought to the notice of members of the company.[1] In that case the auditor may requisition a meeting for the purpose of receiving and considering such explanation of the circumstances connected with his resignation as he wishes to place before it.[2] The auditor is further entitled to require the company to circulate with the notice of the meeting a copy (of reasonable length) of any statement which he wishes to make.[3]

1 CA 1985, s 390.
2 Ibid, s 391.
3 Ibid, s 391(2).

8.99   The directors must proceed to convene a meeting within 21 days of the requisition, failing which they may be liable to fine, either on indictment or summary conviction.[1] If the auditor's notice is not sent out with the notices of the meeting, he may read his statement to the meeting.[2] Copies of the auditor's statement need not be sent out where the court is satisfied that the purpose of the statement is to secure needless publicity for defamatory matter.[3]

1 CA 1985, s 391(4).
2 Ibid, s 391(5).
3 Ibid, s 391(6).

8.100   In addition, the court enjoys a reserve power on the motion of a director or member to order a meeting to be held if it is impracticable to call a meeting in the normal way, by requisition.[1] The court may exercise its power either of its own motion, or on the application of any director, or member of the company who would be entitled to vote at the meeting.[2] The court may order that the meeting be called, held and conducted in such manner as it thinks fit. It may in particular direct that one member of the company present in person or by proxy shall be deemed to constitute a meeting. The power has been used to resolve a case where directors, who comprised two of the three shareholders, refused to attend a meeting so that a requisite quorum of two could not be obtained.[3] The court's function is to determine whether on the facts, a meeting could be held without a court order. Similarly, the court could order a meeting of a two member company to be called where one member had died.[4] Any meeting held and conducted in accordance with a court order is deemed to be a duly called, held and conducted meeting of the company.[5]

---

[1] CA 1985, s 371.
[2] Ibid.
[3] *Re El Sombrero Ltd* [1958] Ch 900; See also *Re HR Paul & Son* (1975) 118 Sol Jo 166.
[4] *Jarvis (Motors) Harrow Ltd v Carabott* [1964] 3 All ER 89, [1964] 1 WLR 1101.
[5] CA 1985, s 371(3).

8.101 Notice of a general meeting is given to all members entitled to attend and vote thereat. Save as otherwise provided in the articles, preference shareholders with no voting rights are not entitled to be summoned to general meetings.[1] The time and procedure for calling meetings will be regulated by the articles of association, but there are important statutory limitations to what the articles may contain, and, if Table A articles are used, these are reflected in the articles.

---

[1] *White v Bristol Aeroplane Co* [1953] Ch 65; *Re MacKenzie & Co Ltd* [1916] 2 Ch 450.

8.102 The Companies Act 1985 thus lays down certain minimum periods of notice which must be given. In the case of the annual general meeting of the company,[1] or any meeting called to consider a special resolution,[2] at least 21 days notice in writing must be given. In the case of any other meeting fourteen days notice must be given where the company is a limited company, and seven days notice in the case of an unlimited company.[3] Meetings can competently be called within these time limits, and it is of course possible for the company's articles to specify longer time limits. It is not clear whether the periods of notice so prescribed must be clear of the day of service and of the day of meeting. In England, it would seem that the notice period must be clear of both;[4] in Scotland, it need be clear of the day of service only.[5] The sensible course is obviously to opt in practice for the longer period.

---

[1] CA 1985, s 369(1).
[2] Ibid, ss 369(1)(b) and 378(2).
[3] Ibid, s 369(1)(b); note that Table A, art 38 reproduces these time limits.
[4] *Re Hector Whaling Ltd* [1936] Ch 208.
[5] *Neil McLeod & Sons Ltd Petitioners* 1967 SC 16.

8.103 Notwithstanding the minimum notice provisions, a meeting called at shorter notice than that provided for in the articles is deemed to have been duly called if, in the case of the annual general meeting, all the members entitled to attend and vote agree to this. In the case of any other meeting the agreement of a majority holding at least ninety-five per cent in nominal value of the shares carrying voting rights or, where the company has no shares, members having ninety-five per cent of the voting rights concur.[1] As a leading authority notes, this provision does not authorise the majority to waive service of a notice altogether, or to dispense with any formality in the notice, such as that a particular resolution will be moved as an extraordinary resolution.[2]

[1] CA 1985, s 369(3) and (4).
[2] *Buckley on the Companies Acts* (14 edn, 1982) p 374.

8.104   Notice must be given to all members entitled to attend and vote at the meeting. If Table A articles are employed, the accidental omission to give notice of a meeting to, or the non-receipt of notice of a meeting by, any person entitled to receive notice shall not invalidate the proceedings at that meeting.[1] Failure to give notice because of an error on the part of directors, e g where they were under the erroneous impression that the petitioner had ceased to be a member of the company, does not fall within the article.[2] On the other hand, failure to give such notice because certain addressograph plates had been mislaid did come within the section.[3]

[1] Table A, reg 39.
[2] *Musselwhite v CH Musselwhite & Son Ltd* [1962] Ch 964.
[3] *Re West Canadian Collieries Ltd* [1962] Ch 370.

8.105   The manner of service of a notice of general meeting is regulated by the articles. So far as they make no provision, the manner provided for in Table A applies, that is, by personal service or by post sent to the member's registered address, or to the address, if any within the United Kingdom supplied by him to the company for the purpose of giving notice.[1]

[1] CA 1985, s 370 and Table A, reg 112.

8.106   Adequate notice of the business to be transacted at the meeting must be given. The leading decision is *Baillie v Oriental Telephone and Electric Co Ltd*.[1] The directors of the company used the majority voting power of that company in a subsidiary to award themselves substantial remuneration as directors of that company. Later, on being advised that the scheme should have been approved by Oriental's shareholders, they called an extraordinary general meeting to approve the remuneration and to alter the articles to enable the directors to receive remuneration for their services in respect of subsidiary companies. The notice gave a grossly inaccurate picture of the amount of remuneration in relation to the profits of the company. The court held that the resolution had to be set aside because the notice failed to put shareholders in a position to know what they were being asked to vote about. In *Normandy v Ind Coope & Co Ltd*,[2] a notice which failed to specify that resolutions to make certain pension and retirement payments to managing directors and to increase the emoluments and allowances of other directors would be proposed was held to be invalid. The pecuniary interest of a director in the matter of a special resolution to be proposed is always a matter of which notice must be given.[3] A notice must disclose all relevant facts upon which the members can exercise an informed business judgment.

---

[1] [1915] 1 Ch 503.

[2] [1908] 1 Ch 84.

[3] *Tiessen v Henderson* [1899] 1 Ch 861; see further discussion concerning extraordinary and special resolutions, paras 8.122 to 8.126, below.

Presence at meeting: proxies

8.107 Members entitled to attend and vote at general meetings of the company may do so either in person or by proxy. Special provisions apply for the appointment of a representative by a corporation which is a member of a company, and he may exercise the same power as a member present in person.[1] Proxies are instruments executed by voting members of a company in favour of another person, enabling that person to exercise the member's voting rights. By CA 1985, s 372 any member of a company, who is entitled to attend and vote at meetings of the company, may appoint another person, whether a member or not, to attend and vote instead of him. A proxy appointed to attend and vote instead of a member of a private company also has the same right as the member to speak at the meeting. Unless the articles provide otherwise, the above provisions do not apply to a company not having a share capital; a member of a private company may appoint only one proxy to attend at any given meeting, and a proxy is not entitled to vote, except on a poll.[2]

---

[1] CA 1985, s 375; note that this facility also applies in respect of meetings of creditors.

[2] Ibid, s 372(1) and (2).

8.108 Every notice calling a meeting of a company having share capital must contain a reasonably prominent statement that the member is entitled to appoint a proxy or proxies to attend and vote instead of him.[1] This provision applies both to general meetings and to class meetings.[2] The instrument appointing a proxy is to be in writing.[3] Where Table A articles are employed, two sample forms of proxy are given, the one general in form, the other cast in a form suitable where it is desired that the proxy holder be required to cast his principal's vote either for or against a resolution.[4] The company's articles may not contain any requirement that the instrument appointing a proxy or any document necessary to show its validity be received by the company more than 48 hours before a meeting or adjourned meeting in order that the appointment be effective thereat.[5] This provision is faithfully reproduced in Table A.[6]

---

[1] CA 1985, s 372(3).

[2] Ibid, sub-s (7).

[3] See Table A, reg 60.

[4] Table A, regs 60 and 61.

[5] CA 1985, s 372(5).

[6] Table A, reg 62.

8.109   Proxies are normally solicited, either by management, or on its behalf, or on behalf of dissentient members who seek to oppose the management. In this respect, management enjoys considerable power. In *Peel v London and North Western Rly Co*,[1] the court held that management was not only entitled, but was bound, to send out circulars explaining their policy, was entitled to solicit votes in support of that policy, and could pay the necessary expenses from company funds. This is, however, subject to an important limitation; the company may not send out invitations to appoint a proxy to some only of the shareholders, and to do so is a summary conviction offence on the part of any officer of the company who knowingly or wilfully permits their issue.[2] Furthermore, as will be seen, the company is under a duty to circulate resolutions properly requisitioned by its members.

---

[1] [1907] 1 Ch 5.
[2] CA 1985, s 372(6); no liability attaches where he issues the form to a member at his request in writing.

8.110   While a proxy may not vote except upon a poll unless the articles provide otherwise, he may always vote upon a poll.[1] Where voting by proxy generally is allowed, the chairman must count the proxy holder's vote as one vote, and not according to the number of members whose votes he holds.[2] As to a poll, the company's articles may not exclude the right to demand a poll at a general meeting on any question other than the election of a chairman of the meeting or the adjournment of a meeting. Furthermore there are, as will be seen, limits to the extent to which articles may make a demand for a poll ineffective.[3] Members can, in giving a proxy, indicate how they wish their representative to vote in respect of particular resolutions.[4] It is by no means certain that the proxy holder is bound to cast his votes in the manner prescribed by the member, though the better view would seem to be that as he is the member's agent, he must abide by the instructions of the member.[5] It would seem, however, that the chairman of the meeting need not inquire whether the proxy holder has followed the member's instructions.[6]

---

[1] CA 1985, s 136(2)(c).
[2] *Ernest v Loma Gold Mines Ltd* [1897] 1 Ch 1.
[3] CA 1985, s 373.
[4] Ibid, s 374; *Buckley*, op cit at p 380 states that this provision was inserted to meet the difficulties of trustee and nominee shareholders.
[5] See *Oliver v Dalgleish* [1963] 3 All ER 330, [1963] 1 WLR 1274.
[6] *Second Consolidated Trust Ltd v Ceylon Amalgamated Tea and Rubber Estates* [1943] 2 All ER 567; *Cousins v International Brick Co Ltd* [1931] 2 Ch 90; *Oliver v Dalgleish*, above.

8.111   The purpose of requiring proxies to be lodged by the member with the company is to enable the company to determine their validity in advance. Where such instrument is not lodged in time, the proxy may not vote the shares in question, nor may he do so at an adjourned meeting of the company.[1] Where a proxy is not stamped in due form, the chairman is entitled to reject votes cast by the proxy in respect of them. On the other hand, it is not ultra vires of the company to accept such proxies.[2] But while the company obviously may scrutinise proxy forms lodged with it, it is not certain whether a member can require the company to allow the member to inspect proxy forms, though there is Commonwealth authority which suggests that members have a right to inspect.[3]

1 *McLaren v Thomson* [1917] 2 Ch 261.
2 *Marx v Estates and General Investments Ltd* [1975] 3 All ER 1064, [1976] 1 WLR 380.
3 *Armstrong v Landmark Corpn* (1967) 85 WN (Pt 1) (NSW) 238.

8.112 The authority given by a proxy is valid until it has been revoked in writing, and notice of revocation given to the company.[1] Even where a proxy has been given and has not been revoked, the member may still appear and vote in person on a poll, in which case the proxy cannot be used.[2]

1 Table A, reg 63; even though the principal becomes mentally disordered or dies the proxy remains valid until the company is notified.
2 *Cousins v International Brick Co Ltd* [1931] 2 Ch 90.

8.113 CA 1985, s 370, sets out a number of general rules which apply to meetings, so far as the articles do not make other provision. In practice, the articles, whether in the form of Table A or otherwise, do make extensive provision for the conduct of meetings.

8.114 S 370 and Table A provide, as has been seen, for the service of notice of meetings.[1] Generally speaking, under Table A articles, the right to call a meeting vests in the directors, and this power is a fiduciary power, to be exercised in the best interests of the company.[2] By CA 1985, s 368 and Table A, reg 37, power is given to the members to requisition a meeting. The conditions are that the requisitionists hold not less than one-tenth of the paid up capital of the company which carries the right to vote at meetings of the company.[3] Reg 37 does permit any director or any member of the company to convene a general meeting if, at any time, there are not sufficient directors in the UK to form a quorum.

1 Table A, reg 111.
2 Table A, reg 37, and see *Pergamon Press Ltd v Maxwell* [1970] 2 All ER 809.
3 See *Buckley*, op cit, p 372; there appears to be an ambiguity in the drafting; *Buckley* argues that the phrase 'one-tenth of the paid up capital' means 'shares having paid up thereon one-tenth of the total capital paid up on all the shares carrying voting rights, and not one-tenth of such shares as are fully paid up . . .' It is submitted that this is correct, but draftsmen of articles may wish to note that s 370(3) is clearer.

8.115 Two members personally present shall be a quorum. Where the company's articles are in the form of Table A, a meeting is quorate if two members are present, each being a member or a proxy.[1] This is effect means that a single member who holds the proxy of another or others may not exercise all the powers of the general meeting.

1 CA 1985, s 370(4); Table A, reg 40.

8.116 Adjournments is a subject dealt with in the articles rather than the Act. Table A, reg 45 gives the chairman the power, with the consent of any meeting at which a quorum is present, to adjourn the meeting. No business is to be transacted at the adjourned meeting other than business which might properly have been transacted at the meeting from which the adjourned meeting took place. The articles may provide for the immediate taking of a poll on the question of adjournment. Where the article so specifies, it is meant that the poll shall be taken as soon as practicable under the circumstances.[1] If the chairman improperly stops a meeting, the meeting can itself resolve to go on with the business for which it was convened and appoint a fresh chairman accordingly.[2] On the other hand, where the articles provide (as does reg 45) that the chairman may adjourn the meeting with the members' consent, he cannot be required by the members to adjourn.[3]

---

[1] *Jackson v Hamlyn*, [1953] Ch 577.
[2] *National Dwelling Society v Sykes* [1894] 3 Ch 159; in exceptional circumstances the chairman can adjourn the meeting, *John v Rees* [1969] 2 All ER 274.
[3] *Salisbury Gold Mining Co Ltd v Hathorn* [1897] AC 268.

8.117   Any member elected by the members present at a meeting may be chairman thereof. It is his duty to preserve order, conduct proceedings regularly, and take care that the sense of the meeting is properly ascertained with regard to any question before it.[1] He has prima facie authority to decide all incidental questions which arise at the meeting and which must be decided at the time. His entry in the minute book of the result of a poll or of his decisions on all such questions is prima facie evidence of that result or the correctness of that decision.[2] He has power, with the vote of the majority, to stop debate after the resolutions have been reasonably discussed.[3] Under Table A articles, in the case of a public company the chairman of the board of directors is to act. The articles also make provision for the chairmanship when the chairman is not available or will not act, and where no director is present and willing to act.[4] In such cases the members may choose one of their number to act as chairman.

---

[1] *National Dwelling Society v Sykes*, above.
[2] *Re Indian Zoedone Co* (1884) 265 Ch D 70.
[3] *Wall v London & Northern Assets Corpn* [1898] 2 Ch 469; *Wall v Exchange Investment Corpn* [1926] Ch 143.
[4] Table A, regs 42–43; CA 1985, s 370(5).

8.118   CA 1985, s 370(6) provides that save where the company's articles otherwise provide, in the case of a company originally having a share capital, each member shall have one vote in respect of each share or each ten pounds of stock held by him, and in any other case every member shall have one vote. Voting rights are, however, extensively dealt with under the articles. If Table A articles are employed, on a show of hands every member present in person shall have one vote, whilst on a poll every member has one vote for each share of which he is the holder.[1] The terms of issue may restrict the voting rights of shares, as is done with preference shares, and may also be imposed so as to create non-voting equity shares as well, though this is today much disapproved of. Provision is made under Table A for receiving the votes of members of unsound mind.[2] No member may vote his shares unless all calls on them are paid up.[3] Objection can only be taken to the qualification of any voter at the meeting or adjourned meeting where the vote objected to is given or tendered. Table A, reg 58 provides that the chairman's decision on this matter is final and conclusive, and this seems to be the common law rule as well.[4] The right to vote enures to the registered shareholder; the company is not to inquire into the beneficial ownership of shares.[5] Thus, a trustee may vote trust shares.[6]

[1] Table A, reg 54; reg 55 deals with joint votes.
[2] Ibid, reg 56.
[3] Ibid, reg 57.
[4] *Wall v London & Northern Assets Corpn*, above. There is an exception to the rule where the chairman's decision was procured by fraud.
[5] *Pender v Lushington* (1877) 6 Ch D 70.
[6] *Siemens Bros & Co v Burns* [1918] 2 Ch 324.

Polls

8.119 Resolutions at meetings are normally passed orally or by a show of hands, but a poll may be demanded. Provision for polls is made by CA 1985, s 373 and in the articles of association as well. On a poll, a member prima facie has one vote for each share or each ten pounds of stock which he holds.[1]

[1] CA 1948, s 370(6) and Table A, regs 46 and 54.

8.120 By s 373 the company's articles cannot exclude the right to demand a poll at a general meeting, save in respect of the election of the chairman and the adjournment of the meeting. Furthermore, the articles cannot make ineffective a demand for a poll which is made either by not less than five voting members, or by a member or members representing not less than one-tenth of the total voting rights of all members having the right to vote at the meeting, or by a member or members holding voting shares, being shares on which an aggregate sum has been paid up equal to not less than one-tenth of the total sum paid up on all the shares conferring that right. Table A articles are more liberal; a poll can be demanded by the chairman, or by two members having the right to vote at the meeting, or by a member or members holding a one-tenth interest of the sort specified in the Act.[1] The power of the chairman to demand a poll is subject to an obligation to exercise it in such a way as to give effect to the real sense of the meeting.[2] On a poll, a member need not cast all his votes in the same way.[3] A resolution adopted at a poll takes effect from the date when the result of the poll is ascertained.[4]

[1] Table A, reg 46.
[2] *Second Consolidated Trust Ltd v Ceylon Amalgamated Tea & Rubber Estates Ltd* [1943] 2 All ER 567; here, he should have allowed a poll where there was no quorum present and the members appointing proxies wanted to vote against a resolution which those present favoured.
[3] CA 1985, s 374.
[4] *Holmes v Keyes* [1959] Ch 199.

Resolutions

8.121 Where business of a special nature is to be transacted at a meeting, the directors may and usually will circulate with the notice calling the meeting an explanation of the business and their reasons for calling the meeting. Provision is also made for the circulation of resolutions proposed by members.[1] Resolutions adopted by a company are of three kinds.

---

[1] CA 1985, ss 376 and 377.

Special resolutions

8.122   A special resolution is required in several instances, both under the Companies Act and Table A or other articles of association. Some instances are given in Table 1 below.

Table 1: Matters requiring special resolution

8.123

CA 1985, s 99	alteration of articles
s 17	alteration of conditions in memorandum which could have been in articles
s 35	reduction of share capital
ss 53, 55	re-registration of public company as private company (note s 54 also).
s 95	to disallow statutory pre-emption.
s 307	limited company making directors liability unlimited
s 308	directors assignment of office
s 572	voluntary winding up
s 582	winding up — power of liquidator to accept shares etc; as consideration for sale of company's property
Table A, reg 34	reduction of share capital, capital redemption reserve, or share premium account.

8.124   A special resolution must be passed by not less than three-fourths of those members who are entitled to vote, either personally or by proxy, where proxies are allowed.[1] This resolution must be passed at a general meeting of which not less than 21 days notice, specifying the intention to propose the resolution as a special resolution, has been given.[2] If a majority in number, holding not less than ninety-five per cent in nominal value of the shares with voting rights, or, in the case of a company not having a share capital, the same percentage of members with voting rights so agree, a special resolution may be passed although shorter notice has been given.[3] Such a resolution will, however, be ineffectual unless the members passing it appreciate that the notice given for the reduction of capital was short notice.[4]

---

[1] CA 1985, s 378.
[2] On the period of notice, and s 379(1) and Table A, reg 38.
[3] CA 1985, s 378(3).
[4] *Re Pearce Duff & Co Ltd* [1960] 3 All ER 222, [1960] 1 WLR 1014.

8.125   The notice of intention to propose a special resolution must identify the intended resolution by specifying either the text or the entire substance of the resolution which it is intended to propose. If the resolution is to be validly passed, it must be the same resolution as that identified in the preceding notice, so an amendment to the previously circulated text of a special resolution can be put to and voted on at a meeting only if the amendment involves no departure from the substance of the circulated text.[1] On the other hand, purely technical errors, such as misdescribing a proposal for a special resolution as an extraordinary resolution do not affect its validity so long as the statutory provisions relating to special resolutions are complied with.[2]

[1] *Re Moorgate Mercantile Holdings Ltd* [1980] 1 All ER 40, [1980] 1 WLR 227.
[2] See *McCurdy v Gorrie* (1913) 32 NZLR 769.

Extraordinary resolutions

8.126 An extraordinary resolution must be passed by the majority required for a special resolution, at a general meeting of which notice specifying the intention to propose the resolution as an extraordinary resolution has been given.[1] The period of notice required may be specified by the articles, but it must be not less than fourteen days.[2] An extraordinary resolution may be passed to wind-up the company under CA 1985, s 572(1)(c). In computing the majority on a poll on an extraordinary or special resolution, the number of votes actually for or against the resolution must be counted. The votes exercised, not voting rights possessed, are relevant here.

[1] CA 1985, s 378, and see *MacConnell v E Prill & Co Ltd* [1916] 2 Ch 57.
[2] This follows from the general notice provision relating to general meetings; CA 1985, s 369.

Ordinary resolutions

8.127 These resolutions are passed by a majority of those present and voting at a general meeting. In some instances, special notice is required of an ordinary resolution. These include: resolutions for the supersession of the auditor;[1] for the removal of a director;[2] and for the appointment of an over-age director.[3] Under CA 1985, s 379, the resolution is ineffective unless notice of intention to move it has been given *to the company* not less than 28 days before the meeting.[4] The company must give its members notice at the same time and in the same manner as it gives notice of the meeting. If, after notice has been given to the company, a meeting is called for a date 28 days or less after notice has been given, then, although it has not been given within the specified time, it is deemed to comply with the Act.[5]

[1] CA 1985, s 388.
[2] Ibid, ss 303 and 304.
[3] Ibid, s 293(5).
[4] Ibid, s 379.
[5] Ibid, s 379(3).

8.128 Resolutions passed at an adjourned meeting take effect from the date on which they were passed.[1] Unless a poll is demanded, a declaration that a special or extraordinary resolution has been passed shall be conclusive evidence of the fact.[2] Where the declaration shows on its face that it is invalid, the resolution is not protected by the statute; in other cases the declaration is conclusive.[3]

[1] CA 1985, s 381.
[2] Ibid, Table A, reg 47.
[3] *Re Hadleigh Castle Gold Mines Ltd* [1900] 2 Ch 419; *Re Caratal (New) Mines Ltd* [1902] 2 Ch 498.

8.129   Particular problems surround the question of amendments to a resolution, the text of which has been circulated. Whatever the resolution, no amendment should, it is submitted, be accepted which renders the resolution business of which the members have not had notice.[1] This would, from the point of view of validity, be subject to exception in a case where all members agree to the altered resolution. In the case of extraordinary and special resolutions, the power to amend is doubtless more restricted, but provided that the amendment does not alter the resolution it should be acceptable.[2]

[1] *MacConnell v E Prill & Co Ltd* [1916] 2 Ch 57.
[2] *Torbock v Lord Westbury* [1902] 2 Ch 871.

8.130   In general, the agenda for a general meeting will be settled by the directors. CA 1985 does, however, make provision for the circulation of members' resolutions. Any number of members representing not less than one-twentieth of the total voting rights of all the members having, at that time, a right to vote at the meeting, or not less than one hundred members holding shares on which there has been paid up on an average sum per member of not less than one hundred pounds, may require the company to circulate notice of any resolution which they propose to move, and to circulate to members a general statement of not more than one thousand words with respect to it.[1] Such matter is to be circulated at the requisitionists' expense, unless the company otherwise resolves. The company or any person aggrieved may apply to the court for an order that the company be not bound to circulate any statement, on the ground that it is being so circulated in order to secure needless publicity for defamatory matter.[2] In such case, the court, if it finds for the objectors, may require the requisitionists to pay all or part of the costs. There does not seem to be any case law on the provision. In principle, it would seem that the objectors must show both that the material is defamatory, and that its circulation is needless.[3]

[1] CA 1985, s 376(1) and (2); on formal matters like the deposit of the requisition, see sub-s (4).
[2] Ibid, s 377(1) and (5).
[3] Cf *Buckley* op cit, Vol 1, p 384; but the general rule is that he who asserts must prove.

8.131   Notice of such a proposed resolution is given in the same manner as notice of the general meeting, and at the same time, but where this is not practicable, it is to be given as soon as practicable thereafter.[1] Once notice is properly given, the resolution may properly be dealt with at the general meeting.[2] It is a finable offence, punishable either on indictment or summary conviction, for an officer to make default in complying with these provisions.[3]

---

[1] CA 1985, s 376(3).
[2] Ibid, sub-s (6).
[3] Ibid, sub-s (7).

8.132 Copies of certain categories of resolutions must be registered. If a copy of a resolution of the kind enumerated below has not been registered, those dealing with the company are not entitled to assume that it has been passed. These resolutions, which must be registered within fifteen days of their adoption are:[1]

(a) special resolutions;
(b) extraordinary resolutions;
(c) resolutions agreed to by all the members but which would otherwise have been ineffective for their purposes unless they had been passed as special resolutions or as extraordinary resolutions;
(d) resolutions or agreements agreed to by all the members of some class of shareholders, but which would otherwise have been ineffective for their purpose unless they had been passed by some particular majority or otherwise in some particular manner, and all resolutions which effectively bind all the members of any class of shareholders though not agreed to by all those members;
(e) resolutions requiring the company to be wound up voluntarily, passed under CA 1985, s 572(1)(a)–(c);
(f) resolutions by the directors of the company, that an old public company should be re-registered as a public company,[2] and that a company's memorandum be altered so that it may be re-registered as a private company.[3] Where articles are registered, a copy of every such resolution for the time being in force must be attached to copies of the articles issued after the passing of the resolution.[4]

It is a finable offence on the part of the company and every officer thereof who fails to comply with the registration requirements.[5]

---

[1] CA 1985, s 380(1) and (2); s 380(2) approves some form other than the printed form.
[2] CC(CP)A 1985, s 2(1)(g).
[3] CA 1985, s 146(2).
[4] Ibid, s 380(2).
[5] Ibid, sub-s (6); note that by virtue of sub-s (7), the offence provisions also apply to liquidators.

Minutes

8.133 Every company is required to keep minutes both of general meetings and of directors' meetings.[1] These need not be kept in any particular form, but where a bound book is not used, adequate precautions must be taken against falsification.[2] Any minute purporting to be signed by the chairman of the meeting at which such proceedings took place or by the chairman of the next succeeding meeting, is prima facie evidence of those proceedings.[3] This is important for the rights of individuals can be affected by the contents of the minutes.[3] The minutes are not necessarily the only admissible evidence of what transpired at a meeting, either as between the company, or as between the company and third parties. The wording of the section speaks of a rebuttable, not an irrebuttable presumption.[4]

[1] CA 1985, s 382.
[2] Ibid, s 722.
[3] See, e g, *Re Llanharry Hematite Iron Ore Co Ltd* (1864) 4 De G J & Sm 426 where the chairman was as a result of the minute entry bound to take shares.
[4] Cf *Kerr v John Mottram Ltd* [1940] Ch 657.

8.134   The company's general meeting minute books are open to inspection by any member without charge, and a member is entitled to copies. It is an offence to refuse inspection and the court may by order compel inspection.[1]

[1] CA 1985, s 383.

Unanimous acquiescence

8.135   Where a company adopts articles in the form of Table A a resolution in writing signed by all the members for the time being entitled to receive notice of and to attend and vote at meetings is as valid and effective as if the resolution had been passed at a duly convened general meeting.[1]

[1] Table A, reg 53.

8.136   Even if the company's articles are not in this or a similar form, in some cases the courts will treat the unanimous agreement or tacit acquiescence of all the members to a course of conduct as equivalent to the approval of the resolution by a properly convened general meeting. The matter must of course be one which is competent to the company.[1] The principle applies to matters which can only be dealt with by special or extraordinary resolution, as it does to matters which can be dealt with by ordinary resolution.[2] The matter is of particular importance in the case of closely held private companies. Thus where the articles provided that the directors should not vote in respect of matters in which they were interested, but all the directors who were also the only shareholders voted in favour of such a transaction, the matter was treated as having validly been determined by the members.[3] Even where some only of the members actively acquiesce, the remainder may lose their right to object by reason of the effluxion of time which can give rise to a finding that they acquiesced.[4] The power of the members voting unanimously is of an overriding nature, which can be exercised as an alternative to the procedures specified by the Companies Act.[5] The assents may be obtained wholly informally, without the holding of a meeting at all.[6]

[1] *EBM Co Ltd v Dominion Bank* [1937] 3 All ER 555, PC, qualifying *Re George Newman & Co Ltd* [1895] 1 Ch 674.
[2] *Cane v Jones* [1981] 1 All ER 533 (where the agreement amounted to an alteration of the articles); *Re MJ Shanley Contracting Ltd (in Voluntary Liquidation)* (1979) 124 Sol Jo 239 (extraordinary resolution for winding up).

3 *Re Express Engineering Works Ltd* [1920] 1 Ch 466.
4 *Re Bailey Hay & Co Ltd* [1971] 3 All ER 693.
5 See further, HW Higginson, 'Waiver of Requirements of the Companies Acts', *The Law Society's Gazette* 30 November 1983, pp 3085–3086.
6 *Re Duomatic Ltd* [1969] 2 Ch 365, [1969] 1 All ER 161.

8.137 It should, however, be noted that there are cases where unanimous ratification will not suffice. These are cases where what is done affects the interests of persons other than shareholders.[1] The authorisation given to a company to alter its objects by special resolution is of this character and there are other examples as well.[2]

1 In general see, HW Higginson, loc cit.
2 E g under CA 1985, s 4; see also ibid, ss 303 and 304 concerning the removal of directors where the director is entitled to advance notice and to be heard. A difficult case dealt with by Higginson is that of long-term service agreements under CA 1985, s 319.

INVESTIGATIONS AND INSPECTIONS

8.138 Investigations and inspections are of three types. First, there are preliminary inspections carried out by the Department of Trade and Industry informally, but under statutory powers; secondly, there are formal investigations carried out by the Department of Trade; and thirdly, there are investigations carried out by the company into share ownership.

Preliminary inspections

8.139 The power of the Department to conduct a preliminary inspection applies to an extensive list of companies. This comprises all companies registered under the Companies Act; to companies registered but not formed under previous Companies Act; to certain unregistered companies including companies formed by statute; and to a body corporate formed outside Great Britain which is carrying on or which has at any time carried on business in Great Britain.[1]

1 CA 1985, s 447(1)(a)–(d).

8.140 Such body corporate may be required by the Department to produce specified books and papers, or may at any time if it thinks there is good reason so to do, authorise any officer of the Department, on producing his authority, to require the body corporate to produce to that officer forthwith, any books or papers which he may specify.[1] The power is subjectively worded; it is submitted that a decision of the Department to authorise their officer to call for books and papers, cannot be challenged for want of reasonable grounds.[2] In addition, any person who appears to be in possession of such books or papers may be required to produce them, but without prejudice to any lien which the possessor may have.[3]

1 CA 1985, s 447(2) and (3).
2 Thus the principle in *R v IRC, ex p Rossminster* [1980] AC 952, would not apply.
3 CA 1985, s 447(4).

8.141   The above power includes a power to take copies of or extracts from any books or papers so produced, and to require the person in possession or any other person who is or was an officer or employee of the company to provide an explanation of them.[1] If the books and papers are not produced, the person from whom production was required may be required to state, to the best of his knowledge and belief, where they are.[2] Failure to comply with such a request is an offence punishable on summary conviction. The person concerned has a defence if he can prove that the books and papers were not in his possession or under his control and that it was not reasonably practicable for him to comply with the requirement.[3] A statement made by a person in compliance with the inspection provisions may be used in evidence against its maker in civil or criminal proceedings.[4] A departmental inspection is in effect an investigatory procedure; the Department's officers must act fairly, but a company or individual cannot decline to produce material on the ground that the Inspector is biased against him or it.[5]

---

[1] CA 1985, s 447(5)(a).
[2] Ibid, s 447(5)(b).
[3] Ibid, s 447(6) and (7).
[4] Ibid, s 447(8).
[5] *R v Secretary of State for Trade, ex Perestrello* [1980] QB 19, [1980] 3 All ER 28.

8.142   The Department of Trade and Industry may also obtain a search warrant from justices where there are reasonable grounds for believing that matter of which production has been demanded is in the premises specified.[1] Such warrant is valid for a period of one month.[2] Papers or documents seized may be retained for three months, or if criminal proceedings under a series of specified enactments (as to which see para 8.143, below) until the conclusion of those proceedings.[3]

---

[1] CA 1985, s 448(1) and (2).
[2] Ibid, s 448(3).
[3] Ibid, s 447(4). It is an offence to obstruct entry, s 448(5).

8.143   Material obtained either as a result of departmental direction or under a search warrant under CA 1985, s 447 or sundry other enactments, is protected from disclosure unless the company under inspection consents in writing to its disclosure.[1] There are exceptions to confidentiality where disclosure is required for the following purposes:

(a)   in respect of a prosecution under or arising out of CA 1985, or sundry other Acts,[2] or any criminal proceedings for an offence entailing misconduct in connection with the management of the body's affairs or misapplication or wrongful retainer of its property;

(b)   in respect of criminal proceedings arising out of the Exchange Control Act 1947 (the operation of this statute is currently suspended but there are fugitive criminals against whom proceedings could still be brought in the event of their return to the UK);

(c)   for the purposes of the examination of any person by an inspector appointed under certain statutory powers;[3]

(d)   for the purpose of enabling the Secretary of State to exercise any of his functions under sundry statutory provisions in respect of the company under inspection;[4] and

(e) for the purpose of proceedings in respect of obstructing a search warrant.

Ancillary provisions make it an offence to destroy, mutilate or falsify records,[5] or knowingly or recklessly[6] make false explanations or statements. There is a saving from disclosure on grounds of legal professional privilege, and a limited protection for bankers in respect of customers' records.[7]

---

[1] CA 1985, s 449. By the latter provision a competent authority to whom disclosure may always be made includes the Director of Public Prosecutions, the Lord Advocate, any constable and any procurator-fiscal. The result is that a constable investigating an offence involving the company may be given access to information or documents obtained by a Department of Trade inspector without regard to the limitations in heads (a) to (g) of s 111(1).

[2] Companies Securities (Insider Dealing) Act 1985 and Insurance Companies Act 1982.

[3] E g under CA 1985, ss 431, 432, 442 or 446.

[4] E g the CA 1985, Companies Securities (Insider Dealing) Act 1985, Prevention of Fraud (Investments) Act 1958 and Insurance Companies Act 1982.

[5] CA 1985, s 450.

[6] Ibid, s 451; it is submitted that in this context 'recklessly' includes a person who makes a statement not knowing whether it is false or not, but who would have appreciated the possibility of its falsity had he addressed his mind to the question; see *R v Caldwell* [1982] AC 341; *R v Lawrence* [1982] AC 510; *R v Seymour* [1983] 2 AC 493.

[7] CA 1985, s 452.

Formal investigations

8.144 The Department of Trade may appoint inspectors either on the motion of the company or a specified proportion of the members or on its own motion. It may also be required to appoint inspectors by the court.

8.145 Where members or the company wish to requisition an investigation, the Department of Trade may appoint inspectors to inspect and report, as follows:[1]

(a) where the company has a share capital, on the application of either not less than 200 members or of members holding not less than one-tenth of the issued shares;

(b) where the company has no share capital, on the application of not less than one-fifth of the company's registered members; and

(c) in any case, on the application of the company.[2] The application must be supported by such evidence as the Department of Trade and Industry may require showing that the applicant(s) have good reason for the investigation. The Secretary of State may require security for costs at present in a maximum sum of £5,000.[3]

---

[1] CA 1985, s 431.

[2] Ibid, s 431(c). No special resolution is required.

[3] Ibid, s 431(4).

8.146 The Department of Trade must appoint inspectors if the court so orders.[1] It may appoint inspectors if it appears to the Department that there are circumstances suggesting that the affairs of the company either are being or have been[2] conducted with intent to defraud its creditors or the creditors of any other person or otherwise for a fraudulent or unlawful purpose or in a manner which is unfairly prejudicial to some part of the members (the commonest ground for intervention), or that any actual or proposed act or omission of or on behalf of the company is or would be prejudicial to the members, or that the company was formed for an unlawful purpose. The grounds for ordering an investigation also include that persons connected with its formation or management have been guilty of fraud, misfeasance or misconduct towards it or its members, or that its members have not been given all the information with respect to its affairs that they might reasonably expect.[3] The powers of investigation are not defeated by reason of the company's being wound up voluntarily.

[1] CA 1985, s 432(1). It is submitted that a court could order such an inspection as an interim order in proceedings under CA 1985, s 459.

[2] But not that they may or will be so conducted, save in respect that the section mentions actual or proposed acts or omissions. One could not thus ask for an inspection simply in order to forestall a takeover bid at the instance of existing controllers who fear manoeuvres by the bidder if successful.

[3] CA 1985, s 432(2).

8.147   Inspectors appointed under these provisions also have powers, where necessary, to investigate and report on related companies, that is, companies which are, or at any relevant time have been, the company's subsidiary or holding company or a subsidiary of its holding company or a holding company of its subsidiary.[1]

[1] CA 1985, s 433.

8.148   The Department of Trade and Industry also has a discretionary power to appoint inspectors to investigate and report on the membership of any company, and otherwise with respect to the company for the purpose of determining the true persons who are or have been financially interested in the success or failure of the company or able to control or materially influence its policy.[1] Presumably, in the light of the provisions of CA 1985 enabling the company to investigate its own shareholding, the Department's powers are intended for reserve use.[2] The order appointing inspectors may limit the investigation to matters connected with particular shares and debentures.[3]

[1] CA 1985, ss 442 and 443.
[2] CA 1985, s 212.
[3] CA 1985, s 442(2).

8.149   The Department of Trade and Industry is required to appoint an inspector to inquire into matters relating to particular shares or debentures where the requisition is supported by sufficient members[1] and where it is satisfied that the application is not made for a vexatious purpose.[2] It is for the applicants to define the ambit of investigation which can only be abridged by the Department where it is satisfied that it is unreasonable for the matter to be investigated. The powers of the inspector extend beyond inquiries into legally binding arrangements and into arrangements which have been or are likely to be observed in practice.[3]

---

[1] CA 1985, s 442(3); the percentages are those required under CA 1985, s 431(2)(a) and (b).
[2] Ibid, s 442(3)(a).
[3] Ibid, s 442(4).

8.150 The powers of inspectors are wide. There is no statutorily prescribed procedure to which they must adhere; the courts have held simply that they must act fairly.[1] Nonetheless inspectors, conscious of the inquisitorial nature of their procedures and the adverse effect which their finding may have, have adopted practices which now appear in the relevant departmental handbook.[2] In particular, inspectors should put to a witness any points that they propose to consider which may involve any criticism of the witness, but not every point of detail.[3] Witnesses are provided with transcripts of their evidence. They are given full opportunity to develop their own version of events, are informed of criticisms to be made of their conduct, and invited to comment on them. They are allowed to be legally represented, and may be given the opportunity to comment on provisional conclusions. They are not, however, either allowed to cross-examine other witnesses or to have the transcript of those witnesses' evidence.

---

[1] *Re Pergamon Press Ltd* [1970] 2 All ER 449; affd [1971] Ch 388.
[2] Department of Trade, *Handbook of the Companies Inspection System* (1980) contains a full account; reference may also be made to LH Leigh, *The Control of Commercial Fraud* (1982).
[3] This is not, however, required as a matter of law; see *Maxwell v Department of Trade and Industry* [1974] QB 523.

8.151 Inspectors have wide powers to compel the production of documents and evidence. Officers and agents of the company and any other body corporate whose affairs are being investigated are under a duty to produce books and documents which are in their custody or power relating to those bodies, to attend before inspectors when required to do so, and otherwise to give to the inspectors all the assistance in connection with the investigation which they are reasonably able to give.[1] Persons not formally connected with the company under investigation who the inspectors consider have relevant information may be placed under similar obligations, and this could include such City institutions as the Take-Over Panel.[2] Under certain circumstances directors or past directors of an entity under investigation may be required to produce documents relating to a bank account maintained by him jointly or with another person provided certain statutory conditions are met. These concern, very broadly, undisclosed payments or the benefit of undisclosed contracts and transactions with directors.[3] These are not necessarily payments tainted by fraud, but they involve some taint of moral turpitude at least.

---

[1] CA 1985, s 434(1).
[2] Ibid, s 434(2); Department of Trade, *Handbook of the Companies Inspection System* (1980) gives guidance on this.
[3] CA 1985, s 435.

8.152 Evidence given by a person to an inspector, whether sworn or unsworn, is admissible in subsequent proceedings brought against its maker, whether civil or criminal.[1] Thus, unless protected from disclosure by reason of the fact that they are confidential documents which the public interest requires to be excluded from evidence, transcripts of evidence, correspondence and the like are admissible.[2]

[1] CA 1985, s 434(5).
[2] *London and County Securities Ltd v Nicholson* [1980] 3 All ER 861, [1980] 1 WLR 948.

8.153 Inspectors, in addition to making their final report, may make and may be required to make interim reports to the Department of Trade.[1] An inspector may inform the Department at any time of circumstances tending to show that an offence has been committed.[2] Reports are in general printed and published, and copies sent to the company under investigation,[3] persons affected by its findings, etc.[3] The inspectors' report is evidence of the opinion of the inspectors in relation to any matter contained in the report.[4] The report may thus be relied upon by a contributor who moves to wind up the company, and the report is not mere hearsay. It may, however, be challenged by evidence at the instance of the respondent to such a petition.[5]

[1] CA 1985, s 437(1).
[2] Ibid, s 433(2).
[3] Ibid, s 437(3) gives the categories of persons who may obtain the report whether on payment or otherwise.
[4] Ibid, s 441.
[5] In *Re St Piran Ltd* [1981] 3 All ER 270.

8.154 The expenses of and incidental to an investigation are met by the Department of Trade in the first instance. The Department may, however, recoup the costs of investigation from designated persons.[1] These include: a person who is convicted on a prosecution arising out of the investigation, or who is ordered to pay damages or restore property in a civil action; or a body corporate which benefits from a recovery;[2] or a body corporate which did not request the investigation;[3] or the applicant or applicants for an investigation under CA 1985, s 431.[4] A person required to indemnify the Department may also be required to indemnify applicants for an investigation.[5]

[1] CA 1985, s 439.
[2] Ibid, s 439(2).
[3] Ibid, s 439(3).
[4] Ibid, s 439(5).
[5] Ibid, s 439(8).

8.155 A public company may itself investigate interests in its own shares. Thus by CA 1985, s 212, a public company may by notice in writing require any person whom the company knows or has reasonable cause to believe to be, or, at any time during the three years immediately preceding the date on which the notice is issued to have been interested in voting shares of the company, to confirm that fact or not, and if it be confirmed, to disclose details of his interest. The notion of an interest in shares includes such matters as family and corporate interests, the mutual interests of members of concert parties, and of options to subscribe for shares.[1] The company's power to inquire is wide; it includes power to make inquiries of any person whom it considers to have been or to be interested in the company's voting capital.

[1] CA 1985, s 212(6).

8.156 A person may by notice be required to give particulars of his own past or present interest in shares during the period specified in the notice. The company may also require particulars of any other interest of which the person knows, whether present or past in addition to the interest in respect of which the notice was issued and which subsists or subsisted at the same time as the latter.[1]

[1] CA 1985, s 212; note that the section also contains provisions concerning the matters to be furnished in particulars.

8.157 Interests disclosed as a result of investigations are to be registered in the register of share interests together with the fact that a requirement to disclose was imposed and the date thereof.[1]

[1] CA 1985, s 213.

8.158 Members holding at the date of a requisition not less than one-tenth of the paid up voting capital of the company may requisition an investigation into share ownership.[1] On deposit of a requisition in proper form, the company must institute an inquiry in the manner specified in the requisition.[2] There are two safeguards against dilatory investigations. First, where the investigation is not completed within three months of the requisition, the company must make an interim report with further such reports at three monthly intervals.[3] Secondly, in the event of default, the Department of Trade could be requested to investigate under its general powers noted above. An investigation is regarded as concluded when the company has made all such inquiries as are necessary or expedient for the purposes of the requisition, and in the case of each such inquiry whether the company has received a response or the time for a response has elapsed.[4] Within fifteen days of the conclusion of the investigation, the company must make a copy of the report available at its registered office.[5] Requisitionists must be notified of this.[6]

[1] CA 1985, s 214.
[2] Ibid, s 214(4).
[3] Ibid, s 215(2).
[4] Ibid, s 215(6).
[5] Ibid, s 215(7).
[6] Ibid, s 215(5); see also on retention and making available for inspection, s 215(7) and s 219.

8.159 If a person fails, having been so requested, to give details of his interest in shares, the company may apply to the court for an order that the shares be placed under restriction.[1] This applies only to shares in which the person is interested, not in which he is believed to be interested. The result is that a freezing order cannot be made in respect of shares, the ownership of which is doubtful. In this context restrictions once imposed by the court can only be removed by the court.[2] In particular the court could deny to a person whose shares were frozen, the benefit of any unfair advantage obtained as a result of his failure to disclose.[3]

---

[1] CA 1985, s 216.
[2] Ibid, s 456.
[3] For further details, see LH Leigh and HC Edey, *Companies Act 1981, Text and Commentary* (1981) paras 330 and 332. Note also that the CA 1985 contains penalty provisions and consequential provisions.

Preface to chapters 9 and 10: Note on accounting and auditing standards

Michael Renshall

Interaction of the Companies Act and accounting and auditing standards

9.01 Although the Companies Act makes no reference to accounting and auditing standards it is impossible to construe British corporate financial reporting and auditing practice by reference to the statute alone. The Act is underpinned for practical purposes by an elaborate structure of generally accepted accounting and auditing concepts, many of which — but by no means all — are codified in official Statements of Standard Accounting Practice (SSAP's) and Auditing Standards and Guidelines issued with the authority of the recognised British and Irish accountancy bodies.[1] These statements, as explained below, are of binding effect on members of the accountancy bodies who come within their scope.

---

[1] The bodies, collectively designated as the Consultative Committee of Accountancy Bodies (CCAB) are: The Institute of Chartered Accountants in England and Wales, Institute of Chartered Acountants of Scotland, Institute of Chartered Accountants in Ireland, The Chartered Association of Certified Accountants, the Institute of Cost & Management Accountants and the Chartered Institute of Public Finance & Accountancy. Accounting standards are outlined by the first one and Auditing Standards and Guidelines are authorised by the first four bodies.

9.02 The official statements — SSAPs and Auditing Standards and Guidelines — are supported in their turn by a substantial body of diverse pronouncements of an advisory nature. In the chapters on accounting and auditing which follow reference is made, where appropriate, to such pronouncements as an aid to interpretation and practice.[1] Explanations of abbreviations used will be found in the list of abbreviations in the preliminary part of this work.

---

[1] In addition to SSAPs, exposure drafts (EDs) and technical releases (TRs) are issued. Both the latter are non-binding but assist in the interpretation of best practice. The most convenient sources of the literature are the annual publications 'Accounting Standards' and 'Auditing and Reporting' published by the Institute of Chartered Accountants in England and Wales and the occasional bulletin 'True and Fair' published by the Auditing Practices Committee.

Accounting standards and the Accounting Standards Committee

9.03 The history of background of accounting standards are described as follows in 'Accounting Standards 1985–86':

'Accounting Standards in the United Kingdom and Ireland are established by the Councils of the six major accountancy bodies acting on the proposals of the Accounting Standards Committee ('ASC').

ASC (originally known as the Accounting Standards Steering Committee) was set up in January 1970 by the Council of the Institute of Chartered Accountants in England and Wales with the object of developing definitive standards for financial reporting.

The Institute of Chartered Accountants of Scotland and the Institute of Chartered Accountants in Ireland became members of the Committee in 1970, the Association of Certified Accountants and the Institute of Cost and Management Accountants joined in 1971 and the Chartered Institute of Public Finance and Accountancy in 1976.

From 1 February 1976 ASC was reconstituted as a joint committee of the six member bodies who act collectively through the Consultative Committee of Accountancy Bodies ('CCAB')[1]"

[1] Accounting Standards 1984–85, published by The Institute of Chartered Accountants in England and Wales 1984 page 9.

9.04   ASC's objectives are to propose for approval of the Councils of the governing bodies definitive standards of financial accounting and reporting. Its objectives encompass (a) fundamentals of financial accounting, (b) definition of terms used, (c) application of fundamentals to specific classes of business and (d) the form and content of financial statements, including presentation and disclosure.

Authority and scope of accounting standards

9.05   The authority and scope of accounting standards are set out in the 'Explanatory Foreword' to accounting standards as follows:
'Statements of standard accounting practice ("accounting standards") describe methods of accounting approved by the Council of The Institute of Chartered Accountants in England and Wales (in association with the Councils of The Institute of Chartered Accountants of Scotland, The Institute of Chartered Accountants in Ireland, the Chartered Association of Certified Accountants and The Institute of Cost and Management Accountants and the Chartered Institute of Public Finance and Accountancy) for application to all financial accounts intended to give a true and fair view of financial position and profit or loss.
Disclosure of significant departures
Significant departures in financial accounts from applicable accounting standards should be disclosed and explained. The financial effects should be estimated and disclosed unless this would be impracticable or misleading in the context of giving a true and fair view. If the financial effects of departures from standard are not disclosed, the reasons should be stated.
Obligation for chartered accountants[1] to observe accounting standards or justify departures
The Council expects members of the Institute who assume responsibilities in respect of financial accounts to observe accounting standards.
   Where this responsibility is evidenced by the association of their names with such accounts in the capacity of directors or other officers the onus will be on them to ensure that the existence and purpose of standards are fully understood by non-member directors and other officers. They should also use best endeavours to ensure that the standards are observed or, if they are not observed, that significant departures from them are disclosed and explained in the accounts. The effect of such departures should, if material, be disclosed unless this would be impracticable or misleading in the context of giving a true and fair view.

Where members act as auditors or reporting accountants the onus will be on them not only to ensure disclosure of significant departures but also to the extent that their concurrence is stated or implied, to justify them.

The Council, through its Professional Standards Committee, may inquire into apparent failures by members of the Institute to observe accounting standards or to disclose departures therefrom.'[2]

---

[1] The statement quoted is addressed by the Institute of Chartered Accountants in England and Wales to its members. The same rules apply, mutatis mutandis, to the members of all the other governing bodies previously listed (Ed).

[2] Op cit, p 189.

Auditing standards and auditing guidelines

9.06 Auditing Standards and Auditing Guidelines are issued by the Councils of The Institute of Chartered Accountants in England and Wales, The Institute of Chartered Accountants of Scotland, the Institute of Chartered Accountants in Ireland, The Chartered Institute of Public Finance and Accountancy and The Chartered Association of Certified Accountants. The first standards and guidelines were promulgated in April 1980.

9.07 The Explanatory Foreword to Auditing Standards and Guidelines explains their status and authority as follows:

'Auditing Standards prescribe the basic principles and practices which members [of the relevant bodies] are expected to follow in the conduct of an audit. Unless otherwise indicated in the text, Auditing Standards apply whenever an audit is carried out. Each Auditing Standard consists of a text to which there may be added an explanatory note.

Explanatory notes have the same status and purpose as Accounting Guidelines (see below).

Auditing Guidelines give guidance on
  (a) procedures by which the Auditing Standards may be applied;
  (b) the application of the Auditing Standards to specific items appearing in the financial statements of enterprises;
  (c) techiques currently being used in auditing;
  (d) audit problems relating to particular commercial or legal circumstances or to specific industries;
but do not prescribe basic principles and practices.

Members [of the relevant bodies] are advised that a court of law may, when considering the adequacy of the work of an auditor, take into account any pronouncements or publications which it thinks may be indicative of good practice. Auditing Standards and Guidelines are likely to be so regarded.

Members of the accountancy bodies [listed above] who assume responsibility as auditors are expected to observe Auditing Standards. Apparent failures by members to observe Auditing Standards may be enquired into by the appropriate committees established by the Councils of the accountancy bodies, and disciplinary action may result.'[1]

---

[1] Auditing and Reporting 1984/85, published by The Institute of Chartered Accountants in England and Wales 1984, pages 3 and 4.

9 Accounting requirements — law and practice

Derek Foster and Alwine Jones

ACCOUNTING RECORDS

Legal requirements: summary

9.08 CA 1985 requires every company to keep accounting records. These records must fulfil the following purposes:

(a) they should be sufficient to show and explain the company's transactions;

(b) they should enable the directors to ensure that any balance sheet or profit and loss account prepared by them complies with the requirements of the Act, including the requirement to give a true and fair view;

(c) they should disclose with reasonable accuracy, at any time, the financial position of the company at that time.[1]

---

[1] CA 1985, s 221(2).

9.09 The Act prescribes the following minimum contents of accounting records:

(a) entries from day to day of all sums of money received and expended by the company, and the matters in respect of which the receipt and expenditure takes place;

(b) a record of the assets and liabilities of the company; and

(c) if the company's business involves dealing in goods, the accounting records should contain the following:

    (i) statements of stock held by the company at the end of each financial year;

    (ii) all statements of stocktakings from which any such statement in (i) above has been prepared;

    (iii) except in the case of goods sold by way of ordinary retail trade, statements of all goods sold and purchased. These statements must show the goods, buyers and sellers in sufficient detail to enable the goods, buyers and sellers to be identified.[1]

The Auditing Practices Committee took counsel's opinion in 1977 on the interpretation of this requirement which was introduced in the CA 1976. The main points of that opinion are discussed below.[2]

---

[1] CA 1985, s 221(3) and (4).

[2] For a summary, see 'True and Fair', issue no 6.

Accounting records

9.10 Counsel pointed out that the CA 1976 did not specify what form the accounting records should take. The previous requirement under CA 1948 was that a company should keep 'books of account'. The change in the wording in CA 1976 implied that these records were no longer required to be in book form. But this is not to say that an accumulation of documents is sufficient. The records should after all be sufficient to disclose the financial position of the company at any time.[1] This necessitates that the information is adequately organised.

---

[1] CA 1985, s 221(2)(a).

Financial position

9.11 Counsel interpreted the CA 1976 requirement to mean that the accounting records should disclose more than the company's cash position, but need not be sufficiently detailed to give a true and fair view of the state of the company's affairs at any time. The concept of true and fair necessarily incorporates information which is not contained in the records themselves, and so such an interpretation would not be practically feasible. Rather he interpreted it to imply that the records should be sufficient for the directors to be able to prepare a statement of the company's assets, liabilities, and pre-tax results with reasonable accuracy.

One implication of this is that the company's stock position must be reasonably estimatable at any time. But this does not necessarily mean that the company should be required to maintain continuous stock records. A reasonable estimate of the company's stock position might be arrived at by other means: one example being the use of gross margins.

'Disclosure' of financial position

9.12 The requirement that the accounting records should be sufficient to 'disclose' the financial position of the company need not, in counsel's opinion, be interpreted too strictly. It need not be taken to mean that the financial position needs to be 'displayed' after each transaction is recorded. Again, the emphasis is on availability and organisation of the necessary information, rather than its immediate entry in the records.

'At any time' — interpretation

9.13 Counsel believed that this phrase should be taken literally. Consequently the directors should be in the position where they could prepare a statement of the company's financial position[1] at any selected date. The requisite information should be readily available, and the inference is that the accounting records should be updated on a fairly regular basis and the information in them be organised in an orderly way. It does not however mean that the transactions need be recorded instantaneously; the directors should be given reasonable time to prepare such a statement.

---

[1] See para 9.08, above.

The contents

9.14   Counsel's opinion was obtained on three problems of interpretation regarding the contents of the records:

    (a) The cash book should contain entries on a day to day basis of monies received and expended by the company. Does this mean that entries should be recorded on a daily basis?

    (b) What is meant by a 'record of' assets and liabilities?

    (c) What stock records are required to be maintained in accordance with s 221(4)?

The paragraphs below summarise Counsel's interpretation of the legislation.

Recording of receipts and expenditure

9.15   Instantaneous recording of transactions was not regarded by Counsel as necessary to fulfil the legal requirements, nor is it practical. What the requirement means is that entries should be made separately, and recorded by date.

The matters in respect of which the transactions have taken place must also be disclosed. But again, this provision should not be given too stringent an interpretation. For example, a record of the day's total takings would be sufficient in the case of a retail shop.

Record of assets and liabilities

9.16   A record should be maintained of all the company's assets and liabilities. These includes debtors, creditors, stocks and plant. Thus the company's records should contain sufficient information from which to determine the company's assets and liabilities. But Counsel emphasised that this need not mean that the company's records must be updated instantaneously.[1]

---

[1] See para 9.13, above.

Companies dealing in goods: stock records

9.17   The additional records which must be maintained by a company whose business involves dealing in goods, are listed at paragraph 9.09(c), above.

The phrase 'statements of stock' held by the company was interpreted by Counsel to mean simply a summary, supporting the amount included in the accounts in respect of stock.

The section also requires that 'statements of stocktaking' from which any such statement has been prepared, should be retained. Counsel did not interpret this to mean that records of every stocktaking conducted during the year must be kept. He was of the opinion that it only refers to those stocktaking results which support the year end stock summary. This might of course include results of stocktakes conducted other than at the year end; for example, if the company counts its stock on a cyclical basis. But it is not intended to encompass those situations where companies undertake frequent stocktaking for their own purposes — for example where a retailer might conduct a stock count of certain lines to determine reorder quantities.

The Act does not specify what form these 'statements of stocktaking' should take. It is generally interpreted fairly broadly; Counsel advised that the stocklists themselves or the summary sheets prepared from these would in most cases answer this description.

The requirement to maintain statements of all goods sold and purchased extends to all companies except as regards goods sold by way of ordinary retail trade.[1] But if a company purchases goods by way of ordinary retail trade, then it must maintain records of goods purchased which comply with the provision.

The term a 'sale by way of ordinary retail trade' is not defined. Counsel suggested the following definition:

'A commercial transaction carried out by a person (the retailer) in the normal course of his business whereby goods are sold or supplied to members of the public (consumers) and are acquired by the purchasers otherwise than for the sole purpose of resale, or re-supply for a valuable consideration.'

In all other cases the records must show the goods, buyers and sellers in sufficient detail to enable the goods, buyers and sellers to be identified. The intention was in Counsel's view, to ensure that the substance of the transaction is properly recorded. Thus, as regards the goods themselves, if the identity of the individual product is not of crucial importance to the transaction, product type identify should be sufficient. Only if goods differ substantially from each other, should each particular item be identified. All companies are required to keep a record of assets and liabilities, and for most companies this will entail maintaining a purchase ledger and sales ledger to ascertain creditors and debtors. In this case, the buyers' and sellers' identities will normally be available from the ledger records.

---

[1] CA 1985, s 221(4)(c).

Accounting records: availability for inspection

9.18 S 222 sets out the requirements in this area.

(a) A company must keep its accounting records at the company's registered office, or at any other place as the directors think fit.

(b) The requirements are different if the company keeps its records at a place outside Great Britain. Then, accounts and returns relating to the business should be sent to Great Britain. These accounts and returns must:
   (i) disclose, with reasonable accuracy, the financial position of the business at intervals not exceeding six months, and
   (ii) enable the directors to ensure that the company's balance sheet and profit and loss account comply with the requirements of the CA 1985 as to the form and content of company accounts.

The accounting records, or in case (b) the accounts and returns, must at all times be open to inspection by the company's officers. The term 'officer' is defined to include the company's directors, secretary and managers.[1] The term 'managers' in this context is taken to refer to the more senior management involved in policy decisions.

In addition several cases have concluded that an auditor should generally be regarded as an officer for Companies Act purposes. In *R v Schacter*[2] the Court of Appeal held that an auditor appointed to office under the Companies Acts should be regarded as an officer of the company. Only if an auditor is merely appointed ad hoc and for some limited purpose should he not be regarded as an officer.[3]

S 222(4) requires that a company must retain its accounting records for a minimum period from the date on which they are made. In the case of a private company, this minimum period is three years. In the case of a public company, the minimum retention period is six years.

---

[1] CA 1985, s 744.
[2] (1960).
[3] See para 10.38, below.

Accounting records: penalties for non-compliance

9.19   If a company fails to keep accounting records as required, every officer who is in default is guilty of an offence unless he shows:

(a) that he acted honestly, and
(b) that in the circumstances in which the business was carried on, the default was excusable.[1]

Moreover, if an officer fails to take all reasonable steps for the preservation of the records, or has intentionally caused failure to preserve them, he is guilty of an offence.[2]

A person guilty of an offence under s 223 is liable to imprisonment or a fine, or both.[3]

---

[1] CA 1985, s 223(1).
[2] Ibid, s 223(2).
[3] Ibid, s 223(3).

A COMPANY'S ACCOUNTING REFERENCE PERIOD AND FINANCIAL YEAR

Establishment of accounting reference date

9.20   The CA 1985 defines a company's financial year by reference to its 'accounting reference period' and 'accounting reference date'.[1] Every company is required to establish an accounting reference date with the registrar of companies. This is the date in each successive calendar year on which the company's accounting reference period will end. The directors must notify the registrar of the company's accounting reference date within six months of incorporation. Failing this, the company's accounting reference date is taken as 31 March every year until formally altered.[2]

---

[1] CA 1985, s 227.
[2] Ibid, s 224.

Financial year

9.21 The directors must prepare a profit and loss account in respect of each accounting reference period.[1] The period covered by the profit and loss account is the company's financial year. A balance sheet must also be prepared, as at the date to which the profit and loss account is drawn up.[2]

The financial year is determined by reference to the company's accounting reference date. It must:

(a) commence on incorporation, or on the day after the date to which the previous statutory profit and loss account was prepared, and

(b) end on the accounting reference date, or on any date not more than seven days before or after the company's accounting reference date.[3] This modification is for convenience, since it enables the directors to draw up accounts to a particular day in the week which is practical for them.

---

[1] CA 1985, s 227(1).
[2] Ibid, s 227(3).
[3] Ibid, s 227(2).

9.22 Provided that there are no alterations to a company's accounting reference date, the situation is straightforward: a company's first accounting reference period will run from incorporation to its accounting reference date. This must be a period of more than 6 months, and not more than 18 months. Subsequent accounting reference periods and financial years will be twelve months in length subject to the seven day adjustment referred to above, and run from one accounting reference date to the next.[1]

---

[1] CA 1985, s 224(4).

Alteration of accounting reference date

(a) *General provision*

9.23 During an accounting reference period, a company may give notice to the registrar of a change in its accounting reference date. The notice must specify the new accounting reference date on which that and each subsequent accounting reference period will end.[1] The date of an accounting reference period cannot be changed retrospectively. The only exceptions to this rule are in the circumstances described in (b) below.

(b) *Group companies*

A company which is either a subsidiary or a holding company of another company may give notice of a change which will take effect in respect of the previous accounting reference period, and all successive periods. It may do this on two conditions:

(i)   that the new accounting reference date coincides with that of the other company, and

(ii) that the period allowed for laying and delivery of accounts in respect of the latest completed accounting reference period has not expired.[2] The old accounting reference date is the relevant one for determining whether the period for laying and delivery has expired or not.

---

[1] CA 1985, s 225(1).
[2] Ibid, s 225(2) and (3).

9.24   This exception can be of assistance if a company wants to change its accounting reference date retrospectively. The company may set up a new subsidiary with an accounting reference date coinciding with the desired date. It will then be entitled to give notice to the registrar of a change in its own accounting reference date to bring it into line with that of its new subsidiary. This change may take effect in respect of the holding company's previous accounting reference period, provided that the period allowed for laying and delivery of its accounts in respect of that period has not expired.

9.25   A change in accounting reference date, whether it has effect as regards the current or the previous accounting reference period, will necessarily result in an alteration to the length of that period. Consequently the notice to the registrar must state whether the original accounting reference period:

(a) is to be treated as shortened, thus ending on the first occasion when the new accounting reference date falls after the beginning of the original accounting reference period, or

(b) is to be treated as extended, thus ending on the second occasion when the new accounting reference date falls after the beginning of the original accounting reference period.[1]

---

[1] CA 1985, s 225(4).

Accounting reference period shortened

9.26   The following points should be noted in connection with a shortened accounting reference period:

(a) where changes are made to the current accounting reference period notice need not be given before the new accounting reference date. For example, a company which had an original accounting reference date of 30 September, might wish to change the date to 30 June. Here, provided notice is given to the registrar in the prescribed form before 30 September, that accounting reference period will end on 30 June of the same year. In practice, problems could arise because of the time limits for the laying and delivery of accounts. In order to forestall this, the rules regarding the laying and delivery of accounts are adapted in the case of a shortened accounting reference period.[1]

(b) There are no restrictions with regard to the frequency with which a company may shorten its accounting reference period. Nor are there in general any restrictions on the length of a shortened accounting reference period.

But the situation with regard to a company's initial accounting reference period is unclear. S 224(4) states that the initial accounting reference period must be between six and 18 months in length. However s 224 is 'subject to' the alteration rules of s 225, which provides no minimum length for a shortened accounting reference period. In principle, it seems a company could procure an initial accounting reference period of less than six months by notifying the registrar of an alteration to the company's accounting reference date during its first accounting reference period (or within the period allowed for laying and delivering accounts in the case of a group company).[2]

---

[1] See para 9.211, below.
[2] CA 1985, s 225(2).

Accounting reference period lengthened

9.27 There are restrictions as to the length of an extended accounting reference period and the frequency with which a company may extend its accounting reference periods.

(a) *Length*

A notice to extend the current or previous accounting reference period has no effect if the period, as extended, would exceed 18 months.[1]

(b) *Frequency of extension*

An extension is not permitted unless one of the following conditions apply:

(i)   no earlier accounting reference period has been extended; or
(ii) the notice is given not less than 5 years after the date on which any earlier period which was extended has come to an end; or
(iii) the company is a subsidiary or holding company of another company, and the new accounting reference date coincides with that of the other company.[2]

---

[1] CA 1985, s 225(5).
[2] Ibid, s 225(6). See para 9.23(a), above.

Overseas companies

9.28   An oversea company[1] is similarly required to prepare a balance sheet and a profit and loss account in respect of each accounting reference period. The same rules apply here with the following exceptions.

(a) *First accounting reference period*

The date of establishment of a place of business in the UK is regarded as equivalent to the date of incorporation of a UK company. Thus the first accounting reference period for an oversea company must begin on a date not later than the date on which a place of business was established in the UK, and must be a period of not less than six or more than 18 months.[2]

(b) *Duration and frequency of extension*

Oversea companies are subject to the same limitation on the length of an extended accounting reference period as UK companies are, i e a maximum of 18 months. But whereas UK companies are also subject to restrictions on the frequency with which their accounting reference periods can be extended, these limitations do not apply to oversea companies.

[1] See para 1.04, above.
[2] CA 1985, s 701(3) and (4).

FORM AND CONTENT OF ACCOUNTS

Introduction

9.29   An individual company's accounts must in general comply with Sch 4 to the Act. There are however different requirements in respect of special category companies (insurance, banking and shipping companies) and these are discussed below.[1]

If at the end of its financial year a company has subsidiaries it must also prepare group accounts.[2] The group accounts are required to comply with Sch 4 insofar as the provisions are relevant to a group, but the holding company is exempt from the requirement to present a profit and loss account, provided certain conditions are met.

[1] See paras 9.156 and 10.03, below.
[2] CA 1985, s 229.

True and fair view

9.30   A company's balance sheet must give a true and fair view of its state of affairs at the end of its financial year, and the profit and loss account must give a true and fair view of its profit or loss for the financial year.[1]

(a) If the balance sheet and profit and loss account drawn up in accordance with the statutory requirements would not provide sufficient information to give a true and fair view, then the additional information necessary for a true and fair view must be presented in the balance sheet or profit and loss account, or in a note to the accounts.[2]

(b) If, owing to special circumstances in the case of any company, compliance with any of the requirements of Sch 4 would prevent the accounts giving a true and fair view (notwithstanding any additional information provided in accordance with s 228(4)) the directors must depart from the requirement so far as is necessary to give a true and fair view.[3]

The ASC obtained Counsel's opinion in September 1983 on the meaning of true and fair, with particular reference to the accounting standards.[4]

---

[1] CA 1985, s 228(2).
[2] Ibid, s 228(4).
[3] Ibid, s 228(5).
[4] *Accountancy*, November 1983, p 154.

True and fair

9.31 In practice the major instances in which the true and fair override principle is applied are the instances in which the statutory provisions do not accord with a relevant SSAP or with industry practice. In general such instances are likely to be acceptable to the courts but this is not to say that the courts are under any obligation to endorse these departures. Care must be taken to give the details of the departure and its effect.

Particular problems have arisen in the following areas, where the treatment recommended by the SSAP does not accord with the legislation:

(a) foreign currency translation;[1]
(b) long term contracts;[2]
(c) investment properties.[3]

Some industries also encounter specific problems in connection with the true and fair override principle in the context of their business.

Accounts can depart from the statutory requirements without the authority of a SSAP, provided that such a departure is necessary for compliance with generally accepted accounting principles. But such instances tend to be rarer, not least because their justification is more difficult without the authority of a SSAP to back them up.

---

[1] See para 9.84, below.
[2] See para 9.101, below.
[3] See para 9.93, below.

Schedule 4: outline

9.32 The Sch 4 requirements are basically the accounting and disclosure requirements which were introduced by CA 1981. Additional matters requiring disclosure in the notes to the accounts are contained in Sch 5 and 6. Sch 4 is in seven parts as shown below:

Part I   Lays down general rules for the form and content of accounts. Companies must choose from the prescribed formats as to how they will present their balance sheets and profit and loss accounts.

Part II   Sets out the accounting principles and rules which must be applied in determining the amounts which are to be included in the accounts for certain items.

Part III   Sets out further disclosure requirements which if not given in the accounts must be set out in the notes to the accounts.

Part IV   Contains special provisions where the company is a holding or a subsidiary company.

Part V   Contains special provisions for investment companies.

Part VI   Contains special provisions where the company has entered into arrangements subject to merger relief.

Part VII   Contains definitions of the terms used in the Schedule.

Paragraphs 9.33 to 9.110, below deal with the requirements of Parts I and II of the Schedule.

Part I — General rules and formats

9.33   Section A of Part I deals with the general rules which are to be applied in adopting the formats. Section B contains the formats for the balance sheet and profit and loss account. There are four possible profit and loss account formats, and two possible balance sheet formats. Once a company has chosen its balance sheet and profit and loss account formats it must adopt the same formats in succeeding years unless in the opinion of the directors there are special reasons for a change.[1]

---

[1] CA 1985, Sch 4, para 2(1).

GENERAL RULES

Rigidity of the formats

9.34   Once a format has been chosen, the items must appear in the order and under the headings and subheadings given in the format concerned.[1] However, the formats may be adapted under any of the following conditions:

(a) Level of detail. Items may be shown in greater detail than required by the formats and new headings may be inserted for assets, liabilities, income or expenditure which are not covered by the formats.[2] This is subject to the restriction that certain items may not be treated as assets in a company's balance sheet (see para 9.56, below).

(b) Non-applicability of headings. A heading or sub-heading must be omitted if there is no amount to be shown for that item in respect of the current, or the preceding, financial year.[3]

(c) Headings prefixed by Arabic numerals. Headings and sub-headings in the formats are prefixed by one of the following:

— Letters
— Roman numerals
— Arabic numerals

Those which are prefixed by letters or Roman numerals can only be adapted under the circumstances in (a) or (b) above. Headings prefixed by Arabic numerals on the other hand are allowed greater flexibility.

Change of order and wording. Headings and sub-headings prefixed by Arabic numerals and their arrangement must be adapted, 'if the special nature of the company's business' requires it.[4] This provision has led to such headings being adapted liberally in practice. Strictly changes should not be made unless they are required because of the special nature of the business. Adaptation is not optional: the fact that a different wording appears preferable is not enough.

Extent of disclosure. Items prefixed by Arabic numerals may be combined if either:

(i) Their individual amounts are not material to assessing the state of affairs or profit or loss of the company for that year, or
(ii) The combination facilitates that assessment. In this case, the individual amounts of any items so combined shall be disclosed in a note.[5]

The latter alternative effectively means that items can be combined on the face of the balance sheet or profit and loss account, if doing so would aid clarity. However, there is no overall exemption from disclosure, since the detail must be given in the notes.

Wide advantage is taken of this provision in practice. It is common for many of the profit and loss account headings to be combined on the face of the profit and loss account, with detailed note disclosure. Similarly, the detailed analysis of fixed assets, debtors, creditors and stocks required is often not given on the face of the balance sheet, but rather in the notes to the accounts.

If items are combined because they are not material ((i) above), disclosure in the notes is not required. The term 'material' is not defined in this context, and it is a matter for the judgment of those preparing the accounts to decide whether amounts are immaterial or not.

---

[1] CA 1985, Sch 4, para 1.
[2] Ibid, Sch 4, para 3.
[3] Ibid, Sch 4, paras 3(5) and 4(3).
[4] Ibid, Sch 4, para 3(3).
[5] Ibid, Sch 4, para 3(4).

Consistency

9.35 The directors have a choice of format in respect of the company's first financial year for which it is preparing accounts under Schedule 4. In subsequent financial years, they must adopt the same format, unless in their opinion there are 'special reasons' for changing it. If a change is made, then the particulars of and reasons for the change in format must be detailed in the notes to the accounts in which the format is first adopted.[1] The corresponding amounts would need to be restated in the new format. There is no definition of 'special reasons'.[2]

---

[1] CA 1985, Sch 4, para 2.
[2] CA 1985, Sch 4, para 2(1).

Corresponding amounts

9.36   For every item shown in a company's accounts, the 'corresponding amount' for the preceding financial year must be shown. This 'corresponding amount' may not be properly comparable with the amount in the current financial year. In this case, the former amount should be adjusted, and the particulars of the adjustment, and the reasons for it, should be included in a note to the accounts.[1]

---

[1] CA 1985, Sch 4, para 4.

Set-off

9.37   In the balance sheet, asset items and liability items may not be set off against each other and, in the profit and loss account, income and expenditure items may not be set off against each other.[1] The rule against set-off is stated categorically and appears absolute. A number of items which were commonly set off under the CA 1948, have ceased to be so. Intercompany balances provide one example of this.[2]

However, a strictly literal interpretation could have the result that, for example, gains or losses on the sales of fixed assets or investments would not be included net in the profit and loss account. Instead, the sales proceeds and the net book value would have to be disclosed separately under the income and expenditure headings. In practice, the profit and loss account tends to disclose only the net gain or loss.

---

[1] CA 1985, Sch 4, para 5.
[2] See para 9.64, below.

The formats

9.38   The 'general rules' discussed in paras 9.33 to 9.37, above must be applied to the formats which appear in Part I, Section B, of the Schedule. There are two possible balance sheet formats, and four profit and loss account formats. The following paragraphs deal with some practical considerations that arise in connection with the formats. It is important to bear in mind however, that there is scope for judgment within the framework of the general rules. The Act offers some definitions of the headings, and these are contained in Part VII of the Schedule. But many items are not defined, and those that are often allow for flexibility. How to classify items within the formats then, may often be a question for the judgment of the directors.

The profit and loss account

9.39 There are four possible formats for the profit and loss account. Formats 1 and 2 are most widely used in the UK, although the directors are free to make the initial choice between the various formats.

All formats have the same headings for income items, but they differ with regard to the classification of expense items. Formats 1 and 3 require a 'functional' analysis of expenditure (cost of sales, distribution costs, administrative expenses etc). Formats 2 and 4 however simply require classification according to the type of expenditure, for example, staff costs and depreciation.

Headings

9.39A In both Formats 1 and 2, all the headings are prefixed by Arabic numerals. This allows considerable flexibility[1]. In particular:

(a) the headings may be changed if they are inappropriate to the special nature of the company's business, and

(b) the headings may be combined and the detail disclosed in the notes.

In practice, companies frequently combine various headings on the face of the profit and loss account and relegate the detail to the notes. This effectively means that the profit and loss account itself continues to be presented much as it was before the CA 1981 was implemented.

The following items must at the minimum be disclosed on the face of the profit and loss account:

(a) Profit or loss on ordinary activities before taxation, and

(b) Amounts set aside or proposed to be set aside to, or withdrawn or proposed to be withdrawn from, reserves, and

(c) Aggregate amount of dividends paid and proposed.[2]

In addition, the figure for extraordinary items is generally disclosed on the face of the profit and loss account, although the legislation permits their disclosure in the notes. For the SSAP 6 requirements, see 9.44 to 9.48, below.

---

[1] See para 9.34(c), above.

[2] CA 1985, Sch 4, para 3(6) and (7).

The choice of format — the profit and loss account

9.40 The following are amongst the factors which might influence the initial choice of format.

(a) *Type of business*

The nature of a company's business might mean that one of the formats is more appropriate for the company, although there is no onus on the directors to choose that particular format. Profit and loss account Format 2 for example is suitable for a manufacturing company in that the headings are more appropriate to the nature of their business.

(b)   *Commercial significance*
Profit and loss account Format 1 requires disclosure of the company's cost of sales, and gross profit. Format 2 does not require such overt disclosure. This is because the gross profit figure does not have to be openly disclosed, since the heading 'other external charges' could incorporate items which would not normally be classified under cost of sales. This might sometimes appear commercially more advantageous. Format 1 nevertheless appears the most popular of the formats. The 1983–84 ICAEW Survey of Published Accounts noted that 28 out of 36 of the public companies included in the survey adopted Format 1.

'Turnover' and 'other operating income'

9.41   Turnover is defined as 'the amounts derived from the provision of goods and services falling within the company's ordinary activities, after deduction of:

(a)   trade discounts,
(b)   value added tax, and
(c)   any other taxes based on the amounts so derived'.[1]

Sometimes it may not be clear whether a particular item would more appropriately be classified as 'turnover' or 'other operating income'. (Format 1, item 6). The crucial distinction is that the income should arise from 'the provision of goods or services' in order to qualify as turnover. Thus, agency commissions and rents receivable will come within this class, if they fall within the company's ordinary activities.

---

[1] CA 1985, Sch 4, para 95.

Turnover: the set-off rule

9.42   Trade discounts must be deducted in arriving at turnover.[1] Trade discounts are generally interpreted as including volume discounts, but not settlement discounts or promotional discounts.

This provision runs contrary to the general rule that there should be no set-off. But otherwise the set-off rules continue to apply. Thus, for example, any commissions receivable included in turnover should be the gross amounts receivable before deducting any disbursements, such as sub-commission payable. Companies acting as agents however should only include their commissions receivable in turnover, and not the gross sales.

---

[1] CA 1985, Sch 4, para 95(a).

Expenditure

9.43   The four profit and loss account formats differ most markedly as regards the headings for the various expense categories.

(a) Formats 1 and 3 allocate the major categories of expenditure according to function, as follows:

Cost of sales
Distribution costs
Administrative expenses

The Schedule states that the above headings 'should be stated after taking into account any provisions for depreciation or diminution in value of assets'.[1] This means that these items will have to be allocated over the three headings, and some allocation of other major expense items, for example staff costs, will probably be necessary.

Other than this, the CA 1985 gives no guidance as to how the expenses should be allocated over the above headings. In practice the following are usually incorporated under the following headings.

Cost of sales commonly includes
Changes in stocks and work in progress
Direct materials
Other external charges
Direct labour and production overheads

Distribution costs commonly includes
Sales staff's wages and commissions
Advertising
Transport costs
Agents' commissions payable
Travel costs
It is not clear where selling costs should be disclosed in the formats. In practice they are generally included under distribution costs.

Administrative expenses commonly includes

Professional fees
Payroll costs for administrative staff

However, the detailed allocation is left to the discretion of the directors. It should of course be reasonable, and also applied on a consistent basis from year to year.

(b) Formats 2 and 4 do not require the same detailed allocations to be made as Formats 1 and 3. The following points should be noted in connection with these formats.

(i) *Other external charges and other operating charges*
There is no definition of either heading in the Schedule, although they are the only two headings which do not apply to a specific type of expenditure; thus expenditure not covered by the other headings in the formats must be allocated between these two headings unless additional headings are to be inserted. (See 9.34(a) above). In practice most of this expenditure tends to be

allocated under 'other external charges'. 'Other operating charges' tends to be the heading to which costs which cannot be said to arise from an external source are allocated, for example bad debts written off.

(ii)   *Staff costs*
Staff costs are defined in Part VII of Schedule 4. They are the costs incurred in respect of people employed by the company under contracts of service during the year. The costs include wages and salaries, social security costs, and other pension costs. This includes executive directors' remuneration.

(iii)   *Diminutions in value: fixed assets*
Formats 1 and 3 have headings for amounts written off tangible and intangible fixed assets. All the formats have a heading for amounts written off investments. The question whether all diminutions in value are realised losses and should therefore be charged to the profit and loss account is discussed in paragraphs 65 to 68 below.

(iv)   *Current assets: amounts written off*
Under Formats 2 and 4, any exceptional amounts written off assets should be categorised separately. Amounts which are neither exceptional nor extraordinary are generally categorised under 'other operating charges'.

---

[1] CA 1985, Sch 4, part I (notes as the profit and loss account formats).

Extraordinary items

9.44   Extraordinary income and extraordinary charges are required to be disclosed separately in the profit and loss account, whichever format is adopted.

The Act gives no definition of these. SSAP 6 and the current exposure draft on extraordinary items and prior year adjustments, ED36, state that extraordinary items are those items which derive from events or transactions that fall outside the ordinary activities of the company, and which are both material and expected not to recur frequently or regularly.

Some examples given in ED36 include:

(a)   the discontinuance of a significant business segment;
(b)   the sale of an investment not acquired with the intention of resale;
(c)   provision made for the permanent diminution in value of fixed assets, because of unusual events during the period;
(d)   the expropriation of assets.[1]

However, the exposure draft stresses that whether an item is extraordinary will depend upon the particular circumstances. Consequently, what is an extraordinary item in one company's books may not be so in another's.

---

[1] ED36, para 8.

Extraordinary items: disclosure

9.45 All four formats show extraordinary income and extraordinary charges in a position in the profit and loss account following the ordinary results, and ED36 accords with this presentation, stating that extraordinary items should be shown after the figure for minority interests, but before deducting any appropriations.

The other mandatory disclosure requirements still hold. For example, the total for staff costs must be disclosed, at least in the notes to the accounts, whichever format is adopted. Thus if an item relating to staff costs is also extraordinary, the accounts would have to include it under extraordinary charges, and also make it clear in the notes that it is a part of the total staff costs for the year.

Generally, extraordinary items are shown on the face of the profit and loss account. There is no specific requirement by the Schedule to do this, and under the Schedule, they may be included in the notes. However presentation on the face of the profit and loss account is in keeping with the intention of the legislation. This is because Arabic headings should only be combined if their combination facilitates the assessment of the company's profit or loss for the financial year; it is unlikely that relegating the disclosure of extraordinary items to the notes would have this effect.

With regard to disclosure, ED36 states:

(a) each individual extraordinary item should be described and shown separately, either on the face of the profit and loss account, or in the notes;
(b) individual items of income and expenditure might derive from a single extraordinary event. If so, they constitute a single extraordinary item, and should be aggregated, with the balance being shown in extraordinary income or extraordinary charges, as appropriate;
(c) although the *net* result of a number of extraordinary items may not be significant, it may be necessary to show extraordinary income and extraordinary charges on the face of the profit and loss account, in order for the accounts to give a true and fair view.

Offset against retained reserves

9.46 The preface to ED36 states that:

(a) retained profits brought forward should not be included in the profit and loss account to offset extraordinary items;
(b) extraordinary items, since they are covered by the formats prescribed by Sch 4, cannot be accounted for as a reserve movement.

Extraordinary items: taxation

9.47 Both ED36 and the law state that the taxation attributable to extraordinary items should be shown separately.[1] The tax attributable to extraordinary items should be calculated by computing the tax charges with and without extraordinary items, and attributing the difference to extraordinary items.

---
[1] ED36 para 11 and CA 1985, Sch 4, para 54.

Exceptional items

9.48   Items are regarded as exceptional by virtue of their size or incidence, although they fall within the ordinary activities of the company. The legal interpretation is similar to the definition given in ED36.

As noted above, Formats 2 and 4 have a separate heading for 'exceptional amounts written off current assets'. Exceptional bad debts or provisions against stocks should therefore be categorised here if either of these formats is used. Otherwise there is no other heading in the formats for exceptional items. ED36 states that exceptional items should be shown on the face of the profit and loss account, and described as exceptional, where this is necessary for a true and fair view. In other cases, they should be shown in a note to the accounts, and be distinguishable as exceptional items.[1] If they are disclosed in a note, then they should be classified under the most appropriate heading in the profit and loss account. If either Format 1 or Format 3 is adopted then this will probably involve classifying the item under cost of sales, administrative expenses, or distribution costs. If either Format 2 or 4 is used and the item does not relate to a write-off against current assets the heading 'other operating charges' will probably be the most appropriate. Alternatively, a new heading could be inserted.

ED36 gives some examples of items which might fall to be classified as exceptional. These include:

(a)   redundancy costs, relating to continuing business segments;
(b)   reorganisation costs unrelated to the discontinuance of a business segment;
(c)   previously capitalised development expenditure written off other than as part of a process of amortisation;
(d)   profits appropriated to employee share schemes;
(e)   profits or losses on the disposal of fixed assets;
(f)   abnormal charges for bad debts and write-offs of stocks and work-in-progress;
(g)   abnormal provision for losses on long-term contracts;
(h)   surpluses arising in the settlement of insurance claims; and
(i)   amounts received in settlement of insurance claims for consequential loss of profits.[2]

---
[1] ED36, para 37.
[2] ED36, para 6.

Balance sheet

9.49   There are two choices of format for the balance sheet. Format 1 adopts a 'vertical' presentation, and Format 2 is 'horizontal'. The headings and sub-headings are the same, whichever format is adopted. The following points should be stressed regarding the arrangement of the headings within these formats.

(a) *Adaptability*

Several of the balance sheet headings are prefixed by letters or Roman numerals and consequently cannot be adapted. An exception is the heading 'revaluation reserve', which must be disclosed in the specified place within the formats, but need not be disclosed under that name, although it is prefixed by a Roman numeral.[1]

(b) *Totals*

The 'horizontal' format obviously dictates where the balance sheet total must be drawn. Under the vertical presentation however there is no provision as to where the total should be drawn, but because of the principle that headings must be shown in the prescribed order, no long term creditors can be disclosed underneath the headings for share capital and reserves, as was the case under CA 1948.

Some companies have however adopted the practice of totalling the balance sheet at 'total assets less current liabilities' (item G in Format 1). This means that longer term creditors are included above the headings for share capital and reserves but in the same total.

(c) *Net current assets*

Format 1 (the vertical presentation) requires that a total for net current assets should be disclosed. This is not necessary under Format 2.

In fact the net current assets figure disclosed under Format 1 can often be misleading, and the order of the headings cannot be changed to compensate for this. There are two reasons for this:

(i) *Debts due after more than twelve months*

'Current assets' include debts due after more than twelve months (see below). The Schedule requires that the effect on the net current assets figure of such items should be disclosed if material.

(ii) *Provisions*

There is no legal requirement that 'provisions' should only include items due after more than twelve months, (although it is sometimes regarded as best practice). Again then, the net current assets figure could be distorted in that it might not reflect some liabilities which could be incurred within twelve months.

---

[1] CA 1985, Sch 4, para 34(2).

Alternative positions in the formats

9.50 Both formats contain some headings which may be disclosed in one of two places. These headings are as follows:

(i) Called up share capital not paid
(ii) Prepayments and accrued income
(iii) Accruals and deferred income

There is no guidance in the legislation as to when the alternative positions should be adopted.

Fixed assets

9.51   All assets must be classified as *either* fixed *or* current. Under the CA 1948 Act, assets which were regarded as neither fixed nor current could be disclosed separately but this is no longer permitted. Notably, investments were often categorised in this way. Fixed assets are those which are intended for use on a 'continuing basis' in the company's activities. Any assets not intended for such use are to be classified as current.[1]

This distinction has given rise to some anomalous situations, e g loans made by the company can be classified under 'fixed assets' provided that they are in the nature of an investment, and are thus intended for use on a continuing basis in the company's activities. Otherwise, debts due to the company are required to be disclosed under 'debtors' in 'current assets'. This could lead to the situation where amounts not recoverable within twelve months are included as current assets. The amount falling due after more than one year must be shown separately for each heading under debtors, but is still included in the 'current assets' group.[2] If the amounts are sufficiently material, then the relevant amounts could be disclosed on the face of the balance sheet to minimise distortion.

---

[1] CA 1985, Sch 4, para 77.
[2] CA 1985, Sch 4, Note 5 to balance sheet formats.

Intangible assets

9.52   Intangible assets include:

(1) development costs;
(2) concessions, patents, licences, trademarks and similar rights and assets;
(3) goodwill;
(4) payments on account.

Development costs

9.53   These can only be included in the balance sheet 'under special circumstances'.[1] There is no guidance in the Act as to what constitutes 'special circumstances'. In practice, provided that the costs fulfil the conditions in SSAP 13, whereby development costs may be capitalised and amortised, this is taken to be satisfactory. The following information should be given in the notes to the accounts:

(a) the period over which the amount of those costs is being or is to be written off, and
(b) the reasons for capitalising the development costs in question.[2]

S 269 states that development costs are to be treated as a realised loss for the purpose of computing distributable profits. This provision will not apply if the directors can give special reasons why they should not be so treated. Conformity with the conditions for deferral set out in SSAP 13 can generally be regarded as sufficient justification for not treating them as realised losses.[3]

---

[1] CA 1985, Sch 4, para 20(1).
[2] CA 1985, Sch 4, para 20(2).
[3] SSAP 13, paras 7–9.

Concessions, patents, licences, trademarks, and similar rights and assets

9.54 These can only be included if:

(a) the assets were acquired for valuable consideration, or
(b) the assets in question were created by the company itself.[1]

---

[1] CA 1985, Sch 4, Note 2 to the balance sheet formats.

Goodwill

9.55 Goodwill may only be included as an asset in a company's balance sheet, to the extent that it was acquired for valuable consideration.[1] Sch 4, para 21(2) states that this consideration should be reduced by provisions for depreciation calculated to write off that amount systematically over a period chosen by the directors. This period should not exceed the useful economic life of the goodwill in question. The directors must disclose the period chosen, and the reasons for choosing that period, in a note to the accounts. The requirement to write off goodwill does not apply to consolidation goodwill arising in the consolidated balance sheet of a group.[2] However the EEC Seventh Company Law Directive, when enacted, will introduce this requirement for consolidation goodwill, and this is anticipated in SSAP 22.

SSAP 22
(a) SSAP 22 states that the preferred accounting treatment for goodwill is immediate write off against reserves. It does not, however, debar amortisation through the profit and loss account over the useful economic life as an alternative. One instance in which this treatment might be used is where the company has insufficient reserves against which the goodwill can be written off.

  The SSAP provisions are not inconsistent with the legislation; the legislative provisions deal only with the situation where goodwill is carried as an asset in the balance sheet, and the possibility of immediate write off is permitted.
(b) The legislation contains no guidance for determining the useful economic life of goodwill. Reference should be made to Appendix 1 to SSAP 22 for indications of factors to be taken into account in determining the useful economic life.
(c) The question of goodwill written off against reserves impinges on the problem of realised and unrealised profits. The elimination of goodwill constitutes a reduction in realised reserves to the extent that the goodwill is considered to have suffered an actual diminution in value.

But in all other cases, SSAP 22 recommends that goodwill which is written off immediately should initially be written off to unrealised reserves with an amount being transferred from unrealised to realised reserves so as to reduce realised reserves on a systematic basis over the economic life.

This appears to imply that goodwill may be written off to the revaluation reserve, but legally the position is in doubt.[3]

---

[1] CA 1985, Sch 4, Note 3 to the formats.
[2] CA 1985, Sch 4, para 66.
[3] See para 9.110, below.

Costs which must not be shown as assets

9.56   As noted above, new headings may be inserted for items which are not covered by the formats.

However Sch 4 specifically excludes the following items from being treated as assets in a company's balance sheet:

(1)   preliminary expenses;
(2)   expenses and commission on any issue of shares or debentures;
(3)   research costs.[1]

---

[1] CA 1985, Sch 4, para 3(2).

(a) Preliminary expenses. There is no legal definition of preliminary expenses. In practice they are regarded as being those costs involved in setting up a company, which would not be incurred in setting up an unincorporated business. Start-up costs, or pretrading expenditure, are not generally classified as preliminary expenses. However if start-up costs fall within the definition of development expenditure, they may be included under that heading in the balance sheet.

Preliminary expenses can alternatively be written off to the share premium account.

(b) Share or debenture issue expenses. These expenses may be written off either through the profit and loss account or against the share premium account. This item would normally include expenses such as Stock Exchange listing costs and any professional fees which are related to a share issue.

(c) Research costs. Research costs are not defined in the legislation. Again, in practice guidance should be taken from the SSAP 13 definition.

Tangible fixed assets

9.57   Sch 4 give the following four subheadings for the analysis of tangible fixed assets:

(1)   land and buildings;
(2)   plant and machinery;

(3) fixtures, fittings, tools and equipment;
(4) payments on account and assets in course of construction.

In practice many companies adapt these headings, or add additional ones to suit their circumstances. It will be recalled that even though these sub-headings are prefixed by Arabic numerals, they should only be adapted if the special nature of the company's business requires it.[1]

---

[1] CA 1985, Sch 4, para 3(3) and see para 9.34, above.

Investment properties

9.58 There are three possible headings under which investment properties may be categorised:

(1) fixed assets — land and buildings;
(2) fixed assets — investments;
(3) current assets — investments.

The question whether such properties should be categorised as fixed or current depends on the 'continuing use' criteria. Generally if the company is intending to sell them in the near future, they should be included under current assets. (This is a provision which extends to all fixed assets, and not just investments.) Otherwise, if they are being held for letting, or if they are in the process of being developed, they should be included in the balance sheet as fixed assets. In this case, they are generally categorised under the heading of 'land and buildings'. This is because the heading 'land and buildings' is analysed in the notes over freehold, long leasehold or short leasehold.

For the problems which arise on the valuation of investment properties under SSAP 19 see below.[1]

---

[1] Para 9.93.

Tangible assets: the set off rules

Regional development grants

9.59 One of the possible accounting treatments under SSAP 4 for a capital-based regional development grant is to offset the grant against the cost of the asset. Alternatively the grant could be included as a deferred credit in the balance sheet. It is questionable whether the former treatment is still accept-able in the light of the set-off prohibition in the legislation.[1] The grant may be viewed as an integral part of the cost of the asset: consequently deducting it from the original purchase price or production cost of the asset represents the substance of the transaction correctly. An opposing view is that 'cost' is defined in the legislation as purchase price or production cost and so any such deductions cannot be viewed as an integral part of cost. If this view is taken, the RDG will have to be shown separately, as a deferred credit.

---

[1] CA 1985, Sch 4, para 5, and see para 9.37, above.

9.60 The situation has become further complicated, since, as from 28 November 1984, the rules for RDGs have changed. Previously all such grants were directly related to capital expenditure. Now, grants are available for approved projects. Broadly, a project will be approved if it creates new, or expands existing, productive capacity, or changes a product or production process. If this project provides jobs, then applicants will automatically receive the higher of:

(a) a job grant of £3000 per job provided; *and*
(b) a capital grant of fifteen per cent of capital expenditure, subject to a maximum £10,000 per job provided.

Therefore, in the case of different projects involving different numbers of jobs created, but the same capital expenditure, a company may receive either a job or a capital-based grant. Capital-based grants are conceptually similar to the old capital-based RDG's; therefore the principles outlined in above will continue to be relevant. The question is whether the job-based grants should be treated as revenue grants, or whether they should also be accounted for by one of the methods described in para 9.61, below. But it is difficult to see why the basis of calculating the grant should determine its accounting treatment. Consequently, the methods outlined above are likely to continue to apply to grants calculated under the new rules.

Assets under lease or hire purchase

9.61 Under SSAP 21 assets acquired under hire purchase or on a finance lease should be capitalised in the lessee's balance sheet. Before the introduction of SSAP 21 and the Companies' Act 1981, some companies used to disclose assets subject to hire purchase in the balance sheet net of the outstanding creditor. Such a treatment is no longer acceptable, neither under SSAP 21 nor because of the rule against set off in Schedule 4 paragraph 5, under the terms of the legislation. Instead the related creditor should be analysed under the headings for creditors.

Investments

9.62 The Companies' Act 1981 introduced a requirement for a detailed breakdown of the items included under investments which was more extensive than that under any previous requirements in the UK.
The following analysis must be given:

Shares in group companies
Loans to group companies
Shares in related companies
Loans to related companies
Other investments, other than loans
Other loans
Own shares

These headings are prefixed by Arabic numerals, and consequently they may, if immaterial, or for the purpose of assisting appraisal, be combined and the detailed analysis disclosed in a note. The notes to the accounts must also give details of any movements on the investments during the year.[1]

---

[1] CA 1985, Sch 4, Balance sheet formats B111.

Related companies

9.63 The Companies' Act 1981 introduced the concept of a 'related company'. This is defined as 'any body corporate (which is not in the same group as that company) in which that company [i e the investor company] holds on a long-term basis a qualifying capital interest for the purpose of securing a contribution to its own activities by the exercise of any control or influence arising from that interest'. 'Qualifying capital interest' refers to a right to vote in all circumstances at general meetings. Where a company holds 20% of the nominal value of the shares carrying such a right, there is a presumption that the investing company holds a qualifying capital interest.

The definition of a related company is very similar to that of an associated company in SSAP 1. There are however differences between the two, the most significant of which are:

(a) Under SSAP 1, an interest in a company has to be 'substantial' before the company will be deemed an associate. But a company will qualify as 'related' if the interest is sufficient 'to secure a contribution to the company's activities by the exercise of control or influence arising from that interest'. It would thus seem possible for a company to be related but not an associate, as defined by SSAP 1.

(b) Under SSAP 1, the interests of all the members of the group should be taken into account in determining whether a company is an associate. This is not stated with reference to related companies in the legislation: paragraph 92 to Schedule 4 simply refers to the investing company's holding a qualifying capital interest, and there is no stipulation that the interests of other members of the group should be taken into account.

Strictly, the legal terminology should be used in the statutory accounts and the companies referred to as 'related'. In practice many sets of accounts continue to use the term 'associated', no doubt because it is a more familiar term. Where the term 'associated' is used, reference should be made in the notes to the fact that such companies are also related companies (assuming of course that they fulfil both definitions.)

Intercompany balances

9.64 Under the 1948 Act, it was a common practice to arrive at a net balance for each group company and then to offset debit and credit balances with the various companies. The net balance was then included under 'interests in subsidiaries' in the balance sheet. The set off rules mean that this treatment is no longer acceptable.

Any intercompany balances now should be split up into their constituent elements, and included in the balance sheet as follows:

	Category (references are to balance sheet Format 1)
Shares in group companies	Fixed assets (BIII 1)
Long term loans to group companies	Fixed assets (BIII 2)
Long term loans from group companies	Creditors: amounts falling due after more than one year (H6)
Intergroup current accounts realisable within one year	Current assets (CII 2)
Intergroup current accounts payable within one year	Creditors: amounts falling due within one year (E6)

As with non-group loans, the current portion of any loan from a group company should be included as part of current liabilities. In the absence of any evidence to the contrary, a loan should be treated as current.

The distinction between a current account and a loan may in some circumstances be a fine one. However, as a general rule, a loan is unlikely to have some formal documentation setting out the terms.

Own shares
The 1981 Companies Act introduced the requirement that if a company purchases its own shares, it must cancel them on purchase. This means that the only situation in which a company may hold its own shares is when it has acquired them for no consideration. This will be the case if they are acquired by way of a gift, or by forfeiture. The 1980 Companies Act introduced the requirement that if a company acquires its own shares by way of forfeiture then it must generally dispose of them within three years.[1]

Other investments
This heading should incorporate holdings of listed and unlisted securities, other than holdings in group or related companies. It might also include term deposits with banks or building societies, if they fulfil the continuing use criterion. Similarly, investments in non-corporate entities could be included here.

---

[1] CA 1985, s 146(2) and see para 4.19, above.

Current assets

Set-off

9.65   The valuation rules relating to current assets are discussed more fully below (9.100 and following). However one aspect of these has implications for the classification of items in the balance sheet. This is the requirement that current assets should be stated at their net realisable value, if this is lower than cost.[1] Consequently if a provision is made in respect of an asset which is expected to realise less than the purchase price or production cost, it should be netted off the cost of the asset. This overrides the general requirement that there should be no set-off.[2] This means that bad debt provisions, loss provisions on long term contracts, and obsolescence provisions on stocks, should all be netted off the assets to which they relate. The acounting treatment is similar with regard to provisions for depreciation and other diminutions in value in respect of fixed assets. There is no requirement to disclose the amount written off current assets as there is in the case of fixed assets. If current assets which have been written down to net realisable value subsequently recover all or part of their original cost, the amount provided must be written back to the extent it is no longer necessary.[3]

---

[1] CA 1985, Sch 4, para 23(1).
[2] Ibid, Sch 4, para 5.
[3] Ibid, Sch 4, para 23(2).

Stocks

9.65A The heading 'stocks' is analysed into various subheadings in the formats. These are more specific than under SSAP 9, which states that stocks should be categorised into 'categories appropriate to the business'. It might be necessary to adapt the sub-headings if the special nature of the company's business demands it.[1]

---

[1] CA 1985, Sch 4, para 3(3).

Payments on account

9.66 The sub-heading under 'stocks' for 'payments on account' refers not to payments received from customers, but to payments made in advance to suppliers for goods not yet received.

This raises the question of how to account for payments received on account from customers in respect of long term contract work in progress. SSAP 9 states that these payments should be deducted from long-term contract work in progress.

A sub-heading is included under creditors for 'payments on account', and the notes to the formats state that 'payments received on account of orders shall be shown for each of these items insofar as they are not deductions from stocks'. This implies that payments on account may be offset against long term contract work in progress, but that it is necessary to look at each contract in turn when offsetting payments received. Those that result in a net credit balance should be included in creditors, whereas the others can be netted off stocks. The aggregate amount of payments received on account should not be offset against the aggregate amount of work in progress.

Debtors

9.67 Both formats analyse debtors over a series of subheadings as follows:

1. Trade debtors
2. Amounts owed by group companies
3. Amounts owed by related companies
4. Other debtors
5. Called up share capital not paid
6. Prepayments and accrued income

Items (5) and (6) may be included in alternative positions within the formats.

The question of amounts due after more than 12 months being included in debtors has already been discussed (para 9.51, above).

Prepayments and accrued income

9.68 'Prepayments' commonly include such items as rent or subscriptions. If the item is of a trading nature, however, it might be more appropriate to include it under trade debtors. Either classification appears permissible under the legislation, provided that it is consistently applied.

'Accrued income' is a term which was introduced by the CA 1981. It is generally taken to include some of those items which were conventionally, prior to the CA 1981, classified as 'sundry debtors' i e amounts due but not yet received. Examples include interest due on loans or other items which are not included within the company's normal trading activities.

Amounts owed to related companies

9.69 The CA 1985 requires disclosure of amounts owed to or by related companies. The definition of a related company in paragraph 92 of Schedule 4 is discussed in paragraph 9.63 above.

Cash at bank and in hand

9.70 In practice this conventionally includes bank deposits repayable on demand, but not term loans with a bank nor deposits with any other financial institutions, such as building societies. These are generally included under 'current asset investments'.

If a company operates several accounts with the same bank, with a legal right of set-off, the question arises whether it is permissible to show the net balance due to or from the bank on the balance sheet. The answer is not a straightforward one. If the balances were repayable on demand, or all repayable on the same date, set-off would seem acceptable. A situation in which set-off would appear unacceptable, would be one in which any amount due to the bank was repayable before the term deposit matured.

Another disclosure problem could arise if the company is a member of a group, and that group has one bank account which is used by all members of the group, with the bank retaining a memorandum column for each company. Generally in such a situation each company accepts liability for the total balance. The usual accounting treatment is for each individual company to include its own balance in its individual balance sheet, but to include a note to the accounts explaining the situation and the extent of its liability.

Creditors

9.71 Under Format 1, creditors must be analysed on the face of the balance sheet between amounts falling due within one year and amounts falling due after one year. This is because the two captions are designated by letters (Format 1 E and H). Under Format 2, this analysis is not required on the face of the balance sheet because the information is incorporated within one balance sheet caption C, under liabilities. However, the same detail must be disclosed in a note.[1]

---

[1] CA 1985, Sch 4, Note 13 to balance sheet Format 2.

No set repayment date

9.72 If there is no set repayment date, then it should be treated as becoming payable at the earliest possible date that the creditor could demand repayment, or on demand. This will apply in the following situations:

(a) *Group balances*

Often a subsidiary will have a loan from its holding company, but there will be no agreement as to when this loan should be repaid. Prior to the CA 1981, such items were included in long-term liabilities, on the assumption that the amount would not become repayable in the foreseeable future. Under Schedule 4 however, unless there is any specific agreement to the contrary, such amounts should strictly be included under 'creditors: amounts falling due within one year'.

(b) *Debenture loans*

Debenture loans can sometimes be redeemed on alternative dates. If this is the case, it should be assumed that the loan will be repayable at the earliest redemption date under normal circumstances.

(c) *Bank overdrafts/loans*

If a bank loan is repayable on demand, then it should be included under amounts payable within one year. If a company has a loan facility for a term of years, then the balance sheet disclosure will depend upon the terms of the agreement. Only if the bank cannot withdraw the facility before the expiry of the term, should that part of the advance which falls due after one year be included in 'amounts falling due after more than one year'.

(d) *Creditors: amounts falling due by instalments*

Certain debts may be payable in instalments with some instalments payable within one year, and some payable after one year. In this case, the amounts should be analysed, and disclosed in the balance sheet under the relevent categories.

Trade creditors and accruals

9.73   CA 1985 requires that 'trade creditors' be disclosed separately from accruals and deferred income. None of these terms is defined. An accrual is often regarded as an amount due but not yet invoiced at the year end. Under this definition goods received but not invoiced at the year end should be included in accruals. In fact, many companies consider it gives a more meaningful picture to include these amounts under trade creditors.

Either classification appears permissible. The method chosen should however be applied consistently from year to year.

'Deferred income' refers to income which has been received in advance of, and is being carried forward to match against, the relevant expenditure in a future period. An example is government grants which may be classified under this heading.

Other creditors, including taxation and social security

9.74   Note 9 to the formats states that 'the amounts for creditors in respect of taxation and social security shall be shown separately from the amount for other creditors'. There is no definition within the Act as to what 'taxation and social security' should comprise, but the natural meaning suggests that all taxes should be included. In practice, companies tend to include PAYE, employees, and employers, NIC, ACT payable, and VAT within this heading. This means that the heading could include both amounts due directly from the company, and amounts which it has collected from third parties.

(a) *Corporation tax*
Corporation tax payable could be included within the heading 'other creditors including taxation and social security costs'. But because it requires separate disclosure in the notes, it is usually included under a separate heading. Whether it should be included under creditors — amounts falling due within one year', or 'creditors — amounts falling due after one year' will depend on the payment date.

It is not generally included under 'provisions', although there is a subheading under 'provisions' for 'taxation including deferred taxation'. An argument could be made out for including it here, since there is some uncertainty as to the amount payable until the assessment is agreed by the Revenue. However it is generally accepted that only deferred taxation should be included under provisions.

(b) *Dividends*
There is no specific sub-heading in the formats for this item. It can either be included under the heading of 'other creditors, including taxation and social security', or given a separate heading. Generally most companies adopt the latter practice.

Provisions for liabilities and charges

9.75   These are defined as 'any amount retained as reasonably necessary for the purpose of providing for any liability or loss which is either likely to be incurred, or certain to be incurred, but uncertain as to the amount or date on which it will arise'.[1] This is a wider definition than that in the CA 1948. There a provision was defined as 'any amount written off or retained by way of providing for depreciation, renewals or diminution in value of assets or retained by way of providing for any *known* liability of which the amount cannot be determined with substantial accuracy'. The new definition covers general provisions for liabilities which are likely to emerge but which cannot be quantified with accuracy.

---

[1] CA 1985, Sch 4, para 89.

Short or long term provisions

9.76 The position of 'provisions for liabilities and charges' at 'I' under Format 1 excludes them from the net current assets figure. This treatment implies that they are long term in nature. However there is no statutory requirement that items included under 'provisions for liabilities and charges' should be confined to long term items nor is there any requirement that the effect of any short term provision on the figure for net current assets be disclosed in a note.

It is generally regarded as best practice to include in provisions only those items which are of a long term nature, for example, as the format suggests, the deferred tax provision (I2). Any items which are likely to become payable within the next twelve months are best included as a separate heading under 'creditors: amounts falling due within one year'. If they are recorded under 'provisions', then if material the true and fair requirement would necessitate that the effect on net current assets be disclosed.

Provisions: the set-off rules

9.77 The set-off rules might seem to indicate that the component parts of a provision would have to be analysed out and included in the balance sheet under the appropriate headings. A provision for anticipated closure costs for example is usually a net figure arrived at after offsetting all the anticipated expenses against any income that would result from realising the assets. Similarly a deferred taxation provision is arrived at by offsetting the anticipated corporation tax payable in respect of timing differences against any ACT recoverable.

Generally, it is thought more meaningful to continue to show the net figure in such cases, whilst the liability is still sufficiently uncertain and therefore for it to rank as a provision.[1]

It is when the liability ceases to be a provision that its component parts should be shown gross. This is at the stage when the element of uncertainty is eliminated.

---

[1] CA 1985, Sch 4, para 89.

Capital and reserves

9.78 The following reserves are prefixed by Roman numerals, and should thus be disclosed separately on the face of the balance sheet in the following order:

Share premium account
Revaluation reserve
Other reserves
Profit and loss account

The terminology used in the CA 1985 must be kept to, with the exception of the 'revaluation reserve' which may be disclosed under another appropriate name, but must be disclosed in the same place in the balance sheet.[1]

---

[1] CA 1985, Sch 4, para 34(2).

9.79 'Other reserves' includes all reserves not covered by the other headings. It can include both distributable and non-distributable reserves. Some reserves are statutorily non-distributable but reference should also be made to the company's articles in determining whether reserves are distributable or not. There is no legal requirement to distinguish between distributable and non-distributable reserves in the accounts, although some companies include such an analysis in the notes to their accounts.

ACCOUNTING PRINCIPLES

9.80 The amounts to be included in respect of all items in a company's accounts are to be determined in accordance with certain statutory accounting principles. These are set out in paragraphs 10–14 of Schedule 4 and are as follows:

(a) *Going concern*
The company shall be presumed to be carrying on business as a going concern.

(b) *Consistency*
Accounting policies shall be applied consistently from one financial year to the next.

(c) *Prudence*
The amount of any item shall be determined on a prudent basis and in particular

  (i) only profits realised at the balance sheet date shall be included in the profit and loss account, and
  (ii) all liabilities and losses which have arisen, or are likely to arise, in respect of the financial year to which the accounts relate shall be taken into account, including those which only become apparent between the balance sheet date and the date on which the balance sheet is signed on behalf of the board of directors.

(d) *Accruals*
All income and charges relating to the financial year to which the accounts relate shall be taken into account, without regard to the date of receipt or payment.

(e) *'Separate valuation'*
  In determining the aggregate amount of any item, the amount of each individual asset or liability that should be taken into account shall be determined separately.

If it appears to the directors that there are special reasons for departing from any of these principles they may do so, but the particulars of the departure, the reasons for it, and its effect must be stated in a note to the accounts.[1]

This exemption from compliance with the accounting principles is different from the exemption from the legislative requirements in order for the accounts to give a true and fair view.[2] The directors in preparing accounts may depart from the accounting principles if they consider that there are special reasons for so doing, without the departure being necessary in order for the accounts to give a true and fair view. However, the requirement at s 228(5) overrides all the Schedule 4 requirements. Consequently, accounts which do take advantage of the 'special reasons' exemption must still be true and fair.

---

[1] See para 9.84(c), below.
[2] CA 1985, s 228(5).

9.81 These principles essentially restate the fundamental accounting concepts in SSAP 2, although the wording is not the same. A new principle, or one that is not stated specifically in the standards, is (e) — the separate valuation principle. This principle is relevant to the accounting treatment of several categories of assets and liabilities. In particular, it prohibits the 'portfolio method' of valuation for investments. Before the introduction of this provision, investments were often included in the balance sheet at an aggregate value, and, provided that the total book value of all the investments was not less than their value in aggregate, no adjustment was made. In this situation, some of the investments could have had a value below their book value, and others a value above book value. Schedule 4 however requires that a provision must be made in respect of a fixed asset if it suffers a permanent diminution in value. Consequently, investments must be looked at on an individual basis to ensure that the statutory requirements are being met. The separate valuation principle applies equally to other assets included in the balance sheet, for example, stocks.

Realised profits

9.82 It is the accounting principle which requires items to be determined on a prudent basis which has caused the most problems, and in particular the requirement that only profits realised at the balance sheet date should be included in the profit and loss account. An attempt to clarify the definition of realised profits is included in paragraph 91 of the Schedule:

'Realised profits are . . . such profits as fall to be treated as realised profits in accordance with principles generally accepted with respect to the determination for accounting purposes of realised profits at the time when those accounts are prepared'.

9.83 The legislation does not define the term 'generally accepted principles'. The question of a suitable definition was made more pressing because the concept of realisation is linked with that of distributability: only profits which have been realised may be distributed by way of dividend or otherwise to shareholders.[1]

In the light of this, the CCAB issued guidance for the determination of realised profits in September 1982.[2]

---

[1] CA 1985, s 263(3) and Sch 4, para 91. See also paras 4.71 and 4.72, above.

[2] TR 481: 'The determination of realised profits and disclosure of distributable profits in the context of the Companies Acts 1948 to 1981', *Accountancy* October 1982 pp 122-3.

Realised profits: CCAB guidance

9.84   A summary of the guidance in TR481 is as follows:

(a) Profits which are required by SSAPs to be recognised in the profit and loss account should normally be treated as·realised unless the SSAP specifically indicates that they should be treated as unrealised (see (c) below).

(b) Profits may be recognised in the profit and loss account in accordance with a policy which is not the subject of a SSAP, or exceptionally in accordance with a policy which is contrary to a SSAP. Provided that the accounting policy is consistent with the accounting principles in Schedule 4, then the profit will be regarded as a realised profit.

(c) Schedule 4, paragraph 15, states that the directors may depart from any of the accounting principles, 'if there are special reasons' for doing so. If they do depart from any of the principles, then they must give particulars of the departure, the reasons for it and its effect in a note to the accounts.

The fact that the accounts would fail to give a true and fair view could constitute a special reason for departure from the accounting principles. SSAP 20 provides an example. Under SSAP 20, unrealised exchange gains on unsettled long term monetary items can be taken to the profit and loss account. This treatment is a departure from the accounting principle that only realised profits should be included in the profit and loss account. Paragraph 65 of SSAP 20 states that the need to show a true and fair view constitutes a special reason for departure from this principle.

9.85   The CCAB·issued further guidance concurrently with this, entitled 'The determination of distributable profits in the context of the Companies Acts 1948 to 1981.'[1] Although this deals primarily with the question of distributability, it is relevant in the context of determining what profits should be treated as realised, when their accounting treatment is not covered by a SSAP. The guidance looks at the following areas which require special consideration:

(a) *Provisions*

Certain provisions are to be treated as realised losses:

(i) Any amounts written off by way of providing for depreciation or diminution in value of assets, and

(ii) Any amount retained as reasonably necessary for the purpose of providing for any liability or loss which is likely to be incurred, or certain to be incurred but uncertain as to amount or as to the date on which it will arise.[2]

For the exceptions to the rule in (i) above, see para 9.86, below.

(b) *Revaluation of assets*

A surplus over original cost recognised on the revaluation of any asset is unrealised and must be credited to the revaluation reserve.[3] However, there are no statutory requirements as to whether the surplus that represents the writing back of past depreciation or diminutions in value should be regarded as realised or unrealised. This is the difference between the cost and the net book value of the asset at the time of revaluation. The CCAB left the question unresolved in TR 482.

However, ED37 'Accounting for depreciation' addresses this problem, and states that depreciation charged prior to the revaluation should not be written back to the profit and loss account. Rather, the difference between the net book amount prior to the revaluation and the revalued amount should be transferred to the revaluation reserve.[4]

(c) *Depreciation and revalued assets*

Where a fixed asset is valued upwards, the difference between the depreciation based on the revalued amount and the historical cost depreciation represents a realised profit.[5] For the accounting treatment of this, see paragraph 9.107 below.

(d) *Disposals of revalued assets*

On the disposal of a revalued asset, any surplus over cost becomes realised. This means that the surplus should be released from the revaluation reserve to reserves representing realised profits. This accords with ED36 'Extraordinary items and prior year adjustments', which states that any unrealised reserve should be released on the disposal of an asset and included in the profit and loss account.

In the same way, any loss which had been treated as unrealised should on disposal of the assets be redesignated as a realised loss. This could arise, for example, if the unrealised loss had initially arisen on a revaluation of all fixed assets: it would then have been debited to the revaluation reserve.[6] On disposing of this asset however the unrealised loss must be transferred from the revaluation reserve.

(e) *Development costs*

Development costs shown as an asset are normally to be treated as a realised loss for distribution purposes. But if the directors can justify the costs being carried forward not being so treated, this requirement does not apply. They will normally be able to do so if the costs are carried forward in accordance with SSAP 13.

---

1 TR 482, *Accountancy*, October 1982, pp 123–126.

2 CA 1985, s 275.

3 Ibid, Sch 4, para 34, and para 9.109, below.

4 ED37, para 22.
5 CA 1985, s 275(2).
6 Ibid, s 275(1), and para 9.88, below.

Provisions for diminution in value

9.86   Schedule 4, para 19(2) requires that a provision for diminution in value must be made if a fixed asset suffers a permanent diminution in value. A similar provision may be made if a fixed asset investment suffers a temporary diminution in value, but the directors are not under any obligation to do so.[1]

Such provisions are generally regarded as realised losses irrespective of whether they are permanent or temporary. There are however two possible exceptions to this:

(a) where the provision is the reversal of a previous upward revaluation, or

(b) where the provision has arisen on a revaluation of all fixed assets.

1 CA 1985, Sch 4, para 19(1).

Reversals of upward revaluation

9.87   If a provision for diminution in value simply represents the reversal of a previous upward revaluation, then it can be treated as an unrealised loss and debited to revaluation reserve.[1] The previous upward valuation would have represented an unrealised profit and as such would have been credited to revaluation reserve. Schedule 4, paragraph 34(3) states that the revaluation reserve must be reduced to the extent that it is no longer necessary.

1 TR482, para 19.

Revaluation of all fixed assets

9.88   Section 275(1) states that a provision for diminution in value arising on a revaluation of all fixed assets excluding goodwill is an unrealised loss; it can thus be debited to the revaluation reserve. This does not mean that every fixed asset will have to be formally revalued and the revalued amount put through the books. A revaluation of the company's fixed assets will be deemed to have taken place, if, in respect of those assets which have not actually been revalued:

(a) the directors have considered the value of each of the assets, and

(b) they are satisfied that the aggregate value of those assets is not less than the aggregate amount at which they are stated in the accounts.[1]

This subsection distinguishes between 'revaluing' a fixed asset, and 'considering the value'. To revalue an asset implies that the book amount of the asset is actually altered: to consider its value does not.

1 CA 1985, s 275(5).

9.89   It is generally agreed that a temporary diminution in value arising in the circumstances outlined in paragraph 9.88 above may give rise to an unrealised loss.

But the question of a permanent diminution in value is a more controversial one. Generally, it would be contrary to the accounting principle of prudence to regard a permanent loss as unrealised.

Valuation rules

9.90   Part II of Schedule 4 contains the valuation rules which determine the amount at which items included in the accounts should be stated. Section B contains the 'historical accounting rules', and Section C details the 'alternative accounting rules' which permit the inclusion of certain assets in the accounts at a revaluation or on a current cost basis. A company does not have to adopt one set of rules exclusively: the Act permits selected revaluations of assets under the alternative accounting rules.

Historical cost accounting rules

Fixed assets

9.91   Fixed assets must, subject to the alternative accounting rules, be stated at their purchase price or production cost, less any provision for depreciation or diminution in value.[1]

---

[1] CA 1985, Sch 4, paras 17 and 18.

Depreciation

9.92   For a fixed asset having a limited useful economic life, the amount of the purchase price or production cost less any estimated residual value must be reduced by provisions for depreciation calculated to write the net amount off systematically over the useful economic life of the asset.[1] ED37 offers definitions of 'useful economic life', and 'residual value'. A fixed asset's useful economic life is the period over which the present owner will derive economic benefit from its use.[2] The 'residual value' is the realisable value at the end of the asset's useful economic life, based on prices prevailing at the date of acquisition, or revaluation where this has taken place.[3] Realisation costs should be deducted in arriving at residual value.

---

[1] CA 1985, Sch 4, para 18.
[2] ED37, para 11.
[3] ED37, para 12.

Investment properties

9.93   SSAP 19 states that investment properties should not be subject to periodic charges for depreciation, except for any property held on a lease with an unexpired term of 20 years or less. This results in a departure, in order to show a true and fair view, from the statutory requirements to provide depreciation. This affects property companies and other companies with investment properties.

Because the 'true and fair' override principle is being applied, the details of the departure from the statutory requirements and its effect should be disclosed in a note to the accounts. To state the effect would necessitate quantifying how much depreciation would have been charged, had the statutory requirements been met. This may not always be possible. The British Property Federation has formulated guidance for the wording of a note which should be included in the accounts in these circumstances. This is as follows:

'In accordance with SSAP 19

(i) Investment properties are revalued annually and the aggregate surplus or deficit is transferred to a revaluation reserve, and
(ii) No depreciation or amortisation is provided in respect of freehold investment properties and leasehold investment properties with over 20 years to run.

The directors believe that this accounting policy results in the accounts giving a true and fair view. Depreciation or amortisation is only one of the many factors reflected in the annual valuation, and the amount which might otherwise have been shown cannot be separately identified or quantified.'

ED37: Non-depreciation of assets

9.94 There are some rare cases in which non-depreciation of fixed assets would not run contrary to the statutory requirements. ED37 states that, in certain very restricted instances, it may not be appropriate to charge depreciation in respect of what would normally be a depreciable asset. This could arise if an asset is maintained to such a standard that

(a) the estimated residual value is equal to or greater than its net book amount, or
(b) its estimated useful economic life is either infinite, or such that any depreciation charge would be insignificant.[1]

For an asset to be treated in this way, maintenance should be undertaken on a regular basis and the cost charged to the profit and loss account. The question of obsolescence, as well as the physical condition of the asset, should be borne in mind in assessing whether any depreciation should be charged.

---

[1] ED37, para 25.

Diminutions in value

9.95 Sch 4, para 19 contains the following provisions with regard to permanent and temporary diminutions in value:

(a) The amount to be included in respect of the fixed asset should be reduced accordingly, and

(b) Any provisions not shown in the profit and loss account should be disclosed (either separately or in aggregate) in a note to the accounts, and

(c) If the reasons for which the provision was made cease to apply, then the provision should be written back to the extent that it is no longer necessary.

For the question of whether a diminution in value constitutes a realised or unrealised loss see para 9.99, below.

Permanent and temporary diminutions in value

9.96 The legislation gives no guidance as to what it is to be regarded as a permanent diminution in value. Certainly paragraph 19(3) admits of the possibility that a permanent diminution in value could reverse, since it discusses the accounting treatment should this arise. In practice, a diminution in value is regarded as permanent if it is unlikely to reverse in the foreseeable future.

Fixed assets: diminutions in value

9.97 The legislation is silent as to how to determine whether a fixed asset has diminished in value. In practice this depends on the type of assets and the particular circumstances.

(a) *Tangible and intangible assets*

For tangible assets which have a finite useful life and are being depreciated, such a situation would arise if the net book value were seen to be unrecoverable in full. SSAP 12 and ED37 suggest that this could arise for reasons such as obsolescence, or a fall in demand for a product. Similarly, if the book value of an intangible fixed asset is deemed to be irrecoverable, it should be written down.

(b) *Investments*

There are several ways in which the 'value' of an investment might be assessed, net asset value being one. But there may be many occasions when the real value of the investment will be higher than this — in particular where the net asset value does not reflect the profits capability of the business. Only if the book or carrying amount of the investment has diminished should consideration be given to making a provision. This would be the case if either:

(i) the net asset value had dropped, due to accumulated losses, or

(ii) there was a permanent reduction in the level of profitability, which no longer supports the original goodwill paid, i e where the real value has dropped below cost.

Both cases effectively result in a fall in the real value of the business, and would necessitate a provision if the book amount were affected. But even in these cases a provision might not be necessary, unless the future prospects of the company mean that the situation is unlikely to reverse.

Group or business reconstructions are a potential problem area. For example, the net tangible assets of a subsidiary might be transferred elsewhere in the group at book value, leaving behind a shell company in respect of which substantial goodwill was paid on acquisition. Here the substance of the reorganisation is that no loss has arisen, and the goodwill inherent in the original cost is still present on a group basis. Consequently no permanent impairment has arisen. However in this situation the directors would have to acknowledge that the shell company is an integral part of the business for which it was acquired and that it will not be disposed of whilst this business is being carried on by the group.

9.98   Two practical points should be noted here. Although not connected with the valuation of subsidiaries they are relevant when a subsidiary transfers its assets to its holding company at under market value.

- (a) Such a transfer may be construed as a distribution to the holding company, as defined by s 263. The directors would therefore have to consider whether the company is legally in a position to make a distribution.
- (b) Similarly transfers of assets at under market value could be interpreted as constituting financial assistance under Section 151 of the Act.

Diminutions in value: accounting treatment

9.99   The question of whether a diminution in value represents a realised loss and thus should be charged to the profit and loss account was discussed in paras 9.86–9.89, above. The following is a summary of the conclusions reached:

- (a) All provisions which are simply the reversal of a previous upward valuation are unrealised losses and should be debited to the revaluation reserve.
- (b) All other provisions which do not 'appear on a revaluation of all fixed assets' are realised losses, whether they are permanent or not, and therefore must be charged to the profit and loss account.
- (c) Provisions for temporary diminutions in value appearing on a 'revaluation of all fixed assets' are unrealised. As such, they can be charged against the revaluation reserve. If there is no credit balance on the revaluation reserve, a debit balance may be set up. For the meaning of 'revaluation' in this context, see para 9.88, above.
- (d) The question of whether a permanent diminution in value could give rise to an unrealised loss was discussed in paras 9.86–9.89, above. The conclusion reached was that such a diminution should always be treated as realised and charged to the profit and loss account.

There appears to be no statutory restriction on setting up a debit balance on the revaluation reserve since Schedule 4, para 34(1) states that any deficits on revaluation must be debited to the revaluation reserve.

Current assets

9.100   Current assets should be included at purchase price, or production cost. But if the net realisable value of the current asset is lower than its purchase price or production cost, then the asset should be included at its net realisable value. As with fixed assets, any provisions should be written back to the extent that they are no longer necessary.[1]

---

[1] CA 1985, Sch 4, paras 22 and 23.

Long term contract work in progress

9.101 Under SSAP 9, long term contract work in progress should be stated in the accounts at cost plus any attributable profit, less any foreseeable losses, less any progress payments received and receivable.[1] Profit taken to the profit and loss account in accordance with this accounting standard is not inconsistent with the law, since the profit can properly be regarded as realised and therefore distributable (see 9.84 above for a summary of CCAB guidance on this subject). However the inclusion of attributable profit in the valuation of a current asset is not permitted by the valuation rules. Therefore, including the attributable profit will entail a departure from the legal requirements in order to give a true and fair view.

The CA 1985 requires a note explaining the departure from the legislation and quantifying its effect when the true and fair override is applied. The effect in this case would be the effect on the profit and loss account i e the value of profit included in long term work in progress. But there are two opposing views regarding whether such a quantification is possible, or meaningful. These views can be summarised as follows:

(a) The figure included in the balance sheet under SSAP 9 for long term contract work in progress comprises three distinct elements — cost, attributable profits (or foreseeable losses), and progress payments received or receivable. Each of these elements should be considered separately. Since it is the inclusion of the profit which contravenes the valuation rules, the amount of that profit is quantifiable and should be disclosed.

(b) Alternatively, the figure in the balance sheet for long term contract work in progress can be viewed as a single net valuation (although separate disclosure is required under SSAP 9 of progress payments included). There is a departure from the valuation rules in including a profit element in the balance sheet but this profit is a net amount, since progress payments contain an element of profit which is deducted from the attributable profit taken. Quantification of the 'net' profit included in the balance sheet figure would not be possible with any degree of accuracy. Nor is it likely to be a material figure: if progress payments are kept up to date, there will not be a significant amount of profit taken on unbilled work.

There are arguments in favour of both approaches and the ASC is considering the matter.

---

[1] SSAP 9, para 27.

Purchase price or production cost

9.102 The purchase price of any asset should be obtained by adding to the actual price paid, any costs incidental to its acquisition.[1] References to purchase price include references to any consideration (whether in cash or otherwise) given by the company in respect of the asset in question.[2] This explains how to construe purchase price when applying the above rules to certain assets, for example debtors, which have no purchase price in the ordinary sense of the word. 'Purchase price' for a debtor is represented by the amount charged for the goods or services supplied.

The production cost of an asset includes the cost of raw materials and consumables used in its production, together with the amount of any costs directly attributable to its production.[3] A reasonable proportion of indirect cost and interest on capital borrowed to finance the production may also be included in production cost, to the extent that these relate to the period of production. The fact that interest is included, and the amount of that interest, must be disclosed in a note to the accounts.[4]

Distribution costs may not be included in the production cost of any asset.[5] The following points should be noted in relation to SSAP 9:

(a) Schedule 4 permits 'a reasonable proportion' of indirect costs to be included in arriving at the production cost of assets. Under SSAP 9, such costs are required to be included in respect of stocks.

(b) The option of including interest costs in the production cost of stocks also causes problems under SSAP 9. In the SSAP, interest is viewed as a financial cost, and therefore it should not normally be included in the cost of stock. The SSAP allows interest costs to be included on long term contracts however, provided that certain conditions are met.

(c) SSAP 9 states that 'cost' includes costs incurred in bringing the stocks to their 'present location and condition'. This has been taken to include the costs incurred in distributing the stocks to warehouses and retail outlets. In practice companies have continued to include these 'internal' distribution costs in the production cost of their stocks. External distribution costs i e those incurred in distributing the goods from the company to customers are not generally included in the cost, since they cannot be viewed as being incurred in bringing the product to its present location and condition.

---

[1] CA 1985, Sch 4, para 26(1).
[2] Ibid, Sch 4, para 90.
[3] Ibid, Sch 4, para 26(2).
[4] Ibid, Sch 4, para 26(3).
[5] Ibid, Sch 4, para 26(4), and see (c) below.

Valuation of stocks and fungible assets

9.103   The purchase price or production cost of any asset shown under the heading 'stocks' in a company's balance sheet, and any assets which are 'fungible assets' (whether fixed or current) may be determined by any of the following methods for assets of the same class:

(a) FIFO (first in, first out)
(b) LIFO (last in, first out)
(c) weighted average price, and
(d) any other method similar to the above.[1]

Fungible assets are defined as 'those which are substantially indistinguishable one from another'.[2]

The overriding principle is that the method chosen must be one which appears to the directors to be appropriate for the company. Notably, the legislation permits LIFO as an acceptable method; this is not however a method which is considered appropriate under SSAP 9.

---

[1] CA 1985, Sch 4, s 27(2).
[2] Ibid, Sch 4, s 27(6).

9.104 Where the amount shown in respect of any stocks or fungible assets differs materially from the 'relevant alternative amount;, then that difference must be disclosed in a note to the accounts for each balance sheet item so affected. In this context, the relevant alternative amount means replacement cost at the balance sheet date. The most recent actual purchase price or production cost before that date may be used, but only if it appears to the directors to constitute the more appropriate standard of comparison for each type of asset under consideration.[1]

This difference need only be stated if assets are included in the balance sheet under any of the methods described in para 9.103 above. The paragraph applies only to stocks and fungible assets (fixed or current) for which the specified methods are used. The requirement does not extend to any assets which are stated at their actual purchase price or production cost, which would apply for contracts.

The requirement to determine the 'relevant alternative amount' for stocks and fungible assets could necessitate a considerable amount of extra work unless the company prepares current cost accounts. In practice, if the company has a fast stock turnover, the difference between the book value and the relevant alternative amount is unlikely to be material, and therefore will not require disclosure. If however the company has slow-moving stocks, then there may be a material difference if price levels have risen significantly. Suitable methods for arriving at the relevant alternative amount include, for example, the use of indices.

---

[1] CA 1985, Sch 4, s 27(5).

Miscellaneous provisions

(a) *Price or cost unknown*
9.105 Where there is no record of any prices, expenses or costs necessary for determining the purchase price or production cost of an asset, (or such a record cannot be obtained without unreasonable expense or delay), then the purchase price or production cost may be taken to be the value ascribed to the asset in the company's earliest available record.[1]

(b) *Assets included at a fixed amount*
Tangible fixed assets, or current assets appearing under the heading 'raw materials and consumables', may be included in the accounts at a fixed quantity and value, provided that:

(i)   their overall value is not material to assessing the company's state of affairs, and

(ii) their quantity, value and composition are not subject to material variation.[2]

This practice is commonly adopted for such items as loose tools. Any additional purchase of such assets would then be charged to the profit and loss account.

(c) *Excess of money owed over value received*
If the amount repayable on a debt owed by a company is greater than the consideration received in the transaction giving rise to the debt, the amount of the difference may be treated as an asset.

This would apply if, for example, debentures were redeemable at a premium (or issued at a discount).

If this accounting treatment is adopted, then the amount treated as an asset must be written off by reasonable amounts each year and must be completely written off before final repayment. The current amount must either be shown as a separate item in the company's balance sheet or disclosed in a note to the accounts.[3]

---

[1] CA 1985, Sch 4, para 28.
[2] Ibid, Sch 4, para 25.
[3] Ibid, Sch 4, para 24.

Alternative accounting rules

9.106   Instead of being valued under the historical cost accounting rules, certain assets may be valued at market value, or current cost, as follows:

(a) Intangible fixed assets, other than goodwill, may be stated at current cost.

(b) Tangible fixed assets may be stated at a market value determined at the date of their last valuation, or at their current cost.

(c) Fixed assets investments may be included at either:
   (i)   market value at the date of their last valuation, or
   (ii) at a value determined by the directors. Where such a basis is used, particulars of and the reasons for adopting it should be disclosed in a note to the accounts.

(d) Current asset investments may be stated at their current cost.

(e) Stocks may be included at their current cost.[1]

As noted above, these provisions allow for selective asset revaluation as well as full current cost accounts. 'Current cost' is not defined, but may be taken to be equivalent to the current cost accounting convention as described in SSAP 16, in which assets are appraised at their current value to the business rather than original cost.

---

[1] CA 1985, Sch 4, para 31.

Depreciation under the alternative accounting rules

9.107 Where an asset has been revalued in accordance with the above rules, the depreciation charge for the revalued assets should be based on the revalued amount.[1]

However, paragraph 32(3) of Schedule 4 states that the depreciation charge in the profit and loss account in respect of revalued assets may, alternatively, be based on their historical cost. In this case, any difference between the historical cost depreciation and the depreciation based on the revalued amount should be shown separately in the profit and loss account or in a note to the accounts.

There are two ways in which the alternative treatment under paragraph 32(3) has been implemented in practice:

(a) Depreciation based on the revalued amount is charged to the profit and loss account. The difference between this figure and the depreciation based on the historical cost may be shown as a transfer from the revaluation reserve to the profit and loss account, since this excess depreciation is not regarded as a realised loss for distribution purposes.

(b) An alternative practice is simply to charge the depreciation based on the historical cost amount to the profit and loss account and charge the additional depreciation direct to the revaluation reserve.

However, method (b) would not accord with ED37 since ED37 states explicitly that the profit and loss account charge should be based on the carrying value of the asset.[2]

---

[1] CA 1985, Sch 4, para 32(1).
[2] ED37, para 16.

Additional information to be disclosed

9.108 Where items have been revalued in accordance with the alternative accounting rules, the items affected and the basis of the valuation used must be disclosed in a note to the accounts. Moreover, the following additional information must be given in respect of each balance sheet item affected, except in the case of stocks:

(a) the comparable amounts determined according to the historical cost accounting rules, both in respect of cost and depreciation (or provisions for diminution in value) or

(b) the difference between those amounts, and the amounts actually shown in the balance sheet or in a note to the accounts.[1]

If the company does not have a record of the original historical cost of an asset, the earliest value at which it was recorded in the books should be taken as cost.[2]

---

[1] CA 1985, Sch 4, para 33.
[2] Ibid, Sch 4, para 28.

Revaluation reserve

9.109   The amount of any revaluation in accordance with the above rules must be credited or debited to a revaluation reserve. This reserve must be disclosed in the place indicated in the balance sheet formats, but need not be shown under that name.

The credit balance on the revaluation reserve must be reduced to the extent that it is no longer necessary, under the company's accounting policies. An amount may only be transferred from the reserve to the profit and loss account if either:

(a) it was previously charged to that account, or

(b) it represents realised profits.[1]

An example would be the surplus over cost on the sale of a revalued fixed asset as suggested in ED36, or the excess of depreciation over the historical cost amount as discussed in para 9.107, above.

---

[1] CA 1985, Sch 4, para 34.

Goodwill and the revaluation reserve

9.110   Under SSAP 22, the preferred accounting treatment for goodwill is immediate write off against reserves. The SSAP recommends that goodwill should initially be written off to unrealised reserves. However, the suitability of the revaluation reserve has been questioned, because of the restrictions on write-offs imposed by paragraph 34(3). This states that the revaluation reserve shall be reduced 'to the extent that amounts standing to the credit of the reserve are no longer necessary *for the purpose of the accounting policies* adopted by the company'.

On one interpretation the accounting policies concerned can only relate to valuations and would not cover the writing off of goodwill. On another, if the accounting policy of the company is to write off goodwill against revaluation reserves then paragraph 34 permits this. The legal position has not yet been resolved.

NOTES TO THE ACCOUNTS

9.111   Schedules 4, 5 and 6 deal with information which must be included in the notes to the accounts. The information required for note disclosure for individual companies is summarised below:

Schedule 4 Part III

      1 Disclosure of accounting policies

      2 Information supplementing the balance sheet and profit and loss account

Schedule 5 Part II   Information regarding shareholdings in companies other than subsidiaries

     Part IV   Identification of ultimate holding company

     Part V   Directors' emoluments

     Part VI   Higher paid employees

Schedule 6   Loans and other transactions involving directors

Disclosure for directors' emoluments and transactions are dealt with in chapter 6. The note disclosure requirements for group accounts are dealt with superately, below.

Accounting policies

9.112   The accounting policies adopted by the company in determining the amounts to be included in respect of items shown in the balance sheet and in determining the profit or loss of the company should be stated. This must include the policies for the depreciation and diminution in value of assets and the basis for translating amounts in foreign currencies.[1]

SSAP 2 has a similar requirement. This is that the accounting policies followed for dealing with items which are judged material or critical in determining the profit or loss for the year, and in stating the financial position of the company, should be disclosed.[2]

---

[1] CA 1985, Sch 4, paras 36 and 58(1).
[2] SSAP 2, para 12.

Information supplementing the profit and loss account

Turnover

9.113   If, in the course of a financial year, the company has carried on business of two or more classes that, in the opinion of the directors, differ substantially from each other, there should be stated in respect of each class:

(a) the amount of turnover attributable to that class, and
(b) the amount of the profit or loss of the company before taxation which is, in the opinion of the directors, attributable to that class.[1]

The requirement in (b) means that the costs would have to be allocated over the various classes of business. Similarly, if the company has supplied markets that differ substantially from each other, the amount of turnover attributable to each market should be stated. 'Market' in this context means a market delimited by geographical bounds.[2]

Both these requirements could necessitate a detailed analysis of the turnover figure. But the following points should be stressed:

(i)   In both cases, an analysis only has to be given if the markets or classes of business 'differ substantially from each other' in the directors' opinion. Similarly, if the amounts attributable to the different markets or different classes of business are not, in the directors' opinion, material, then no analysis is necessary, and
(ii) If the directors believe that the disclosure of any of the information required by paragraph 55 would be seriously prejudicial to the interests of the company, then paragraph 55(5) exempts them from

disclosure. The fact that the information has not been disclosed for this reason must however be stated.

---

1 CA 1985, Sch 4, para 55(1).
2 Ibid, Sch 4, para 55(2).

Income and expenditure

9.114   Paragraph 53 contains details of items which must be separately disclosed in the notes to the profit and loss account. These include:

(a) Interest payable. This figure should be analysed over
 (i) Interest on all bank loans and overdrafts, and other loans wholly repayable within 5 years of the balance sheet date, and
 (ii) Interest on all other loans.
 Interest on group loans however should be disclosed separately.
(b) the amount of income from listed investments.[1] SSAP 8 requires that income credited to the profit and loss account should include the related tax credits.
(c) The net rental income from land and buildings if it forms a substantial part of the company's income.
(d) The amount charged to the revenue for the hire of plant and machinery. SSAP 21 draws a distinction between operating leases and finance leases. Broadly, the latter are leases so constructed as to transfer all or most of the risks and rewards of ownership to the lessee. With operating leases, the rental payments should be charged to the profit and loss account. Finance leases and assets acquired under hire purchase should be capitalised, and depreciation and interest charges in respect of them should go through the profit and loss account. These figures are not generally included in the amount charged to revenue for the hire of plant and machinery.
(e) The amount of remuneration for the auditors should be disclosed. This should include any expenses payable to the auditors.

---

1 See para 9.129, below.

Depreciation and diminutions in value

9.115   The legislation requires that a provision for diminution in value of fixed assets should be disclosed in the notes, if not disclosed in the profit and loss account. In addition to this, SSAP 12 requires that the provision for depreciation of tangible fixed assets should be disclosed in the notes to the profit and loss account.

The fact that fixed assets include investments and intangibles means that any amounts written off these items must also be disclosed. Both the amounts written off in the current financial year, and the cumulative amounts written off must be disclosed.

Staff details

9.116   The following information should be given:

(a) The average number of people employed during the year
(b) The average number of people so employed within each category of employees.[1]

There is no exemption from this disclosure on grounds of immateriality. The average number must be calculated by:

(i) taking the number of persons employed under contracts of service by the company in each week during the financial year
(ii) adding the weekly totals, and
(iii) dividing the total by the number of weeks in the financial year.[2]

The number includes directors, if they are employed under contracts of service by the company. Moreover, it includes those employed worldwide, and not just those within the UK.

The categories should be such as the directors may select, having regard to the manner in which the company's activities are organised. Thus the categories may be analysed by function (administration, sales etc) or by division, in line with the analysis of turnover.

---

[1] CA 1985, Sch 4, para 56(1).
[2] Ibid, Sch 4, para 56(2) and (3).

9.117 In addition, the following information should be disclosed in respect of these employees:

(a) the aggregate amount of wages and salaries paid or payable in respect of that year to those persons, and
(b) the aggregate amount of social security costs incurred by the company on their behalf. Social security costs comprise employers' national insurance contributions and any similar costs overseas.
(c) Other pension costs incurred on the company's behalf should also be disclosed.[1] ED32 suggests certain items which should be disclosed in respect of pension costs (see para 9.141, below).

---

[1] CA 1985, Sch 4, para 56(4).

Higher paid employees

9.118 Schedule 5 Part VI deals with information concerning higher paid employees. Disclosure must be made of the number of employees who receive in excess of £30,000 p.a. The information must be given in ascending bands of £5000.

Unlike the employee information discussed in paras 9.116 and 9.117, above, this disclosure relates only to employees of the holding company when group accounts are prepared, although many companies give the information on a group basis. Similarly, details of directors' emoluments only relates to directors of the holding company.

Taxation

9.119   The legislative requirements for the disclosure of the charge for taxation remain broadly the same as they did prior to the CA 1981. The only change introduced was that taxation charged on extraordinary items should be distinguished from taxation charged on ordinary activities. In practice, extraordinary items are shown net of attributable taxation on the face of the profit and loss account, and the detailed analysis is given in a note.

Schedule 4, paragraph 54 contains the disclosure requirements for the note on taxation. These are as follows:

    (a)   the amount charged for UK corporation tax before relief for overseas taxation. The basis of the charge and the rate used should be stated.
    (b)   any relief for overseas taxation.
    (c)   the charge for UK income tax.
    (d)   the total charge for overseas taxation, both relieved and unrelieved.

Also particulars should be given of any special circumstances which affect the liability in respect of taxation on profits, income or capital gains for the current or succeeding financial years.[1] One example is the availability of tax losses which have been utilised in the year, and the balance that could be utilised in the future.

---

[1] CA 1985, Sch 4, para 54(2).

SSAP 8 and SSAP 15

9.120   The SSAP requirements should also be borne in mind. SSAP 8 (corporation tax) requires some additional disclosures, including the amount of any irrecoverable advance corporation tax. A revised version of SSAP 15 (deferred tax) was issued in June 1985. Disclosure required by this includes the amount of any provision for deferred taxation relating to ordinary activities included in the profit and loss account. Any deferred taxation in respect of extraordinary items should be shown separately. The deferred tax balance should be analysed over its major components in a note to the balance sheet. The total amount of any deferred taxation which has not been provided for should also be shown, again analysed over its major components.

Information supplementing the balance sheet

Share capital and debentures

9.121   These requirements are contained in paragraphs 38 to 41 of Schedule 4. The following details should be given in the notes in respect of each class of shares or debentures issued during the year:

    (a)   reasons for making the allotment
    (b)   classes of shares or debentures allotted
    (c)   for each class, the consideration received should be given. In addition, in respect of shares issued, the number allotted together with their aggregate nominal value must also be disclosed. If debentures have been issued, the amount issued should be stated.

It should be stressed that any allotment of shares, issue of convertible securities, or conversion of securities into shares must be validly authorised by the company in general meeting, or by the articles.

Capitalisation of interest

9.122 Paragraph 26(3) of Schedule 4 states that interest on capital borrowed to finance the production of an asset, to the extent that it accrues in respect of the period of production, may be included in the production cost of the asset. If so, the fact that the interest has been included, and the amount, must be disclosed in a note.

Fixed assets

9.123 The disclosure requirements apply to all fixed assets. This includes intangibles and investments as well as tangible fixed assets.

The note disclosure requirements relating to all fixed assets are detailed in paragraphs 42 to 44 of Schedule 4. The following disclosures should be made for all fixed asset categories:

(a) Their aggregate purchase price or production cost, or gross valuation determined under one of the alternative accounting rules. (See para 9.106, above)
(b) In respect of provisions for depreciation or diminution in value:
  (i) the cumulative amount at the beginning and end of the year
  (ii) the amount provided during the year
  (iii) the amount of any adjustments made during the year in respect of the disposal of any assets, and
  (iv) the amount of any other adjustments made during the year.
(c) The effect in respect of each fixed asset item as a result of:
  (i) any revaluation made in accordance with the alternative accounting rules, and
  (ii) any acquisitions, disposals or transfers during the year.

Revaluations

9.124 For each fixed asset (except listed investments) which is shown at a valuation, the notes to the accounts should state

(a) for valuations which have been made during the current year, the names or qualifications of the valuers and the bases of the valuation
(b) for valuations which have been made in a previous year, the years and the amounts of the valuations[1]
(c) in the year of the revaluation, the effect on depreciation should be disclosed if it is material.[2]

In addition, the comparable historical cost amounts in respect of cost and depreciation, or the difference between the historical and the alternative amounts must be stated.[3] If the original cost is not known, then the earliest value at which the asset was recorded in the books should be taken as cost.

---

[1] CA 1985, Sch 4, para 43.
[2] SSAP 12, para 21.
[3] CA 1985, Sch 4, para 33.

Tangible fixed assets

9.125 For land and buildings held as fixed assets the following should be shown separately

   (a) freeholds
   (b) long leaseholds (leases with 50 years or more to run from the balance sheet date), and
   (c) short leaseholds.[1]

---

[1] CA 1985, Sch 4, para 44.

9.126 The SSAP disclosures relating to tangible fixed assets should also be included in the notes.

(a) *SSAP 12* (depreciation)
The following disclosures are required by SSAP 12
   (i) The useful lives or depreciation rates, and the method of depreciation used[1] (i e straight line or reducing balance). This disclosure is usually given in the accounting policy note.
   (ii) If the rate or method of depreciation is changed, this will not require a prior year adjustment. This is because it is regarded as a change in accounting estimate rather than a change in accounting policy. But SSAP 12 requires that the effect of the change should be disclosed if it is a material amount.[2]

(b) *SSAP 19 — Investment properties*
An 'investment property' is defined in paragraph 7 of SSAP 19 as an interest in land and/or buildings

   (a) in respect of which construction work and development have been completed, and
   (b) which is held for its investment potential, any rental income being negotiated at arms length.

This excludes property owned and occupied by the company, or let to and occupied by another group company.

   Investment properties must be revalued annually and the following additional information should be disclosed:

   (i) If the valuer is an employee or officer of the company, then this fact must be stated.[3]
   (ii) SSAP 19 states that depreciation must not be charged on investment properties.[4] However the particulars of, and reasons for, the departure from the legal requirements should be stated. The British Property Federation suggested a wording for such a note, and this is given in 9.93 above.

---

[1] SSAP 12, para 22.
[2] SSAP 12, para 20.
[3] SSAP 19, para 12.
[4] SSAP 19, para 10.

Goodwill

9.127 Where goodwill acquired by a company is shown, or included as an asset in the company's balance sheet, the period chosen for writing off the consideration for the goodwill, and the reasons for choosing that period, must be disclosed in a note.[1]

---

[1] CA 1985, Sch 4, para 21(4) and see para 9.55, above.

Investments

9.128 All the general requirements relating to disclosure of information on fixed assets apply to fixed asset investments, including investments in subsidiaries and related companies.

The major consequences of this are

(a) both the gross amounts and the amounts written off investments must be disclosed in the notes to the accounts
(b) movements on the gross amounts, and on provisions in respect of investments must be disclosed
(c) fixed asset investments may be included at market value, or directors' valuation under the alternative accounting rules. If the directors' valuation is used, then details of the method of valuation and the reasons for adopting it must also be stated.

Listed investments

9.129 The aggregate amount of listed investments should be stated. This amount should be divided between those with permission to deal on the UK Stock Exchange and others.[1] It should be noted that investments dealt with on the Unlisted Securities or Over-the-Counter markets are not listed investments.

Further information may be needed in respect of listed investments:

(a) The aggregate market value of listed investments must be disclosed if this is different from book value.
(b) If the market value is greater than the Stock Exchange value for any investments, then the Stock Exchange value for those investments must be disclosed.[2]

---

[1] CA 1985, Sch 4, para 45(1).
[2] CA 1985, Sch 4, para 45(2).

Substantial shareholdings

9.130 Additional information is required if the company holds in another body corporate either

(a) more than ten per cent of the nominal value of any class of equity share capital, or
(b) more than ten per cent of the allotted share capital, or

(c)   share capital having a total book value in excess of ten per cent of the company's assets.

The following information must be given in respect of these companies.

(i)   Name.
(ii)   Country of incorporation if outside the UK. The notes should also state whether the company is registered in England or Scotland, if this is different from the country of registration of the holding company.
(iii)   The description and proportion of the nominal value of the allotted shares of each class held must also be stated.[1]

Corresponding amounts are not required for this information. Moreover, if the number of such companies is large then only those that principally affect the results or assets need be detailed. The notes however must state that information has only been provided in respect of those companies.

---

[1] CA 1985, Sch 5, part II.

9.131   If the company holds more than twenty per cent of the allotted share capital in the other company, then the aggregate amount of its capital and reserves and its profit or loss should be stated. This information must relate to the other company's most recent financial year which ends on or before that of the investing company.

However, if any of the following circumstances apply, this information is not required:

(a)   the investment is in a subsidiary company and the subsidiary's accounts are included in the group accounts, or
(b)   the investment is equity accounted, or
(c)   the body corporate is not required to file its balance sheet with the registrar and does not publish its balance sheet in the UK or elsewhere, and the investment is in less than 50% of the allotted share capital (unlimited companies could come into this category), or
(d)   it is immaterial.

Current assets

Stocks

(a) *Replacement cost*
9.132   The CA 1981 introduced a new requirement. For each category of stock, if the balance sheet amount differs materially from the replacement cost at the balance sheet date, then the amount of the difference must be stated in the notes to the accounts.[1] The most recent actual purchase price or production cost may be used if the directors consider that this is a more appropriate standard of comparison. This requirement only applies if stocks are included in the accounts at any of the permitted approximations to cost, for example FIFO or LIFO. It does *not* apply to stocks which have been included at their actual cost i e their purchase price or production cost.

(b) *Long term contracts*

SSAP 9 requires that the attributable profit be included in the balance sheet figure for work in progress. This constitutes a departure from the legislative provisions. The situation is discussed in para 9.101, above.

---

[1] CA 1985, Sch 4, para 27(3).

Goods sold subject to reservation of title

9.133 Normally, no disclosure need be made in the accounts of a company which has purchased goods subject to reservation of title. However, where

(a) there are doubts about the ability of a business to continue as a going concern, but the accounts have been prepared on a going concern basis, and
(b) a significant amount of the liabilities are subject to reservation of title,

disclosure of the position may be necessary in order to give a true and fair view. Because of the difficulties in determining the legal position in relation to individual suppliers, and in quantifying the sums involved, it will generally only be practicable to give a general nature of the position.[1]

---

[1] See para 4.81, above.

Debtors

9.134 The following items should be disclosed in the notes:

(a) for each item included under debtors, the amount falling due after one year should be shown separately.[1]
(b) Details of loans to directors or officers should be given, as should the details of any material transactions with directors or other officers. The legislative requirements in connection with this have been discussed in chapter 6, above.
(c) Similarly, if the company has given financial assistance to employees for the purchase of shares in the company, the aggregate of any such loans outstanding should be disclosed in the notes.[2]

---

[1] CA 1985, Sch 4, Note 5 on balance sheet formats.
[2] CA 1985, Sch 4, para 51(2).

Creditors

9.135 The following information should be given for each item shown under creditors:

(a) For creditors which are not payable by instalments, the amount due after five years
(b) For creditors which are payable by instalments any of which fall due after five years:

    (i) the total amounts payable, and

    (ii) the amounts payable after five years[1]

(c) For all items in (a) and (b), the terms of repayment and the rate of interest should be stated. However, if this is likely to result in a statement of excessive length, then it is sufficient to give a general indication of the terms of repayment and the rates of interest.[2]

(d) If the Format 2 balance sheet is used, then any amounts falling due within one year must be shown separately for each of the items under creditors.[3]

The general rule applies that a loan or instalment on a loan must be treated as falling due on the earliest date on which the lender could require payment. Thus any loan with no fixed repayment terms must be treated as immediately repayable. For example a loan to a company from its holding company would generally have to be included under the heading 'creditors — amounts falling due within one year', unless there were some formal agreement with the holding company to the effect that the amount would not be recalled within one year.

---

[1] CA 1985, Sch 4, para 48(1).
[2] Ibid, Sch 4, paras 48(2) and (3).
[3] Ibid, Note 13 to the balance sheet formats.

9.136 Creditors for taxation and social security should be disclosed separately[1] as should the aggregate amount of any proposed dividend, excluding ACT. ACT on proposed dividends should be disclosed as a current tax liability.

---

[1] CA 1985, Sch 4, Note 9 to the balance sheet formats.

Secured creditors

9.137 If any of the creditors are secured, the following information must be given:

(a) the amount which is secured, and

(b) the nature of the security given.[1]

By 'the nature of the security' is meant such details as whether the charge is fixed or floating.

---

[1] CA 1985, Sch 4, para 48.

Reserves and provisions

9.138 The movements on each reserve during the current year must be given. Thus the following should be disclosed

(a) the opening balance

(b) transfers to and from the reserve

(c) the source and application of such transfers, and

(d) the closing balance.[1]

Comparative figures are not required in this case. Similar disclosures should be given for any provisions included in the balance sheet, if they are material. The term 'provision' is defined in paragraph 89 of Schedule 4 as 'any amount retained as reasonably necessary for the purpose of providing for any liability or loss which is either likely to be incurred, or certain to be incurred but uncertain as to the amount, or as to the date on which it will arise'.

[1] CA 1985, Sch 4, para 46(2).

Guarantees and other financial commitments

Capital commitments

9.139 Where practical the estimated amounts should be given

(a) of capital expenditure contracted for but not provided, and

(b) of capital expenditure which has been authorised by the directors but which has not been contracted.[1]

[1] CA 1985, Sch 4, para 50(3).

Contingencies

9.140

(a) Particulars must be given of any charge on the assets of the company to secure the liability of any other person. Where practical, the amount secured should be stated.[1] An example would include the situation where a holding company had guaranteed the overdraft of a subsidiary.

(b) for other contingent liabilities for which provision has not been made, the following information should be given:

(i) the estimated amount of the liability

(ii) its legal nature, and

(iii) whether any valuable security has been provided by the company for this commitment. If so, details of the security should be given.[2]

The legal requirements should be viewed in the light of SSAP 18 (contingent liabilities). This states that an accrual provision should be made for a contingent liability if the likelihood of its arising is probable. When no contingent liability is accrued, then SSAP 18 requires detailed particulars to be disclosed unless the possibility of the loss is remote.

The particulars which are required under SSAP 18 are similar to those required under the legislation. But in addition to the legislative requirements, details should be given of any uncertainties which might affect the ultimate outcome. The taxation implications should also be disclosed, if they are necessary for a proper understanding of the financial position.

¹ CA 1985, Sch 4, para 50(1).
² CA 1985, Sch 4, para 50(2).

Pension commitments

9.141   Particulars of any pension commitments included under any provision shown in the company's balance sheet should be disclosed. Similarly particulars of any such commitments for which no such provision has been made should be disclosed.

Separate disclosure is required where any such commitments relate to pensions payable to past directors.[1]

ED32 suggests disclosures for pension costs. The major ones in ED32 are

(a) the nature of the pension scheme
(b) the way in which it is funded
(c) the accounting policy
(d) brief actuarial information, and
(e) amounts charged in the profit and loss account.

¹ CA 1985, Sch 4, para 50(4).

Other financial commitments

9.142   Particulars should also be given of any other financial commitments which have not been provided for, and which are relevant to assessing the company's state of affairs.[1] The wording of this suggests that it is referring to payments which the company is legally bound to make in the future. In general, only major commitments which are likely to have a material impact on the company's affairs are disclosed.

¹ CA 1985, Sch 4, para 50(5).

9.143   SSAP 21 has detailed disclosure requirements for lease and hire purchase commitments.[1] Obligations under finance leases and hire purchase contracts should be disclosed separately from other obligations and liabilities, either on the face of the balance sheet or in the notes to the accounts. The net obligations should be analysed between amounts payable in the next year, amounts payable in the second to fifth years after the balance sheet date, and the aggregate amount payable thereafter.

The SSAP also requires that operating lease commitments for the next financial year should be disclosed, analysed over the commitment relating to operating leases which

(a) expire within the next financial year
(b) expire within the second to fifth years inclusive from the balance sheet date, and
(c) expire more than five years after the balance sheet date.[2]

The leases in respect of land and buildings should be shown separately from the other operating leases.

In addition paragraph 54 of SSAP 21 requires the disclosure of commitments existing at the balance sheet date in respect of finance leases which have been entered into, but whose inception occurs after the year end.

---

[1] SSAP 21, paras 49–57.
[2] SSAP 21, para 56.

9.144 SSAP 21 thus prescribes an accounting treatment for a major source of off balance sheet finance. Under SSAP 21 both the assets acquired under finance leases, and the liabilities which relate to them must be reflected in the company accounts.

THE DIRECTORS' REPORT

9.145 Every company must prepare a directors' report for each financial year. Except for those companies which are defined as special category companies (see para 9.201, below) the contents of this report are as set out in section 235. In addition, the report must contain the details specified in Schedule 7 to the CA 1985.

9.146 The 1981 Act introduced several changes regarding the directors' report, including some new disclosure requirements. Some of those have given rise to problems of interpretation often because the legislation does not specify how detailed the disclosure should be. Paras 9.147 to 9.155 deal with particular problems which have arisen as a result of the CA 1981 changes.

Business review

9.147 The directors' report must contain a 'fair view of the development of the business of the company and its subsidiaries during the financial year, and of their position at the end of it'.[1] The CA 1985 gives no indication of how extensive such a review should be, nor what it should include; obviously it is envisaged that it should incorporate at least a brief indication of the company's results for the year together with information about any important events which have taken place during the year, including any acquisitions or closures. But wider issues, such as economic and market conditions, may arguably also be necessary to help explain how the company has performed during the financial year.

The fact that the legislation is not specific about the level of detail required means that in practice the extent of the disclosures is left to the discretion of the directors. With public companies, a detailed review is often included in the chairman's statement with a summary in the directors' report. But in some cases, a reluctance to divulge too much commercial detail in the published accounts has resulted in the chairman's statement also only containing a summary.

---

[1] CA 1985, s 235(1)(a).

Future developments

9.148 The directors' report should give an indication of 'any likely future developments in the business of the company and its subsidiaries'.[1] A broad statement about future developments together with any major changes projected, rather than a quantified forecast, is usually taken as sufficient to satisfy this requirement. This is sometimes incorporated into the business review section.

The directors should be aware that even broad statements indicating future profitability could constitute a profit forecast as defined by the City Takeover Code.[2] This would need to be reported on in any subsequent takeover.

---

[1] CA 1985, Sch 7, para 6(b).
[2] City Takeover Code, Section K.

Post balance-sheet events

9.149 Particulars of any important events affecting the company, or any of its subsidiaries, which have occurred since the end of the year should be included in the directors' report.[1] Similarly SSAP 17 requires that the statutory accounts should incorporate or refer to any events which have occurred between the end of the financial year, and the date on which the accounts are signed by the directors. There are two significant differences between the legal and the SSAP 17 requirements:

(a) SSAP 17 distinguishes between adjusting and non-adjusting post balance sheet events. Adjusting events are matters which should be taken into account in preparing the financial statements, although occurring after date, and separate disclosure is not required in respect of them. Non-adjusting events should not give rise to changes in amounts in financial statements, since they relate to conditions which did not exist at the balance sheet date. The legislation does not make such a distinction; consequently the implication is that both adjusting and non-adjusting events should be disclosed in the directors' report. It should be emphasised that the legislation only requires disclosure in respect of 'important' events.

(b) Paragraph 9 of SSAP 17 states that disclosure should be made in the notes to the accounts in the case of non-adjusting post balance sheet events. This contrasts with the legal requirement that such disclosure be made in the directors' report. To avoid duplication of information, it is advisable to follow the legal requirements and disclose the full details of the events in the directors' report, with a cross reference in the notes.

SSAP 17 has disclosure requirements which are more detailed than the legislative requirements. These are:

(i) the nature of the event
(ii) an estimate of the financial effect, or a statement that it is not practical to make such an estimate, and
(iii) an explanation of the taxation implications when necessary for a proper understanding of the financial position.[2]

These SSAP disclosure requirements relate to non-adjusting post balance sheet events: the effects of adjusting post balance sheet events should be reflected in the financial statements, as stated in the SSAP.

---

[1] CA 1985, Sch 7, para 6a.
[2] SSAP 17, paras 24 and 25.

Research and development

9.150   An indication of the research and development activities of the company and its subsidiaries should be given. Again the scope of this requirement is not made explicit within the legislation, and in practice the information given in the report tends not to be detailed, since companies are often reluctant to disclose such sensitive information to competitors.

---

[1] CA 1985, Sch 7, para 6(c).

Directors' Interests

9.151   Another change introduced by the CA 1981 is that information about directors' interests in share and loan capital may be given in the notes to the accounts rather than in the directors' report.[1] In practice, companies generally still include this information in the report. The following points should be emphasised:

(a) directors' interests in any group company must be given, specifying the company concerned.
(b) details must be given for each director; and there are no exceptions on the grounds of immateriality. If the director does not have any such interests, this should be stated.
(c) Directors' interests include beneficial and non-beneficial interests, and also any share options.
(d) there is no legal requirement to distinguish between beneficial and non-beneficial interests. However listed and USM companies are required by The Stock Exchange to disclose this information.[1]

There are however certain cases in which directors' interests need not be disclosed. The most common are in the accounts of a wholly owned subsidiary, where either

(a) the person concerned is a director of both the subsidiary and its holding company, or
(b) the company concerned is a subsidiary of a company incorporated outside the UK.[2]

---

[1] CA 1985, Sch 7, para 2.
[2] SI 1985/802.

Employee details

9.152   Before the CA 1981, the directors' report had to contain information concerning the number of employees. However, now these details should be given in the notes to the accounts. But the following information about the company's policy towards its employees should be disclosed in the directors' report:

(a)   If the company's weekly average number of employees throughout the year exceeded 250, the company's policy with regard to the employment of disabled persons.[1]

(b)   The 1982 Employment Act introduced the requirement to disclose the steps the company has taken to involve the employees in the company's management. Again this requirement only extends to companies employing more than 250 people on average throughout the year. The details required include the company's policy to provide their employees with information of concern to them as employees, and to encourage the employees' involvement by such means as an employee share scheme.[2]

(c)   The Health and Safety at Work Act 1974 gave the Secretary of State the right to prescribe that the directors' report should contain information about arrangements in force for securing the health and safety at work of its employees. As yet no such disclosure is required; however Schedule 7 Part IV of the CA 1985 affirms that the Secretary of State still has the power to exercise that right.

---

[1] CA 1985, Sch 7, part III.
[2] CA 1985, Sch 7, part V.

The directors' report and the auditor

9.153   Before the CA 1981, the directors' report was not included within the scope of the auditors' opinion. Now, however, the auditors have to consider whether in their opinion the information contained in the report is consistent with the accounts.[1]

The Auditing Practices Committee has issued guidance on the auditors' duty in relation to the directors' report and other financial information issued with audited financial statements.[2] This guidance emphasises that the auditors do not have a statutory duty to form an opinion as to the directors' report: their statutory duty only extends to checking its consistency with the audited financial statements.

---

[1] CA 1985, s 237(6).
[2] Auditing guideline: Financial information issued with audited financial statements.

Guideline: the auditors' statutory duties

9.154   If they find any inconsistencies, and these still remain after discussion with the directors, the auditors should determine whether any amendments should be made to the directors' report, or to the financial statements. The latter situation is unlikely, since the auditors will probably review the directors' report after having performed most of their audit work. If, however, they do decide that the financial statements are incorrect, then the audit report may need qualifying. It must also refer to the inconsistency.

If, as is more likely, it is the directors' report which, in the auditors' opinion, needs amending then the audit report should simply refer to the inconsistency as required by s 237(6).

Guideline: The auditors' non-statutory duties

9.155 The guideline goes on to consider the auditors' non-statutory responsibility in relation to the directors' report. It indicates that the auditor should review the directors' report to determine whether it contains any misleading information. If it does he should discuss the matter with the directors, to see if the problem can be eliminated.

If the problem is not eliminated, then the auditor should consider what action he should take. In very rare cases, he may decide that the financial statements are incorrect, and that an audit qualification is necessary. If however he decides that the directors' report is misleading, he has no statutory duty to comment in his report. In situations where he considers that the matter is potentially so misleading that it would be inappropriate for him to remain silent, he should seek legal advice on what action he should take. He has the following courses of action open to him

(a) he can attend the general meeting and, exercising his right to be heard under s 387(1), draw the attention of the meeting to the points in the directors' report which he considers misleading

(b) he might decide to refer to the matter in his report. Counsel however has advised that the qualified privilege (i e the defence to an action for defamation) which an audit report usually enjoys may not extend to such comments.

GROUP ACCOUNTS

9.156 If a company has subsidiaries at the end of its financial year, it must prepare group accounts. These are defined as 'accounts which deal with the state of affairs and profit or loss of the company and its subsidiaries'.[1]

The group accounts must be approved by the directors when the balance sheet of the holding company is signed. They must be laid before the members in general meeting, and a copy must be filed with the registrar.

---

[1] CA 1985, s 229(1).

9.157 The legislative requirements deal with the form and content of group accounts, and exemptions from the requirement to produce group accounts. The specific provisions of the CA 1985 are summarised below.

S 229   (1) The requirement to produce group accounts
           (2)–(4) Exemptions
           (5)–(7) The form of group accounts

S 230	(1) The content of group accounts
	(2)–(6) True and fair view
	(7) Coterminous year ends
	(8) Modifications which require Secretary of State approval

| S 736 | Definition of a subsidiary |

| Sch 4 | Part IV Content of accounts where the company is a holding company or subsidiary |
| | Part VI Merger relief |

| Sch 5 | Parts I and III Particulars of subsidiaries |

9.158   However, a holding company which is a special category company may prepare group accounts which comply with ss 257 to 262 of and Schedule 9 to the Act. Moreover, holding companies of special category companies may also prepare their group accounts in accordance with these sections. But a holding company which opts to do this but is not itself a special category company must prepare a 'hybrid' set of accounts, since only the group accounts and not the company's own accounts may be prepared under the special category rules. In effect, this means that the group accounts will comply with the Companies' Act as follows:

(a) Directors' report — Schedule 4
(b) Company balance sheet and related notes — Schedule 4
(c) Consolidated balance sheet, profit and loss account and related notes — Schedule 9.

In practice several 'hybrid' groups do prepare sets of accounts to the above specification. But it is equally common for the group accounts to comply wholly with Schedule 4. In the latter case, the subsidiary is generally included in the group accounts under the equity method of accounting.

The SSAPs and the EEC 7th Directive

9.159   The current legislation does not address many of the problems which arise in practice with group accounting. In particular, it is silent on the accounting treatment of changes arising in the composition of the group and the treatment of goodwill. SSAP 14 addresses this problem, and the SSAPs on goodwill and accounting for business combinations (SSAPs 22 and 23 respectively) go a long way towards clarifying the position.

Moreover, eventually the SSAP requirements relating to the calculation, disclosure and treatment of consolidation difference will become statutory requirements. The EEC 7th Directive on group accounts is compatible in most respects with the accounting standards. This directive does not however have to be introduced in the UK until January 1988, and then it need not be implemented for a further two years.

The following paragraphs deal with the current legislative and SSAP requirements. The implications of the 7th Directive are discussed under the relevant headings.

Subsidiary: the legal definition

9.160   Section 736 of the CA 1985 contains the definition of a subsidiary.[1] To summarise the definition:

One company, A, is regarded as the subsidiary of another company, B, if, but only if

(a) The company B
  (i) is a member of A, and controls the composition of A's board of directors; or
  (ii) holds more than half in nominal value of A's equity share capital, or
(b) A is a subsidiary of any company which is B's subsidiary.

The following points should be noted:

(i)   One company is regarded as controlling the composition of the board of directors of another company, if and only if the former company can by the exercise of some power appoint or remove all, or a majority of, the board of directors.[2]
(ii) 'Equity share capital' is defined as the company's issued share capital, excluding any part thereof which, neither as respects dividends nor as respects capital, carries any right to participate beyond a specified amount in a distribution.[3]
(iii) In determining whether the company is a subsidiary of B, any shares held by another subsidiary of B should be treated as being held by B, as should any nominee shareholdings.[4]

---

[1] The definiton of a subsidiary for tax purposes differs from the legal definition (Taxes Act 1970, s 532).

[2] CA 1985, s 736(2).

[3] Ibid, s 744.

[4] Ibid, s 736(4).

9.161   The EEC 7th Directive adopts this parent company concept of a group, but differs in the detailed definition of a subsidiary. Under the provisions of the Directive, a company is a subsidiary of another if that other holds a majority of the shareholders' voting rights. This differs from the current UK criterion that the majority of the equity share capital (without distinction as to voting right) should be held. Also, there is an additional requirement under the Directive that a company should be treated as a subsidiary of a shareholder if that shareholder controls, either alone or pursuant to an agreement with other shareholders, a majority of the votes. Those companies which have shareholdings which were specially devised not to make the company a subsidiary might well find that their original intention is thwarted by this definition: it will result in a number of companies becoming subsidiaries when they are not at present; and it could result in their being subsidiaries of more than one parent.

The alternative requirement, concerning control of the composition of the board (9.160(b) above), is included in the Directive.[1] However, the definition is slightly different, and it might give rise to practical problems in unusual cases.

---

[1] 7th Directive, Article 1(b).

Legal exemptions from the obligation to prepare group accounts

9.162   There is no legal requirement to produce group accounts if the holding company is itself a wholly owned subsidiary of another body incorporated in the UK.[1] The same exemption applies under SSAP 14.

The legislation also permits a subsidiary to be excluded from group accounts if the directors of the holding company are of the opinion that

(a) its inclusion would be impractical; or

(b) it would be of no real value to members of the holding company in view of the insignificant amounts involved, or it would necessitate a disproportionate amount of expense or delay; or

(c) the result would be misleading; or

(d) the result would be harmful to the business of the company or any of its subsidiaries; or

(e) the business of the holding company and that of the subsidiary are so different that they cannot reasonably be treated as a single undertaking.[2]

Department of Trade and Industry approval is necessary in the cases of (d) and (e).[3]

For the SSAP 14 exemptions from preparing consolidated accounts, see para 9.170, below.

---

[1] CA 1985, s 229(2).
[2] Ibid, s 229(3).
[3] Ibid, s 229(4).

9.163   If group accounts are not prepared or if some subsidiaries are not included therein, the following information must be included in the notes to the holding company's accounts

(a) the reasons why the subsidiaries have not been dealt with in the group accounts.

(b) details of any qualifications in the audit reports of these subsidiaries; also details of any note in their accounts, which, but for that note, would have been the subject of a qualification. In the latter case, the details need only be given when these items have not been dealt with in the holding company's accounts and are material to the holding company's accounts.

(c) the aggregate amount of the total investment of the holding company in the shares of its subsidiaries, stated by way of the equity method of valuation.[1]

Point (c) does not apply if the holding company is itself a wholly owned subsidiary of a company incorporated in the UK.[2]

If any of the above information is unobtainable, a note to that effect should be included.[3]

---

[1] CA 1985, Sch 4, para 69(2) and (3).
[2] Ibid, Sch 4, para 69(4).
[3] Ibid, Sch 4, para 69(5).

9.164   The exemptions from preparing group accounts under the 7th Directive differ in some respects from the current exemptions. Some of the most important differences are as follows:

(a) *Exemptions for subgroups*
The present exemption for a holding company which is itself a wholly owned subsidiary of another company incorporated in the UK will be extended to cover any holding company which is the wholly owned subsidiary of a company incorporated within the EEC. Moreover, if the subgroup's parent holds 90% or more of the shares in the intermediate parent, a similar exemption will apply. This is conditional on the remaining shareholders' approving the exemption.

   This subgroup exemption only applies if the EEC holding company prepares accounts (which will have to be filed in the UK) and has them audited in accordance with the Directive. Given this, the exemption is mandatory.[1]

   The effect of this exemption is that a UK group wholly owned by a non-EEC parent, (for example, American or Swiss) will have to continue to prepare consolidated accounts, whereas one owned by an EEC parent will not.

   The extension of this exemption will mean that UK law will no longer be able to require the consolidation of a subgroup owned by a UK parent which is itself the wholly owned subsidiary of an EEC parent. The Directive does however permit a requirement for a limited amount of sub-consolidation information.

(b) *Size exemptions*
Member states have the option to introduce exemptions for groups coming within a certain size range. These exemptions only apply if none of the members of the group has any securities listed on a Stock Exchange.

(c) *Other grounds for exclusion from group accounts*
There are certain other grounds on which a subsidiary may be excluded.[2] These are similar in some respects to those under the current UK legislation (See para 9.162, above.) Notably, however, the current exclusions on the grounds of impracticality or harm to the business are not included under the 7th Directive. In practice this is unlikely to cause many significant problems.

---

[1] 7th Directive Article 7.1.
[2] 7th Directive Articles 13 and 14.

The form of group accounts

9.165   In practice group accounts generally consist of a single set of consolidated accounts, comprising

   (a)   a consolidated balance sheet
   (b)   a consolidated profit and loss account
   (c)   a consolidated statement of source and application of funds, and
   (d)   the balance sheet of the holding company

together with the related notes.

The holding company profit and loss account need not be included in the group accounts, provided that the consolidated profit and loss account shows how much of the consolidated profit or loss for the financial year is dealt with in the accounts of the company. Where advantage is taken of this dispensation, that fact must be disclosed in a note to the group accounts.

Financial years

9.166   Both the legislation and SSAP 14 require that the financial years of the holding company and its subsidiaries should be coterminous, unless there are good reasons why this is not practical.[1] Obviously failure to implement this requirement may result in some distortion, and could even result in failing to present a true and fair view.

But there may be circumstances in which it is impractical for the financial year of the holding company and its subsidiaries to coincide. For example, overseas subsidiaries might be unable to comply with the holding company's timetable if their accounts had to be drawn up to the same date.

If for whatever reason the financial years do not coincide, the group accounts should incorporate the subsidiary's accounts for the last financial year ended before the date of the holding company's balance sheet.[2] If this procedure is not followed Secretary of State approval is required.

[1] CA 1985, s 230(7)(a) and SSAP 14 para 17.
[2] Ibid, s 230(7b).

9.167   SSAP 14 offers two alternatives in the case of non-coterminous year ends

(a) The legislative procedure outlined above. If this is followed, any abnormal events in the subsidiary's books occurring between its year end and that of the holding company should be adjusted for.
(b) Alternatively special financial statements could be drawn up for the subsidiary which coincide with the financial year of the holding company. Because it does not accord with the legislative requirements, this procedure requires Secretary of State approval.

Where the financial years are not coterminous, the following information should be included in the group accounts:

(i)   the reasons why the company's directors consider that the subsidiary's financial year should not coincide with that of the holding company
(ii)   the dates on which the subsidiary's financial year ends and
(iii) the names of the principal subsidiaries involved.[1]

[1] SSAP 14, para 18.

9.168   Section 229(5) of the CA 1985 states that group accounts should normally take the form of consolidated accounts; group accounts may however be presented in another form, if this is better for

(a) presenting the same or equivalent information about the state of affairs and profit or loss of the company and its subsidiaries; and

(b) presenting the information so that it may be readily appreciated by the company's members

Given these conditions other acceptable forms of group accounts are

(i) more than one set of consolidated accounts dealing with the company and one group of subsidiaries, and with other groups of subsidiaries, or

(ii) separate accounts dealing with each of the subsidiaries, or

(iii) the company's individual accounts, with a statement expanding the information about the subsidiaries. This statement will generally consist of an abridged set of the subsidiaries' accounts, or

(iv) any combination of these forms.[1]

In practice probably the most common example of accounts which are not fully consolidated is a set of consolidated accounts excluding one subsidiary, together with a summary of that subsidiary's results.

All sets of group accounts must give the same or equivalent information as that required for consolidated accounts[2].

---

[1] CA 1985, s 229(6).
[2] Ibid, Sch 4, para 68.

9.169 SSAP 14 is also less flexible than the legislation. Its states that group accounts must comprise consolidated accounts, unless certain specific exceptions apply. These are as follows:

(a) the subsidiary's activities are so dissimilar that consolidated accounts would be misleading, or

(b) the holding company does not exercise voting control over the subsidiary, or has restrictions imposed on its ability to appoint the majority of the board, or

(c) the subsidiary operates under severe restrictions which impair control, or

(d) control is intended to be temporary[1]

The SSAP goes on to state that if a company prepares group accounts in a form other than consolidated financial statements the directors must justify their accounting treatment. Moreover, they must state their reasons for concluding that the resulting accounts give a fairer view of the financial position of the group as a whole.

---

[1] SSAP 14, para 2.

9.170 Some of the common situations in practice in which group statements take a form other than consolidated accounts are discussed below:

(a) The most common is if the activities of a subsidiary are so different from those of the rest of the group that its consolidation would be misleading. Both SSAP 14 and the Directive require non-consolidation in these circumstances, as does the current legislation, which is less prescriptive with regard to the requirement for consolidated accounts. The most difficult practical problem lies in determining whether its activities are so dissimilar that consolidated accounts would be misleading.

Generally, exclusion on the grounds of dissimilar activities is confined to cases where the subsidiary's business involves the preparation of accounts drawn up on a basis which cannot sensibly be combined with that applying to other group companies. For example, a group which principally manufactured and distributed goods might include a bank. Aggregating the assets and liabilities of the bank with those of the manufacturing company could produce a balance sheet which gave a distorted view, so there are arguably grounds for not including the bank in the consolidation.

(b) Another common reason for exclusion from consolidation is that the control exercised by the holding company is temporary. Again, the Directive and SSAP 14 require non-consolidation here. This should be interpreted as relating to the intention only at the time of acquisition, rather than meaning that the subsidiary should be deconsolidated when the decision to dispose of it is taken subsequently.

Such an interpretation is endorsed by paragraph 32 of SSAP 14. This defines the effective date for accounting for both acquisitions and disposals as being the earlier of
(i) the date at which consideration passes, or
(ii) the date on which an offer becomes or is declared unconditional.

(c) A company might be legally a subsidiary requiring incorporation in the group accounts, but in effect only an associate. For example a company might be the subsidiary of two different companies. This would be the case if one company (A), held more than 50% of its equity share capital, whereas another company (B) controlled the composition of its board. In this case, B would not be entitled to more than 50% of its profits. Therefore consolidating its results in B's accounts would be misleading, since it is in substance an associate of B.

Group accounts: the accounting treatment

9.171   As noted in para 9.159, above, the Act does not deal comprehensively with the accounting treatment of subsidiaries in group accounts. Currently the SSAP requirements must be relied upon. However, the 7th Directive will give statutory authority to many of the current SSAP requirements.

The most significant areas covered by the SSAPs but only touched on by current UK law are the accounting treatment of business combinations and the treatment of goodwill arising on acquisition. But in addition the SSAPs do leave some questions unclarified; in particular, the subject of fair value accounting. The various accounting requirements are discussed in paras 9.172 to 9.191, below.

Accounting for business combinations

9.172 SSAP 23 deals with accounting for business combinations, which arise when one or more companies become subsidiaries of another company. The two different methods of accounting for these combinations are acquisition accounting and merger accounting. The SSAP restricts merger accounting to share for share exchanges. It does this by prescribing certain conditions which must be fulfilled before merger accounting can be applied. SSAP 23 also discusses the method of accounting for mergers and the accounting method for acquisitions. The differences between the two methods result in the consolidated accounts for a combination which has been treated as a merger looking very different from the accounts of a combination treated as an acquisition.

The 1981 Act introduced a dispensation from the requirement to set up a share premium account provided that certain conditions were met, and in doing this it effectively legalised merger accounting (see para 9.179 below on merger relief). The 7th Directive deals in more detail with merger accounting and the requirements are in the main the same as those in SSAP 23.

The detailed requirements and their practical implications are discussed below.

The conditions for merger accounting

9.173 Under SSAP 23, a business combination may be accounted for as a merger if all of the following conditions are met:

(a) the combination results from an offer to the holders of all the equity shares, and the holders of all the voting shares which are not already held by the offeror; and

(b) the offeror has secured as a result of the offer a holding of
  (i) at least 90% of all equity shares, and
  (ii) the shares carrying at least 90% of the votes of the offeree, and

(c) immediately prior to the offer, the offeror does not hold
  (i) 20% or more of all the equity shares of the offeree, or
  (ii) shares carrying 20% or more of the votes of the offeree, and

(d) not less than 90% of the fair value of the total consideration given for the equity share capital (including that given for shares already held) is in the form of equity share capital, and not less than 90% of the fair value of the consideration given for voting non-equity share capital (including that for shares already held) is in the form of equity and/or voting non-equity share capital.[1]

An offer is defined as any offer made by, or on behalf of, a company (the offeror) for shares in another company (the offeree). A number of separate offers constituting in substance a composite transaction is considered to be a single offer.[2]

Merger accounting is optional given that the above conditions apply: therefore a combination may be accounted for as an acquisition even if these conditions prevail. Any combination which does not meet all the above conditions must be accounted for as an acquisition. When the Seventh Directive is enacted, it appears that merger accounting will be available on a more limited basis than it is at present.

---

[1] SSAP 23, para 11.
[2] SSAP 23, para 7.

9.174   The SSAP goes on to discuss the accounting treatment in the group accounts. It does not specifically address the treatment in the company's individual accounts, but guidance on this is provided in the Appendix to the SSAP. For the sake of clarity the treatment in the company's individual accounts and in the group accounts are discussed together below.

Merger accounting

9.175   In the offeror's accounts, the normal treatment is to record the investment in the offeree at the nominal value of the shares which the offeror issues in exchange.

If there is additional consideration in some form other than equity shares, the fair value of such consideration should be added to the nominal value of the shares issued.

On consolidation only slight adjustments are necessary:

(a)   It is not necessary to adjust the carrying value of the assets and liabilities of the offeree to fair value, either in the offeree's accounts or on consolidation. Adjustments however should be made to achieve uniformity of accounting policies between the combining companies.[1]

(b)   In the group accounts, the offeree's profits or losses for the period when the merger first takes place should be included for the entire period. The corresponding amounts should be restated as though the companies had been combined throughout the previous period, and at the previous balance sheet date.[2] Consequently, the results of the offeree company are brought into the group accounts retrospectively.

(c)   One difference that may arise on consolidation is the difference between the carrying value of the investment, and the nominal value of the shares transferred to the offeror company. If the carrying value is less, then the difference should be treated as a consolidation reserve; if it is greater, then the difference should be treated as a reduction of reserves.[3]

---

[1] SSAP 22, para 18.
[2] SSAP 23, para 19.
[3] SSAP 23, para 20.

Acquisition accounting

9.176   The Appendix to the SSAP states that, if a combination is acquisition accounted, then the investment should be recorded at cost in the offeror company's books. Cost is defined as 'the fair value of the consideration given'.

On consolidation the following points should be noted:

(a)   The fair value of the consideration given i e the cost, should be allocated between the underlying net tangible and intangible assets, other than goodwill, on the basis of the fair value to the offeror company.[1] This may be done by adjusting the values in the books of the offeree company; alternatively the adjustments can be left until the consolidation stage.

(b) Any difference between the purchase consideration and the total of the fair values ascribed to the net assets will represent goodwill.[2]
(c) The results of the offeree company should be brought into the group accounts from the date of the acquisition only.[3]

These differences mean that the consolidated accounts will look very different if a merger approach is adopted instead of an acquisition approach. Paras 9.177 to 9.181 below deal with some of the major differences.

---

[1] See below.
[2] SSAP 23, para 16.
[3] SSAP 23, para 17.

Share premium account

9.177 On a merger the investment should be recorded in the offeror company's books at the nominal value of the shares issued by the offeror company. Therefore no share premium account will be created. Accounting for a combination as an acquisition, on the other hand, could result in the creation of a share premium account, if the shares are being issued at a value in excess of their nominal value. (But see para 9.179, below). Therefore this method of accounting can result in the creation of a sizeable non-distributable reserve.

9.178 Merger accounting was not lawful until the introduction of the 1981 Companies Act. This allowed relief from the requirement to set up a share premium account in certain situations.[1]

To qualify for this relief, the issuing company (the offeror) must have acquired at least a 90% holding in the equity share capital of another company (the offeree) in consequence of the allotment of its own equity shares. The consideration must have been provided by either:

(a) the issue or transfer to the issuing company of equity shares in the other company, or
(b) the cancellation of any such shares not held by the issuing company.[2]

It is not necessary that all of the 90% holding is acquired in total as a consequence of this allotment. However, the relief is available only in respect of the shares issued in the transaction which takes a holding to 90%, and not in respect of shares already held which count towards 90%.

---

[1] See chapter 4, above.
[2] CA 1985, s 131.

9.179 This relief is generally referred to as 'share premium account relief', or, somewhat confusingly, as 'merger relief'. The latter title is confusing because a company might choose to take advantage of this relief when it is not merger accounting for a business combination. There are two sets of circumstances under which this may occur:

(a) the combination might qualify as a merger under SSAP 23 but might nonetheless have been accounted for as an acquisition. (Merger

accounting is optional under the SSAP given that the relevant conditions apply.)[1]
(b) The conditions in SSAP 23 under which a company might merger account are more restrictive than the legal conditions under which a company can take advantage of merger relief. Therefore, the combination might qualify for statutory merger relief although it does not fulfil the SSAP 23 conditions. For example a business combination can only be classified as a merger under SSAP 23 if the offeror did not have a prior holding of more than 20% (para 9.173(c), above). Merger relief however can apply irrespective of the size of the prior holding, although the relief is not available in respect of this prior holding.

---

[1] See para 9.173, above.

Preacquisition profits

9.180   In an acquisition, the preacquisition profits of the acquired company are frozen at the date of the acquisition, and are generally regarded for accounting purposes as non-distributable. In a merger, on the other hand:

(a) the retained earnings of the two companies are aggregated in the consolidated balance sheet, and
(b) their profit and loss accounts are aggregated for the whole year. Thus the results of the acquired company which arose before the combination are included. The corresponding amounts are similarly aggregated, and the historical summaries restated.

Obviously then, provided that the companies are profitable, merger accounting will result in the consolidated distributable profits appearing better than they would if acquisition accounting were adopted. This explains the attraction of merger accounting.

Value of assets acquired

9.181   Under the merger accounting rules, no adjustment need be made to the asset values of the offeree company; they are simply brought into the consolidated accounts at their book amounts.

However, with acquisition accounting, these assets must be assigned fair value in the consolidated balance sheet, which will commonly differ from the book amount, often materially.[1]

This difference will affect the consolidated results, since the depreciation charge and any profits or losses on disposals will obviously be different if the book values are adjusted. It is likely that the fair values of the assets will be higher than their book values: consequently profits on disposal are likely to be greater in the case of merger accounting, and this will tend to boost the consolidated results further.

---

[1] See para 9.186, below.

Practical implications

9.182   These differences outlined in paras 9.177 to 9.181 have two major implications in practice.

(a) They can invalidate comparability in that they can produce very different results for combinations which are in essence similar.
(b) The conditions for merger accounting are such that the directors can frequently effectively choose the most desirable reporting method by making adjustments to the mechanics of the deal. Merger accounting is likely to be preferred because of the favourable effect on future reported profits, without real regard to the substance of the deal.

Vendor placings

9.183   A business combination might achieve classification as a merger rather than as an acquisition by means of a vendor placing. With this, the business combination is effected by way of a share for share exchange including arrangements for the offeree's shareholders to place for cash the offeror's shares which they receive in exchange for their own.

The combination thus meets all the conditions set out in SSAP 23 for merger accounting.[1] But because the original shareholders can place for cash the shares which they receive in the offeror company, there will not be continuity in the shareholders' interests.

---

[1] See para 9.173, above.

Vendor rights issue

9.184   A vendor rights issue is a refinement of a vendor placing: the existing shareholders of the offeror company are given rights to subscribe for the placing of the shares by the offeree company shareholders. Therefore, in a vendor rights issue, the cash to finance the purchase is raised from the acquiring company's shareholders, but indirectly, allowing the company to account for the transaction as a merger rather than as an acquisition.

9.185   The suitability of the merger method depends on what the true test of a merger is taken to be. One school of thought takes continuity in the shareholders' interests as the essential criterion. On this interpretation, the combinations described in 9.182–3 above are in substance acquisitions. A contrary view is that combinations can be treated as mergers provided that no resources leave the group. This results in more combinations being regarded as mergers in the true sense of the term, including vendor rights issues and vendor placings.

Fair value accounting

9.186   There is as yet no formal guidance on fair value accounting. However, the principle behind it is that the acquisition of a subsidiary is effectively the purchase of a conglomeration of assets and liabilities. Therefore in the consolidated accounts these can be included at their individual cost to the group rather than at their book value in the company being acquired. This cost to the group is effectively the price paid for the individual assets, based on the assessment of their worth. Such an approach will affect the future reported earnings in the consolidated profit and loss account: for example, the depreciation charge on a fixed asset, if based on the cost to the group (i e the fair value at the time of acquisition by the group) will be different to the depreciation charge based on the original cost to the subsidiary.

Goodwill

9.187   SSAP 22 deals with the accounting treatment of goodwill. It states that goodwill should not be carried in the balance sheet of the company or group as a permanent item. There are two possible methods of accounting for purchased goodwill:

   (a) the preferred method is immediate write-off against reserves
   (b) alternatively, goodwill may be systematically amortised through the profit and loss account over its useful economic life. The amount written off must be charged before arriving at the profit or loss on ordinary activities.

One important point arising from the standard is that, although consolidation goodwill must either be amortised or written off immediately in the group accounts, there is no requirement to reduce the carrying value of the relevant investment shown in the holding company balance sheet by a similar amount, provided that there has been no permanent impairment in value.

Negative goodwill is defined as the excess of the fair values of the separable net assets acquired, over the fair value of the consideration given. SSAP 22 requires that this should be credited directly to reserves. Although there is no specific requirement, in practice negative goodwill is likely to be disclosed as a separate unrealised reserve. It may then be transferred to realised reserves in line with the depreciation or realisations of the assets acquired in the business combination which gave rise to the negative goodwill in question.

SSAP 22 requires that the accounting policy followed in respect of goodwill be explained in a note to the accounts. If material, the amount of goodwill on each acquisition should be disclosed. Where the amortisation treatment is adopted, the disclosure requirements are the same as for other fixed assets: the cost, accumulated amortisation and net book value at the beginning and end of, and the movements in, the period must be shown. Disclosure is required of the amortisation period for each major acquisition, the reasons for choosing that period, and also the amount of goodwill written off through the profit and loss account in a financial period. Any unamortised amount of goodwill should be shown as a separate item under intangible fixed assets.

Effective date of acquisition or merger

9.188   This is defined in SSAP 14 as being the earlier of:

   (a) the date on which the consideration passes, and
   (b) the date on which an offer becomes or is declared unconditional.[1]

This definition applies, even if the acquiring company has the right under the agreement to share in the profits of the acquired business from an earlier date.

If the combination is being accounted for as an acquisition, then the results of the acquired company should be brought into the group accounts from the date of the acquisition only. In merger accounting, however, the results should be aggregated for the entire period.

Often, financial statements drawn up to the effective date are not available. In order to arrive at the subsidiary's figures up to the effective date for an acquisition, it may therefore be necessary to apportion the results in the audited financial statements on an appropriate basis. Time or turnover might provide such a basis. Alternatively, if reliable interim accounts are drawn up, or the latest audited financial statements are drawn up to a date sufficiently near the effective date, these could be used.

---

[1] SSAP 14, para 32.

SSAP 23 Disclosure requirements

9.189 SSAP 23 requires the following disclosure be made in respect of all material business combinations, whether they are accounted for as acquisitions or mergers:

(a) names of combining companies
(b) details of consideration given
(c) the accounting treatment adopted for the business combination
(d) the nature and amount of any significant accounting adjustments required to achieve consistency of accounting policies.

9.190 Where there are material mergers in a period, SSAP 23 requires the following details be disclosed:

(a) The fair value of the consideration given by the issuing company
(b) an analysis of the current year's attributable profit before extraordinary items between the periods before and after the effective date of the merger
(c) an analysis of the attributable profit before extraordinary items (i) of the current year, up to the effective date of the merger, and (ii) of the previous year, disclosing that of the issuing company and that of the subsidiary
(d) an analysis of each extraordinary item, including which of the merger parties it relates to, and whether it is pre- or post-merger

Merger relief: statutory disclosures

9.191 In addition, certain statutory disclosures are required when the company has entered into arrangements subject to merger relief. These are:

(a) the name of the new subsidiary company, and the number, nominal value and class of its shares issued, transferred or cancelled in the transaction
(b) particulars of the accounting treatment adopted in the company's

accounts, including that in any group accounts, in respect of such issue, transfer or cancellation, and

(c) where the company prepares group accounts, particulars of the extent and manner in which the disclosed group profit or loss for the year of the merger is affected by the results of the subsidiary for the period before the transaction

(d) the number, nominal value and class of shares issued by the holding company in the transaction

(e) any profit or loss which is included in the group results and which arises from the disposal of any shares in the subsidiary, any fixed assets of the subsidiary, or any shares in any other company which owned any such fixed assets or shares (insofar as any profit or loss relates to such items). This disclosure is required in the accounts of the year of merger and of the two subsequent financial years.

Group Accounts: the true and fair view

9.192   Group accounts must comply with the schedules to the CA 1985 as regards disclosure, in so far as these are applicable to group accounts.

As for individual accounts, the group accounts, together with any notes, must give a true and fair view of the state of affairs of the company and its subsidiaries. The requirement to give a true and fair view overrides both the Schedule 4 requirements, and all other matters which must be included in the group accounts or in the notes to those accounts. Consequently any additional information necessary for a true and fair view must be provided in the group accounts or in a note to them. Only if the additional information would still not result in a true and fair view being given should the directors depart from the legal requirements. In this case, the directors must give full details of the departure, including the reasons for it and its effect.[1]

---

[1] CA 1985, s 230.

Argyll Foods case

9.193   The question of a true and fair view in the context of group accounts is a crucial one, in the light of the Argyll Foods case in 1982.[1] Here, the directors included in the consolidated balance sheet a company which did not become a subsidiary until shortly after the end of the financial year, on the grounds that the terms were agreed and that they already had effective control. Moreover, ·

(a) they already had a substantial shareholding at the year end, and

(b) the company was a subsidiary by the time the accounts were finalised.

The notes to the accounts contained full details of the departure from the Companies Act and SSAP 14, including the directors' reasons for the departure and a summarised balance sheet of the new subsidiary. The auditors referred to the situation in their report, and stated that, in their opinion, the accounts were not rendered misleading by the non-compliance.

The Department of Trade and Industry prosecuted the company for non-compliance with s 150 and s 152 of the Companies Act 1948. Their argument was that there could be no compromise over the definition of a subsidiary, and that only subsidiaries owned at the year end could be included in group accounts. The decision was that the financial director was guilty of contravening ss 150 and 152, concerning the presentation of the accounts.

The implications of the outcome of the *Argyll Foods* case are far reaching. The case demonstrated that the DTI will not allow a breach of the detailed provisions of the Companies Act, unless the breach is necessary to give a true and fair view. The directors were not allowed to breach detailed provisions so that they could prepare accounts that they considered better or more informative. In the *Argyll* case, the accounts could have been presented in a way that gave a true and fair view, and still complied with the Companies Acts.

[1] For details of this case see *Accountancy* August 1981, p 19 and June 1982, pp 80–81.

Contents of group accounts

9.194   The form and content of group accounts and the related notes should comply with Schedule 4, so far as this is applicable to group accounts in the form in which those accounts are prepared.[1] This provision is subject to the true and fair override.

[1] CA 1985, s 230(1).

9.195   If the group accounts take the form of consolidated accounts, they should comply as far as practicable with the requirements of the CA 1985 as if they were the accounts of an actual company.[1] They should combine the information contained in the individual accounts, but with such adjustments as the directors of the holding company think necessary.[2] There are no examples in the Schedule of what adjustments might be considered necessary on consolidation. In practice they include the elimination of minority interests, pre-acquisition profits, and inter-company balances, profits and dividends.

If the group accounts are not presented as consolidated accounts, they must give the same or equivalent information as that required in the case of consolidated financial statements.

[1] CA 1985, Sch 4, para 62.
[2] Ibid, Sch 4, para 61.

9.196   The following disclosure requirements do not apply to the group accounts. Consequently, disclosure need only be made of the holding company details.

(a) The information about shareholdings in companies other than subsidiaries will only apply to the holding company's accounts.[1]
(b) Schedule 5 Part V relates to the details of the chairman's and directors' emoluments, pensions and compensation for loss of office. Disclosure is only required for holding company directors.

(c) Disclosure of the number of employees remunerated at the higher rates only applies to holding company employees.[2]

(d) Particulars of loans and other transactions need only be given in respect of the directors and officers of the holding company.[3]

---

[1] CA 1985, Sch 5, Part II.
[2] Ibid, Sch 5, Part VI.
[3] Ibid, Sch 6.

Company's own accounts

9.197 Schedule 4 Part IV contains special provisions where the company is a holding company or subsidiary:

(a) The balance sheet headings for amounts attributable to group companies should be analysed between:
  (i) Amounts attributable to any holding company or fellow subsidiary of the company
  (ii) Amounts attributable to any subsidiary of the company.
  This analysis can be made either on the face of the balance sheet or in the notes.[1]

(b) Where the company is a holding company, the number, description and amount of the shares in, and debentures of, the company held by its subsidiaries should be disclosed. Where the subsidiary is concerned as a personal representative or trustee (provided no beneficial interests exists) this disclosure is not required.[2] Such shareholdings are in fact prohibited except under special circumstances.

---

[1] CA 1985, Sch 4, para 59.
[2] Ibid, Sch 4, para 60.

9.198 The following information must be disclosed in the holding company's accounts in respect of any companies which are its subsidiaries at the year end:

(a) the name of the subsidiary

(b) its country of incorporation if outside the UK. The notes should also state whether the company is registered in England or Scotland, if this is different from the country of registration of the holding company.

(c) the description and proportion of the nominal value of each class of shares held. This must be analysed over shares held by the holding company itself, and shares held by other subsidiaries.

If the company has so many subsidiaries that this would be impractical, then disclosure need only be made in respect of principal subsidiaries. However, the notes to the accounts must make it clear that this has been done, and the full details must be filed with the annual return.

The details need not be disclosed in respect of the preceding year.[1]

In addition, SSAP 14 paragraph 33 requires that an indication of the nature of the business of principal subsidiaries should be given.

---

[1] CA 1985, Sch 4, para 58(3).

9.199 Schedule 5 Part III deals with financial information required in respect of subsidiaries. This is that the holding company accounts should state:

(a) the aggregate amount of the subsidiary's capital and reserves, and
(b) its profit or loss for the financial year.

There are several exemptions from this disclosure and these are dealt with in paragraph 17 of Schedule 5. Most importantly, the information need not be given if the subsidiary's accounts are included in the group accounts, nor if the investment of the company in the shares of the subsidiary is included in the company's accounts by way of the equity method of accounting.

9.200 There are additional disclosures required by SSAP 14. Briefly, these are:

(a) *Accounting policies*
The accounting policies should be uniform throughout the group, or consolidation adjustments should be made to achieve uniformity. If this is impractical, then disclosure should be made of the different policies used, and the reasons therefore. An indication of the effect on the results and net assets of the adoption of different policies should be given.

The accounting policies for the consolidation of subsidiaries, acquisitions and disposals, and the treatment of consolidation goodwill should also be disclosed.

(b) *Minority interests*
Minority interests in the share capital and reserves of the companies consolidated should be disclosed as a separate amount in the consolidated balance sheet and should not be shown as part of shareholders' funds. In the consolidated profit and loss account, the minority interests in the consolidated profit after tax but before extraordinary items, should be disclosed. Minority interests in extraordinary items should be deducted from the related amounts.

(c) *Changes in composition of the group*
Where there are material additions to or disposals from the group, the consolidated accounts should contain sufficient information about the results of the subsidiaries acquired or disposed of to enable the shareholders to appreciate the effect on the consolidated results.[1]

---

[1] SSAP 14, para 30.

SPECIAL CATEGORY COMPANIES

9.201 Certain companies and groups do not have to prepare their accounts in accordance with Schedule 4. 'Special category' companies may instead prepare accounts in accordance with Schedule 9. Special category companies include banking, shipping and insurance companies. Moreover, holding companies which have a subsidiary which falls into this category have the option of preparing their group accounts under Schedule 9. Where a holding company is not itself a special category company but has a subsidiary which is, the holding company's own accounts would have to be prepared under Schedule 4, but its group accounts could be prepared under Schedule 9. Accounts prepared in accordance with Schedule 9, are referred to in the CA 1985 as 'special category' accounts.

9.202   The following definitions apply in this context:

(a) 'Banking company' means a company which is a recognised Bank under the Banking Act 1979 or is a licensed institution within that Act.
(b) 'Insurance company' means an insurance company to which Part II of the Insurance Companies Act 1982 applies.
(c) 'Shipping company' means a company which, or a subsidiary of which, owns ships or includes among its activities the management or operation of ships, and which satisfies the Secretary of State that it ought, in the national interest, to be treated under Part VII of the CA 1985 as a Shipping Company.[1]

Separate EEC Directives are being developed for banking and insurance companies. Exempt shipping companies will be required to conform with Schedule 4 by 1988.

---

[1] CA 1985, s 257(1).

9.203   Where a company's individual accounts are special category.

(a) the balance sheet must give a true and fair view of the state of affairs as at the end of the financial year, and
(b) the profit and loss account must give a true and fair view of the company's profit or loss for the financial year.

The balance sheet and profit and loss account must comply with the requirements of Schedule 9, so far as applicable.[1]

Special category group accounts must give a true and fair view of the state of affairs and profit or loss of the company and the subsidiaries dealt with by those accounts as a whole: if prepared as consolidated accounts, they must comply with the requirements of Schedule 9, so far as applicable. If they are not prepared as consolidated accounts they must give the same or equivalent information.

Both individual and group special category accounts must contain a note to the effect that they are prepared in accordance with Schedule 9.

---

[1] CA 1985, s 258(1)–(2).

Form and content of special category accounts

9.204   The disclosure requirements are contained in Schedule 9, and are the same as those formerly under Schedule 8A. Banks continue to have certain further exemptions, provided that they have obtained Secretary of State approval. These exemptions are detailed in Part III to Schedule 9.

There are consequently no statutory formats for special category accounts. Nor do the accounting principles and rules have statutory force, although most are regarded as best practice. Further, there are many specific disclosure requirements for Schedule 4 accounts which do not apply for special category companies.

PREPARATION, LAYING AND DELIVERY OF ACCOUNTS

Procedure on completion of accounts

9.205 The directors must prepare a profit and loss account in respect of each financial year, and a balance sheet as at the last day of the financial year.[1]

The company's balance sheet must be signed on behalf of the board by two of the directors of the company, or if there is only one director by that one.[2] However, a company's articles may require the signature of more than two directors.

The company's profit and loss account and any group accounts of the holding company must be annexed to the balance sheet, and must be approved by the directors before the company's balance sheet is signed. In this context there is no legal requirement to sign the consolidated balance sheet, although it is common practice to do so.

---

[1] CA 1985, s 227.
[2] Ibid, s 238(1).

Laying and delivery of accounts

9.206 The directors must, in respect of each financial year, lay the company's accounts before the company in general meeting.[1] The company's accounts consist of:

(a) *Holding companies*
    (i)   the company's balance sheet
    (ii) the directors' report
    (iii) the auditor's report, and
    (iv) the group accounts
    together with the related notes.

(b) *Individual companies*
    (i)   the company's profit and loss account
    (ii) the company's balance sheet
    (iii) the directors' report, and
    (iv) the auditor's report
    together with the related notes.

In addition SSAP 10 requires for all but the smallest companies a statement of source and application of funds.

Copies of these documents must be sent not later than 21 days before the date of the meeting, to

    (i)   every member of the company
    (ii) every holder of the company's debentures, and
    (iii) all others who are entitled to receive copies.[2]

(But see para 9.215, below),

A copy of these accounts must also be delivered to the registrar of companies.[3] It must be annexed to the company's annual return which must be submitted within 42 days from the AGM. Under certain circumstances, the company may instead deliver modified accounts to the registrar. (For the regulations relating to this, see paras 9.216 to 9.233, below).

If the accounts are not in English, then the directors must attach a certified translation into English.[4] There is however no requirement for the accounts to be in £ sterling.

---

[1] CA 1985, s 238.
[2] Ibid, s 240(1).
[3] Ibid, s 241(3).
[4] Ibid, s 241(3b).

Unlimited companies

9.207   Unlimited companies are exempt from the requirement to file accounts with the registrar, if all of the following conditions are met:

(a) during the accounting reference period the company must not at any time have been the subsidiary of a limited company, nor have been under the control of two or more limited companies, and

(b) it must not at any time during the accounting reference period have been the holding company of a limited company, and

(c) it must not at any time during the accounting reference period have been a promoter of a trading-stamp scheme within the meaning of the Trading Stamps Act 1964.[1]

The references in (a) and (b) above to a company that was limited are to any body corporate, the liability of whose members was at that time limited. This includes non-UK registered companies.

---

[1] CA 1985, s 241(4).

Period allowed for laying and delivery of accounts

9.208   The period allowed after the end of the accounting reference period for laying and delivering accounts is seven months for public companies, and ten months for private companies.[1] There are however certain exceptions to this rule which are summarised in paras 9.209–9.212, below.

---

[1] CA 1985, s 242(2).

Companies with overseas business or interests

9.209   A UK registered company which carries on business or has interests outside the UK may claim an extension to the period by three months. In order to claim this extension the directors must give to the registrar of companies notice in the prescribed form:

(a) stating that the company carries on such business or has such interests, and
(b) claiming an extension of three months to the period allowed.[1]

But in order to qualify for the extension, the claim must be made before the period normally allowed has expired.

---

[1] CA 1985, s 242(3).

First accounting reference period exceeding 12 months

9.210 If the company's first accounting reference period exceeds twelve months, then the time allowed for laying and delivery is reduced by the number of days by which the accounting reference period exceeds twelve months. The time allowed for laying and delivery, however, must not be reduced below three months.[1]

---

[1] CA 1985, s 242(4).

Accounting reference period shortened

9.211 Where the company's accounting reference period has been shortened it may result in the directors' having less time to prepare the accounts. For this reason the period for laying and delivery in such cases is the longer of:

(a) the period normally allowed[1] but in relation to the new financial year i e commencing with the new accounting reference date, and
(b) the period of three months beginning with the date on which the notice concerning the alteration is given.[2]

---

[1] See para 9.208, above.
[2] CA 1985, s 242(5).

Overseas companies

9.212 Overseas companies are required to deliver a copy of their accounts in respect of each accounting reference period to the registrar of companies. This must, if necessary, have a certified translation into English attached to it. As with UK registered companies, unlimited overseas companies are exempt from this requirement provided that they meet the conditions set out in para 9.207, above.

Overseas companies have a longer period after the end of their accounting reference period in which to deliver accounts to the registrar. The period normally allowed is 13 months; however if their first accounting reference period exceeds 12 months, the time for laying and delivery is shortened as with UK companies.[1]

---

[1] CA 1985, ss 700–703.

Secretary of State's powers

9.213   The Secretary of State may, if he thinks fit, give written notice to the company extending the time allowed for laying and delivery of accounts. This provision extends to overseas companies.

Penalties for non-compliance

9.214   Penalties for non-compliance with these regulations attach to every person who was a director immediately before the end of the time allowed for laying and delivery.[1] The penalty is a fine up to an aggregate of £400, plus £40 for each day of default. If a person is charged with an offence, it shall be a defence to prove that he took all reasonable steps for securing that the requirements should be complied with.

Penalties also attach to the company in respect of a failure to deliver accounts to the registrar.

---

[1] CA 1985, s 243.

Shareholders' right to obtain copies of accounts

9.215   As noted in para 9.206, above certain persons are entitled to receive copies of the company's accounts. However, documents are not required to be sent

(a) to a member or debenture holder of whose address the company is unaware
(b) to more than one of the joint holders of any shares or debentures, none of whom are entitled to receive notices of general meetings.
(c) in the case of joint holders of shares or debentures some of whom are and some of whom are not entitled to receive such notices of general meetings, to those who are not so entitled.[1]

However, any member of the company and any holder of the company's debentures, including those above, is entitled to be furnished on demand with a copy of the company's accounts.[2]

---

[1] CA 1985, s 240.
[2] Ibid, s 246.

MODIFIED ACCOUNTS

9.216   The directors of a limited company are required to deliver a copy of the company's accounts to the Registrar of Companies, and to lay a copy before the members in General Meeting.[1]

Normally the form and content of both sets of accounts must comply with Schedule 4 to the Act. However if certain conditions[2] are met the company will qualify as a small or medium-sized company. In such a case, the directors may prepare modified accounts for submission to the Registrar of Companies in respect of certain financial years. These modified accounts are required to comply with Schedule 8 to the CA 1985 rather than with Schedule 4. The advantage in exercising the option is that the disclosure requirements of Schedule 8 are much less extensive than those of Schedule 4; thus greater confidentiality can be maintained. However, the disadvantage is that Schedule 4 format accounts must still be laid in full before the members in General Meeting. The directors will have to decide whether the increased confidentiality which can be obtained by exercising the option is outweighed by the more extensive preparations involved.

Two points which relate to a company's entitlement to file modified accounts should be emphasised.

(a) In a company's first financial year, the directors will be able to file modified accounts if the company fulfils the qualifying conditions in that year. In subsequent financial years, fulfilling the qualifying conditions in respect of a financial year will not automatically entitle a company to file modified accounts in respect of that year. The detailed rules are set out in para 9.220, below.

(b) The circumstances under which a company may deliver modified accounts in respect of a financial year are less straightforward if the company is required to prepare group accounts under s 229 for that year. Paras 9.218–9.225, below deal with the situation where the company is not a holding company. Paras 9.226–9.228, below deal with modified accounts where the company is a holding company.

---

[1] CA 1985, s 241.
[2] See para 9.218, below.

Ineligible companies

9.217 Some types of company áre precluded from taking advantage of these provisions relating to modified accounts.[1]

These ineligible companies are

(a) public companies
(b) banking, insurance and certain shipping companies (as defined for Sch 9 purposes)
(c) companies which are members of an 'ineligible group'.

A group is classed as ineligible if its ultimate holding company or any subsidiary of that company

(i) falls into category (a) or (b) above;
(ii) is a body corporate which is a banking or insurance company;
(iii) is a body corporate which has the power to offer its shares or debentures to the public, and may lawfully exercise that power. This definition extends to any public company, including those registered overseas.

---

[1] CA 1985, s 247(2) and (3).

The qualifying conditions: individual companies

9.218   Two or more of the following conditions must be satisfied in a financial year before a company may qualify as small or medium-sized.[1]

	Small company	*Medium-sized company*
Turnover not exceeding	£1.4m	£5.7m
Balance sheet total not exceeding	£0.7m	£2.8m
Average number of employees not exceeding	50	250

An EEC Council Directive adopted in November 1984 allows for a revision of the current thresholds to the extent of an increase of 55% in balance sheet total and 60% for turnover. Implementation of this revision is optional and the DTI is at present considering whether the balance sheet and turnover thresholds in the UK should be increased.

Turnover
The qualifying limits only apply where the company's financial year is 12 months in length. If the company's financial year is less than or greater than 12 months, the turnover figures should be pro-rated on an annual basis.[2]

Balance sheet total
The balance sheet total referred to above is that comprising items A to D of the Format 1 balance sheet: that is, it is the total of the company's assets before deducting any creditors or provisions.[3]

Average number of employees
This figure is to be arrived at by

  (i)   taking the number of persons employed by the company in each week during the financial year
 (ii)   adding the weekly totals
(iii)   dividing the total by the number of weeks in the financial year.[4]

---

[1] CA 1985, s 248(1) and (2).
[2] Ibid, s 248(5).
[3] Ibid, s 248(3).
[4] Ibid, s 248(4).

Entitlement to file modified accounts

First financial year

9.219   If a company qualifies as small in respect of its first financial year, it may deliver small company accounts. Similarly, if it fulfils the qualifying conditions for a medium-sized company it may deliver accounts modified as for a medium-sized company.[1]

---

[1] CA 1985, s 249(2).

Subsequent financial years

9.220 After its first financial year, a company may deliver accounts modified as for a small company in respect of a financial year, if it qualifies as small in that and the immediately preceding financial year. The same procedures apply to the delivering of accounts modified as for a medium-sized company.[1]

There are also provisions to cater for companies that fluctuate in and out of the qualifying conditions, as follows

(a) A company may cease to fulfil the qualifying conditions in the current financial year. Provided however that in the previous year
 (i) the company did qualify, and
 (ii) it was entitled to deliver modified accounts in respect of that year, then it will be entitled to deliver modified accounts for the current financial year.[2] Only if it fails to qualify again in the following financial year, will it lose its entitlement.

(b) A company may not have fulfilled the qualifying conditions in the preceding financial year, but still have been entitled to deliver modified accounts in respect of that year. This will be the case if the situation in (a) above prevailed. In this case, if it fulfills the conditions in respect of the current financial year, it will retain its entitlement to deliver modified accounts.[3]

It should be noted that it does not have to be the same two conditions that are satisfied in successive years — each year is looked at on its own merits.

---

[1] CA 1985, s 249(4).
[2] Ibid, s 249(5).
[3] Ibid, s 249(6).

Change in status: summary

9.221 The above rules for financial years subsequent to the first might appear cumbersome. In practice their application to the current financial year is straightforward, provided that the following approach is adopted.

(i) *Entitlement to file accounts modified as for a small company*
1 Was the company entitled to file modified small company accounts in respect of the preceding financial year? If the answer is no, then the company will not be so entitled in respect of the current financial year, irrespective of its status in the current year.

2 If the company was so entitled, then it will retain its entitlement for the current financial year, provided that:

(a) it fulfilled the qualifying conditions for a small company in the preceding financial year, and/or
(b) it fulfils the qualifying conditions for a small company in the current financial year.

(ii) *Entitlement to file accounts modified as for a medium-sized company*
It should be observed that a company which qualifies as 'small' will

automatically qualify as 'medium-sized'. Thus the question of entitlement to deliver accounts modified as for a medium-sized company can be approached as follows:

1   Was the company entitled to deliver modified accounts (either as for a small, or for a medium-sized company), in respect of the preceding financial year? If not, then it will not be entitled to deliver modified accounts for the current year.

2   If the company was so entitled, then it will be entitled to file accounts modified as for a medium-sized company for the current year if at least one of the following conditions are met.

   (a) It fulfilled the qualifying conditions for a medium-sized company in the preceding financial year.
   (b) It fulfils the qualifying conditions for a medium-sized company in the current financial year.

In fact it follows from (i) above that an expanding company might qualify as medium, but not small, in respect of the current financial year, but still be able to file small company accounts.

Table 1 provides an example of how the rules might operate in practice when a company's status is changing.

The contents

9.222   Schedule 8, Part I contains details of the exemptions for modified accounts for small and medium-sized companies respectively.[1] Modified accounts must include the following additional information:

   (a) A directors' statement to the effect that the company is entitled to deliver accounts modified as for a small/medium-sized company, and
   (b) A report of the auditors stating that, in their opinion, the directors are so entitled.

The provisions of this Schedule are discussed in more detail below. It should be stressed again at this point that the Schedule 8 requirements relate only to the accounts which are to be delivered to the Registrar of Companies: the accounts which are laid before the members in General Meeting must comply with Schedule 4.

---
[1] CA 1985, Sch 8, paras 2–11.

Accounts modified as for a small company

9.223   The exemptions for small companies are quite extensive.

   (a) The directors must deliver a signed balance sheet to the Registrar of Companies. This balance sheet is required to follow either Format 1 or 2, as for a Schedule 4 balance sheet, but only those items to which a letter or Roman numeral is assigned need be disclosed.[1] In addition, the aggregate amount of debtors falling due after one year must be

Table 1

Financial Year	Conditions satisfied	Entitlement to file modified accounts
1 (First financial year)	Small	Since this is the company's first financial year, it will be entitled to file small company accounts in view of the fact that it qualifies as small.
2	Small	The company will be entitled to deliver small company accounts, since it satisfies the conditions in 9.218 for two successive years.
3	Medium	Again the company retains its entitlement to file small company accounts, since the conditions 1 and 2(a) in (i) are satisfied.
4	None	Although the company satisfies neither set of qualifying conditions it will be entitled to file medium-sized company accounts. The conditions 1 and 2(a) in (ii) are fulfilled.
5	Medium	The company can file accounts modified as for a medium-sized company. In this year it satisfies the conditions 1 and 2(b) in (ii).

disclosed, and, if the Format 2 balance sheet is adopted, the figure for creditors should be analysed between:
  (i) amounts falling due within one year
  (ii) amounts falling due after more than one year.[2]
(b) No profit and loss account is required.[3]
(c) No directors' report is required.[4]
(d) The notes on accounting policies (including foreign currency), share capital, particulars of allotments and details of indebtedness as required by Schedule 4, must still be included. Moreover the Schedule 4 requirement that comparatives must be included for the preceding financial year continues to apply. The other notes required by Schedule 4 are exempt.

Schedule 5 requirements
Parts I–IV of Schedule 5, which are basically group disclosure requirements, remain applicable.

However, small company modified accounts are exempt from the disclosure requirements of Parts V and VI of this Schedule. These requirements relate to directors' and higher paid employees' emoluments.

Schedule 6 requirements (details of directors' loans and transactions).
  These disclosures are also required for modified accounts.

---

[1] CA 1985, Sch 8, para 2.
[2] Ibid, Sch 8, para 6.
[3] Ibid, Sch 8, para 3.
[4] Ibid, Sch 8, para 3.

Accounts modified as for a medium-sized company

9.224   The exemptions in the case of a medium-sized company are:

(a) Several items in the profit and loss account format may be combined, under the heading 'gross profit or loss'.

The items to be combined are as follows.

Format 1

1	Turnover
2	Cost of sales
3	Gross profit or loss
4	Other operating income

Format 2

1	Turnover
2	Change in stocks of finished goods and work in progress
3	Own work capitalised
4	Other operating income

5(a)   Raw materials and consumables
 (b)   Other external charges

Format 3

A1   Cost of sales
B1   Turnover
B2   Other operating income

Format 4

A1   Reduction in stocks of finished goods and work in progress
A2(a) Raw materials and consumables
  (b) Other external charges
B1   Turnover
B2   Increase in stocks of finished goods and work in progress
B3   Own work capitalised
B4   Other operating income[1]

In all these cases, the figure for gross profit includes other operating income. Of the Schedule 4 formats, only Format 1 discloses a gross profit figure, but this does not include other operating income. Thus, a company filing accounts modified as for a medium-sized company could be in the position where these accounts show a higher gross profit figure than that in the shareholders' accounts.

(b) Neither disclosure nor analysis of turnover is required.[2]

Otherwise, the profit and loss account must comply with Schedule 4. The balance sheet, directors' report and remaining notes to the accounts must comply with Schedules 4–7.

---

[1] CA 1985, Sch 8, para 7(1) and (2).
[2] Ibid, Sch 8, para 8.

Modified accounts: small and medium-sized

9.225   The above paragraphs have dealt with the differing disclosure requirements for small and medium-sized companies in respect of the profit and loss account and balance sheet, and also the directors' report and notes to the accounts. The following three points apply both to small and to medium-sized companies.

(i) *Statements of standard accounting practice*

The SSAPs apply only to those accounts which are intended to give a true and fair view of the financial position, and profit or loss. Because of the exemptions available, a company's modified accounts may not give a true and fair view, although they will be based on the accounts presented to the shareholders. Although the shareholders' accounts are required to comply with the SSAPs, modified accounts need not so comply themselves. This means that the disclosure requirements of the SSAPs need not apply to modified accounts: for example, no statement of source and application of funds will be required. However, the principles for calculating the amount at which items are stated in the accounts should be the same as required by SSAPs.

(ii) *Directors' statement*

The balance sheet delivered to the Registrar must be signed by two directors of the company (or, where the company has only one director, by that director). Immediately above their signatures on the balance sheet there must be a statement by the directors that 'they rely on Sections 247 to 249 of the Act as entitling them to deliver accounts modified as for a small or (as the case may be) for a medium-sized company.'[1]

(iii) *Report of the auditors*

The modified accounts delivered to the Registrar must be accompanied by a special report of the auditors. This should state that in their opinion:

(a) the directors are entitled to deliver modified accounts in respect of the financial year, and
(b) any accounts comprised in the documents delivered as modified accounts are properly prepared in accordance with the CA 1985.[2]

The full text of the auditors' report on the accounts laid before the shareholders must also be reproduced in this special report. Illogically, because this reports on the truth and fairness of the accounts, it will not relate directly to the modified accounts themselves.

Moreover, page references in the auditors' report on the shareholder accounts will be repeated in the report on the modified accounts but will have no context. Similarly, if the auditors' report on the shareholder accounts is qualified and in that context refers to a note, it is quite likely that this note will not need to be repeated in small company modified accounts.

An example of the special audit report required for modified accounts is as follows.

REPORT OF THE AUDITORS TO THE DIRECTORS OF LIMITED

Under Schedule 8 paragraph 10(1) of the Companies Act 1985

We have examined the accounts on pages A to B which have been modified, in the manner permitted for a small company/medium sized company, from the accounts of the company prepared for its members for the year ended   , 19 .

In our opinion, the directors are entitled to deliver modified accounts in respect of the year ended   , 19   and the modified accounts are properly prepared in accordance with Schedule 8 of the Companies Act 1985.

We set out below the text of our report dated   , 19   to the members on the unmodified accounts for the year ended   , 19 .

'We have audited the accounts on pages C to D in accordance with approved auditing standards.

In our opinion the accounts, which have been prepared under the historical cost convention, give a true and fair view of the state of the company's affairs at 19   and of its profit and source and application of funds for the year then ended and comply with the Companies Act 1985.'

Ltd.

Date (of report on modified accounts)

---

[1] CA 1985, Sch 8, para 9.
[2] Ibid, Sch 8, para 10.

Modified accounts: holding company

Holding company's accounts

9.226   The provisions relating to modified accounts are more restrictive if the company is required to prepare group accounts under s 229 in respect of a financial year. If this is the case, then the holding company must fulfil the requirements of s 250. But in addition it may only deliver individual accounts modified as for a small company, if the group (the holding company and its subsidiaries) is in that year a small group i e the group aggregates fall within the conditions for a small company. Similar rules apply with regard to accounts modified as for a medium-sized company.

The group account figures must fulfil two or more of the qualifying conditions set out in para 9.218 above, before the group qualifies as small or medium-sized. The group account figures are:

(a)   in the case of consolidated accounts, the figures shown in those accounts[1]
(b)   if the group accounts are not consolidated, the group figures must be calculated as if consolidated accounts had been prepared.[2]

In addition, if any subsidiary has been omitted from the group accounts on grounds other than impracticability, the relevant figure for the subsidiary must be included in the group calculations.[3]

---

[1] CA 1985, s 250(3)(a).
[2] Ibid, s 250(3)(b).
[3] Ibid, s 250(4).

Group accounts

9.227   If the directors are entitled to deliver modified accounts for the holding company, they may also deliver modified group accounts. Whether the group as a whole qualified in preceding years is irrelevant. Modified group accounts must fulfil the disclosure requirements of Schedule 8 Part II if the accounts are consolidated. Moreover, if the accounts are not consolidated, they must give the same or equivalent information as required by Schedule 8, Part II. Schedule 8, Part III also applies to modified group accounts.

Contents of modified group accounts

9.228   The exemptions are the same as those which apply to the individual company accounts (see paras 9.223 and 9.224, above). Similar provisions also apply to the directors' statement and the auditors' report.

Directors' statement. In the case of modified group accounts, the directors' statement on the holding company balance sheet should include the following:

(a) that they have relied on ss 247 to 249 of the Act as entitling them to deliver accounts modified as for a small or (as the case may be) for a medium-sized company, and

(b) that the documents delivered include modified group accounts, in reliance on s 250 of the Act.[1]

Auditors' report. This must include the statement that in their opinion

(a) the company is entitled under section 250 of the Act to deliver modified group accounts, and

(b) these documents have been properly prepared.[2]

---

[1] CA 1985, Sch 8, para 21.
[2] Ibid, Sch 8, para 22.

DORMANT COMPANIES

9.229   A company may pass a special resolution making itself exempt from the obligation to appoint auditors. It may do so in the following circumstances:

(a) at any time before the first general meeting at which the accounts as required by s 241 are laid. To take advantage of this, the company must always have been dormant. Public limited companies and special category companies do not qualify for this exemption.

(b) At a general meeting at which accounts, as required by s 241, are laid. Two conditions must be met here:

(i) The company must have been dormant since the end of the financial year, and

(ii) The directors must have been entitled to deliver small company accounts in respect of that financial year. A company which would have been entitled to file small company accounts but is a member of an ineligible group, can still take advantage of the exemption. This provision automatically excludes public limited companies and special category companies.

9.230 A company is dormant 'during any period in which no transaction occurs which is for the company a significant accounting transaction'. A company which has been dormant ceases to be so on the occurence of any such transaction, and will lose its exemption from the obligation to appoint auditors. In this situation, the directors may appoint an auditor to hold office until the conclusion of the next general meeting; if they fail to exercise that power, the company in general meeting may exercise it.

Significant accounting transactions

9.231 The question of whether a company is dormant hinges on what constitutes a significant accounting transaction. Section 252(5) defines this as 'a transaction which is required by s 221 to be entered in the company's accounting records'. However transactions which arise from the taking of shares by a subscriber in pursuance of an undertaking of his in the memorandum are to be disregarded. The definition is wide-ranging — for instance, if a company has to pay its own fee for filing accounts with the Registrar, it will not be dormant.

Laying and delivery of unaudited accounts ·

9.232 Companies which are exempt from the obligation to appoint auditors in respect of a financial year need not include an auditors' report with their statutory accounts for that financial year. This will apply if either:

(a) The company was exempt throughout the financial year, or
(b) The company became so exempt by virtue of a special resolution passed during the year, and retained the exemption until the end of the year.

A report by the company's auditors need not be included with the accounts which are laid before the members in general meeting, or those delivered to the Registrar of Companies. If the auditors' report is omitted from the accounts delivered to the Registrar, then the balance sheet should contain a statement by the directors immediately above their signatures, to the effect that the company was dormant throughout the financial year. If modified accounts are delivered, then the special audit report otherwise required in the case of modified accounts need not be included. Similarly, the directors do not need to include a statement on the balance sheet concerning the company's eligibility to file modified accounts.[1]

---

[1] See CA 1985, Sch 8, paras 9 and 10 and para 9.225(ii), above.

Agency companies

9.233 Cases where a company is acting solely as agent on behalf of a principal should be reviewed carefully. In most cases, the agent will be required to keep records of its transactions on behalf of the principal, and such records are regarded as accounting records; consequently the company will not be dormant and will have to prepare audited accounts.

Sometimes, non-trading companies within a group hold the legal title to a property, but another group company occupies it and pays the property expenses. The question of whether the non-trading company is dormant, will depend upon whether it is acting as nominee. If so, the property should be carried in the balance sheet of the actual owner and, if there are no other transactions, the nominee will be dormant. If however the company is not acting as nominee the property should be carried in its balance sheet. If the property includes buildings, depreciation or revaluations might need to be entered in the company's books. Consequently the company would not be dormant.

ABRIDGED ACCOUNTS

Introduction

9.234   Sections 254 and 255 deal with the publication requirements for a company's accounts, and establish a distinction between 'full' and 'abridged' accounts. The rules are designed to make the reader aware that in these cases he is not being presented with all the information necessary for a true and fair appraisal of the company's affairs.

This is done by drawing the distinction between 'full' and 'abridged' accounts, and then by establishing different publication requirements for the two, so as to emphasise to the reader that he is not being presented with 'full' accounts in the latter case.

Abridged accounts: the legal definition

9.235   Section 255(1) defines abridged accounts as 'any balance sheet or profit and loss account relating to a financial year of the company, or purporting to deal with any such financial year, otherwise than as part of full accounts (individual or group).'

Full accounts are defined in s 254. They are the accounts, for a group or individual company, which are required to be laid before the company in general meeting and delivered to the Registrar. It should be emphasised that modified accounts, which may be filed for a small or medium-sized company, are also included within the definition of full accounts.

The publication requirements

9.236   The auditors' report must always be included when full accounts are published.[1] When the company publishes abridged accounts, however, the directors must not include the audit report, but must incorporate a statement indicating:

(a) That the accounts are not full accounts.
(b) Whether full individual or full group accounts have been delivered to

the Registrar of Companies. If the company is unlimited and therefore exempt from the requirement to deliver accounts to the Registrar, a statement must be included that the company is exempt.

(c) Whether the company's auditors have made a report under section 236 on the company's accounts and

(d) Whether this report was unqualified.[2]

---

[1] CA 1985, s 254(2) and (4).
[2] Ibid, s 255(3).

9.237 In practice, a report is regarded as 'unqualified' for these purposes provided that the accounts comply with the legislation (one requirement of which is that they should present a true and fair view). In certain circumstances, a report may be qualified solely on the grounds of non-compliance with a SSAP which is not required for a statutory true and fair view. The accounts might still present a true and fair view, and fulfil all the other legal requirements. In such a case, no reference need be made to the qualification in the s 255(3) statement.

The situation in which this is most likely to apply at the present time is if the accounts have failed to comply with SSAP 10 (Statement of Source and Application of Funds).

Meaning of 'publication'

9.238 The definition of abridged accounts only becomes relevant in the context of publication, since it is only in the case of abridged accounts published by the company that the s 255(3) statement need be given.

Section 742(5) defines publication: 'A company is to be regarded as publishing any balance sheet or other account if it publishes, issues, or circulates it, or otherwise makes it available for public inspection in a manner calculated to invite members of the public generally, or any class of members of the public, to read it'.

The publication rules of ss 254 and 255 (see para 9.236, above) only apply to full or abridged accounts which are published by the company itself. Financial information relating to the company published by any other source would not be subject to these requirements.

Abridged accounts generally include interim and preliminary reports of results issued by companies, insofar as these include information relating to a financial year.

Conventionally the term publication has come to have a wide interpretation. In particular it has come to include the issue of employee reports and shareholder circulars, and it is common for abridged accounts within these documents to include a s 255(3) statement.

Although the scope is wide, the legislation obviously does not aim to include every issue of summarised financial information by a company under the heading of 'publication'. This could lead to the situation where, for example, the directors' providing the company's bank with financial information might constitute publication and hence necessitate the inclusion of a s 255(3) statement. Obviously, this would be impractical, but where to draw the line depends on the circumstances. As a general rule though, provided that

(a) the information is issued to specific persons,
(b) it is confidential in nature, and
(c) the restricted status of the information is clear,

it would not generally be regarded as published material.

Abridged accounts: the scope

9.239

(a) *Period covered*

Abridged accounts must relate to or purport to deal with a company's (or group's) financial year, that is, the period in respect of which the directors of a company must prepare accounts for presentation to the members at the annual general meeting.

(b) *Context*

Information which is published as part of a company's full accounts will not comprise abridged accounts. This includes all information within the same document as the full accounts, for example, five or ten year historical summaries.

(c) *Entity*

The provisions apply to abridged accounts which relate to a company, or to a group of companies, as defined in the CA 1985 for reporting purposes.

The practical consequences

9.240   Set out below are some instances of documents which prima facie could be taken to constitute abridged accounts, and how they are classified in practice. Obviously these examples are not exhaustive.

(a) *Supplementary information*

Listed companies commonly include supplementary information in the same document as their full accounts. For example, the document might include five year financial summaries, or 'highlights' pages, neither of which on their own would constitute full accounts.

Provided however that the information is published as part of or as an attachment to the company's full accounts, it will not comprise abridged accounts[1]. For this reason, any such supplementary information need not incorporate a s 255(3) statement.

(b) *Divisional accounts*

Results for a particular division within a company might be published. These would not generally comprise abridged accounts, since abridged accounts must relate to a company or to a group of companies i e a reporting entity as provided by the CA 1985. Of course this exception might not prevail if the results for all the divisions within a company were given, since this could amount to disclosing the results for the whole company.

(c) *Preliminary announcements*

As noted, preliminary announcements issued by listed companies as required by The Stock Exchange appear to fall within the definition of abridged accounts, although in practice many are published without the inclusion of a s 255(3) statement.

(d) *Interim announcements*

These do not relate to a full financial year. So, except to the extent that they include comparative figures for the last full financial year, they would not come within the scope of the definition. If such comparatives are included the same considerations apply as with preliminary announcements.

(e) *Prospectuses and public offer documents*

Prospectuses and public offer documents, including shareholder circulars, will usually be regarded as published information (see para 9.238, above). Historical financial summaries are often included in an accountant's report within these documents. However, since the directors have an overall responsibility for the document, this information is regarded as being published by the company. In practice most published offer documents include a s 255(3) statement relating to historical summaries.

The Stock Exchange requirement for the full text of any audit qualification to be reproduced would appear to be in conflict with the legal requirements.[2] In practice The Stock Exchange accepts an extract from the audit report setting out the substance of the qualification.

(f) *Employee reports*

As noted in para 9.238, above, reports to employees are regarded as published information. Consequently the inclusion of financial information, if it resembled a profit and loss account or balance sheet, would necessitate a s 255(3) statement, although again points (a)–(c) in para 9.238, above would be relevant.

---

[1] CA 1985, s 255(1).
[2] 'Admission of Securities to Listing', section 5.25(d).

10 Audit and auditors

Michael Renshall

POWERS AND DUTIES OF AUDITORS

Legal duties

10.01 The directors of every company are required to lay before the members in general meeting in respect of each financial year a copy of the annual accounts for that year, consisting of the profit and loss account and balance sheet, group accounts if the company has subsidiaries, the directors' report and the auditor's report.[1]

---

[1] CA 1985, s 241(1).

10.02 The auditor must report to the members of the company on the accounts examined by him.[1] This report must be attached to the balance sheet and, except for certain unlimited companies, must be filed together with the accounts, with the Registrar of Companies.[2]

---

[1] CA 1985, s 236(1).
[2] Ibid, s 241(3).

10.03 The auditor's report must state (a) whether, in his opinion, the balance sheet of the company (and of the group in the case of group accounts) and profit and loss account (of the company or group, whichever is appropriate) give respectively a true and fair view of the state of affairs at the balance sheet date and of the profit or loss for the financial year (of the company or of the group, as appropriate) and (b) whether the accounts have been properly prepared in accordance with the Companies Act 1985.[1] Special category companies (banking, insurance and shipping companies) are permitted to take advantage of exemptions from the statutory disclosure requirements by virtue of ss 258 to 262 and Part III of Sch 9 (see chapter 9); in this case the auditor is not required explicitly to state whether the accounts give a true and fair view but whether they have been properly prepared in accordance with the Companies Act 1985.[2] The effect of the latter exemptions is not to relieve the accounts of special category companies from the requirement to give a true and fair view in general terms, but to relieve them from some specific disclosure requirements of the Act. Where while the absence of the information in question might impair the true and fair view given by the accounts of non-exempt companies, in the case of banks and insurance companies it is specifically provided that their accounts shall not be deemed not to give a true and fair view by reason only of the fact that they have availed themselves of exemptions permitted by the Act.[3]

---

[1] CA 1985, s 236(2).
[2] Ibid, s 262(2).
[3] Ibid, Sch 9, paras 27(4) and 28(2).

10.04 In addition to the auditor's principal duty to report whether the accounts give a true and fair view and comply with the CA, s 237 lays down certain additional requirements:

º   The auditor is required to make such investigations as will enable him to form an opinion as to whether proper accounting records have been kept by the company and proper returns received from branches not visited by him, and whether the accounts are in agreement with those records. If proper accounting records have not been kept or the records are not in agreement with the accounts the auditor is required to say so in his report.[1]
º   The auditor must report if he has not received all the information and explanations necessary for the purposes of his audit.[2]
º   The auditor must consider whether the information given in the directors' report relating to the financial year is consistent with the accounts; if the auditor is of the opinion that the information is not consistent he must state this fact in his report.
º   The auditor must report certain statutory information relating to directors' emoluments and transactions if that information has not been included in the accounts. This includes particulars of chairman's and directors' emoluments (Parts V and VI of Schedule 6) and particulars of loans and other transactions favouring directors and officers (Parts I to III of Schedule 6).

---

[1] CA 1985, s 237(2).
[2] Ibid, s 237(4).

10.05 The Companies Act does not prescribe the procedures to be followed by the auditor in the performance of his duties, the standard of care required of him, or the extent of any liability he may owe to members and third parties who rely on his report. These matters have been left to the courts to decide and are briefly discussed in paras 10.06 and 10.36 to 10.39 below.

Legal powers

10.06 The Act gives the auditor powers necessary to enable him to perform his duties. The auditor has a right of access at all times to the books, accounts and vouchers of the company and is entitled to require from the officers of the company such information and explanations as he considers necessary for the performance of his duties.[1] He is entitled to attend any general meeting of the company and to receive notices of, and other communications relating to, any general meeting and to be heard at any general meeting on any part of the business which concerns him as auditor.[2] Where the company is a holding company with subsidiaries incorporated in the UK, that subsidiary and its auditor have a duty to provide any information and explanations which the holding company's auditor may reasonably require.[3] Where the subsidiary is incorporated overseas the holding company must take all steps as are reasonably open to it to obtain from the subsidiary the information and explanations required.[4] Finally it should be noted that it is a criminal offence for any officer of a company knowingly or recklessly to make a statement to the auditor which is misleading, false or deceptive in any material particular.[5]

---

[1] CA 1985, s 237(3).
[2] Ibid, s 387(1).
[3] Ibid, s 392.
[4] Ibid, s 392.
[5] Ibid, s 393.

APPOINTMENT OF AUDITORS

10.07 At each general meeting at which accounts are laid before the members, every company must appoint an auditor (or auditors) to hold office from the conclusion of that meeting until the conclusion of the next general meeting at which accounts are laid.[1] If an auditor is not appointed at the general meeting the office of auditor falls vacant and the company is required to give notice within a week of this fact to the Secretary of State who may appoint a person to fill the vacancy.[2] It is an offence not to give such notice.[3] In practice the vacancy is normally filled by exercise of the directors' powers.[4] Dormant companies (that is, those that are not public or special category companies, have had no accounting transactions during the period, are entitled to deliver for filing modified accounts appropriate to small companies, and are not required to produce group accounts) are entitled to pass a special resolution not to appoint auditors.[5]

---

[1] CA 1985, s 384(1).
[2] Ibid, s 384(5).
[3] Ibid, s 384(5).
[4] See para 10.08, below.
[5] CA 1985, s 252: see also paras 9.229–9.233, below.

10.08 The first auditor of a company may be appointed by the directors at any time before the first general meeting at which audited accounts are presented to hold office until the conclusion of that meeting.[1] If the directors fail to exercise these powers, the company in general meeting may do so.[2] The directors or the company in general meeting may also fill any casual vacancy in the office of auditor.[3] If there are joint auditors a casual vacancy in the office of one does not affect the power of the survivor or survivors to continue acting.[4]

---

[1] CA 1985, s 384(2).
[2] Ibid, s 384(3).
[3] Ibid, s 384(4).
[4] Ibid, s 384(4).

10.09 A resolution for the appointment as auditor of a person other than the retiring auditor, the filling of a casual vacancy, the reappointment of a retiring auditor appointed by the directors to fill a casual vacancy or the removal of an auditor before the expiration of his term of office requires special notice.[1]

---

[1] CA 1985, ss 386(1) and 388(1); see also paras 10.13 to 10.16, below.

10.10 When a new auditor is to be appointed to replace an existing auditor, he is required if he is a member of one of the recognised accountancy bodies[1] to ascertain from the retiring auditor whether there are any professional reasons why he should not accept the appointment. Unless he receives a satisfactory response the incoming auditor is required to consider his position before accepting the appointment. The member is advised to decline nomination if the existing auditor informs him that the company has refused authority to discuss the company's affairs with the proposed new auditor. This procedure is imposed by the ethical requirements of the UK accountancy bodies, not by statute.[2]

---

[1] See para 10.26, below.
[2] ICAEW Members Handbook 1.309.

10.11 Although under English law partnerships are not separate legal entities, it is the general practice (unless the articles provide otherwise) to appoint auditors in the name of their firms and not as individuals. In England the effect of appointing auditors in the firms name is to appoint as auditors all those partners who are qualified for appointment on the day the appointment is made.[1] An event which subsequently disqualifies one of the partners does not in itself automatically disqualify the remainder. A person who is appointed a partner subsequent to the date of appointment of the firm as auditors would not in law rank as an appointed auditor until his firm's appointment is next formally ratified by the company. Formerly, when automatic reappointment of auditors applied, the situation could arise that a company could find itself without lawfully appointed auditors because all those ranked as partners at the time of first appointment had since ceased to be partners. Problems of this nature are rare today, and transient at most, because of the requirement for companies to appoint (or reappoint) auditors at each general meeting at which accounts are laid before the members.[2]

---

[1] See report of the Company Law Committee 1962, Cmnd 1749, paragraph 427.
[2] See para 10.07, above.

10.12 Under Scottish law a partnership is a legal entity. A Scottish firm is qualified for appointment as auditors only if all partners are individually qualified for such appointment.[1]

---

[1] CA 1985, s 389(8).

REMOVAL OF AUDITORS

10.13 A company may remove an auditor from office by an ordinary resolution of members in general meeting notwithstanding anything in any agreement between the company and the auditor.[1] Removal does not deprive the auditor however of any right he may have to compensation or damages in respect of the termination of his appointment.[2] Special notice must be given of any resolution to remove an auditor.[3] Under the special notice requirement 28 days notice must be given to the company which in turn must give 21 days notice to the members.[4] Once the company receives notice of such a resolution it must send a copy of it to the auditor.[5]

[1] CA 1985, s 386(1).
[2] Ibid, s 386(3).
[3] Ibid, s 388(1).
[4] Ibid, s 379.
[5] Ibid, s 388(2).

10.14 An auditor who is proposed to be replaced or removed is entitled to make written representations (not exceeding a reasonable length) and the company is required to state, in the notice of resolution, that such representations have been made and send a copy of the representations to every member of the company to whom notice of the meeting is or has been sent.[1] If copies of the auditor's representations are not sent to the members (either because they were received too late by the company or because of the company's default) the auditor may require such representations to be read out at the meeting.[2] There are sanctions to prevent auditors abusing this right. If, on application, the court considers that the right to make representations is being abused to secure needless publicity for defamatory matter then the representations need not be sent or read out. The court may order that the costs of such an action be paid in whole or part by the auditor, notwithstanding that he is not party to the application.[3]

[1] CA 1985, s 388(3).
[2] Ibid, s 388(4).
[3] Ibid, s 388(5).

10.15 An auditor who has been removed before the expiry of his term of office may attend the general meeting at which his term of office would otherwise have expired and any general meeting at which it is proposed to fill the vacancy caused by his removal.[1] He may be heard at any such meeting on any part of the business which concerns him as former auditor of the company.[2]

[1] CA 1985, s 387(2).
[2] Ibid, s 386(10).

10.16 The company must register the resolution removing the auditor with the Registrar of Companies within fourteen days of the passing of the resolution.[1]

[1] CA 1985, s 386(2).

RESIGNATION OF AUDITOR

10.17 An auditor may resign before his term of office expires by depositing a notice in writing to that effect at the company's registered office.[1] His resignation becomes effective on the date he lodges such notice or on such later date as may be specified in the notice. The auditor's notice of resignation is not effective unless it contains either a statement to the effect that there are no circumstances connected with his resignation which the auditor considers should be brought to the notice of members or creditors of the company, or a statement of any such circumstances.[2]

---

[1] CA 1985, s 390(1).
[2] Ibid, s 390(2).

10.18 The company must send the auditor's notice of resignation to the Registrar within fourteen days and, if the auditor has made a statement as to the circumstances connected with his resignation, must send a copy of the statement to all those who are entitled to receive copies of the statutory accounts (members and debentures holders) within the same time period.[1] If the company fails to comply, it and every officer of the company who is in default is guilty of an offence and liable to a fine.[2]

---

[1] CA 1985, ss 390(6) and 240(1).
[2] Ibid, s 390(7).

10.19 If on application to court within fourteen days of receipt of the notice of resignation by the company, the court decides that the statement is being used to secure needless publicity for defamatory matter then the statement need not be sent out.[1] Following the court order the company must send a statement setting out its effect to all those entitled to receive a copy of the auditor's statement;[2] the penalties for failure to perform this duty are the same as for failure to send out the auditor's statement.[3]

---

[1] CA 1985, s 390(5).
[2] Ibid, s 390(6)(a).
[3] Ibid, s 390(7).

10.20 If the auditor has made a statement giving the circumstances of his resignation[1] he is entitled to call on the directors to requisition an extra-ordinary general meeting to explain further the circumstances surrounding his resignation.[2] If the directors fail to convene a meeting within 21 days of receiving the auditor's requisition any director who has failed to take all reasonable steps in the matter is guilty of an offence and liable to a fine.

---

[1] CA 1985, s 390(2)(b).
[2] Ibid, s 391(1).

10.21 The auditor may also require the company to circulate a statement in writing of the circumstances connected with his resignation before the general meeting at which his term of office would otherwise have expired or before any general meeting at which it is proposed to fill the vacancy caused by his resignation or convened on his requisition.[1] If a written statement, not exceeding a reasonable length, is made by the auditor and it is received in time, the company is required to state in the notice of the meeting that a statement has been made and send a copy of the statement to every member to whom notice is or has been sent.[2] There are provisions for application to the court where the right to send a statement is being abused which are similar to those referred to above.[3] If the directors do not send out the written statement, the auditor may require it to be read out at the meeting.

[1] CA 1985, s 391(2).
[2] Ibid, s 391(3).
[3] See para 10.19, above.

10.22   An auditor who has given notice of resignation retains his right to attend, and receive any notice or communication relating to, the meetings referred to above. He is also entitled to be heard at such meetings on any matter which concerns him as former auditor of the company.[1]

[1] CA 1985, s 391(7).

REMUNERATION OF AUDITORS

10.23   The auditor's remuneration (including sums paid in respect of expenses) is fixed by the company in general meeting or in such manner as the company in general meeting may determine.[1] It is common practice for the general meeting to give authority to the directors to fix the auditor's remuneration. Where the auditor is appointed by the directors (for example as first auditor or to fill a casual vacancy) or by the Secretary of State[2] the directors or the Secretary of State may fix the remuneration.[3]

[1] CA 1985, s 385(1).
[2] See para 10.07, above.
[3] CA 1985, s 385(2).

10.24   The amount of auditors' remuneration (including sums paid in respect of expenses) charged in the profit and loss account must be separately disclosed in the company's accounts.[1]

[1] CA 1985, Sch 4, para 53(7).

QUALIFICATION FOR APPOINTMENT AS AUDITOR

Introduction

10.25   To qualify for appointment the auditor must be either (a) a member of a body of accountants established in the United Kingdom and recognised by the Department of Trade and Industry or (b) individually authorised by the Secretary of State for Trade and Industry as having similar qualifications obtained outside the United Kingdom.[1] Officers and servants of the company being audited, employees and partners of such officers and servants, and bodies corporate are disqualified from acting as auditor.[2]

---

[1] CA 1985, s 389(1)(a).
[2] Ibid, s 389(6); and see paras 10.31–10.35, below.

Members of a United Kingdom body of accountants

10.26 The accounting bodies recognised by the Secretary of State for Trade and Industry under the Act are the Institute of Chartered Accountants in England and Wales, the Institute of Chartered Accountants in Scotland, the Chartered Association of Certified Accountants and the Institute of Chartered Accountants in Ireland.[1] These bodies require that their members are adequately qualified for the task of auditing through practical experience and appropriate tests of competence. Under their internal rules members who wish to perform audits must obtain practising certificates, which are issued only after they are able to show that they have obtained suitable experience subsequent to their admission to membership. In addition, the four recognised bodies have strict ethical standards and are parties to a joint disciplinary scheme, which are designed to ensure the independence of the auditor and provide for inquiry into and sanctions against professional misconduct or where it is alleged there has been a lapse in standards of professional work.[2]

---

[1] CA 1985, s 389(3).
[2] ICAEW Members Handbook 1.1.

Individual authorisation

10.27 The Department of Trade and Industry may authorise as auditors individuals who have obtained similar qualifications outside the United Kingdom to those of the UK bodies.[1] In this case it is the individual auditor who is authorised and not the professional body of which he is a member. Authorisation may be refused if it appears that the country in which the qualification was obtained does not confer corresponding privileges on UK individuals.[2]

---

[1] CA 1985, s 389(1)(b).
[2] Ibid, s 389(5).

10.28 Within the European Community, the European Commission has sought to harmonise auditors' qualifications. The Eighth Company Law Directive, which has been approved by the member states, lays down minimum qualifications for auditors. The final date for the introduction of legislation in each member state is 31 December 1987 but implementation of the legislation may be delayed until 1 January 1990.[1]

---

[1] Eighth Council Directive on the approval of persons responsible for carrying out the statutory audits of accounting documents (84/253/EEC).

10.29 Formerly, persons who had obtained adequate knowledge and experience either (a) in the course of their employment by a member of one of the recognised UK accountancy bodies or (b) by practising as an accountant before 6 August 1947, might be authorised by the Secretary of State to act as an auditor.[1] No new authorisations under category (a) have been permissible since 18 April 1978.[2]

[1] CA 1985, s 389(1)(b).
[2] CA 1976, s 13(4).

10.30 A person who retains an authorisation granted under section 13(1) of the Companies Act 1967 is qualified to act as auditor of an unquoted company.[1]

[1] CA 1985, s 389(2). The authorisation relates to persons who were wholly or mainly occupied in practising as accountants and at 3 November 1966 were the duly appointed auditors of an exempt private company as defined by CA 1948.

10.31 The auditor also has to satisfy sections 389(6) to (9) covering disqualified persons (see below).

DISQUALIFIED PERSONS

10.32 The Act ensures minimum standards of auditors' independence by disqualifying certain persons from acting as auditor notwithstanding that they may possess the necessary professional qualifications. An officer or servant of the company, or a person who is a partner of or in the employment of an officer or servant of the company is not qualified for appointment as auditor of that company.[1] A body corporate may not be an auditor.[2] These disqualifications extend to acting as auditor of the company's holding or subsidiary company or of a subsidiary of the company's holding company.[3]

[1] CA 1985, s 389(6).
[2] Ibid, s 389(6)(c).
[3] Ibid, s 389(7).

10.33 It is an offence to act as an auditor if a person knows he is disqualified or if he fails to resign without reasonable excuse if to his knowledge he becomes disqualified during his term of office.[1] It is a defence if, while knowing of facts which would give rise to his disqualification in law, the auditor was not aware of his disqualification because he has no knowledge of the statutory provisions.[2]

[1] CA 1985, s 389(9).
[2] *Secretary of State v Hart* [1982] 1 All ER 817.

10.34 The four recognised UK accountancy bodies have issued ethical guidelines which are designed to reinforce the legal requirements for independence. For example, the guidelines bar auditors from being shareholders of companies they audit, and there are suggested limits to the percentage of an auditor's fee income which may be derived from one client.[1]

10.35 The law does not bar an employee of an auditor from being an officer or servant of the company, and in former times it was not unknown for an employee of an audit firm to act as a director or secretary of the company. This practice is now barred for auditors who are members of the four recognised accounting bodies by their ethical guidelines which prohibit auditors from having such relationships.[1]

¹ ICAEW Members Handbook 1.2.

LEGAL LIABILITY OF AUDITORS

10.36 An auditor is in a contractual relationship with the company he audits and contractually bound to carry out the terms of his engagement (which may by agreement between the parties specifically extend beyond the statutory requirements). Failure to do so would constitute a breach of contract and may render the auditor liable for damages suffered in consequence by the company. Although the auditor reports to the shareholders, it should be noted that he is contractually engaged by the company, not by its members, and his contractual responsibility is to the company itself. The auditor must apply proper standards of professional competence to the conduct of his audit, that is, the standards of care and skill to be expected of a reasonably careful and skilful auditor.[1]

¹ *Re London and General Bank* [1895] 2 Ch 673.

10.37 An auditor owes a duty of care to third parties with whom he is not in a contractual relationship if he knows, or ought to know, that those persons will, or are likely to, place reliance on his work, and may be liable in negligence for loss or damage suffered by them in consequence of such reliance.[1]

¹ *Hedley Byrne & Co Ltd v Heller & Partners Ltd* [1964] AC 465; *JEB Fasteners Ltd v Marks Bloom & Co* [1981] 3 All ER 289.

10.38 An auditor may also incur civil or criminal liability if in the course of his work as auditor he is held in breach of specific statutes. Although an auditor may not be an officer of any company he audits,[1] and the auditor is not included in the list of persons specified in the definition of officer (i e director, manager or secretary),[2] he may nevertheless be held liable as an officer for certain purposes. Thus an auditor has been held liable under the sections relating to delinquent directors for damages for misfeasance or breach of trust appearing in course of winding-up[3] and criminally liable as an officer for breach of the Theft Act and for falsification of records under the winding-up provisions.[4] An auditor may be held liable if he is party to the making of a misleading, false or deceptive statement contrary to s 12 of the Prevention of Fraud (Investments) Act 1958.[5]

¹ CA 1985, s 389(6).
² Ibid, s 744.

3 Ibid, s 631 and *Re Landau and General Bank* [1895] 2 Ch 673; *Re Kingston Cotton Mill* [1896] 2 Ch 279. *Re City Equitable Fire Insurance Co* [1925] Ch 407.
4 *R v Shacter* [1960] 2 QB 252.
5 *R v Wake and Stone* (1954 unreported).

10.39   In proceedings (civil or criminal) against an auditor (whether or not he is an officer) in respect of alleged negligence, default, breach of duty or breach of trust, the court may relieve him wholly or in part of any liability, if it considers that he has acted honestly and reasonably, and that having regard to all the circumstances of the case (including those connected with his appointment) he ought fairly to be excused.[1] If an auditor apprehends that any claim may be made against him on these grounds he may apply to the court for relief.[2] Recourse to these provisions appears rare, if not unknown.

1 CA 1985, s 727(1).
2 Ibid, s 727(2).

FORMS OF AUDITORS' REPORTS

10.40   There is no statutorily prescribed format or formulation for the audit report although, as noted above, the law specifies the matters to be covered in the report. An Auditing Standard issued by the Councils of the Consultative Committee of Accountancy Bodies gives a recommended form of wording and guidance on how reports should be worded where the auditor considers it necessary to qualify his opinion. In the latter circumstances the wording depends on whether the substance of the qualification is fundamental or less important, though still material, and whether the auditor is qualifying his opinion because of disagreement with an item in the accounts or uncertainty about its effects. Example 1 sets out the commonly adopted form of unqualified audit report.

10.41   The Act defines a qualified audit report as one which 'is not a report without qualification to the effect that in the auditor's opinion the accounts have been properly prepared in accordance with this Act'.[1] Auditing Standards classify qualified audit reports into four categories.

- *Disclaimer.* In a disclaimer of opinion the auditor states that he is unable to form an opinion as to whether the financial statements give a true and fair view.
- *Adverse.* In an adverse opinion the auditor states that in his opinion the financial statements do not give a true and fair view.
- *'Subject to'.* In a 'subject to' opinion the auditor effectively disclaims an opinion on a particular matter which is not considered fundamental.
- *Exception.* In an 'except for' opinion the auditor expresses an adverse opinion on a particular matter which is not considered fundamental.[2]

1 CA 1985, s 271(3).
2 ICAEW Members Handbook, Auditing and Reporting, Section 3.103. Qualifications in audit reports.

10.42 Where a small or medium company wishes to file modified (i e abbreviated) accounts (see paras 9.216–9.228, above) the auditor must report whether in his opinion the company is eligible for this concession.[1] Where such a company files modified accounts with the Registrar of Companies, a special auditor's report is required stating that, in the opinion of the auditor, the requirements for exemption have been met and reproducing the auditor's report on the full accounts. Example 2 sets out the recommended form of special report on modified accounts.[2]

---

[1] CA 1985, Sch 8, para 10(1) and see para 9.225, above.
[2] See paras 9.216–9.228, above.

OTHER RESPONSIBILITIES

10.43 In addition to the requirements to examine statutory accounts and report on their truth and fairness and their compliance with the Act, the Act requires the auditor to produce reports or statements in certain other circumstances as discussed below.

Auditors' and accountants' reports to be set out in prospectus

10.44 S 57 states that every prospectus has to set out the reports specified in Part II of the Third Schedule of the Act. Paragraph 16 of the Schedule states that the auditor must report on the profits or losses and assets and liabilities of the company (or group) for each of the five financial years preceding the issue of the prospectus. In the case of listed companies the provisions of s 57 are overridden by the requirements of The Stock Exchange (contained in the 'Yellow Book' — Admission of Securities to Listing) which also require the auditors to report on five years' accounts. The auditor is also required to consent to his name appearing in the prospectus.[1]

---

[1] CA 1985, s 61(1) — see Yellow Book p 3.14 para 1.8.

Re-registration of a private company as a public company

10.45 A private company having a share capital may be re-registered as a public company provided certain formalities are observed and documents filed with the Registrar of Companies. A copy of a written statement by the auditor of the company is required stating that in his opinion the relevant balance sheet (a balance sheet prepared within seven months of the company's application to re-register) shows that at the balance sheet date the amount of the company's net assets was not less than the aggregate of its called-up share capital and undistributable reserve.[1] A copy of the relevant balance sheet together with an unqualified audit report thereon must be filed. If the report was qualified it may still be possible for the company to re-register provided that the auditor states that the qualification is not material for the purpose of determining, by reference to that balance sheet, whether the company's net assets were not less than the aggregate of its called-up share capital and undistributable reserves.[2] Example 3 shows a form of audit report to the Registrar on re-registration of a private company as a public company.

---

[1] CA 1985, s 43(3)(b).
[2] Ibid, s 46(5).

Allotment of shares by a public company otherwise than for cash

10.46   Except in the case of a takeover or merger, a public company may allot shares as fully or partly paid up otherwise than for cash only if a person qualified to be appointed as auditor of the company (in practice generally the auditor himself) reports on the value of the non-cash assets to the company, and a copy is sent to the proposed allottee.[1]

---

[1] CA 1985, s 103(1).

10.47   This report is required to state:

    (a) the nominal value of the shares;
    (b) the amount of any premium payable on those shares;
    (c) the description of the consideration, the method and date of valuation and, where valued by someone other than the auditor, his name and experience and the reason for his employment;
    (d) the extent to which the nominal value of the shares and any premium are to be treated as paid up by the consideration.

10.48   Example 4 shows a form of independent accountants' report on the issue of shares by a plc for non-cash consideration.

10.49   Transfer of non-cash assets to a public company by a subscriber to the memorandum or a person who was a member at the date of the company's re-registration as a public company.

10.50   Broadly s 104 does not allow a company, within two years of its registration (or re-registration as a public company) to acquire, from a subscriber to the memorandum or, where the company has re-registered as a public company, from a member at the date of re-registration, non-cash assets amounting to more than one-tenth of the company's nominal share capital unless (a) the agreement has been approved in general meeting and (b) the non-cash asset has been valued and reported on.

10.51   The report required is the same in all material respects as that required under s 103 and must be given by the auditor or independent accountants entitled to act as auditor (see Example 4).

Distributable profits

10.52   Where an auditor has given a qualified report on a set of accounts on which a proposed distribution is to be based the auditor is required to state in writing whether, in his opinion, the subject of the qualification is material for the purposes of determining whether the distribution would be in contravention of the Act[1] (see Example 5).

---
[1] CA 1985, s 271(4).

Directors' transactions involving recognised banks

10.53   Recognised banks and their holding companies are required to maintain a register of certain transactions involving directors and make this register available for inspection by members of the company.[1] A statement of transactions which subsisted during the financial year is also required.

---
[1] CA 1985, s 343.

10.54   The auditor is required to examine the statement and report whether it contains the relevant particulars; if it does not then his report must include them. The report is annexed to the statement.[1]

---
[1] CA 1985, s 343(6).

Financial assistance for acquisition of own shares by a private company

10.55   A private company may, in certain circumstances, provide financial assistance for the acquisition of its own shares.[1] The directors are required, inter alia, to make a statutory declaration which, broadly, states that in their opinion the company will be able to pay its debts following the giving of the assistance and for the following twelve months.[2]

---
[1] CA 1985, ss 155–158.
[2] CA 1985, s 156(2)(b).

10.56   The auditor is required to report to the directors that he is not aware of anything to indicate that the opinion expressed by the directors is unreasonable in all the circumstances[1] (see Example 6).

---
[1] CA 1985, s 156(4).

Purchase of own shares by a private company out of capital

10.57   A private company may also purchase its own shares out of capital in certain circumstances. Among other requirements section 173(3) requires the directors to make a statutory declaration specifying the amount of the permissible capital payment and to state that, in their opinion, the company is, and will remain for at least one year, solvent.

10.58   A report by the auditor similar to that required under section 156(4) is required by section 173(5) (see Example 6) except that the auditors must also state that the specified capital payment is in their view properly determined in accordance with sections 171 and 172.[1]

---
[1] See paras 4.35–4.41, above.

EXAMPLE 1

COMMON FORM OF UNQUALIFIED AUDIT REPORT

AUDITORS' REPORT TO THE MEMBERS OF . . .

We have audited the accounts on pages . . . to . . . in accordance with approved Auditing Standards.[1]

In our opinion[2] the accounts, set out on pages . . . to . . .
which have been prepared under the historical cost convention as modified by the revaluation of land and buildings[3] give a true and fair view of the state of the company's affairs at 31st December 19— and of its profit and source and application of funds[4] for the year then ended and comply with the Companies Act 1985.[5, 6, 7]

---

[1] Extra-statutory statement, wording derived from 'The Audit Report' Auditing Standard (ICAEW Auditing and Reporting 1984/85, Section 3.102, paragraphs 3 and 11).

[2] CA 1985, s 236(2).

[3] Extra-statutory statement suggested by Auditing Standard 'The Audit Report' (supra).

[4] Extra-statutory statement. The source and application of funds statement is not a statutory requirement but is required by SSAP 10.

[5] CA 1985, s 236(2).

[6] The report quoted relates to an individual company's accounts. The same formulation, mutatis mutandis, is used when reporting on group accounts.

[7] The fact that the report is unqualified signifies that the auditor is satisfied that proper accounting records have been kept by the company, that he has received all the information and explanations necessary for the purpose of his audit and that in all other respects the accounts comply with the Act. See para 10.04, above.

EXAMPLE 2

FORM OF SPECIAL AUDIT REPORT ON MODIFIED ACCOUNTS

AUDITORS' REPORT TO THE DIRECTORS UNDER PARAGRAPH 10 OF SCHEDULE 8 OF THE COMPANIES ACT 1985

In our opinion the company satisfies the requirements of sections 247 to 249 of the Companies Act 1985 for exemption as a [small/medium-sized] company in respect of the year ended 31 December 198-, and in particular, the modified accounts have been properly prepared in accordance with Schedule 8 of that Act. We are not required to express an audit opinion on the truth and fairness of these modified accounts.

We reported, as auditors of XYZ Ltd, to the members on [date] on the company's financial statements prepared under s 236 of the Companies Act 1985 for the year ended 31 December 198-, and our audit opinion was as follows:

'We have audited the financial statements on pages . . . to . . . in accordance with approved Auditing Standards.

In our opinion the financial statements, which have been prepared under the historical cost convention, as modified by the revaluation of land and buildings, give a true and fair view of the state of the company's affairs at 31 December 198- and of its profit and source and application of funds for the year then ended and comply with the Companies Act 1985.[1, 2]

ABC & Co
[date]

---

[1] CA 1985, ss 247 to 249 and Sch 8.

[2] Form of wording suggested by the Auditing Practices Committee of CCAB — see 'The Companies Act 1981 and the auditor' (1981), pp 10 to 11 (statutory references updated).

EXAMPLE 3

**FORM OF AUDIT REPORT TO THE REGISTRAR ON
RE-REGISTRATION AS A PUBLIC COMPANY**

An example[1] of an appropriate form of statement by the auditor where he has expressed an unqualified opinion on the financial statements or where he has qualified his report but the qualification is not material, is set out below:

AUDITORS' REPORT TO THE REGISTRAR OF COMPANIES UNDER S 43(3)(B) OF THE COMPANIES ACT 1985

We have audited the financial statements of XYZ Limited for the year ended 31 December 19.. in accordance with approved Auditing Standards and have

* *(1)   expressed an unqualified opinion thereon
* *(2)   expressed a qualified opinion thereon. The subject of our qualification is not material for the purpose of determining whether at the date of the balance sheet the net assets of the company were less than its called-up share capital and undistributable reserves.

In our opinion the balance sheet as at 31 December 19.. shows that at that date the amount of the company's net assets was not less than the aggregate of its called-up share capital and undistributable reserves.[2]

---

[1] Form of wording suggested by the Auditing Practices Committee of CCAB — see 'The Companies Act 1980 and the auditor' (1981), pp 18–19 (statutory references updated).
[2] CA 1985, s 43(3)(b).

EXAMPLE 4

FORM OF INDEPENDENT ACCOUNTANT'S REPORT ON ISSUE OF SHARES BY A PLC FOR NON-CASH-CONSIDERATION

INDEPENDENT ACCOUNTANT'S REPORT ISSUED IN ACCOR-DANCE WITH SECTION 103 OF THE COMPANIES ACT 1985 TO XYZ PUBLIC LIMITED COMPANY

As required by s 103 of the Companies Act 1985, we report on the value of the consideration for the allotment to . . (name of allottee) of fully paid up.

The consideration to be given by . . (name of allottee) is the freehold building situated at . . (address) and X,000 (number) shares, having a nominal value of £1 each, in . . public limited company.

The freehold building was valued on the basis of its open market value by . . (name of valuer) Esq FRICS on . . (date) and in our opinion it is reasonable to accept that valuation.

The shares in . . public limited company were valued by us on . . (date) on the basis of the price shown in The Stock Exchange Daily Official List at . . (date).

In our opinion, the methods of valuation of the freehold building and of the shares in . . public limited company were reasonable in all the circumstances. There appears to have been no material change in the value of either part of the consideration since the valuations were made. On the basis of the valuations, in our opinion, the value of the total consideration is not less than £. . (being the total amount to be treated as paid up on the shares allotted together with the share premium).[1, 2]

---

[1] CA 1985, s 103.

[2] Form of wording suggested by the Auditing Practices Committee of CCAB — see 'The Companies Act 1980 and the auditors' (1981), p 11 (statutory references updated).

EXAMPLE 5

**FORM OF AUDIT REPORT AS TO WHETHER A QUALIFIED
AUDIT REPORT IS MATERIAL FOR DISTRIBUTION PURPOSES**

AUDITORS' STATEMENT TO THE MEMBERS OF XYZ LIMITED
UNDER SECTION 271 OF THE COMPANIES ACT 1985

We have audited the financial statements of XYZ Limited for the year
ended 31 December 19. . in accordance with approved Auditing Standards
and have expressed a qualified opinion thereon.

In our opinion that qualification is not material for the purpose of determining, by reference to those financial statements, whether the distribution
[interim dividend for the year ended . . .] proposed by the company is
permitted under s 271 of the Companies Act 1985.[1, 2]

---

[1] CA 1985, s 271.

[2] Form of words suggested by the Auditing Practices Committee of CCAB — see 'The
Companies Act 1980 and the auditor' (1981), p 23 (statutory references updated).

EXAMPLE 6

**FORM OF AUDIT REPORT RELATING TO FINANCIAL
ASSISTANCE FOR ACQUISITION OF OWN SHARES**

REPORT OF THE AUDITORS TO THE DIRECTORS OF XYZ
LIMITED UNDER SECTION 156(4) OF THE COMPANIES ACT 1985

With reference to the company's proposed financial assistance for the
purchase of 5,000 ordinary shares, we have inquired into the company's state
of affairs as at [date].

We are not aware of anything to indicate that the opinions, expressed by
the directors in Part 2 of the declaration as to the company's liquidity
position are unreasonable in all the circumstances.[1,2]

---

[1] CA 1985, s 156(4).
[2] Form of words suggested by the Auditing Practices Committee of CCAB — see 'The
Companies Act 1981 and the auditor' (1981), p 20 (statutory references updated).

11 Winding-up arrangements and reconstructions

W F Ratford

SECTION 1: INTRODUCTION

11.01 Insolvency law applicable to companies in England and Wales has developed in a haphazard fashion over a long period and the newly consolidated provisions of the Companies Act are supplemented by the principles of common law and equity. In addition, many of the principles of bankruptcy law have been imported into company law, and the conflicting interests of the many parties involved with insolvent companies have given rise to a large body of case law. This Chapter deals principally with the provisions of the Companies Act 1985, but refers to other sources where appropriate.

Liquidations

11.02 The phrase 'liquidation' does not appear in the legislation, and the Companies Act refer throughout to the cumbersome expression 'winding up'. However in this chapter the more common phrase 'liquidation', in any event freely interchangeable, has been adopted.

11.03 The two principal types of liquidation are:[1]

(a) by the court — a compulsory liquidation; (section 2)
(b) voluntary — either as a members' voluntary liquidation or a creditors' voluntary liquidation; (section 3).

---

[1] CA 1985, s 501(1).

11.04 Provisions common to both principal types of liquidation are dealt with in Sections 4, 5 and 6 of this chapter.

11.05 A company that has already passed a resolution for voluntary liquidation may be wound up subject to the supervision of the court.[1] The effect of a court order in these circumstances is to change the liquidation into a compulsory one, with broadly similar provisions applying, and the court has power to impose any conditions upon the conduct of the liquidation as it thinks just. This type of liquidation is now rarely encountered.

---

[1] CA 1985, s 501(1)(c) and ss 606 to 610.

Receiverships

11.06   The types of receivership dealt with in Section 7 are:

(a)   court appointments;
(b)   appointments under statute; and
(c)   appointments under the powers given in a document.

Arrangements and reconstructions

11.07   The principal sections of the Companies Act that are considered in Section 8 are:

(a)   s 425 — court approved schemes of compromise or arrangement.
(b)   s 601 — binding arrangements on creditors in voluntary liquidation; and
(c)   s 582 — transfer of business or property for shares.

Dissolution

11.08   Section 9 of this chapter deals with striking-off and dissolution following a liquidation.

SECTION 2: COMPULSORY LIQUIDATION

11.09   A compulsory liquidation is one instituted by the court as a result of a petition to the court by an interested party. The appropriate courts for such actions are the courts of Chancery Division of the High Court, or certain county courts where the paid up share capital of the company concerned does not exceed £120,000 and its registered office is within the Court's district.[1]

---

[1] CA 1985, s 512.

11.10   The grounds on which a petition can be presented to the court, and the company wound up, are:[1]

(a)   the company has passed a special resolution to that effect;
(b)   the company is unable to pay its debts;
(c)   the number of members is reduced below two;
(d)   the company does not commence business within a year of incorporation, or suspends its business for a year;
(e)   if the company is an old public company under s 1 of the CC (CP)A 1985;
(f)   if the company has been registered as a public company for more than a year since incorporation but has not been issued with a certificate under s 117; and
(g)   the court is of the opinion that it is just and equitable to wind up the company.

---

[1] CA 1985, s 517.

11.11   A petition may be presented by the company itself, a creditor or a contributory.[1] Contributory means every person liable to contribute to the assets of a company on winding-up, including those claiming to be contributories prior to determination of such claims.[2] Contributories include directors with unlimited liability, shareholders to the extent that shares are not fully paid, and directors and shareholders who have been party to a redemption or purchase of own shares out of capital within twelve months before winding-up commenced. A contributory may normally petition only if the number of members has been reduced below two, or if he had acquired shares by allotment or as a result of the death of a previous shareholder, or if he has been a member for at least six months in the previous eighteen months.[3] However, a person who is a contributory by virtue of being a party to the redemption or purchase of the company's shares may petition on the grounds that the company is unable to pay its debts, or that it is just and equitable that the company should be liquidated.[4] There are also powers given to other bodies to petition for a liquidation in special circumstances, including the Secretary of State for Trade,[5] the Official Receiver[6] and the Bank of England.[7]

---

[1] CA 1985, s 519(1).
[2] Ibid, s 507(1).
[3] Ibid, s 519(2).
[4] Ibid, s 519(3).
[5] Ibid, s 519(4) and s 517(b) or (c); s 519(6) and s 440.
[6] Ibid, s 519(7).
[7] Banking Act 1979, s 18.

11.12   The most common form of petition is by a creditor on the grounds that the company is unable to pay its debts. Whilst the court may determine whether a company is unable to pay its debts, a company is deemed to be in this position if an execution of a judgment debt is unsatisfied, or if the company neglects to pay a statutory demand. It is sufficient for a creditor for a debt exceeding £750 to serve a demand for payment at the company's registered office; if the debt is not disputed, the failure to pay within three weeks will constitute inability by the company to pay its debts for this purpose.[1]

---

[1] CA 1985, s 518.

11.13   When the petition has been presented a date for a hearing is fixed and the petition is served at the company's registered office. The petition then has to be advertised in the Gazette, within seven days after it has been served and not less than seven days before the date of the hearing. In addition, an affidavit by the petitioning creditor verifying the petition must be filed with the court within seven days of the petition being presented.

11.14   When the petition is heard in court, the court may grant the petition or dismiss it, adjourn the hearing or make any interim order or other order that it thinks fit.[1] Once the petition has been granted, the liquidation is deemed to have commenced from the date of the presentation of the petition, or if a voluntary liquidation had commenced earlier, from that earlier date.[2]

However, for some purposes the date of the winding-up order has some relevance.

¹ CA 1985, s 520.
² Ibid, s 524.

11.15 After the petition has been granted, the Official Receiver becomes provisional liquidator[1] and takes custody of the company's assets.[2] However, circumstances may arise in which it is necessary for action to be taken in respect of a company's assets or business in the period after the presentation of the petition but before the hearing, and the court has the power to appoint a provisional liquidator during this period.[3] Such an appointment may be made upon the application of the company, a creditor, or a member. Where the Official Receiver has been appointed provisional liquidator in this way he may consider that the nature of the company's assets or business is such that a manager is required to administer the estate and he may apply to the court for the appointment of a special manager, who will be given specific powers by the court.[4] Furthermore, in the interim period, the company, a creditor or a contributory may apply to the court for any proceedings being taken against the company to be stayed.[5]

¹ CA 1985, s 533(2).
² Ibid, s 537(1).
³ Ibid, s 532.
⁴ Ibid, s 556.
⁵ Ibid, s 521.

11.16 The power to appoint a liquidator lies with the court,[1] which can also remove a liquidator[2] or fill any vacancy in the post.[3] A liquidator may also resign from office.

¹ CA 1985, s 531.
² Ibid, s 536(1).
³ Ibid, s 536(3).

11.17 Within one month of the winding up order being made (extended to six weeks where a special manager has acted) the Official Receiver is required to convene separate meetings of creditors and contributories, to determine whether an application be made to the court for the appointment of someone other than the Official Receiver as liquidator.[1] Notices are sent by post, and the meetings are advertised in the Gazette and a local newspaper not less than seven days before they are to be held.

¹ CA 1985, s 533(3).

11.18 The Official Receiver acts as chairman of the meetings, and provides a report on the history of the company and any other information available, and each meeting can make its choice of a liquidator in place of the Official

Receiver. In the event of disagreement on such choice, the court will act as it thinks fit.[1]

---

[1] CA 1985, s 533(4).

11.19   The quorum for each meeting is three,[1] and for a resolution of either meeting to be valid it must be passed by a majority in both number and value of those voting.[2] At the meeting of contributories, the value of votes cast is determined in accordance with the company's articles of association, and at the creditors' meeting by the proofs of debt accepted by the Official Receiver. It should be noted that a creditor that does not submit a proof of debt as directed in the notice convening the meeting is unable to vote.[3] Forms of proxy are required in the prescribed form.[4]

---

[1] WUR 138.
[2] Ibid 134.
[3] Ibid 139.
[4] Ibid 147.

11.20   The meetings are also required to decide whether an application should be made to the court for a committee of inspection, and who should serve on it.[1] The committee must consist of creditors and contributories, or their representatives holding general powers of attorney, in such proportions as agreed at the meetings, any difference being determined by the court.[2] If there is no committee, the liquidator may apply to the Secretary of State for any sanction that would have otherwise been given by the committee.[3]

---

[1] CA 1985, s 546.
[2] Ibid, s 547(1).
[3] Ibid, s 548.

Committee of inspection

11.21   The committee may meet at such times as it decides, failing which meetings must be held at least once a month but the liquidator or any committee member may also call a meeting as and when he thinks it desirable.[1] The quorum of the committee is a majority of the committee, and the committee can act only by a majority of those attending a meeting.[2] The liquidator is required to call meetings of the creditors or the contributories as appropriate if a vacancy in the committee arises, subject to the power of the court to order that the vacancy need not be filled.[3]

---

[1] CA 1985, Sch 17(1).
[2] Ibid, Sch 17(2).
[3] Ibid, Sch 17(6).

11.22   The powers of the committee include the sanctioning of certain of the powers of the liquidator, set out in para 11.27, below, and in addition extend to approving the liquidator's remuneration,[1] consenting to the investment of funds and sale of any investments[2] and sanctioning calls on shares.[3] The committee is also required to audit the liquidator's cash book every three months.[4]

[1] WUR 159.
[2] Ibid 173.
[3] CA 1985, s 567.
[4] WUR 174

11.23 The members of the committee are not entitled to remuneration, and, without leave of the court, they cannot make any direct or indirect profit from the liquidation, nor acquire any assets from the liquidation.[1] They are however entitled to receive reimbursement of reasonable expenses incurred in the performance of their duties.[2]

[1] WUR 161 and 163.
[2] Ibid 195(1).

The liquidator

11.24 Following the meetings of creditors and contributories, the Official Receiver reports to the court to obtain an order for the liquidator's appointment. A liquidator appointed in place of the Official Receiver cannot act until the court order is made and he has notified his appointment to the Registrar of Companies and given security (in the form of a bond) to the satisfaction of the Secretary of State.[1]

[1] CA 1985, s 534.

11.25 A liquidator's duty is to realise the assets of the company and to distribute the funds to those entitled, and while doing so to exercise a high standard of care and diligence and to act impartially. The liquidator is an officer of the company, but also an officer of the court. The assets of the company do not vest in the liquidator, unless a specific order is made.[1]

[1] CA 1985, s 538(1).

Powers of a liquidator

11.26 A liquidator may exercise the following powers without the sanction of the court or the committee of inspection:

(a) sell any of the company's property by public auction or private contract either in whole or in parcels;   s 539 (2)(a)

(b) do all acts and execute deeds, receipts and other documents in the name of the company;   s 539(2)(b)

(c) use the company's seal;   s 539(2)(b)

(d) prove, rank and claim in the bankruptcy, insolvency or sequestration of any contributory and receive dividends;   s 539(2)(c)

(e) draw and endorse bills of exchange/promissory notes in the name and on behalf of the company;	s 539(2)(d)
(f) borrow money on the security of the company's assets;	s 539(2)(e)
(g) take out letters of administration to any deceased contributory;	s 539(2)(f)
(h) appoint an agent to do any business which the liquidator is unable to do himself;	s 539(2)(g)
(i) do all things as may be necessary to liquidate the company and distribute its assets;	s 539(2)(h)
(j) settle the list of contributories; and	s 567 and WUR 80
(k) call meetings of creditors, contributories and the committee of inspection.	s 540(3)

11.27 A liquidator may exercise the following powers only with the sanction of either the court or the committee of inspection.

(a) bring or defend any action or other legal proceeding in the name of and on behalf of the company;	s 539(1)(a)
(b) carry on the business of the company so far as may be necessary for its beneficial winding up;	s 539(1)(b)
(c) appoint a solicitor to assist him in the performance of his duties;	s 539(1)(c)
(d) pay any class of creditors in full;	s 539(1)(d)
(e) make any compromise with creditors, contributories or debtors of the company. It is important to note that a liquidator may not upon his own initiative, without running the risk of becoming personally liable, settle a disputed claim against the company, or accept less than the full amount of any debt due to the company;	s 539(1)(e) and (f)
(f) apply to the court for it to take misfeasance proceedings against past or present promoters, directors, managers, liquidators or officers of the company in order to compel the repayment or restoration of money or property or payment of compensation in respect of any misapplication, retainer, misfeasance or breach of trust. It appears that a receiver appointed by a debenture holder cannot be proceeded against under this provision.	s 631
(g) disclaim, with the sanction of the court, onerous unsaleable property or unprofitable contracts; and	s 618
(h) rectify the register of members, with the leave of the court, and make calls.	s 567(2)

11.28   The remuneration of a liquidator is fixed by the committee of inspection or is at the same level applicable to the Official Receiver under the Companies Fees Regulations.

Administration

11.29   The liquidator may operate a bank account himself only with the approval of the Department of Trade. Such approval will be given upon application by the Committee of Inspection if the particular circumstances of the liquidation require the liquidator to have a special account.[1] Otherwise, the liquidator must pay all sums received by him into the Insolvency Services Account at the Bank of England.[2]

---

[1] CA 1985, s 542(3).
[2] Ibid, s 542(2).

11.30   If the balance held at the Bank of England exceeds £2,000 and the excess is not required for the purposes of the liquidation, the liquidator may request that the surplus is transferred to an interest bearing account.[1] Further, surplus funds that are not required for the immediate purposes of the liquidator may, with the approval of the committee of inspection, be invested in government securities.[2]

---

[1] CA 1985, s 660(5).
[2] Ibid, s 660(2).

11.31   The liquidator is required to submit details of his receipts and payments to the Department of Trade every six months, and a copy of the liquidator's account is filed with the court.[1] There is also a provision for the account to be sent to all creditors and contributories, although this requirement may be dispensed with by the Department of Trade.[2] In addition there is a requirement to file returns with the Registrar, although this is seldom requested.[3]

---

[1] CA 1985, s 543(2).
[2] Ibid, s 543(6).
[3] Ibid, s 641.

11.32   The Department of Trade has a duty to oversee the manner in which a liquidator carries out the liquidation.[1]

---

[1] CA 1985, s 544.

Conclusion of liquidation

11.33   When the liquidator has realised all the assets, and made all necessary distributions, he sends a summary of his receipts and payments to all creditors and contributories, with a notice that he intends to apply for his release.[1] A final account may then be submitted to the Department of Trade,[2] which will give the Order of Release and publish it in the Gazette.[3]

---

[1] WUR 205(1).
[2] Ibid 175(2).
[3] Ibid, 205(2).

11.34   The liquidator may apply to the court, after publishing his release, for an order that the company should be dissolved.[1]

---

[1] CA 1985, s 568.

SECTION 3: VOLUNTARY LIQUIDATION

General

11.35   A voluntary liquidation of a company[1] incorporated under the Companies Act is one instituted by resolution of its shareholders and may take place in the following circumstances:[2]

(a) by ordinary resolution, if the articles provide that either the company should exist for a fixed period only and that period has passed or the company should be dissolved upon a specified event occurring and that event has occurred;

(b) by special resolution, with no pre-conditions; and

(c) by extraordinary resolution affirming that the company cannot continue its business by reason of its liabilities.

Any of these resolutions has to be advertised in the Gazette within fourteen days[3] and filed with the Registrar within fifteen days of its adoption.[4]

---

[1] Not unregistered companies, see CA 1985, ss 665 and 666(4).
[2] CA 1985, s 572.
[3] Ibid, s 573.
[4] Ibid, s 572(3) and s 380.

11.36   In anticipation of winding up, the directors (or where there are more than two, a majority of them) may be able to make a statutory declaration[1] that they have made a full enquiry into the company's affairs and have formed the opinion that the company will be able to pay its debts in full within a specified period, not exceeding twelve months from the passing of the resolution to wind up. If such a declaration, incorporating a statement of the company's assets and liabilities at the latest practicable date, is made within the five weeks prior to the passing of the resolution, and is filed with the Registrar no later than fifteen days after the passing of the resolution, the winding up is a 'members' voluntary liquidation'.[2]

---

[1] WUR, Form 108.
[2] CA 1985, s 577.

11.37   In all other cases, where either a proper declaration has not been made or a declaration has not been filed in time, the liquidation is a 'creditors' voluntary liquidation'.[1] The distinction is important since it affects the ability of creditors to influence the course of the winding up, although many of the procedures are common.

---

[1] CA 1985, s 578.

11.38 A director making a declaration has to have reasonable grounds for the opinion that the company will be able to pay its debts in full in the period specified. If a declaration is made but the company's debts are not paid nor capable of being paid in the period, the onus of proof lies on the director to show that he had reasonable grounds for his opinion[1] and, if he does not, he may be liable to imprisonment or a fine.[2]

---

[1] CA 1985, s 577(5).
[2] Ibid, s 577(4).

11.39 A voluntary liquidation commences at the time of the passing of the resolution by the shareholders[1] and from that time the company exists only for the purposes of winding up even though its corporate state and corporate powers continue until it is dissolved. The company is required to cease to carry on its business, except in so far as it is necessary to benefit the winding up.[2] In practice a business might be allowed to continue for a short period either in a limited way to allow for the disposal of assets, or to facilitate the sale of the company's undertaking as a going concern.

---

[1] CA 1985, s 574.
[2] Ibid, s 575.

11.40 A consequence of the liquidation is that the powers of the directors cease other than as sanctioned by the members or the liquidator in a members' voluntary liquidation, or by the committee of inspection or the creditors in a creditors' voluntary liquidation.[1] Further, transfers of the company's shares require the sanction of the liquidator to be valid, and the status of the members of the company cannot be altered.[2]

---

[1] CA 1985, ss 580(2)·and 591(2).
[2] Ibid, s 576.

Creditors' voluntary liquidation

11.41 The first step towards a creditors' voluntary liquidation takes place at a meeting of the directors of the company, when it would be resolved to call the necessary meetings of members and creditors.

11.42 The directors should appoint one of their number to preside at the creditors' meeting,[1] and, as a matter of good practice, formally approve a statement of the company's affairs that is required to be laid before that meeting.[2]

---

[1] CA 1985, s 588(3)(b).
[2] Ibid, s 588(3)(a).

11.43 There is no statutory format for the statement of affairs, but it should be made up to the latest practicable date and show the estimated realisable values of the company's assets, and the total of creditors' claims with their order of ranking against those assets. The statement does not have to be signed or sworn by the directors, or filed with the Registrar.

Notice to members

11.44 The notice to members of the general meeting at which a resolution for liquidation is to be proposed must be sent to all members giving at least seven days' notice,[1] or such longer period as may be prescribed by the company's articles.[2]

---

[1] CA 1985, s 588(1).
[2] Ibid, s 369(2).

11.45 Notwithstanding the power of members otherwise so to do[1] the period of seven days' notice may not be waived in this case;[2] however, if the period of notice is not given, this will not affect the validity of any resolution passed at the members' meeting.[3] Where the prescribed notice is not given, and the meeting of creditors is not held on the same day as the members' meeting, or the following day, the liquidation is, nevertheless, effective and the liquidator appointed at the members' meeting has authority to act.[4]

---

[1] CA 1985, s 369(3).
[2] Ibid, s 588(1).
[3] Ibid, s 588(6).
[4] *Re Centrebind Ltd* [1966] 3 All ER 889.

Notice to creditors

11.46 The notice of the meeting, together with special and general proxies, should be sent to all creditors listed in the company's records and to all other likely creditors. Sufficient time should be allowed for the preparation of the notices to creditors since they must be despatched by post simultaneously with the notices to members.[1] The meeting must be held on the same day as, or the day following, the members' meeting.[2]

---

[1] CA 1985, s 588(2)(b).
[2] Ibid, s 588(2)(a).

11.47 Notice of the meeting should be sent specifically to creditors that have obtained a judgment against the company or that have caused an execution to be levied against the company's assets as well as the sheriff or bailiff (see para 11.106, below).

11.48 The notice of the creditors' meeting must be advertised in the Gazette and also in at least two local newspapers circulating in the area of the company's registered office or principal place of business.[1] In practice advertisements are often placed in the national as well as the local press.

---

[1] CA 1985, s 588(2)(c).

Members' meeting

11.49   The purpose of the members' meeting is to pass an extraordinary resolution to the effect that by reason of its liabilities the company is unable to continue its business and should, therefore, be wound-up. A majority of 75 per cent of those present and voting is required to pass an extraordinary resolution[1] and the proceedings at this meeting are governed by the articles of the company, including the requirement for a quorum.

[1] CA 1985, s 378(1).

11.50   At the same meeting, the members may nominate a liquidator[1] and appoint not more than five representatives to a committee of inspection.[2] However, the creditors may resolve that all or some of the persons appointed to the committee by the members shall not act unless the court otherwise directs.[3]

[1] CA 1985, s 589(1).
[2] Ibid, s 590(2).
[3] Ibid, s 590(3).

11.51   The members' resolution has to be advertised in the Gazette within fourteen days[1] and filed with the Registrar within fifteen days.[2]

[1] CA 1985, s 573.
[2] Ibid, s 572(3) and s 380.

Creditors' meeting

11.52   The purpose of the creditors' meeting is to appoint a liquidator[1] and to appoint not more than five representatives to a committee of inspection.[2] It is normal practice for the directors to give a report on the events leading up to the liquidation, and for creditors to have an opportunity to question the directors and their actions.

[1] CA 1985, s 589(1).
[2] Ibid, s 590(1).

11.53   A meeting may not act unless at least three creditors entitled to vote are present or represented. If the meeting has to be adjourned for lack of a quorum, it must be adjourned either to the same day in the following week or for such longer period, up to a maximum of 21 days as decided by the chairman.[1]

[1] WUR 138.

11.54   For a resolution to be passed at a creditors' meeting it must be supported by a majority both in number and in value of those voting.[1] It should be noted that a creditor may not vote in respect of any unliquidated (i e unquantified) or contingent debt or any debt the value of which is not ascertained,[2] and that a secured creditor may vote only in respect of the balance of his debt after deduction of his valuation of his security.[3]

[1] WUR 134.
[2] Ibid, 140.
[3] Ibid, 141 to 144.

11.55 If the creditors' nomination for the liquidator differs from the members' nominee, the creditors' choice will take precedence unless the court, upon application within seven days by any director, member or creditor of the company, orders otherwise.[1]

[1] CA 1985, s 589(3).

11.56 A matter of practical importance at a creditors' meeting is to ensure that proxies submitted by creditors are valid. Proxies must be returned to the company's registered office not later than four o'clock in the afternoon of the day preceding the meeting,[1] and the principal rules relating to proxies are:[2]

    (a) a creditor may vote either in person or by proxy;

    (b) general and special proxy forms must be sent to creditors with the notice of the meeting;

    (c) proxies must be in the appropriate forms;[3]

    (d) a creditor may give a general proxy to any person (other than a minor);

    (e) a creditor may give a special proxy to any person (other than a minor) to vote at any specified meeting or adjournment thereof for or against the appointment or continuation in office of any specified person as liquidator or member of the committee of inspection, and on all other matters arising at the meeting; and

    (f) a creditor may appoint the chairman of the meeting or the liquidator to act as his general or special proxy.

[1] WUR 154(2).
[2] Ibid, 146 to 156.
[3] Ibid, Forms 80 and 81.

11.57 A company may by resolution of its directors authorise a person to act as its representative at a creditors' meeting.[1] A copy of the resolution, certified as a true copy by a director or secretary, should be available to be produced to the meeting.

[1] CA 1985, s 375(1)(b).

Committee of inspection

11.58 As noted above, a committee of inspection may consist of up to five members' nominees and five creditors' nominees. The members in general meeting may appoint not more than five of their number to act as members of the committee, provided that the creditors may resolve that all or any of the persons so appointed ought not to be members of the committee, unless the court otherwise directs. At the creditors' meeting the creditors may appoint not more than five of their number to act as a committee.

11.59 The proceedings of the committee are governed by the same rules as apply to a committee in a compulsory liquidation.[1]

---

[1] See paras 11.21 and 11.23, above.

11.60 The powers of the committee include the sanctioning of certain of the general powers of the liquidator[1] and in additon are:

(a) to direct which books shall be kept by the liquidator and to inspect them when so desired;	WUR 172(3)
(b) to sanction the continuation of any powers of the directors of the company;	s 591(2)
(c) to consent to the investment of surplus funds, and the sale of investments;	WUR 173
(d) to fix the remuneration of the liquidator; and	s 591(1)
(e) to authorise the disposal of the books and papers of the company at the conclusion of the liquidation.	s 640(1)(c)

---

[1] See para 11.66, below.

Liquidator

11.61 Within fourteen days of appointment the liquidator must publish a notice to that effect in the Gazette and notify the Registrar.[1]

---

[1] CA 1985, s 600; CFR 1985, Forms 600 and 600a.

11.62 A liquidator's duty is to realise the assets of the company to the best advantage and to distribute the funds to the creditors and members in accordance with their respective rights.[1] He has a responsibility to observe a high standard of care and diligence and to deal fairly and honestly with the creditors and members. The exact status of a liquidator cannot be easily defined. For certain purposes he may be described as a trustee, but he is more properly described as the agent of the company of which he is liquidator. It should be noted that the property of the company does not vest in the liquidator but remains vested in the company. Thus the liquidator undertakes his duties as the agent of a disclosed principal — the company — and in normal circumstances no personal liability will fall upon him. However, the liquidator will be liable for any breach of his statutory duty to conduct the liquidation in a proper manner with due regard to the rights of the various parties involved.

---

[1] CA 1985, s 597.

11.63 The remuneration of a liquidator may be fixed by the committee of inspection or, where there is no committee, by the creditors.[1] The liquidator may not purchase any of the company's assets[2] neither may he be party to any transaction in connection with the continuing business of the company from which he would profit,[3] subject in both cases to exceptions sanctioned by the court.

---

[1] CA 1985, s 591(1).
[2] WUR 161.
[3] Ibid, 162.

11.64 A liquidator may resign from office, or may be removed from office by the court upon application by an interested party.[1] Where a vacancy occurs in the office of liquidator, the creditors may fill the vacancy, except where the original appointment had been by the court.[2] In any event, the court has a general power to fill any vacancy.[3]

---

[1] CA 1985, s 599(2).
[2] Ibid, s 592.
[3] Ibid, s 599(1).

Powers of liquidator

11.65 The powers available to a liquidator in a voluntary liquidation are broadly the same as those applicable in a compulsory liquidation, although certain powers may be exercised without sanction. A liquidator may exercise without the sanction of the court or the committee of inspection, all the powers set out in para 11.26 above, and in addition items (a), (b) and (c) of para 11.27, above.[1]

---

[1] CA 1985, s 598(2).

11.66 A liquidator may exercise the other powers set out in para 11.27 with the sanction of either the court or the committee of inspection, or, where there is no committee, a meeting of the creditors.[1] The sanction of either the court or the committee is also required to enable the liquidator to accept shares as consideration for the sale of the whole or part of the business or property of the company to another company.[2]

---

[1] CA 1985, s 598(1).
[2] Ibid, s 593.

11.67 In the event of any matters arising that cannot be dealt with under the defined powers, a liquidator may seek directions from the court under s 602.

11.68 A liquidator can appoint an agent to do any business which he is unable to do himself.[1] but he cannot delegate his powers generally. He may, therefore, give a power of attorney to do some specific act, but not a general power. If joint liquidators are appointed, the creditors can decide at the time of their appointment that their powers can be exercised by one or more of them. If there is no such decision by the creditors not less than two of the liquidators can exercise their powers.[2] Unless two joint liquidators have authority to act alone, in the event that one of them dies the survivor cannot act until a new liquidator is appointed.[3] Furthermore, the liquidators cannot delegate their powers to one of their number.[4]

[1] CA 1985, s 539(2)(g).
[2] Ibid, s 598(5).
[3] *Re Metropolitan Bank v Jones* (1876) 2 Ch D 366.
[4] *Re London and Mediterranean Bank* (1871) 6 Ch App 206.

11.69 The liquidator is able to operate his own bank account. However, following submission by the liquidator of his periodic returns, the Department of Trade will determine the amount that has been held by the liquidator for a period in excess of six months. The amount so determined must be paid by the liquidator into the Insolvency Services Account at the Bank of England[1] subject to the retention by the liquidator of monies required for his immediate purposes. The investment of funds at the Bank of England follows the rules that apply in compulsory liquidation set out in para 11.30, above.

[1] CA 1985, s 642.

11.70 Where a dividend has been declared, and any dividends remain unclaimed for a period of six months, the monies involved must also be paid into the Insolvency Services Account.[1]

[1] CA 1985, s 642.

Meetings and returns

11.71 If the liquidation continues for more than one year, a general meeting of the company and a meeting of creditors must be held each year within three months of the anniversary of the commencement of the liquidation.[1] This period may, however, be extended with the permission of the Department of Trade. The purpose of these meetings is for the liquidator to present an account of his actions and of the conduct of the liquidation. The liquidator should give fourteen days' notice in writing to the members;[2] only seven days notice need be given to the creditors, but it has to be both in writing and by advertisement in the Gazette and a local newspaper.[3]

[1] CA 1985, s 594.
[2] Ibid, s 369(1).
[3] WUR 129.

11.72 Within 30 days of the first anniversary of the commencement of the liquidation, and at six monthly intervals thereafter, the liquidator is required to file with the Registrar a cash statement (in duplicate) supported by an affidavit, and where applicable a trading account and lists of dividends.[1] The statement also includes additional information on the liquidation.[2]

[1] WUR 197; Forms 92 to 96.
[2] CA 1985, s 641.

11.73 As soon as the liquidation is completed, the liquidator is required to call a general meeting of the company and a meeting of creditors for the purpose of laying before the meetings an account of the liquidation.[1] Whilst it is usual practice for notices to be given in writing, the only statutory requirement is that the notices should be published in the Gazette at least one month before the meetings.[2]

[1] CA 1985, s 595(1).
[2] Ibid, s 595(2).

11.74 The account presented to the meeting, in the prescribed form,[1] must be sent to the Registrar within one week thereafter,[2] together with a return of the meetings.[3] A final return can be made even if there is no quorum present at a meeting.

[1] WUR Form 110.
[2] CA 1985, s 595(3).
[3] WUR Form 112.

Members' voluntary liquidation

11.75 Many of the principles that apply to the administration of a creditors' voluntary liquidation apply also to a members' voluntary liquidation and, where this is the case, only a broad indication of the procedures is given. Where different procedures or principles apply, these are explained in more detail.

11.76 In a members' voluntary liquidation the company in general meeting may appoint one or more liquidators and fix their remuneration;[1] any vacancy in the office of liquidator may be filled in a similar way, subject to any arrangement with the creditors.[2] Within fourteen days of his appointment the liquidator must advertise his appointment in the Gazette and file a notice with the Registrar.[3]

[1] CA 1985, s 580(1).
[2] Ibid, s 581.
[3] Ibid, s 600; CFR 1985 Forms 600 and 600a.

11.77 Other than where there is a scheme of arrangement under section 582 dealing with all the company's assets, a liquidator will realise the assets and deal with creditors' claims. It is of course possible that the total net realisations from the assets might be inadequate to meet all claims; accordingly it is unlikely that a distribution will be made to creditors until all claims have been substantially agreed, and in any event not until the liquidator has both served notices on known potential creditors and advertised for claims in the Gazette.

11.78 If, in the course of the liquidation, the liquidator is at any time of the opinion that the company will not be able to pay its debts in full within the period stated in the directors' declaration, he is required to call a meeting of creditors to present a statement of the company's assets and liabilities.[1] This provision does not affect the status of the liquidator who continues in office unless he chooses to resign, because the creditors have no power to vote either on the continuation of the existing appointment or on the appointment of a new liquidator. However, if the creditors are of the opinion that the liquidator is unsuitable, perhaps because of a conflict of interest, and the liquidator declines to resign, the creditors may either commence proceedings for compulsory liquidation, or apply to the court for the removal of the liquidator.[2]

---

[1] CA 1985, s 583.
[2] Ibid, s 599(2).

11.79 If a members' voluntary liquidation continues for more than a year, a general meeting of the company must be held each year within three months after the anniversary of the commencement of the liquidation.[1] This period may, however, be extended with the permission of the Department of Trade. Such meetings would be summoned by the liquidator giving the normal period of notice of fourteen days, in writing.[2]

---

[1] CA 1985, s 584.
[2] Ibid, s 369(1).

11.80 As soon as the liquidation has been completed, the liquidator is required to call a general meeting of the company, for the purpose of laying before the meeting an account of the winding up.[1] Whilst it is usual practice for written notice to be given to members, the only statutory requirement is that a notice shall be published in the Gazette at least one month before the meeting.[2] The meeting has no formal business other than to receive the account although the meeting could be used to approve the liquidator's remuneration and to authorise the disposal of the company's records.[3] The account presented to the meeting, in the prescribed form,[4] must be sent to the Registrar within one week thereafter, together with a return of the holding of the meeting.[5] It is not necessary for a quorum to be present at the final meeting, and an appropriate return can still be made, although the absence of a quorum must be noted in the return.[6]

---

[1] CA 1985, s 585(1).
[2] Ibid, s 585(2).
[3] Ibid, s 640(1)(b).
[4] WUR Form 110.
[5] Ibid, Form 111.
[6] CA 1985, s 585(4).

SECTION 4: LIQUIDATIONS — GENERAL MATTERS

Distributions in a liquidation

11.81 In both compulsory liquidations and voluntary liquidations, the liquidator should apply the realisations of the company's assets in the following order:

(a) The expenses of the liquidation in the following order:[1]
  (i)   the costs of preserving, getting in or realising the assets;
  (ii)   the taxed cost of the petitioning creditors in a compulsory liquidation;
  (iii) the remuneration of any special manager;
  (iv)   the costs of preparing the statement of affairs (compulsory liquidation only);
  (v)   the court taxed costs of shorthand writers;
  (vi)   the necessary disbursements of the liquidator not included under (i), including any Corporation Tax payable in the liquidation;
  (vii) the costs of any persons properly employed by the liquidator, not covered above;
  (viii) the liquidator's remuneration; and
  (ix)   the expenses of the committee of inspection.
(b) preferential creditors;[2]
(c) creditors secured by floating charges;[3]
(d) unsecured creditors;
(e) deferred interest claims;[4]
(f) post liquidation interest, under the terms of a contract;[5]
(g) claims of employees for benefits under s 719 of the Companies Act;[6]
(h) shareholders, subject to the articles of association.

---

[1] CA 1985, s 604, and WUR 195.
[2] Ibid, s 614(1) and Sch 19.
[3] Ibid, s 196.
[4] See para 11.98.
[5] Where the company is solvent otherwise.
[6] CA 1985, s 659(3).

11.82   If the available assets are insufficient to pay the creditors of any of the above clauses in full, each creditor in the class will receive only a proportion of its claim.

Preferential creditors

11.83   The creditors to be paid preferentially in a liquidation, and in a receivership before the claims of creditors secured by floating charges, are:[1]

(a) any taxes assessed on the company, relating to periods ended prior to the 6th April before the relevant date;
(b) PAYE deductions (both in respect of income tax deductions, and subcontractors' tax) arising in the twelve months before the relevant date;
(c) value added tax and car tax, in respect of the twelve months up to the relevant date;
(d) general betting duty, bingo duty, pool betting duty or gaming licence duty falling due in the twelve months before the relevant date;
(e) local rates due and payable in the twelve months before the relevant date;

(f) national insurance contributions for employees payable during the twelve months before the relevant date;

(g) contributions to recognised pension schemes, arising in the twelve months prior to the relevant date for employer's contributions, and in the four months prior to the relevant date for employees' contributions deducted from wages;

(h) wages, salary or commission of employees in respect of the four months prior to the relevant date, limited to £800 of gross wages in respect of each employee;

(i) all accrued holiday pay due to any employee at the relevant date; and

(j) advances made for the purpose of paying wages or salaries or holiday pay, to the extent that the employees' own preferential claims have been reduced by the disbursement of the advances.

---

[1] CA 1985, Sch 19.

11.84 The relevant date for the purposes of determining preferential claims is:

(a) in a compulsory liquidation — the earliest of the date of the appointment of a provisional liquidator, the winding-up order, or a resolution to wind-up voluntarily;[1]

(b) in a voluntary liquidation, the date of the shareholders' resolution;[2]

(c) in a receivership, the date of the receiver's appointment.[3]

---

[1] CA 1985, Sch 19(1)(a).
[2] Ibid, Sch 19(1)(b).
[3] Ibid, s 196(4).

11.85 The preferential debts rank equally, and if the assets are insufficient to meet them will abate proportionately.[1]

---

[1] CA 1985, s 614(2)(a).

11.86 A person that has guaranteed a preferential debt will stand in the shoes of the creditor if the debt is paid by that person.[1]

---

[1] *Re Lamplugh Iron Ore Co* [1927] 1 Ch 308.

11.87 In a compulsory liquidation where a landlord or other person has distrained in the three months before the winding-up order, the preferential creditors have a first charge on the goods or proceeds; where the landlord or other person pays the preferential creditors under such a charge, he acquires the rights of the preferential creditors so paid.[1]

---

[1] CA 1985, s 614(4).

Claims

11.88   The process of ascertaining the claims of creditors is similar in voluntary and compulsory liquidations, although in the latter case there are additional administrative provisions to consider. It should be borne in mind that the liquidator has a duty to ensure that creditors are aware of their rights to claim.[1] Thus, the liquidator should invite claims, by means of individual notices, from the creditors recorded in the company's books, and in addition from those who could have claims, such as former suppliers, employees, contingent creditors that have contracts with the company and disputed claimants. The liquidator should also seek information from the company's directors and staff.

[1] *Re Armstrong Whitworth Securities Co Ltd* [1943] Ch 673, [1947] 2 All ER 479.

11.89   The liquidator may give fourteen days' notice to the creditors to make their claims or be excluded from the benefit of any distribution that is made before the claims are lodged. Such a notice is given by advertisement in a convenient newspaper and individually to creditors whose claims have not been accepted. In a compulsory liquidation the individual notices must be sent to creditors appearing in the statement of affairs who have not submitted a claim, whilst in a voluntary liquidation the notices must be sent to the last known addresses of any persons who, to the knowledge of the liquidator, claim to be creditors.[1]

[1] WUR 106.

11.90   In a voluntary liquidation there is no specified manner by which creditors have to make claims, although in practice a form acceptable to Customs and Excise for the purposes of obtaining relief for value added tax on bad debts is often used. In a compulsory liquidation, the claim may be either by an unsworn proof of debt, or if the liquidator so requires by a sworn proof of debt.[1] A sworn proof of debt may also be called for in a voluntary liquidation where, for example, there is a dispute as to the existence or quantum of a claim.

[1] WUR 92.

11.91   Generally, the liquidator must deal with claims by creditors within 28 days of receipt, either by accepting or rejecting the claim or by requiring supporting evidence. However, where the liquidator has specified a date by which claims should be made for the purposes of participating in a dividend, the claim must be dealt with within the fourteen days after that date.[1]

[1] WUR 117.

11.92   If the liquidator rejects a claim made by formal proof (either sworn or unsworn), the creditor may appeal to the court within 21 days of the service of the notice of rejection.[1]

[1] WUR 108.

11.93 In a compulsory liquidation, the liquidator is also required to give formal notice of his intention to declare a dividend to creditors that have not claimed and there is a procedure to deal with rejected claims.[1] Such formal notice is often given in a voluntary liquidation, to ensure that no claim can be made against the liquidator personally if insufficient assets remain after a distribution to meet late, unknown, claims. It should be noted that whilst it is in theory possible for a liquidator to give formal notice of a dividend in a compulsory liquidation in order to debar known creditors who do not claim, this procedure cannot be validly implemented in a voluntary liquidation. However in both cases, the only certain method of dealing with creditors that do not claim is to seek directions from the court.[2]

[1] WUR 119.
[2] CA 1985, ss 557 and 602.

11.94 In general, all liabilities incurred by the company prior to the commencement of liquidation can be proved, even though those liabilities may be uncertain, or are future or contingent liabilities. The rules to be applied in ascertaining the claims of creditors are those that apply in a bankruptcy.[1] Certain types of debt are not provable:

(a) debts incurred when the creditor had notice of either the presentation of a winding up petition, or of a resolution for voluntary liquidation;[2]
(b) debts that cannot be fairly estimated;[3]
(c) debts that are unenforceable; and
(d) debts due to the members of the company in their capacity as members.[4]

[1] CA 1985, s 612.
[2] BA 1914, s 30(2).
[3] Ibid, s 30(6).
[4] CA 1985, s 502(2)(f).

11.95 The amount of a liability that can be admitted as a claim may be affected by its nature; in particular,

(a) a debt due in a foreign currency must be converted into sterling at the rate ruling at the commencement of a creditors' voluntary liquidation or on the day a winding-up order is made in the case of a compulsory liquidation.;[1]
(b) claims under contracts that involve future payments (e g directors' service contracts) must be discounted to present values.[2]

[1] *Re Lines Bros Ltd* [1983] Ch 1.
[2] *Re Parana Plantations Ltd* [1946] 2 All ER 214.

11.96 Interest can be proved in a liquidation only in respect of periods prior to the commencement of liquidation, in the following circumstances:

(a) if specifically provided by contract, subject to the limitation noted in para 11.97, below; or
(b) at a rate of four per cent per annum on overdue debts:[1]

(i) payable on a fixed date and arising by virtue of a written instrument; and

(ii) on other debts, from the date of a written demand giving notice that interest will be charged.

---

[1] WUR 100.

11.97   There is an overall limit of five per cent per annum on interest that can be claimed in a liquidation, notwithstanding any contractual arrangements, and there are complex provisions to deal with current accounts and interest payments prior to the commencement of liquidation, and the treatment of debts that are partly secured.[1]

---

[1] BA 1914, s 66.

11.98   Contractual interest in excess of five per cent per annum becomes a deferred claim, payable only if the claims of other unsecured creditors are paid in full.

Contributories

11.99   If the shares of a company in liquidation are not fully paid up, past and present members of the company may be liable as contributories to contribute to the assets of the company.[1] The maximum liability of each member is the amount unpaid on the shares held, or previously held, by him.[2]

---

[1] CA 1985, s 502(1).
[2] Ibid, s 502(2)(d).

11.100   Where a company is limited by guarantee the maximum liability of members is the amount of their contracted contribution.[1]

---

[1] CA 1985, s 502(3).

11.101   Where a member has died, or is bankrupt, any obligation to make a contribution in the liquidation forms a claim against his estate to be dealt with by the executors or trustee as the case may be.[1]

---

[1] CA 1985, ss 509 and 510.

11.102   There are complex provisions to determine the liabilities of past and present members for uncalled capital.[1]

---

[1] CA 1985, s 502(2).

11.103   Where a company that was previously unlimited is re-registered as a limited company, and a liquidation commences within three years of the date of re-registration, the members at the time of re-registration, and those who ceased to be members within the twelve months before re-registration, can be liable without limit for any outstanding debts contracted when they were members.[1]

---

[1] CA 1985, s 505.

11.104 A liability to contribute may also fall upon a director or manager of the company, where that person had held office within the twelve months before the commencement of the liquidation. The potential liability does not include any debt contracted by the company after the person ceased to hold office, and in any event is subject to a court order being made.[1]

---

[1] CA 1985, s 503.

11.105 If the company has within the twelve months prior to the commencement of the liquidation made a payment out of capital for the redemption or purchase of its own shares, a liability for contribution will arise if the assets and other contributions noted above are insufficient to meet liabilities. Those liable are the recipients of the capital payments but the directors who signed the required statutory declaration become jointly and severally liable with those recipients to make the contribution.[1]

---

[1] CA 1985, s 504.

Executions

11.106 There are provisions to allow a liquidator in either a voluntary or a compulsory liquidation to recover goods or proceeds of sale of certain executions.

11.107 When a creditor has issued execution or attached a debt, he is not entitled to retain the benefits of the execution or attachment unless it was completed before the commencement of the liquidation or, if earlier, the date on which the creditor had notice that a meeting was to be held to consider a resolution to wind-up voluntarily. In the latter case, there is, however, provision for the court to allow the execution to stand. The completion of any execution is when the goods are sold, and of an attachment of a debt when payment is made.[1]

---

[1] CA 1985, s 621.

11.108 There are further provisions relating to goods or proceeds of sale in the hands of a sheriff. If the sheriff still holds the goods and receives notice either that a provisional liquidator has been appointed, or that a winding up order has been made, or that a resolution to wind-up voluntarily has been passed, the goods have to be released to the liquidator, subject to the costs of execution being a first charge on the goods.[1] When the judgment debt involved exceeds £250, the sheriff has to hold the proceeds of sale of the goods, less expenses, for fourteen days before paying the judgment creditor. If, during that period, notice is given to the sheriff of a winding up petition or the calling of a meeting to wind-up voluntarily, the proceeds must be held by the sheriff and eventually paid to a liquidator if one is appointed.[2] However, the rights of the liquidator to recover assets or sale proceeds may be set aside by the court.[3]

[1] CA 1985, s 622(1) and (2).
[2] Ibid, s 622(3) and (4).
[3] Ibid, s 622(5).

Distraint

11.109 In a voluntary liquidation, goods taken by distraint cannot be recovered. However, in a compulsory liquidation, where a landlord or other person has distrained on goods in the three months before the date of the winding-up order, the goods or proceeds of sale can be recovered for the benefit of preferential creditors. The person whose distraint is thus avoided acquires the same rights as the preferential creditors so paid.[1]

[1] CA 1985, s 614(4).

Disclaimer

11.110 A liquidator will often discover that an asset of the company is worthless and unsaleable, because of the obligations attaching to it; examples are a lease at a high rent, shares with a liability to pay calls, or land burdened with onerous covenants. The liquidator is able, with the sanction of the court, to disclaim such property, as long as he does so within twelve months of the commencement of the liquidation. The period allowed is extended to twelve months from the time a liquidator becomes aware of the property, if it is discovered after the first month of the liquidation, and the court also has power to extend the time period.[1]

[1] CA 1985, s 618.

11.111 There is also a provision to allow any third party that has an interest in any property to make an application to the liquidator, requiring him to decide whether or not he will disclaim. The liquidator has 28 days in which to make a decision, after which time he cannot disclaim, but it is unclear what happens thereafter.[1]

[1] CA 1985, s 619(2).

11.112 The court has wide powers to place conditions on the disclaimer and can assess damages that will be admitted as a claim in the liquidation.[1]

[1] CA 1985, s 619.

SECTION 5: OFFENCES IN A LIQUIDATION

11.113 A number of offences that may be committed by directors, officers and others arise as a result of a liquidation, some of which impose personal liability for the company's debts.

11.114 The first general provision to consider is that which gives the court power to assess damages against past or present directors of a company in liquidation, and also applies to any person involved in the formation or promotion of the company, managers, officers, and liquidators.[1] If it appears that the company's funds have been misapplied, or the person has been guilty of misfeasance or breach of trust, the court may order restitution to be made as it considers just. Proceedings are instituted upon application by the Official Receiver, the liquidator, a creditor or a contributory, and the provisions apply in addition to any criminal proceedings that may arise.

---

[1] CA 1985, s 631.

11.115 A person who is involved in running the business of a company may also incur a personal liability if the business has been carried on for a fraudulent purpose, or with intent to defraud the creditors of either the company or any other person.[1] An application may be made to the court by the Official Receiver, the liquidator, a creditor or a contributory, and the court can make a declaration that any persons knowingly party to carrying on the company's business in the manner noted above shall be personally liable, without limit, for any of the company's liabilities, as the court thinks fit.

---

[1] CA 1985, s 630.

11.116 In addition to the personal liability noted in para 11.115 above, a criminal offence is also created if the same conditions are met.[1] It should be noted that this provision is applicable whether or not the company is in liquidation.

---

[1] CA 1985, s 458.

11.117 Criminal offences also arise where it can be shown that prior to a liquidation any person, with intent to defraud creditors, has:[1]

(a) made a gift or transfer of, or charge on, or connived at the levying of execution against, the company's property; or
(b) concealed or removed property after, or in the two months before, a judgment has been obtained against the company.

---

[1] CA 1985, s 625.

11.118 There are other provisions under which criminal sanctions can be applied against a past or present officer of a company that goes into liquidation. The principal offences are:[1]

(a) concealing, or fraudulently removing, property to a value of £120 or more, or concealing any debt due to or from the company;
(b) concealing, destroying, or falsifying, any of the company's books and papers;
(c) fraudulently parting with, altering, or making omissions in, company documents; and
(d) disposing of property obtained on credit but not paid for, other than in the normal course of business.

---

[1] CA 1985, s 624(1).

11.119 Certain of the offences noted in paragraph 11.118 apply where officers have been privy to offences by others; certain offences also apply after the commencement of the liquidation.[1]

---

[1] CA 1985, s 624(2).

11.120 A past or present officer also commits a criminal offence if, either prior to or in the course of the liquidation of a company, he makes false or fraudulent representations to obtain the consent of a creditor to an arrangement in connection with the liquidation.[1]

---

[1] CA 1985, s 629.

11.121 There are further provisions, creating criminal offences, to ensure that officers co-operate with the liquidator, or do not falsify the company's books. A past or present officer commits an offence if, in the course the liquidation, he:

(a) makes a material omission in any statement of the company's affairs (this also applies to statements provided prior to the liquidation);[1]
(b) attempts to account for any of the company's property by way of fictitious losses or expenses;[2]
(c) with intent to defraud or deceive, destroys or tampers with the company's books or records, or is privy to the making of false entries in the books;[3]
(d) does not give to the liquidator full information concerning the company's property, or any disposals of property other than in the normal course of business;[4]
(e) does not deliver to the liquidator any of the company's property or records under his control;[5]
(f) fails to inform the liquidator within one month that he knows or believes that a false debt has been proved;[6] or
(g) prevents the production of books or documents relating to the company.[7]

---

[1] CA 1985, s 628.
[2] Ibid, s 626(2).
[3] Ibid, s 627.
[4] Ibid, s 626(1)(a).
[5] Ibid, s 626(1)(b) and (c).
[6] Ibid, s 626(1)(d).
[7] Ibid, s 626(1)(e).

SECTION 6: FRAUDULENT PREFERENCE

11.122 A fraudulent preference arises where, in the six months before a company goes into liquidation, one creditor is paid before another intentionally, in order to give some preference to the recipient.

11.123 The term fraudulent preference is misleading, and 'voidable preference' would seem more appropriate to describe the transaction more accurately. Such a preference may involve no moral blame at all and is certainly not fraudulent in the accepted legal sense, but a preference that can be voided may have been made on grounds with which most people would sympathise.[1]

---

[1] See per Maugham J in *Re Patrick & Lyon Ltd* [1933] Ch 786 at 790.

11.124 Where a transaction (including a conveyance, mortgage, delivery of goods, payment, or other act relating to property) that is in essence a payment is effected by a company unable to pay its debts as they become due from its own money, in the six months prior to the liquidation of a company, with a view to giving one creditor preference over the other creditors, it is deemed a fraudulent preference.[1]

The person preferred may also be someone who is a surety or guarantor for a debt due to a creditor.

---

[1] CA 1985, s 615(1) and BA 1914, s 44.

11.125 Thus, there are three points to be established when considering whether a transaction was a fraudulent preference:

(i) whether the transaction took place in the six months prior to a liquidation;
(ii) whether at the time the company was unable to pay its debts as they fell due; and
(iii) whether there was an intention to prefer.

11.126 The liquidator is the applicant in any proceedings to establish fraudulent preference and thus would be personally liable for any order for costs made against him.[1] The onus of proof lies with the liquidator to establish the conditions noted above.[2]

---

[1] *Re Strand Wood Co Ltd* [1904] 2 Ch 1.
[2] *Peat v Gresham Trust Ltd* [1934] AC 252.

11.127 Ultimately a case to establish fraudulent preference depends upon there being an intention to prefer and the mere fact of preference is not sufficient.[1] Furthermore there must be a dominant intention to prefer, although the intent to prefer need not be the sole intent.

---

[1] *Re Goldsmid, ex p Taylor* [1887] 18 QBD 295.

11.128 It is unlikely that a liquidator will be able to point to specific evidence to support a claim, and the intention of the directors of a company will have to be inferred, taking account of all the circumstances. It will be necessary to persuade the court that it is proper to draw an inference of intent to prefer from the facts, and the case will founder if there is any doubt, since the onus of proof never shifts from the liquidator.

11.129   Bearing in mind that each case will turn on its own facts, past decided cases can give only limited guidance on what does or does not constitute a fraudulent preference. The reasons and circumstances that have been advanced to defeat a fraudulent preference claim include payment in the ordinary course of business or under pressure, payment under an existing contract, belief that there was a legal obligation to pay, and intention to preserve an existing credit facility. However, payments made because of a sense of moral duty, or as a result of pressure by a director, have been held to be preferences.

11.130   If a transaction is shown to be a fraudulent preference, it will be set aside and any payment will be recovered by the liquidator, and will be for the benefit of the general body of creditors and will not constitute an asset subject to any floating charge.[1] The creditor will have a claim in the liquidation for the amount paid to the liquidator.

---

[1] *Re Yagerphone* [1935] Ch 392.

11.131   Where the debt settled by way of a fraudulent preference was secured by property belonging to a third party, that third party would also have obtained the benefit of the preference and, consequently, becomes liable as surety to the person making the repayment.[1]

---

[1] CA 1985, s 616.

SECTION 7: RECEIVERSHIP

11.132   The expression 'receivership' does not appear in the Companies Act, and the term has come to be used to cover the wide variety of types of administration in which a 'receiver' acts. Furthermore the Act deals only with administrative matters in connection with a receiver's appointment over the assets of a company, and much of the law governing receiverships is derived from the consolidation of the practice of the Court of Chancery, and case law. It is beyond the scope of this work to deal other than briefly with what is a complex and wide-ranging topic.

11.133   A receiver may be appointed over the property of a company in a number of ways:

   (a) by the court;
   (b) under statutory powers, principally the Law of Property Act 1925;
   (c) by a debenture holder under a fixed charge; and
   (d) by a debenture holder under a floating charge.

Appointment by the court

11.134 An application may be made to the court for the appointment of a receiver where the assets of a company are considered to be in jeopardy, in order to protect those assets for the benefit of the persons ultimately entitled to them. The application could be by shareholders if there has been neglect in the management of a company's assets and business. Alternatively, the application could be by a debenture holder if an event has occurred that places the assets, and thus the security, in jeopardy, but where that event is not specified in the debenture as a breach.

11.135 The receiver is an officer of the court, and must act within the powers given to him by the court. Before acting, he will be required to provide a guarantee bond as security for his performance. He is personally liable for all contracts into which he enters, although this is subject to a right of indemnity out of the assets under his control in respect of liabilities properly incurred.

11.136 A number of administrative provisions relating to notification of appointment, statement of affairs, annual returns and preferential creditors, which are dealt with in detail below, apply, in appropriate circumstances, to a receiver appointed by the court.

Appointment under statutory powers

11.137 Although there may be specific provisions in a mortgage relating to the appointment of a receiver, and the powers of that receiver, the Law of Property Act 1925 confers certain general powers where the deed is silent.[1]

---

[1] LPA 1925, s 101(1)(iii).

11.138 The statutory power of appointment can be exercised only after the mortgagee has become entitled to exercise the statutory power of sale,[1] that is where either a demand for repayment of principal remains unpaid for three months, or interest is more than two months in arrear, or there is breach of some provision other than the payment of principal or interest.[2]

---

[1] LPA 1925, s 109(1).
[2] Ibid, s 103.

11.139 The receiver is agent for the mortgagor,[1] and his main power is to be able to demand and recover the income arising from the property. He can take possession of vacant property but, unless provided for in the mortgage deed, cannot displace a mortgagor in possession, nor exercise a power of sale. Certain additional powers available to the mortgagee may be delegated to the receiver by means of the appointment document, to enable him to grant leases,[2] accept surrenders of leases[3] and insure the property.[4]

---

[1] LPA 1925, s 109(2).
[2] Ibid, s 99(19).
[3] Ibid, s 100(13).
[4] Ibid, s 109(7).

11.140   Any funds received by the receiver are applied in payment of out-goings on the property including authorised repairs, prior charges, the receiver's costs, and the interest and principal due under the mortgage.[1] Any residue is paid to either a subsequent mortgagee or the mortgagor, subject of course to the receiver's duty as an agent to account to the mortgagor.

---

[1] LPA 1925, s 109(8).

11.141   Again a receiver is subject to the statutory duties, as appropriate, as set out in the Companies Act.[1]

---

[1] See paras 11.149 et seq.

Appointment under a fixed charge

11.142   A debenture deed conferring rights under a fixed charge will specify the assets that are pledged as security and the events that will give the deben-ture holder the right to sell those assets in order to recover monies due to him. These events will be deemed to be breaches of the contractual arrangements, and there is a general power to exercise rights of sale or to appoint a receiver under the Law of Property Act. In addition, or in substitution, powers of sale and appointment may be dealt with specifically in the debenture deed. It is important to note that the powers of a receiver may be limited by the terms of the debenture or by statute.[1]

---

[1] LPA 1925, s 109.

11.143   Fixed charges are usually taken over land and buildings and other fixed assets, although the extent to which such a charge covers plant is open to question. Modern deeds normally incorporate a fixed charge on present and future book debts. Although it is considered best practice to accept such charges, properly constituted, as valid,[1] it could be argued that a charge on debts can fall only within the definition of a floating charge.

---

[1] See *Siebe Gorman & Co Ltd v Barclays Bank Ltd* [1979] 2 Lloyd's Rep 142.

11.144   A receiver under a fixed charge is agent of the mortgagor, although this agency ceases upon the liquidation of the company.

11.145   A receiver appointed under a fixed charge is responsible only for his own costs and for the payment of the amounts owed to his appointing deben-ture holder that are covered by the debenture. Apart from a general duty of care, he does not have any responsibility towards the preferential or other classes of creditors of the company, other than to realise the best possible price for the company's assets at the time when he chooses to sell.

11.146   The receiver is subject to the general requirements of the Companies Act, set out below.[1]

---

[1] See paras 11.149 et seq.

Appointment under a floating charge

11.147 The most common type of debenture given by a company is one that creates a floating charge over non-specified assets, and normally covers the whole of the undertaking of the company. This is a charge on present and future assets that by their nature are constantly changing, and allows the company to deal with those assets in the normal course of business without referral to the debenture holder.[1] The debenture deed will specify the events that will cause the company's licence to deal with the assets to be terminated, and the floating charge is then said to 'crystallise'. One of these events will be the appointment by the debenture holder of a receiver, and from this point the floating charge is equivalent in force to a fixed charge on the assets available at the time.

---

[1] For definition of floating charge, see *Re Yorkshire Woolcombers Association Ltd* (1903), 2 Ch 284. See also para 4.80, above.

11.148 A receiver under a floating charge will be an agent of the company, but again this agency does not survive the commencement of liquidation. A receiver may also be appointed as a 'manager' in order to carry on the business where the undertaking itself is subject to the charge and the powers of management will be set out in the debenture deed.

Receivers generally

Appointment

11.149 The appointment of a receiver is likely to be made under hand, although this will depend upon the provisions of the debenture. The receiver becomes appointed from the time that he (or an authorised representative) physically accepts the appointment document[1] and thus the date of the document is not relevant.

---

[1] *Cripps (Pharmaceuticals) Ltd v Wickenden* [1973] 2 All ER 606.

11.150 Upon appointment, a receiver who is appointed over the whole or substantially the whole of a company's property by or on behalf of the holders of a floating charge is required to give notice to the company at its registered office, or main place of business if different, in the prescribed form.[1] For any type of receivership, the debenture holder, or the person that sought a court appointment, has to give notice to the Registrar within seven days of the appointment.[2]

---

[1] CA 1985, s 495(2)(a), and CFR 1985 Form 495(2)(a).
[2] Ibid, s 405(1), and Form 405(1).

Qualifications

11.151 There are no specific qualifications required in order that a person can act as a receiver or manager, although an undischarged bankrupt is disqualified from acting, other than under a court appointment, by virtue of the offence that arises out of so acting.[1] A body corporate cannot act as a receiver.[2]

[1] CA 1985, s 490.
[2] Ibid, s 489.

Notice

11.152   There is no specific requirement for a receiver to notify creditors and others generally of his appointment, although in practice a receiver will need to communicate with debtors and creditors in order to collect in the company's assets and make arrangements for the continuation of the business if this is the case. However, any correspondence (including orders or invoices) issued by the company, the receiver or the liquidator must contain a statement that a receiver or manager has been appointed.[1]

[1] CA 1985, s 493.

Agency

11.153   The receiver's relationship with the company will be defined in the debenture and he will have power to act as agent for the company. In the event that the company goes into liquidation, the receiver ceases to be an agent and becomes an independent principal.

11.154   As agent the receiver has a duty to keep a full account of his dealings with the company's assets; and to account to the company when required.[1]

[1] CA 1985, s 497(6) and see *Smiths Ltd v Middleton* [1979] 3 All ER 842.

Personal liability

11.155   A receiver or manager is personally liable on any contract entered into by him unless he has specifically contracted without personal liability.[1] However, where the receiver is personally liable, he will be entitled to an indemnity out of the assets of the company,[2] as long as he has acted within his powers and not negligently.

[1] CA 1985, s 492(3)(a).
[2] Ibid, s 492(3)(b).

11.156   If a receiver appointed under a floating charge permits the company to continue to trade, and he is subsequently unable to meet the claims of preferential creditors because the available assets have been dissipated by trading, he may be personally liable to the preferential creditors to the extent of such dissipation.[1]

[1] See *Westminster Corpn v Haste* [1950] Ch 442.

Statement of affairs

11.157   Within fourteen days of the receipt by the company of the notice of an appointment of a receiver of the whole or substantially the whole of the company's property by or on behalf of the holders of a floating charge, a statement as to the affairs of the company has to be submitted to the receiver.[1] The period allowed may be extended by the receiver or the court. The statement has to be in the prescribed form,[2] giving details of the company's assets and liabilities, and be verified by affidavit or statutory declaration of a director and the company secretary.[3] There are provisions to require company employees other than directors to submit the statement.[4] The reasonable costs of preparing the statement are to be paid by the receiver out of the floating charge assets.[5]

---

[1] CA 1985, s 495(2)(b).
[2] CFR 1985 Form 495(3)(a).
[3] CA 1985, s 496(2).
[4] Ibid, s 496(2) and (3).
[5] Ibid, s 496(4).

11.158   Within two months of receiving the statement, the receiver is required to send out the following:[1]

  (a) to the Registrar of Companies, a copy of the statement, a summary of the statement and his comments on the statement;
  (b) to the court (if applicable) a copy of the statement, with comments;
  (c) to the company, a copy of his comments or a notice that no comments have been made; and
  (d) to any trustees for any debentures on whose behalf he was appointed and if possible to the holders of those debentures, a copy of the summary.

---

[1] CA 1985, s 495(3).

Preferential creditors

11.159   Where a receiver is appointed under a debenture containing a floating charge and the company was not in liquidation at the date of his appointment, he is required to pay preferential creditors out of the assets subject to the floating charge coming into his hands, in priority to any payment to the debenture holder.[1] The preferential creditors are those that are preferential in a winding up,[2] and are dealt with in paragraph 11.83. Any payments made by the receiver to preferential creditors may be recouped out of the assets of the company available for payment of general creditors.[3]

---

[1] CA 1985, s 196.
[2] Ibid, s 614 and Sch 19.
[3] Ibid, s 196(5).

Accounts

11.160   Where a receiver is appointed over the whole or substantially the whole of a company's assets by or on behalf of the holders of a floating charge he is required to prepare an abstract of his receipts and payments in the prescribed form[1] for the first twelve months of his appointment and for every twelve months thereafter, with a final return ending on the day he ceases to act.[2] The abstract has to be sent to the company, the Registrar of Companies, and the debenture holders and their trustees within two months of the end of the relevant period.

[1] CFR 1985 Form 497.
[2] CA 1985, s 497.

11.161   In any other case where a receiver is appointed under a charge, the abstract of receipts and payments covers six months' periods, and has to be sent to the Registrar of Companies within one month of the end of the period.[1]

[1] CA 1985, s 498.

Ceasing to act

11.162   Upon ceasing to act a receiver appointed under a charge must give notice to the Registrar,[1] and submit a final abstract of receipts and payments.

[1] CA 1985, s 405(2) and CFR 1985 Form 405(2).

Remuneration

11.163   The basis of a receiver's remuneration may be provided for in the debenture, but in the absence of any reference, his remuneration, together with any expenses incurred, will be limited to five per cent of realisations.[1]

[1] LPA 1925, s 109(6).

11.164   Where no limit is set, as will normally be the case for company debentures, the receiver has a duty towards the company to act properly and the level of his remuneration may be challenged by a liquidator, by application to the court.[1]

[1] CA 1985, s 494.

Applications to the court

11.165   A receiver has the ability to apply to the court for directions on any matter arising in connection with the performance of his functions.[1]

[1] CA 1985, s 492(1) and (2).

Charges

11.166 A company may create a charge in favour of a creditor, or a contingent creditor, over any of its assets. However, it is necessary to consider both the nature of the charge (that is, whether it is fixed or floating) and the assets involved in order to determine whether the charge can be enforced by the creditor.

11.167 A fixed charge is one in which the assets to be charged are specified, and which prevents the company dealing with those assets without the consent of the creditor. A floating charge, however, can cover a class of assets, or the whole of the undertaking of the company, and allow the company to deal in the normal course of business with the assets involved until the occurrence of the events specified in the charge document.

11.168 Certain types of charges have to be registered with the Registrar within 21 days of their creation in order to be effective[1] if the charges are:[2]

  (a) a floating charge on the company's undertaking; or
  (b) granted to secure an issue of debentures; or
  (c) of the nature equivalent to a bill of sale; or
  (d) on uncalled share capital, unpaid calls, land, book debts, ships, aircraft, goodwill, patents, trademarks or copyrights.

---

[1] CA 1985, s 395(1).
[2] Ibid, s 396.

11.169 Charges in other categories do not need to be registered.

11.170 The effect of non-registration of a charge in a category noted above is that the charge will be void against a liquidator and any other creditor of the company, and the money secured by it becomes immediately repayable.[1]

---

[1] CA 1985, s 395(2).

11.171 The primary duty to register a charge rests with the company creating it, but any person interested in the charge (for example, the creditor) can make an application.[1] A company is also required to register charges that are assumed by virtue of the acquisition of charged property.[2]

---

[1] CA 1985, s 399.
[2] CA 1985, s 400.

11.172 A charge may be subject to scrutiny and challenge upon the company being wound up. A charge that is created within six months before a liquidation to secure an existing liability may be a fraudulent preference;[1] the tests to be applied are dealt with in Section 6. However, this is usually of relevance in practice only as regards fixed charges, as there are specific provisions dealing with floating charges.

---

[1] CA 1985, s 615.

11.173   A floating charge created within the twelve months before a liquidation is invalid in the liquidation unless it can be shown that the company was solvent immediately after the creation of the charge, or, if the company was not solvent, the charge is only valid to the extent of monies introduced at the time of or subsequent to the charge.[1] Interest on the new monies is also secured at a rate of 5% per annum.[2] Where the charge secures a running account such as a bank overdraft, the rule in *Clayton's Case*[3] will apply to the effect that a debt existing at the time the charge is created may be extinguished by payments into the account, resulting in the overdraft being deemed to have been advanced after the creation of the charge.

[1] CA 1985, s 617(1).
[2] Ibid, s 617(2).
[3] *DeVaynes v Noble* (1816) 1 Mer 572.

SECTION 8: ARRANGEMENTS AND RECONSTRUCTIONS

General

11.174   There are three matters to be considered under the general heading of arrangements and reconstructions, as follows:

(a) a scheme of arrangement between a company and its creditors or members, or both, under CA 1985, s 425, requiring the consent of the court;

(b) any arrangement between a company that is being wound-up voluntarily and its creditors, under CA 1985, s 601; and

(c) a reconstruction of a company that is being wound up voluntarily, under CA 1985, s 582.

S 425 schemes

11.175   It is possible for a company to carry out under section 425 almost any type of compromise or arrangement, or reconstruction of share capital, within the general limitations imposed by company law and subject always to the sanction of the court.

11.176   The first step in a scheme will be taken by the company or any member or creditor making an application to the court for the court to order meetings of the various parties involved to consider the scheme.[1] Since this provision can be used for a wide variety of purposes, it will be necessary to hold meetings, and thereby obtain the sanction, of all those whose rights are affected by the scheme. If for example it is proposed that the rights attaching to various types of shares are to be changed there will need to be separate meetings of the holders of each type of share. If, however, the rights of creditors are affected, meetings would be required for each class of creditors with different interests. Thus each 'class' for the purpose of such meetings would be comprised of persons whose rights are sufficiently similar for them to have a common view of the proposals. It is the responsibility of the applicants in the scheme to determine in the first instance what meetings should be held.

1 CA 1985, s 425(1).

11.177 The court will order the manner in which notice of the meetings is to be given. The company is required to send with the notice of the meeting a statement explaining the effect of the compromise or arrangement, and stating in particular any material interests of the directors, in any capacity, and the effect of the scheme on them.[1] If the rights of debenture holders are affected, the interests of the trustees of any debenture deed and the effect on them must also be disclosed.[2] Where the notice is given by advertisement, the advertisement must either give these statements or state an address at which the statements can be obtained free of charge.[3]

1 CA 1985, s 426(2).
2 Ibid, s 426(4).
3 Ibid, s 426(3) and (5).

11.178 At the meetings of each class of members or creditors, the scheme must be approved by a majority in number, representing three-fourths in value, of those present and voting, and all classes must so vote for the scheme to be capable of implementation. The court will consider the results of the class meetings and if the provisions of the statute have been complied with, if each class was fairly represented and if the arrangement is a reasonable one it will give its sanction. The scheme is then binding on the company and the members and creditors of all classes,[1] although a copy of the court order sanctioning the scheme has to be delivered to the Registrar of Companies before the scheme can have effect.[2]

1 CA 1985, s 425(2).
2 Ibid, s 425(3).

11.179 As has been noted above, the section can be used for many types of scheme. If the scheme involves the transfer of the whole or any part of the undertaking or property of the company ('the transferor') to another company ('the transferee') the court is given power to make provision for a number of specified matters:[1]

(i)   the transfer of the whole or any part of the undertaking and assets, or liabilities, of the transferor to the transferee;

(ii)   the allotment by the transferee of shares and other securities;

(iii) the continuation, in the name of the transferee, of any legal proceedings either by or against the transferor;

(iv) the dissolution of the transferor without liquidation;

(v)   provision for dissenters: and

(vi) any incidental matters in order to effect the scheme.

1 CA 1985, s 427(3).

11.180   Where the order provides for the transfer of assets and liabilities the transfer shall be effected by the order alone, which may provide that assets are released from any existing charges.[1]

---
[1] CA 1985, s 427(4).

S 601 schemes

11.181   Under s 601 it is possible for a company that is about to be, or is being, wound up voluntarily to enter into any form of arrangement with its creditors. Although there is a right of appeal to the court, an arrangement will be binding:[1]

(a) on the company, if sanctioned by an extraordinary resolution: and
(b) on the creditors, if agreed to by 75 per cent in both number and value of the creditors.

---
[1] CA 1985, s 601(1).

11.182   The scope of the section is limited since it applies only in the context of a voluntary liquidation, and only to 'arrangements' and not to 'compromises' with creditors. Furthermore, in practice, there may be problems in obtaining the required majority of creditors in favour of the scheme, since the majority must be of all creditors and not only those attending a meeting if there is one.

11.183   The procedure to be adopted would be for the directors or the liquidator to call meetings of members and creditors, although there is no specific provision for the latter. Any member or creditor may appeal to the court against the arrangement within three weeks of its completion, and the court has power to amend, vary or confirm the arrangement,[1] but a properly sanctioned arrangement cannot be set aside completely.

---
[1] CA 1985, s 601(2).

11.184   It is useful to draw distinctions between the various methods available for compromises and arrangements in a voluntary liquidation:

(a) A liquidator can enter into a compromise or arrangement with individual creditors, if sanctioned by the committee of inspection or the court.[1] This is only subject to the agreement of each creditor, and thus only assenting creditors can be bound.
(b) An arrangement.that is binding on all creditors can be effected under s 601, with a 75 per cent majority of all creditors.
(c) Both arrangements and compromises that are binding on all creditors can be effected under s 425 with a simple majority in number, and 75 per cent in value, of creditors attending the required meetings, subject of course to court approval.

---
[1] CA 1985, ss 539(1)(e) and 598(1).

Reconstruction under s 582

11.185 A more limited form of reconstruction can be adopted by a company in conjunction with a voluntary liquidation, under s 582. This allows the liquidator to transfer the whole or part of the business or property of the company that is being liquidated to another company, and to receive as consideration shares in the transferee company.[1]

---

[1] CA 1985, s 582(1).

11.186 In a members' voluntary liquidation the sanction of a special resolution of the company is required,[1] but in a creditors' voluntary liquidation the section may be applied only with the sanction of either the court or the committee of inspection.[2] Additionally, if an order for a compulsory liquidation, or a winding up under supervision is made, within a year of the special resolution, the resolution is not valid unless sanctioned by the court.[3]

---

[1] CA 1985, s 582(2).
[2] Ibid, s 593.
[3] Ibid, s 582(7).

11.187 The meeting to consider the special resolution may be held prior to or at the same time as the meeting to consider the winding up resolution.[1] Because of the provisions relating to dissentient shareholders discussed below, the meeting under s 582 is sometimes held a clear seven days before the winding up meeting in order that the level of dissent can be determined, and the resolution may, for commercial reasons, include a provision that it shall not be effective if the level of dissent exceeds a specified proportion of shareholdings.

---

[1] CA 1985, s 582(7).

11.188 A scheme under this section may provide that the shares issued by the transferee company are allotted directly to the members of the company being liquidated. In such a case provision would have to be made for the payment of creditors of the company in liquidation, either out of assets not transferred or by the transferee accepting an obligation to pay them. This procedure could give rise to a liability falling upon the liquidator personally, since the assets of the company would have been distributed to members without regard to the prior claims of creditors.

11.189 Any member of the company who did not vote in favour of the special resolution may dissent from the scheme by giving notice in writing to the liquidator at the company's registered office within seven days, and may thereby require the liquidator either to abandon the scheme or purchase his interest.[1] The price to be paid for the dissenting shareholder's interest is to be determined by agreement, or failing which by arbitration. Since the funds for doing this have to be provided for by special resolution,[2] the terms upon which dissentients are to be dealt with will normally be incorporated in the arrangement as sanctioned by the shareholders. However, the price cannot be specified since it can only be determined as between liquidator and shareholder.

[1] CA 1985, s 582(5).
[2] Ibid, s 582(6).

SECTION 9: DISSOLUTION

Methods

11.190   A company cannot disappear without legal process, and there are three methods available for the dissolution of a company:

(i)   a company that is not carrying on business, and is defunct, may be struck off the register by the Registrar of Companies;
(ii)   a company will be dissolved following a liquidation; and
(iii) the court may order that a company be dissolved without winding up if its undertaking is transferred to another company under a scheme of reconstruction.

Striking off

11.191   Where the Registrar of Companies has reasonable cause to believe that a company is not carrying on business or in operation, he may send a letter by post to the company enquiring if the company is carrying on business.[1] This procedure may be initiated by the Registrar of Companies, usually where the company has not submitted annual returns or accounts. In practice, the directors may request the Registrar of Companies to take the appropriate steps if the company is not trading and has no assets. It will be appreciated that in these circumstances, striking off is a suitable alternative to liquidation, since no costs are incurred.

[1] CA 1985, s 652(1).

11.192   If the Registrar of Companies does not receive a reply to his first letter within one month, he must within fourteen days thereafter send a second letter to the company, by registered post, giving a further period of one month for the company to reply.[1] If there is no response to the second letter, or if a reply confirms that the company is not carrying on business or in operation, the Registrar of Companies may send a notice to the company, which is published in the Gazette, to the effect that the company will be struck off at the expiration of three months from the date of the notice.[2] At the end of the three month period the Registrar may strike the company's name from the register, and the company is dissolved upon the publication of a notice to that effect in the Gazette.[3] The procedure may be halted in the three month notice period if the company shows good cause why the striking off should not occur.

[1] CA 1985, s 652(2).

[2] Ibid, s 652(3).
[3] Ibid, s 652(5).

11.193 A similar procedure to that outlined above can be applied if the company is being liquidated and no returns have been made by the liquidator for six months. The requirement in such a case is not that the company is not in business but that either no liquidator is acting or the affairs of the company are fully wound up.[1]

[1] CA 1985, s 652(4).

11.194 Even though the company has been dissolved, any liability that might attach to either a director, officer or member of the company continues and may be enforced.[1] Furthermore a company that has been struck off the register may still be liquidated by the court,[2] although in practice the first step would be to apply for the restoration of the company to the register.

[1] CA 1985, s 652(6)(a).
[2] Ibid, s 652(6)(b).

11.195 The striking off procedure can be reviewed at any time within twenty years of the publication of the final notice in the Gazette. An application may be made to the court either by a creditor or member, on the grounds either that the company was carrying on business at the time it was struck off, or that it is just that the company's name should be restored.[1] Such a procedure would be adopted if it were discovered that the company had assets, but it is likely that restoration would be conditional upon a liquidation taking place subsequently.

[1] CA 1985, s 653.

Liquidation

11.196 In a voluntary liquidation (either creditors' or members') the liquidator is required to submit a final account to the Registrar of Companies and returns of the final meetings of members and, if applicable, creditors. The company is dissolved three months from the date on which the account and returns are filed, subject to the court making an order deferring the dissolution upon application by an interested party.[1]

[1] CA 1985, ss 585(5) and 595(6).

11.197 In a compulsory liquidation, the liquidator may make an application to the court when the company's affairs have been completely wound up and the company is dissolved from the date of the court order.[1] This procedure is in addition to the requirements of a liquidator in a compulsory liquidation to obtain his release.[2] In practice a formal application for dissolution is not made, and the company is eventually struck off and dissolved under the provisions noted above.[3]

---

[1] CA 1985, s 568.
[2] Ibid, s 545.
[3] Ibid, s 652(4).

Scheme of arrangement

11.198   Where a scheme of arrangement is being effected under CA 1985, s 425, the scheme may provide for the transfer of the whole of a company's undertaking and liabilities to another company.[1] The court has power to order as part of such a scheme that the transferor company be dissolved without winding up.[2]

---

[1] CA 1985, s 427(2).
[2] Ibid, s 427(3)(d).

Bona vacantia

11.199   When a company is dissolved, any remaining assets of the company are deemed to be 'bona vacantia', and thus vest in either the Crown, the Duchy of Lancaster or the Duke of Cornwall.[1] This would be subject to any order made by the court if the company were subsequently restored to the register, and if the assets have been sold the company is able to recover their value.[2] Alternatively, it may be possible for, say, the members of a dissolved company without liabilities to receive assets without applying for the restoration of the company, since it appears to be the practice of the Treasury Solicitor (and the solicitors to the Duchys of Lancaster and Cornwall) to ensure as far as possible that assets are distributed to those entitled to them. The Crown has the right to disclaim any property that could vest in it[3] and any liabilities arising from such disclaimer remain with the company.[4]

---

[1] CA 1985, s 654.
[2] Ibid, s 655.
[3] Ibid, s 656.
[4] Ibid, s 657.

Dissolution declared void

11.200   In addition to the provisions allowing a company's name to be restored to the register after striking off, there are limited provisions to allow for the dissolution of a company to be declared void. A liquidator or other interested person may make an application to the court within two years of the dissolution, and the order by the court makes the dissolution void ab initio.[1]

---

[1] CA 1985, s 651.

Index

Accountant
promoter as 2.01
Accounting
companies acts
interaction with, 9.01
financial year, 9.21–9.22
reference periods
accounting reference date, 9.20
alteration of, 9.23–9.25
retrospective charge, 9.24
group of companies, 9.23
lengthening of, 9.27
overseas companies, 9.28
shortening of, 9.26
Accounting principles
alternative accounting rules, 9.106
additional information, 9.108
depreciation under, 9.107
depreciation and revalued assets, 9.85
development costs, 9.85
diminution in value of assets, 9.86, 9.89
disposals of revalued assets, 9.85
distributable profits, determination of, 9.85
general rules, 9.80–9.81
historical cost accounting
current assets, 9.100
excess of money owed over value received, 9.105
fixed amount, included at, 9.105
fungible assets, 9.103–9.104
long term contract work in progress, 9.101
price or cost unknown, 9.105
purchase price or production cost, 9.102
stock, valuation of, 9.103–9.104
depreciation, 9.92
diminution in value, 9.95
accounting treatment, summary of, 9.99
fixed assets, 9.97
permanent and temporary, 9.96
fixed assets, 9.91–9.99
investment properties, 9.93
non depreciation of assets, 9.94
subsidiaries transferring assets to holding Co, 9.98

Accounting principles—*continued*
provision treated as realised losses, 9.85
realised profits, 9.82–9.83
CCAB guidance, 9.84
revaluation of assets, 9.85
all assets, 9.88
reversals of upward revaluation, 9.87
valuation rules, 9.90
Accounting records
assets and liabilities, 9.16
availability for inspection, 9.18
companies business
dealing in goods where, 9.09
contents, 9.14
financial position, 9.11
'at any time' meaning, 9.13
disclosure of, 9.12
form of, 9.10
minimum contents, 9.09
penalties for non-compliance, 9.19
purposes, legal requirements, 9.08
receipts and expenditure, 9.15
'sale by way of ordinary retail trade', 9.17
'statements of stock' meaning, 9.17
stock records, 9.17
true and fair view, meaning, 9.11
Accounting standards *see* also STATEMENTS OF STANDARD ACCOUNTING PRACTICE
authority and scope of, 9.05
charted accountants
obligation to observe, 9.05
committee, 9.03, 9.04
companies acts, interaction with, 9.02
history of, 9.03
significant departures
disclosure or justification of, 9.05
Accounts
abridged
documents constituting, 9.239
generally, 9.234
legal definition, 9.235
publication
meaning, 9.238
requirements of, 9.238
scope of, 9.239
agency companies, 9.233
auditors, examination of, by, 10.02

435

440   *Index*